TAXAT

D1536681

TAXATION
AND
WELFARE

Arnold C. Harberger
The University of Chicago

Little, Brown and Company
Boston

760360

COPYRIGHT © 1974 BY LITTLE, BROWN AND COMPANY (INC.)

All rights reserved. No part of this book may be reproduced
in any form or by any electronic or mechanical means
including information storage and retrieval systems
without permission in writing from the publisher, except
by a reviewer who may quote brief passages in a review.

Library of Congress Catalog Card No. 73-15066

FIRST PRINTING

Published simultaneously in Canada
by Little, Brown & Company (Canada) Limited

PRINTED IN THE UNITED STATES OF AMERICA

For Anita

Preface

The articles in this volume are the outgrowth of a long-standing interest in both public finance and welfare economics and especially in the considerable area in which these two branches of economics overlap. This area particularly comprehends the analysis of the resource-allocation effects of tax and other policies, a label which is broad enough to cover all the studies presented here.

The format for the volume is more informal than that of most collections of essays, in that I have preceded most chapters by introductory notes. These notes serve different functions. In some cases they merely describe the article's content, and/or the circumstances under which it was originally written. In other cases they incorporate further thoughts on the problem, stemming either from further independent work, or as a reaction to comments received since the original publication. Much of this material summarizes the main points on which my classroom presentation of the issue in question has been modified since the particular chapter was written. This fact may add to this volume's usefulness for public finance classes at the graduate and advanced undergraduate levels.

Since the introductory notes themselves contain material similar to (and usually more extensive than) the summary statements appearing in introductions to similar collections, only the main outlines of the volume follow. Chapters 1–5 are concerned with consumer surplus analysis, in all cases in a general-equilibrium context. Chapter 1 represents a recent restatement of the basic principles underlying the use of consumer surplus concepts for policy analysis, and Chapters 2 and 3 expand and develop this approach to measuring the welfare costs of various distortions in a general-equilibrium context. Chapters 4 and 5, on the other hand, are applications (paradoxically antedating Chapters 1–3 by some years) in which the resource-allocation costs of a set of distortions are measured. Chapter 4 is concerned with measuring the costs generated by monopoly elements in United States manufacturing, whereas Chapter 5 deals with the distortions of foreign trade, capital, and labor markets that characterized the Chilean economy in the late 1950s.

Chapters 6–11 all deal, in one way or another, with the corporation income tax. Chapter 6, which is my contribution to the *International Encyclopedia of the Social Sciences* on the subject, expounds and introduces the general theme, Chapter 7 deals with the incidence of the tax, and Chapter 8 tries to measure its resource-allocation costs, working within the theoretical framework developed in 7. Chapter 9 (written jointly with John G. Cragg and Peter Mieszkowski) returns to the incidence issue in an empirical context, arguing the difficulty of answering the incidence question by means of econometric time-series analysis, and includes a response by Marion Krzyzaniak and Richard A. Musgrave.

Chapters 10–12 deal not with the corporation tax as such, but with specific provisions of United States tax legislation which apply particularly (though not exclusively) to the corporate sector. Chapter 10 considers the effects of the various tax incentives (most particularly stepped-up depreciation schedules and the investment tax credit) which were introduced in 1962–64 as investment stimuli. Chapters 11 and 12, on the other hand, both deal with the special tax treatment of minerals. Each covers the percentage depletion and capital gains options offered by the tax law, but the former chapter focuses on minerals generally, whereas the latter concentrates on estimating the relevant tax incentives for oil and gas alone.

Chapters 13–17 might be labeled as covering "Other Tax Issues." Chapter 13 gives an expository analysis of the value-added tax, culminating in a qualified advocacy for its adoption in the United States. Chapters 14 and 15 both deal with the question of border tax adjustments—the GATT-authorized remission at the border of indirect taxes paid in the production of exported goods, and the corresponding levy of surcharges on imported goods so as to capture from their importers indirect taxes similar in magnitude to those paid on home-produced goods of the same type. These chapters have never before been published, and they treat a topic that seems to have attracted increasing interest in recent years.

Chapters 16 and 17 move away from the United States context, the first to Latin America and the second to Canada. Both deal with tax reform. The first was my contribution to the Second Inter-American Conference on Taxation (Santiago, December, 1962) and sets forth my own thoughts (in this case frequently loaded with value judgments) as to the appropriate directions that tax reform should take in Latin America. This paper has been most noted for its revival and advocacy of the idea of market-enforced self-assessment of property and similar taxes. The last chapter presents a summary evaluation of the reform proposals of the so-called Carter Report on the Canadian tax system, as well as an empirical exercise designed to assess the likely capital-market implications of the Carter proposals. For easier reference, figures, tables, and equations have been renumbered throughout to incorporate the chapter numbers.

In conclusion let me express my thanks to those who have worked most closely with me in the preparation of this volume, without whose help it would probably never have come into being: to David Wall for initially suggesting the idea; to Daniel Wisecarver for helping with the final selection of papers and painstakingly screening them and the final manuscript for errors; and to Alyce Monroe, secretary and helper without peer. I am also grateful to my wife, to whom this book is dedicated, for the multitude of ways, including taxing herself for the welfare of our family, in which she has worked to make this book, along with my other professional activities, possible.

Contents

TAXATION AND WELFARE

I

Although the following article, originally published in the *Journal of Economic Literature* in September, 1971, was the last to be written of those appearing in this volume, it appears as the introductory essay because, more than any of its companion pieces, it deals with the broad conceptual framework of applied welfare economics. In particular, it provides a background against which the material presented in several other chapters (particularly 2, 3, 4, 5, and 8) can be more easily comprehended and digested.

The three postulates concern the use of (a) demand and (b) supply prices (i.e., the ordinates of the relevant curves) as measures of benefit and cost to demanders and suppliers of successive units demanded and supplied, and (c) the adding up of benefits and costs across different members of the community for which the welfare-economic analysis is being undertaken.

It is important in this context to recognize the substantial degree of subtlety and sophistication that the concepts of demand and supply price involve. In a true sense they reflect the value to the demander or supplier of the alternative(s) that he gives up in demanding or supplying an additional unit of a particular good or service. In this way each point along a demand curve reflects indifference on the part of the demander as between having that particular unit at that particular price on the one hand, and whatever else he would have done instead on the other, and similarly for the supply curve. Moreover, the alternatives in question may be monumentally complex: the choice between a teaching job at a midwestern university and one as economist for a real estate firm in Hawaii entails not only vastly different baskets of goods and services that would be consumed in one as against the other place; it can also involve totally different life-styles. The choice can also be probabilistic rather than single-valued, in the sense that taking a job in Hawaii real estate probably reduces the probability of each of a whole host of academic and quasi-academic opportunities that might come one's way, but probably raises the chances that any of a number of good business opportunities (other than the Hawaii job itself) will at some point or another present themselves. Yet complex though the alternatives may be, their value to the individual is summarized in the different (though undoubtedly mutually interdependent) supply prices he places upon the respective opportunities of working in the two very different environments.

The case is similar with demand price. Regardless of whether the choice is simple (e.g., that between a cola drink and ginger ale at a sporting event), intermediate (e.g., choosing a meal from a highly varied and elegant menu), or extremely complex (e.g., adjusting a large portfolio in a constantly changing and obviously probabilistic securities market), we can still attach a simple and very important meaning to demand price. For any particular choice or action, demand price is that one which just barely induces the individual to take the choice or action in question, thereby reflecting the borderline between it and its (possibly numerous and complex) alternatives. For choices involving highly divisible goods and services, the maximization of individual welfare entails carrying demand or supply to the point where, at the margin, demand or supply price equals market price. For choices entailing indivisibilities, the demander's or supplier's optimum, among alternative options, is that one which maximizes the excess of demand price over market price (for demanders) or that which maximizes the excess of market price over supply price (for suppliers).

This way of looking at demand and supply prices allows one to appreciate the scientific merit and the considerable intellectual power of the traditional idea of consumer (and producer) surplus. In fact the main thrust of this article is to go into the intellectual underpinnings of this concept, and to deal with some of the main issues that have been raised concerning it.

In the time since this article was published, the great bulk of the comments that I have received have dealt with postulate (c), which by its equal weighting of the demand and supply prices of different individuals ignores or sets aside questions of income distribution. I deal with this matter in a more technical context in my introduction to Chapter 2, so my present discussion concentrates on the broader issues involved. In the first place, let me state emphatically that I advocate the use of postulate (c) fundamentally (indeed, I should probably say solely) as a technical convention which permits us to separate resource-allocation from distributional effects in the analysis of any given problem. I emphatically do not mean to say or imply thereby that distributional considerations are unimportant, or that economists should refrain from expressing opinions concerning them. In fact, I believe that such opinions can play a vital role in the public debate over many policy issues, especially on the wide range of public programs with explicit distributional orientation.

What I do insist, however, is that we can never expect to achieve a general consensus about the weight that should be attached to the welfare of different groups, and that the tools of economic analysis have in themselves nothing to contribute toward helping us move toward such a consensus. As I have often told my classes, I think I can give a course on how to use the tools of economics to assess the resource-allocation effects of given policies or projects; I cannot, on the other hand, give a course in "how to tell the good guys from the bad guys," let alone indicate ways in which such a judgment could be directly incorporated as an integral part of the technical analysis of a particular public policy or private action.

James Meade's proposed method of assigning distributional weights to the benefits and costs associated with different individuals[1] could perfectly well be incorporated, in place of postulate (c), into the framework proposed here, thus leaving it totally free from the possibility of criticism on distributional grounds. I was constrained not to do this, however, not only because of the impossibility of gaining any general consensus on the relevant weights, but also because of the fact that only in a very small fraction of real-world problems can the benefits and costs of a particular policy, program, or other action be disaggregated among income groups or other categories that might be relevant in the assignment of distributional weights. This is particularly true for the ex ante analysis of policy decisions, where the relevant costs and benefits stretch many years into the future.

Thus in the final analysis I see no relevant or practical alternative to the use of postulate (c), at least for the great bulk of scientific work on the resource-allocation side of applied welfare economics. But this conveys no suggestion or implication that distributional effects should therefore be neglected. It simply means that where they are brought into account, this should be done as a separate part of an overall economic

[1] See J. E. Meade, *Trade and Welfare* (London: Oxford University Press, 1955), Vol. I, Chap. 5, and Vol. II, Chap. 2.

3

analysis of the problem in question (which in many cases may be even more important than the resource-allocation part, but which should not be mixed up with it).[2]

[2] The approach of distinguishing for analytical purposes between the allocative and the distributive aspects of a problem has a long tradition in the public finance literature. For an excellent modern defense of this approach, set in a somewhat broader context than that of my own paper, see Richard A. Musgrave, *The Theory of Public Finance* (New York: McGraw-Hill, 1959), Chaps. 1 and 2.

Chapter 1

Three Basic Postulates

for Applied Welfare Economics:

An Interpretive Essay

I

This paper is intended not as a scientific study, nor as a review of the literature, but rather as a tract — an open letter to the profession, as it were — pleading that three basic postulates be accepted as providing a conventional framework for applied welfare economics. The postulates are: (a) the competitive demand price for a given unit measures the value of that unit to the demander; (b) the competitive supply price for a given unit measures the value of that unit to the supplier; (c) when evaluating the net benefits or costs of a given action (project, program, or policy), the costs and benefits accruing to each member of the relevant group (e.g., a nation) should normally be added without regard to the individual(s) to whom they accrue.

In an era when literally thousands of studies involving cost-benefit analysis or other types of applied welfare economics are underway at any given moment, the need for an accepted set of professional standards for this type of study should be obvious. In proffering postulates (a)–(c) as the basis for such a set of standards, I do not want to overstate their benefits. Just as the road-construction standards that a team of highway engineers must meet can be checked by other highway engineers, so the exercise in applied welfare economics carried out by one team of economists should be subject to check by others. But while the highway engineers can apply professional standards to characteristics such as thickness of base, load-carrying capacity, drainage characteristics, and the like, characteristics such as scenic beauty are beyond their competence as professional engineers. In the same way, any program or project that is subjected to applied-welfare-economic analysis is likely to have characteristics upon which the economist as such is not professionally qualified to pronounce, and about which one economist is not professionally qualified to check the opinion of another. These elements — which surely include the income-distributional and national-defense aspects of any project or program, and probably its natural-beauty aspects as well — may be exceedingly important, perhaps even the

Reprinted with permission from Arnold C. Harberger, "Three Basic Postulates for Applied Welfare Economics," *Journal of Economic Literature*, Vol. IX, No. 3 (September, 1971), pp. 785–797.

dominant factors governing any policy decision, but they are not a part of that package of expertise that distinguishes the professional economist from the rest of humanity. And that is why we cannot expect to reach a professional consensus concerning them. If we are to take a (hopefully justified) professional pride in our work, we also must have the modesty and honesty not to claim for our profession more than we are particularly qualified to deliver. But this does not mean that we need be silent on matters that lie outside the range of our professional expertise; economists should probably participate more rather than less in the public discussion of such matters, but hopefully in a context that recognizes the extra-professional nature of their intervention.

Some readers will undoubtedly recognize that postulates (a)–(c) underlie most analyses that use the concepts of consumer and producer surplus. That being the case, one might ask, what is the need for a tract on the subject? My answer stems from the fact that, as an inveterate practitioner of applied welfare economics along many different lines, I encounter with considerable regularity colleagues who are skeptical of consumer surplus on one or more of several alleged grounds:

(i) Consumer-surplus analysis is valid only when the marginal utility of real income is constant.

(ii) Consumer-surplus analysis does not take account of changes in income distribution caused by the action(s) being analyzed.

(iii) Consumer-surplus analysis is partial-equilibrium in nature, and does not take account of the general-equilibrium consequences of the actions whose effects are being studied.

(iv) Consumer-surplus analysis, though valid for small changes, is not so for large changes.

(v) The concept of consumer surplus has been rendered obsolete by revealed-preference analysis.

While I do not have the impression that the skeptics dominate professional opinion in this area, they are sufficiently numerous (and a number of them sufficiently prestigious) that we surely cannot be said to have achieved a high degree of professional consensus on the subject. Yet I feel, precisely because of the power and wide applicability of the consumer-surplus concept, that a recognizable degree of consensus concerning it would increase, to society's general benefit, the influence on public policy of good economic analysis. More-over, I think that there is a fair chance of convincing a goodly share of the skeptics that postulates (a) to (c) constitute the most reasonable basis on which to seek professional consensus in the area of applied welfare economics. The merit of attaining something like a consensus, and the possibility of helping to induce some movement toward that end, provide the motivation for this tract.

II

Ordinarily, I would consider it quixotic to expect much to result from any such effort. But in this case my hopes are buoyed by the fact that it is easily possible for many skeptics to join the consensus without really changing their minds on any fundamental issues. How can this happen? Because (1) we already have a reasonably well-established consensus on the basic methodology of national-income measurement, (2) it is easy to show that postulates (a)–(c) incorporate a greater degree of subtlety of economic analysis than does national-income methodology, and (3) most of the "objections" to consumer-surplus analysis hold a fortiori with respect to the measurement of national income. If we are prepared to more-or-less agree on national-income methodology (while being mindful of its defects), why should we resist approaching an agreement on a methodology for applied welfare economics (also keeping its defects in mind, but aware at the same time that they are much less serious than those applying to national income)?

Let us consider specifically objections (i), (ii) and (v) above, comparing in each case the force with which the objection applies to consumer-surplus analysis on the one hand, and to the use of national income as an indication of welfare on the other — objections (iii) and (iv) are dealt with in section III below.

Objection (i). I will later show that the assumption of constancy of the marginal utility of real income is not essential for the validity of consumer-surplus measures of welfare. Here, however, I shall only note that the benefits and costs treated in most applications of consumer-surplus analysis (e.g., measures of the efficiency costs of a tax or an agricultural program, cost-benefit analyses of highway or irrigation projects, etc.) involve only a small fraction of a normal year's growth in GNP. Far more vulnerable to the objection that the marginal utility of real income might have changed are observations like "Real GNP doubled between 1950 and 1970," or even "National income will grow by $60 billion next year."

Objection (ii). By the same token, the changes in income distribution resulting from a particular measure being subjected to cost-benefit or consumer-surplus analysis are likely to be minimal by comparison with those that occur from decade to decade, or even from year to year, as a consequence of all causes. If, then, it is felt that "distributional weights" should be applied in the former case, before judgments can be made, it is even more important that they should be incorporated in the latter case.

Objection (v). Consider the case of the coal miner who, racked with silicosis, voluntarily quits a $7-an-hour job in the mine to take a newly available $2-an-hour job clerking in a grocery store. National income goes down, but welfare in all likelihood goes up. In this case consumer-surplus analysis accords with revealed preference, while the movement of national income is in the opposite direction from the change in welfare. The same is true for the textbook case of the housekeeper who marries her employer.

Of course, economists do not truly believe that real NNP or national income is a complete measure of welfare. But it is equally true that in most of the contexts in which changes in these magnitudes, or comparisons of them across

7

regions or countries are dealt with, the discussion carries strong welfare connotations, often to the point where it would be meaningless if those connotations were denied. National income and NNP are, in a very real sense, measures of welfare under certain assumptions, but only to a first order of approximation. No one would deny that many other factors are important — the strength of the social fabric, the quality of life, and certainly the issue of to whom the income accrues — but it is not feasible to build these into a national-income measure. Hypothetically, one might contemplate a national-income measure incorporating "distributional weights," but two obstacles stand in its way: first, the impossibility of achieving a consensus with regard to the weights, and second, the fact that most of the data from which the national accounts are built are aggregates in the first place, and do not distinguish the individuals or groups whose dollars they represent. Giving equal weight to all dollars of income is mathematically the simplest rule, and our data come that way in any event. In a sense, the second obstacle imposes, rather arbitrarily to be sure, a solution to the perplexing difficulties posed by the first. This solution is obviously a far-from-perfect measure of national welfare — indeed it is surprising how little dissatisfaction has been expressed (until quite recently) with its use as such. But even its firmest detractors would probably not deny the usefulness of the national accounts and the necessity for them to be built on the basis of rules or conventions reflecting some degree of professional consensus.

An easy way to see the relationship between national income and the consumer-surplus concept is to consider the first two terms of the Taylor expansion of a utility function

(1.1) $$U = U(X_1, X_2 \cdots X_n)$$

(1.2) $$\Delta U = \sum_i U_i \Delta X_i + \tfrac{1}{2} \sum_i \sum_j U_{ij} \Delta X_i \Delta X_j.$$

Since U_i is a function solely of $(X_1, X_2 \cdots X_n)$, we can write $\sum_j U_{ij} \Delta X_j = \Delta U_i$; with this (1.2) simplifies to

(1.3) $$\Delta U = \sum_i U_i \Delta X_i + \tfrac{1}{2} \sum_i \Delta U_i \Delta X_i.$$

Now, assuming utility maximization in the face of market prices $(P_1 \cdots P_n)$ we have $U_i = \lambda P_i$, where λ represents the marginal utility of income, and

(1.4) $$\Delta U_i = \lambda^0 \Delta P_i + P_i^0 \Delta \lambda + \Delta P_i \Delta \lambda.$$

Substituting from (1.4) into (1.3) we obtain

(1.5) $$\frac{\Delta U}{(\lambda^0 + \tfrac{1}{2} \Delta \lambda)} = \sum P_i^0 \Delta X_i + \tfrac{1}{2} \sum \Delta P_i \Delta X_i + \frac{1}{4} \frac{\Delta \lambda \sum \Delta P_i \Delta X_i}{(\lambda^0 + \tfrac{1}{2} \Delta \lambda)}.$$

Neglecting third-order terms, this yields

(1.5') $$\frac{\Delta U}{\lambda^0 + \tfrac{1}{2} \Delta \lambda} \approx \sum P_i^0 \Delta X_i + \tfrac{1}{2} \sum \Delta P_i \Delta X_i.$$

The first term on the right-hand side of (1.5') measures the first-order change in utility, and can be identified with the change in national income (or, more properly, net national product) expressed in constant prices. The second term

8

measures the second-order change in utility, and can be identified with the change in consumer surplus.[1] The fact that the consumer-surplus concept is associated with a higher-order term in the Taylor expansion of the utility function is simply the mathematical counterpart of the statement made earlier that "postulates (a)–(c) incorporate a greater degree of subtlety of economic analysis than does national-income methodology."

Note, too, that (1.5) in effect converts the change in utility into monetary terms by dividing it by the marginal utility of income. There is obviously no problem when the latter is not changing, but when it does change as a consequence of the action(s) being analyzed, the conversion of utility into money is implicitly carried out at the midpoint of the beginning and ending marginal utilities of income. The criticism[2] that consumer-surplus concepts have validity only when the marginal utility of income is constant must therefore be rejected.

The conversion of utility into money also greatly eases the aggregation problem. Clearly both the first-order and the second-order terms on the right-hand side of (1.5) can be aggregated over individuals without difficulty.

III

In this section I shall discuss objections (iii) and (iv), which were left aside in the comparison between consumer surplus and national-income methodologies in the preceding section. Objection (iii), that consumer-surplus analysis is

---

[1] This is strictly true only when the point of departure is one of full, undisturbed equilibrium. When the starting point is one where distortions are already present, some of the change in consumer surplus is incorporated in the first term. This point will be treated in more detail below.

[2] The origin of this criticism is probably the thought that changes in consumer surplus ought directly to measure changes in utility. That this would be a fruitless pursuit should be obvious — among other things consumer surplus would not be invariant to monotonic transformations of the utility function. However, the measure $1/2 \Sigma \Delta X_i \Delta P_i$ is invariant, with the change in ΔU stemming from a monotonic transformation being offset by the change in $(\lambda + 1/2 \Delta\lambda)$ in the denominator of the left-hand side of (1.5). The following way of stating the same argument avoids the approximation implicit in a two-term Taylor expansion: the change in utility stemming from the change in a policy variable from z_0 to z^* is

$$\Delta U = \int_{z_0}^{z^*} \sum_i U_i(z) \frac{\partial X_i}{\partial z} \, dz.$$

This, being expressed in utils, is not invariant to a monotonic transformation. However, transforming utility into money continuously through the integration process, always at the marginal utility of money prevailing at that point, we have

$$\Delta W = \int_{z_0}^{z^*} \sum_i \frac{U_i(z)}{\lambda(z)} \frac{\partial X_i}{\partial z} \, dz = \int_{z_0}^{z^*} \sum_i P_i(z) \frac{\partial X_i}{\partial z} \, dz.$$

This obviously is invariant under any transformation of the original utility function which leaves unchanged the relevant behavioral reactions to changes in z.

An issue arises in connection with the comparability of measures of welfare loss, when one is comparing moves on two different paths (say T_1 and T_2) away from the undistorted equilibrium. If the marginal utility of the numeraire (here real income) is constant, there is no issue in this regard. However, comparability does not require constancy of the marginal utility of real income, but only "well-behavedness." By this I mean that when real income falls by ΔY as a consequence of the imposition of T_2, its marginal utility should change by the same amount as occurs when real income falls by ΔY as a consequence of a tax T_1.

partial-equilibrium in nature, and fails to take account of general-equilibrium considerations, is totally invalid on a theoretical level, but can fairly be levied against some practical applications.

Taking the theoretical issue first, one need only note that rigorous general-equilibrium formulations of consumer-surplus measurement have long since been a part of the corpus of economic theory. Hotelling [10, 1938], Hicks [7, 1941; 8, 1946; 9, 1956], and Meade [18, 1955, esp. Vol. II] all have derived, in a general-equilibrium framework, measures of welfare change that are consistent with postulates (a)–(c), and many others have followed in their train.[3]

The key to understanding the general-equilibrium nature of the consumer-surplus concept is the following simple measure of welfare change:

$$(1.6) \qquad \Delta W = \int_{z=0}^{z^*} \sum_i D_i(z) \frac{\partial X_i}{\partial z} \, dz.$$

Here D_i represents the excess of marginal social benefit over marginal social cost per unit level of activity i; X_i represents the number of units of activity i; and z is the policy variable, the effects of a change in which we are interested in measuring. The D_i (distortions) can take many forms — about which more will be said below — but here, for simplicity of exposition, I shall assume that all the D_i take the form of taxes. A tax quite obviously drives a wedge between demand price (which under postulate (a) measures the value of the marginal unit to the demander) and supply price (which under postulate (b) measures the value of the marginal unit to the supplier), and this fits most naturally into the framework of this paper.

If a tax is placed on a single good j in the absence of any other distortions, (1.6) becomes

$$(1.7) \qquad \Delta W = \int_{T_j=0}^{T_i^*} T_j \frac{\partial X_j}{\partial T_j} \, dT_j,$$

which is equal to the familiar welfare-cost triangle (*ABC* in Figure 1.1). Though the demand and supply functions of other goods may shift as a consequence of placing a tax on good j, the measure of welfare change is unaffected by such shifts since the distortions D_i in all other markets are, by assumption in this case, zero. However, if taxes on other goods already exist when T_j^* is imposed, the effects of its imposition are given by

$$(1.8) \qquad \Delta W = \int_{T_j=0}^{T_j^*} T_j \frac{\partial X_j}{\partial T_j} \, dT_j + \int_{T_j=0}^{T_j^*} \sum_{i \neq j} T_i \frac{\partial X_i}{\partial T_j} \, dT_j.$$

This is equal to the triangle *ABC* in Figure 1.1 (which generates a negative contribution to welfare) plus, with constant T_is, the expression $\sum_{i \neq j} T_i \, \Delta X_i$ where ΔX_i measures the change in the equilibrium quantity of X_i occasioned by the imposition of T_j^*. Any of the terms in this summation, which is what

[3] See Corlett and Hague [1, 1953]; Harberger [3, 1964; 4, 1964]; Johnson [11, 1960; 12, 1962]; Lange [14, 1942]; Lipsey and Lancaster [15, 1956–57]; Lipsey [16, 1970]; and McKenzie [17, 1951].

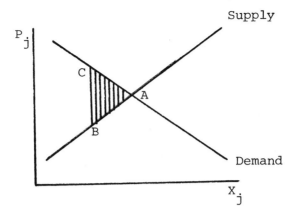

FIGURE I.I

makes the difference between partial- and general-equilibrium approaches when other distortions are present, can be either positive or negative — when the distortion itself is positive (e.g., a tax), a positive contribution is made to the change in welfare if, as a consequence of a new disturbance (in this case the imposition of $T_j{}^*$), X_i increases, and a negative contribution if X_i decreases. When the distortion itself is negative (e.g., a subsidy), the contribution to welfare associated with activity i as a consequence of $T_j{}^*$ is negative if $\partial X_i / \partial T_j > 0$ and positive if $\partial X_i / \partial T_j < 0$. This case is illustrated in Figure 1.2, where it is assumed that both the demand and supply curves of X_k shift as a consequence of the imposition of $T_j{}^*$. If the shift is from the solid demand and supply curves (when $T_j = 0$) to the broken ones (when $T_j = T_j{}^*$), the area $EFGH$ ($= T_k \, \Delta X_k$) is an added loss; if the shift is in the other direction it is an added benefit helping to offset (and possibly actually outweighing) the triangle ABC in Figure 1.1.

This is a convenient place to point out the relationship between the general expression (1.8) for welfare change and the approximation (1.5'). Define $C_i + T_i = P_i$, and assume constant costs of production C_i, with the resource constraint $\sum C_i X_i = Y$, a constant.[4] When a tax is imposed on X_j in the presence of pre-existing taxes on other goods $i \neq j$, we have, substituting $C_i + T_i = P_i^0$ for $i \neq j$, $C_j = P_j^0$ and $T_j{}^* = \Delta P_j$ into (1.5'),

(1.5'') $$\sum P_i^0 \, \Delta X_i + \tfrac{1}{2} \sum \Delta P_i \, \Delta X_i = \sum C_i \, \Delta X_i + \sum T_i \, \Delta X_i$$
$$+ \tfrac{1}{2} \sum \Delta C_i \, \Delta X_i + \tfrac{1}{2} T_j{}^* \, \Delta X_j.$$

Since $\sum C_i \, \Delta X_i = \sum \Delta C_i \, \Delta X_i = 0$ under our assumptions, we have

(1.5''') $$\sum P_i^0 \, \Delta X_i + \tfrac{1}{2} \sum \Delta P_i \, \Delta X_i = \sum T_i \, \Delta X_i + \tfrac{1}{2} T_j{}^* \, \Delta X_j$$

[4] These assumptions are consistent with a situation in which the tax revenues received by the government are redistributed to the private sector via neutral transfers. For a more detailed treatment see Harberger [3, 1964].

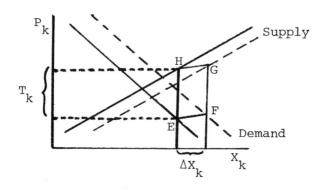

FIGURE I.2

as a measure of the change in welfare stemming from the imposition of T_j^*.[5]
This is precisely what emerges from (1.8) in the case where the demand and
supply curves for X_j are linear. It also shows how, when there are pre-existing
distortions, elements of consumer surplus are present in the expression $\sum P_i^0 \Delta X_i$,
representing the first-order approximation to welfare change.

Let us return to the discussion of objection (iii), that consumer-surplus
analysis neglects general-equilibrium considerations. While it is clear that no
theoretical obstacle stands in the way of taking such considerations into account,
it is in fact rarely done in studies involving applied welfare economics. I do
not want to appear to defend this neglect — indeed, the sooner it is rectified,
the better — but at the same time I want to try to dispel any thoughts that the
job of incorporating general-equilibrium aspects is so big as to be effectively
hopeless. All that job entails is adding to the standard partial-equilibrium
welfare analysis (of the tax T_j^* in our example), an expression $\sum_{i \neq j} D_i \Delta X_i$.
That may look like a formidable task but it need not be. The set of activities
with significant distortions is a subset of the set of all activities; the set of
activities whose levels are significantly affected by the action under study
(e.g., T_j^*) is another subset of the set of all activities. Only their intersection
(see Figure 1.3) is important for the analysis of the effects of the specific policy

[5] Where no pre-existing distortions are present, and a vector of distortions $T^* = (T_1^*, T_2^* \cdots T_n^*)$ is introduced, (1.6) becomes, for linear demand and supply curves, $\Delta W = \frac{1}{2}\Sigma T_i \Delta X_i$, where

$$\Delta X_i = \int_{\mu=0}^1 \left(\frac{\partial X_i}{\partial T} \right) T^* \mu \, d\mu.$$

That is to say, if the final set of taxes is (.5, .2, .1), one can imagine the process of integration taking place through steps like (.05, .02, .01), (.10, .04, .02), (.15, .06, .03), etc. The locus of points traced out by this exercise will define the set of triangles $1/2 T_i \Delta X_i$. As this exercise can in principle be performed for any set of distortions (not just taxes), it is quite general. One must note, however, that the triangles traced out here are not triangles between stable demand and supply curves but rather triangles defined by the loci of marginal social benefit (demand price) and marginal social cost (supply price) as μ goes from zero to one. On this result see Hotelling's equation 19 and the subsequent discussion [10, 1938].

action in question, and it is to be hoped that in most cases the number of elements in it will be of manageable size.[6]

Objection (iv) can be dealt with on several levels. In the first place, there is the issue of the exactness of (1.5); when the basic utility functions are quadratic, the first two terms of the Taylor expansion are all that are needed to describe the function fully; but when the basic utility functions are not linear or quadratic, (1.5) will be an approximation. And (1.5′) is vulnerable even when the utility function is quadratic, because of its neglect of the third term of (1.5). But while (1.5) and (1.5′) thus may contain errors of approximation which will be smaller, the smaller are the changes being studied, (1.6) is not subject to the same charge. The integrals set out there can be taken for curved as well as linear demand and supply curves, or, more properly stated, for curved or linear loci of demand prices and supply prices.

At another level entirely, one might interpret the large-versus-small-changes issue as raising up the old consumer-surplus conundrums about the value attaching to the first units of liquid or the first units of food, etc. I prefer to sidestep this issue on the ground that the problems arising in applied welfare economics typically do not involve carrying people to or from the zero point

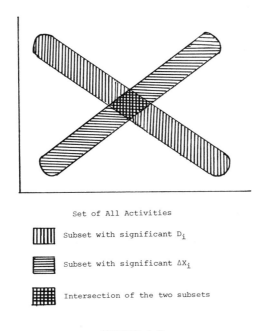

Set of All Activities

Subset with significant D_i

Subset with significant ΔX_i

Intersection of the two subsets

FIGURE I.3

[6] Certain distortions, such as the property tax or the corporation income tax, which apply to a large subset of activities, can be taken into account through the use of shadow prices — e.g., in this case the social opportunity cost of capital. See Harberger [5, 1968 and 6, 1969]. Once the "general" distortions have been dealt with in this way, the remaining ones, it is to be hoped, will be sufficiently small in number so as to keep the problem manageable.

in their demand curves for food or for liquids, and where they do (as, for example, in famine relief programs), it appears more appropriate to approach the problem through assigning a monetary value to the human lives saved or lost, a task which necessarily carries us beyond the narrow confines of consumer-surplus analysis.

At still another level, when large changes are involved, the well-behavedness of functions is less easily guaranteed than when only small changes are present. For example, it is easy to show that the Hicks-Slutsky substitution properties apply to demand functions defined by movements constrained to a locus of the form $\sum C_i X_i = Y$, a constant (FG in Figure 1.4) so long as one is concerned with small changes in the neighborhood of the undistorted equilibrium (e.g., in the neighborhood of A). However, this cannot be shown to be generally true for large changes. For example, Figure 1.4 is so constructed that at both B and E the indifference curves intersecting FG have the same slope. This means that a demand function constrained to the locus FG (with real income being held constant in this sense) will have two quantities associated with the same relative price. Except in the case where the income expansion path at that price coincided with the segment EB between these two quantities, there would have to be some range(s) in that quantity interval in which the own-price elasticity of each good was positive, thus violating one of the Hicks-Slutsky conditions.[7]

There are at least two ways in which analyses based on postulates (a) to (c) can be justified in the face of this possible criticism. At the strictly theoretical level, while some results of some exercises in applied welfare economics may derive directly from the Hicks-Slutsky properties, the validity of equation (1.6) does not depend on the existence of well-behavedness in this sense. Alternatively one may simply take it as a matter of convention that, just as measurements of real national income in a sense are built on a linear approximation of the utility function, so we shall base consumer-surplus and cost-benefit analyses upon a quadratic approximation of that function, incorporating the Hicks-Slutsky properties. This more "pragmatic" approach would presumably be

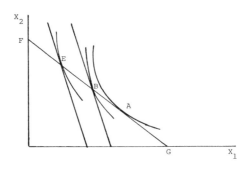

FIGURE 1.4

---

[7] For a further elaboration of this point see Foster and Sonnenschein [2, 1970].

based on the unlikelihood of our encountering cases in which empirical evidence can be mustered showing that such an approximation yields seriously biased numerical estimates of welfare costs and/or benefits.

A final variant of the large-versus-small-changes question concerns the normalization of measures of welfare change to correct for changes in the general price level. Consider the case of a two-good economy with $X_1 C_1 + X_2 C_2 = Y$, a constant. In this context one can analyze the effects of imposing, say, a 100 percent tax on X_1, with no distortion on X_2, or alternatively granting a 50 percent subsidy to X_2 with no distortion in the market for X_1. Assuming that the tax proceeds are returned to the public via neutral transfers and that the money for the subsidy is raised by neutral taxes, we should expect the same real equilibrium to be achieved in both of the alternative situations being compared. We should also, presumably, arrive at the same measure for ΔW. If we set $C_1 = C_2 = 1$, which is simply a question of choice of units and entails no loss of generality, with the 100 percent tax on X_1, the measure of welfare change is $\Delta W = 1/2 \sum \Delta X_i \, \Delta P_i = 1/2 \, \Delta X_1$. Alternatively, with a 50 percent subsidy to X_2, the welfare change measure is $-1/4 \, \Delta X_2$, which is equal to $1/4 \, \Delta X_1$, since under our assumptions $\Delta X_2 = -\Delta X_1$. This ambiguity can readily be resolved through the appropriate choice of a numeraire. When X_1 is the numeraire, the 100 percent tax on it is reflected in the price vector changing from $(1, 1)$ to $(1, 1/2)$, which is exactly what happens when a 50 percent subsidy to X_2 is introduced, so long as X_1 is the numeraire. Likewise, when X_2 is the numeraire, the 50 percent subsidy to it produces the same price vector $(2, 1)$ as is generated by the 100 percent tax on X_1. My own preference as to a conventional way of correcting for changes in the absolute price level is to normalize on net national product = national income. This entails setting $\sum P_i X_i = \sum C_i X_i = Y$, a constant, which in turn implies, since $C_i + T_i = P_i$, that $\sum T_i X_i = 0$. This normalization automatically calls attention to the fact that most problems of applied welfare economics are "substitution-effect-only" problems, a point to which we shall turn in the next section.

IV

In this section I shall discuss some of the complexities that may arise in applications of the analytical approach represented by postulates (a)–(c). Let us first consider in more detail the close relation of the postulates to "revealed preference." Essentially, postulates (a) and (b) state that when demanders (suppliers) pay (get) their demand (supply) price for each marginal unit, the balance of their indifference as between demanding (supplying) that unit and undertaking the relevant available alternative activities has just barely been tipped. In effect, demand and supply prices are measures of the alternative benefits that demanders and suppliers forego when they do what they decide to do.

Equation (1.6) appears to capture all effects of an exogenous policy change, z, that are relevant to our three postulates — and indeed it does except when the exogenous change z in itself alters the resources available to the economy in question, the technological possibilities under which it operates, or the trading conditions that it faces in external markets. So long as the exogenous change does not alter any of these things, all that it entails is the reshuffling of available resources among activities. It is in this sense that "substitution effects only" are involved in expression (1.6) in such cases.

To see that (1.6) does not capture the "income effects" of changes in resources, technology, or trading conditions, let us consider them in turn. Suppose, for example, that the exogenous change is that emigrant remittances, which were previously outlawed under foreign countries' exchange controls, are now permitted. The country receiving the remittances clearly gains, even if no distortions whatsoever are present in its economy. Hence (1.6) fails to capture the direct benefit associated with the remittances, even though in the presence of distortions it would capture the welfare "repercussions" that the receipt of the remittances might engender.

When technological advance occurs, the resources thus freed are enabled to increase total welfare, again even if no distortions are present. In Figure 1.5, the benefit from a technological advance that reduced unit costs from OA to OB would be given by the area $ABCD$ in the absence of other distortions, and by that area plus expression (1.6) in their presence. Expression (1.6) would of course include the area $CDEF$ if a unit tax equal to ED were already in existence on X_1. The exogenous force z in (1.6) would in this case be the reduction in unit cost (price) of producing X_1 and the terms in $\partial X_i/\partial z$ would include movements due to both the income and the substitution effects of this price change.

An exactly similar analysis applies in the case of an improvement in trading conditions in external markets. Here again a measure of the contribution to welfare that would be entailed in the absence of distortions must be added to (1.6), and the $\partial X_i/\partial z$ in (1.6) reinterpreted as above.

I believe that the three cases mentioned — new resources (gifts from outside), new technology (gifts of science and nature), and improved trading terms — or their respective negatives, are the only ones for which estimated first-order income effects must be added to expression (1.6). It is very important to note that such effects are not generated by price changes taking place within the economy under study in the absence of technical change. In this case, unless there are distortions, the benefits to demanders of a fall in price are cancelled

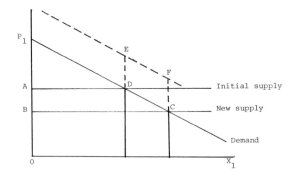

FIGURE 1.5

16

by the costs to suppliers, and vice versa in the case of a rise in price. And when distortions are present, (1.6) captures their effect. Likewise it is important to recognize that no additional term should be added to (1.6) in cases where production moves from a point on the true (outer) production frontier to some interior point as a consequence of the introduction of a new distortion (such as a tax on the employment of a factor in some lines of industry but not in others).

This brings to mind a second subtlety involved in (1.6): it is essential to recognize that the X_i refer to activities, not just products. In the case just mentioned the tax would be on the activity of using, e.g., capital in a certain subset of industries — say the corporate sector. D_i would here be the tax per unit of corporate capital, and X_i its amount. The activities of producing and consuming a given good should be kept analytically separate whenever the distortions affecting them differ;[8] likewise, a given type of activity which is affected by different distortions in different regions should be broken down into as many separate activities as there are different distortions. Perhaps the best guide that can be given in this matter is "identify the relevant distortions and let them define the relevant set of activities."

We now turn to a brief listing of the various types of distortion. (1) Taxes have probably been given sufficient attention already; let me only add that all kinds of taxes (income, excise, property, sales, consumption, production, value-added, etc.) fit easily into the framework presented here. (2) Monopoly profits, in the sense of any return (above the normal earnings of capital) that is obtained as a consequence of artificially restricting sales to a point where price exceeds marginal cost should also clearly be included. Note that for a great many analytical purposes monopoly profits can be treated as a privately imposed and privately collected tax. (3) The excess of price over marginal revenue in any external market in which the society in question has monopoly power is another case. This is a negative distortion which can be offset by an optimal export tax or by the implicit tax imposed by a private export monopoly. Categories (4) and (5) are simply the counterparts of (2) and (3) for the case of monopsony, the distortion in (4) stemming from monopsony profits, and that in (5) from the excess of marginal cost over price in any external market in which the society in question has monopsony power. (6) Externalities of all kinds represent distortions, positive or negative. Pollution of air or water is a negative distortion, which could, under postulates (a)–(c), be offset by a tax per unit of pollutant equal to what people would be willing to pay not to have it, or what they require as compensation in order to put up with it. The congestion of highways and streets represents another negative distortion, which could in principle be offset by an optimum congestion toll reflecting the extra cost (in terms of time, fuel, wear and tear, etc.) imposed upon others as a consequence of the presence of the marginal driver on the road.

Some readers may be inclined to question my classifying all taxes (and all monopoly profits) as distortions, only to go on to point out cases where they can be used to offset other distortions. Why not make special categories for

---

[8] Except in the trivial case of a closed economy or of nontraded goods, where production and consumption are necessarily the same.

17

cases like the optimum tariff, optimum export tax, optimum pollution charge, and optimum congestion toll? My answer is twofold. First, it is overwhelmingly simpler to avoid the special categories, and its cost — if any — is only the acceptance of the idea that distortions can offset each other. But this idea is needed in any event for activities where more than one distortion is present; different distortions applying to a given activity can either reinforce, or wholly or partially offset each other. Second, by avoiding special categories we high-light the fact that we are very unlikely to find optimal taxes and tolls in any real-world context.

V

This brings me back to my main theme: to plead for the "conventionalization" of postulates (a)–(c). Arguing in favor of them are the facts that they are both simple and robust and that they underlie a long tradition in applied welfare economics. They are simple both in the sense that their use entails no more than the standard techniques of received economic theory, and in the sense that the data that their use requires are more likely to be available than those required by alternative sets of postulates (in particular any that involve the full-blown use of "distributional weights").

The robustness of the postulates is another attribute of special importance. They can readily be used to define a set of policies that characterizes a full optimum. This entails no more than introducing taxes, subsidies, or other policies to neutralize distortions (e.g., monopoly, pollution) that would other-wise exist, so that the consolidated D_i affecting each activity are all zero, and raising government revenue by taxes that are truly neutral (lump-sum or head taxes),[9] or (cheating only slightly) by almost-neutral taxes such as Kaldor's progressive consumption-expenditure tax [13, 1955]. The postulates can also, in principle, be used to solve second-best problems such as finding the excise tax rates T_i on a subset of commodities $X_1, X_2, \cdots, X_k$ that entails the mini-mum cost of distortions while still raising a given amount of revenue. But these problems, taken from the theoretical literature, are likely to remain textbook problems. The practitioner of applied welfare economics knows full well that his clients do not come to him in search of full optima or elegant suboptima. He is more likely to be asked which of two alternative agricultural programs is better, or what resource-allocation costs a given tax increase involves, or whether a certain bridge is worth its cost. And to be relevant, his answer must recognize the existence of many distortions in the economy, over whose presence neither he nor his client have control. Most applied welfare economics thus answers questions like "Does this action help or hurt, and by approximately how much?" or "Which of two or three alternative actions helps most or hurts least, and by approximately how much?" — all this in a context in which most (if not all) existing distortions have to be taken as given. It is the fact that the three postulates are able to handle these kinds of questions, as well as more elegant optimization problems, that gives them the robustness to which I refer.

While it is true that there is no complete correspondence between what is

---

[9] The best definition of a head tax is one which must be paid either with money or with the taxpayer's head!

18

traditional and what is right, some weight must be given to the fact that no alternative set of basic assumptions comes nearly as close as postulates (a)–(c) to distilling the fundamental assumptions of applied welfare economics as we know it. These postulates are reflected not only in the general-equilibrium literature referred to in footnotes 5 and 6, but also in the standard practice of down-to-earth cost-benefit analyses [see, for example, 20, U.S. Inter-Agency Committee on Water Resources, 1958]. And it is here, really, that the need for a consensus is greatest. In the United States, cost-benefit (and its counterpart, "cost-effectiveness") analysis received a major boost when the PPB (Planning-Programming-Budgeting) concept was endorsed by President Lyndon Johnson and decreed as official policy by the Bureau of the Budget. And at the state and local level, investment projects and programs are also being scrutinized with an unprecedented degree of care, largely owing to the increasing concern that people have for environmental issues. Moreover, not just the United States is involved in this movement; the concerns about the environment, the worries about "what we are doing to ourselves," the recognition that our resources are too scarce to be wasted on bad programs, have no national limits. There is, indeed, a worldwide trend in which, country by country, an increasing fraction of the key decision-making posts are occupied by economists, and in which increasing efforts are applied to provide a sound economic justification for the projects that governments undertake. Finally, we have seen in the last decade a growing involvement of international organizations in the issues to which this paper is addressed: three regional development banks newly formed for Africa, Asia, and Latin America; increasing resources are devoted by the United Nations Development Programme to project identification and development, and by the World Bank to project financing. The OECD [19, 1968, 1969] has also shown increasing concern in this area.

The developments described above simply highlight the need for a set of standards, of "rules of the game" by which our professional work in applied welfare economics can be guided and judged. The three basic postulates that have been the subject of this essay provide a de minimis answer to this need: their simplicity, their robustness, and the long tradition that they represent all argue for them as the most probable common denominator on which a professional consensus on procedures for applied welfare economics can be based.

And so, having made my plea, let me salute the profession with what might well have been the title of this paper, with what is certainly the key that points to the solution of most problems in applied welfare economics, with what surely should be the motto of any society that we applied welfare economists might form, and what probably, if only we could learn to pronounce it, should be our password:

$$\text{``} \int_{z=0}^{z^*} \sum_i D_i(z) \frac{\partial X_i}{\partial z} \, dz. \text{''}$$

REFERENCES

1. Corlett, W. J., and Hague, D. C. "Complementarity and the Excess Burden of Taxation," *Rev. Econ. Stud.*, 1953, 21(1), pp. 21–30.

2. Foster, E., and Sonnenschein, H. "Price Distortion and Economic Welfare," *Econometrica*, March 1970, 38(2), pp. 281–297.

3. Harberger, A. C. "Taxation, Resource Allocation and Welfare" in National Bureau of Economic Research and The Brookings Institution, *The Role of Direct and Indirect Taxes in the Federal Revenue System*. Princeton: Princeton University Press, 1964, pp. 25–75. [This volume, Chapter 2.]

4. ———. "The Measurement of Waste," *Amer. Econ. Assoc. Pap. and Proc.*, May 1964, 54, pp. 58–76. [This volume, Chapter 3.]

5. ———. "On Measuring the Social Opportunity Cost of Public Funds" in *The Discount Rate in Public Investment Evaluation* (Conference Proceedings of the Committee on the Economics of Water Resources Development, Western Agricultural Economics Research Council, Report No. 17, Denver, Colorado, December 17–18, 1968), pp. 1–24.

6. ———. "Professor Arrow on the Social Discount Rate" in *Cost-Benefit Analysis of Manpower Policies*, edited by G. G. Somers and W. D. Wood. Kingston, Ontario: Industrial Relations Centre, Queen's University, 1969, pp. 76–88.

7. Hicks, J. R. "The Rehabilitation of Consumers' Surplus," *Rev. Econ. Stud.*, February 1941, pp. 108–16. Reprinted in American Economic Association, *Readings in Welfare Economics*. Homewood, Ill.: Richard D. Irwin, Inc., 1969, pp. 325–335.

8. ———. *Value and Capital*. Second edition. Oxford: The Clarendon Press. 1946.

9. ———. *A Revision of Demand Theory*. London: Oxford University Press, 1956, chapters X and XVIII.

10. Hotelling, H. "The General Welfare in Relation to Problems of Railway and Utility Rates," *Econometrica*, July 1938, 6(3). Reprinted in American Economic Association, *Readings in Welfare Economics*. Homewood, Ill.: Richard D. Irwin, Inc., 1969.

11. Johnson, H. G. "The Cost of Protection and the Scientific Tariff," *J. Polit. Econ.*, August 1960, 68(4), pp. 327–345.

12. ———. "The Economic Theory of Customs Unions" in *Money, Trade and Economic Growth*. London: George Allen and Unwin, 1962, pp. 48 ff.

13. Kaldor, N. *An Expenditure Tax*. London: George Allen and Unwin, 1955.

14. Lange, O. "The Foundations of Welfare Economics," *Econometrica*, July–October 1942, 10, pp. 215–228. Reprinted in American Economic Association, *Readings in Welfare Economics*. Homewood, Ill.: Richard D. Irwin, Inc., 1969, pp. 26–38.

15. Lipsey, R. G., and Lancaster, K. "The General Theory of Second Best," *Rev. Econ. Stud.*, 1956–57, 25(63), pp. 11–32.

16. Lipsey, R. G. *The Theory of Customs Unions: A General Equilibrium Analysis*. London: Weidenfeld and Nicholson, 1970.

17. McKenzie, L. W. "Ideal Output and the Interdependence of Firms," *Econ. J.*, December 1951, 61, pp. 785–803.

18. Meade, J. E. *Trade and Welfare*, Vol. II, Mathematical Supplement. London: Oxford University Press, 1955.

19. Organization for Economic Cooperation and Development. *Manual of Industrial Project Analysis in Developing Countries*. Paris, Vol. I, 1968; Vol. II (by I. M. D. Little and J. A. Mirrlees), 1969.

20. United States Inter-Agency Committee on Water Resources. *Proposed Practices for Economic Analysis of River Basin Projects*. Washington: Government Printing Office, 1958.

II

The following chapter was first presented in 1963 at a conference sponsored by the National Bureau of Economic Research and The Brookings Institution and published jointly by them in a volume titled, *The Role of Direct and Indirect Taxes in the Federal Revenue System* the following year. Together with Chapter 3 of this volume, it deals in some detail with the analysis of the welfare costs of taxation in a general-equilibrium context. The initial problem posed was how, in the analysis of a particular tax or set of taxes, to account for the money (or command over resources) raised by the government in that way. On the one hand it could be assumed that the government spent the tax proceeds in some specific way, but unfortunately there is no limit to the number of alternative patterns of additional spending that could thus be assumed. Similarly, it could be postulated for the purposes of the analysis that other taxes were reduced to compensate the extra revenue generated by the tax(es) being studied. But again there is an infinite range of alternative taxes or combinations of taxes that could play this compensating role. On reflection, it becomes obvious that the problem requires some sort of "conventional" solution.

At the end of section I, I proposed the solution that in analyzing the effects of a particular set of taxes we consider as its counterpart a reduction of income taxes of similar incidence by income bracket (see Table 2.1). This solution has the possible virtue of "sounding practical," and it was with this in mind that I introduced it. But it has the theoretical flaws (a) of entailing distributional changes within income brackets (see footnote 5), and (b) of making it difficult to analyze changes in the income tax itself (indeed, I bypass this assumption when dealing with income taxation as such). And in any case its aura of "practicality" is false, in the sense that in no plausible real-world context would it work out that the introduction of a new excise tax (or set of taxes) would be just counterbalanced by a reduction in income taxes neatly designed so as to leave the distribution of the tax burden by income bracket unchanged.

In retrospect, I would prefer to have proposed a more purist convention with respect to "where the tax money goes" — which indeed is the one I have always used in my own thinking on the subject. This solution uses the concept of neutral taxes and transfers, which can be conceived of as classical lump-sum taxes and subsidies. When a new tax or set of taxes is imposed, we conceive of it as being counterbalanced by a pattern of lump-sum subsidies (and possibly lump-sum taxes) which keeps the relative distribution of income unchanged. We thus rule out both (first-order) income effects and income-distribution effects as we study the influence of particular taxes on economic efficiency. In a sense this convention fully isolates the efficiency aspects of the problem under review, so that readers can feel on safer ground with it as the backdrop of the analysis, rather than the "practical convention" mentioned in the text.

As alluded to earlier (see Chapter 1), I find it surprising how many people have an instinctive negative reaction to an analytical apparatus which conceptually separates efficiency from distribution criteria in the analysis of a particular problem. One may perhaps caricature this frequent reaction as saying that if one separates out the efficiency aspect of a problem, it must mean that one implicitly favors the status quo as far as income distribution is concerned. Here I would simply like to introduce some arguments as a counterpoise to that reaction.

Consider first the standard textbook separation of the income and substitution effects of a change in price. As

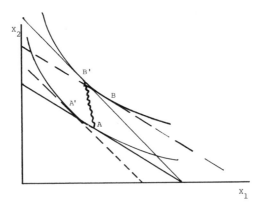

FIGURE 2A

22

depicted in Figure 2A, the total move is from A to B'. Are we to consider the substitution effect as the move from A to A' and the income effect that from A' to B', or should we instead view the income effect as being the move from A to B, and the substitution effect that from B to B'? Obviously there is no ground for choice here — indeed there is no reason in principle why we could not make the separation between income and substitution effects continuously as one varies price from its initial to its final level, as suggested by the zigzag line AB', where "upward" moves represent income effects and "leftward" moves substitution effects.

It is similar with respect to distribution effects. If we let X represent the vector of outputs, D that of the distribution of income, and T that of policy variables (taxes, etc.), and express $X = F(D, T)$, we have four possible points, labeled to correspond to those in Figure 2A.

$$X_a(D_0, T_0)$$
$$X_{a'}(D_0, T_1)$$
$$X_b(D_1, T_0)$$
$$X_{b'}(D_1, T_1).$$

The moves from X_a to $X_{a'}$, and from X_b to $X_{b'}$ are two alternative measures of the efficiency effects of the policy shift from T_0 to R', and there is no way to choose between them analytically. And since the same methodology for measuring efficiency effects (welfare costs) would be applied in either case, it is idle to attribute to the methodology or its users a bias in favor of the status quo.

Section II is an effort to derive analytically but at the same time expound intuitively the basic methodology of welfare-cost measurement. In order to keep the analysis simple and amenable to graphical treatment, it is limited to the case of a linear resource constraint. (However, the counterpart of this analysis for the case of a nonlinear constraint is presented in "The Measurement of Waste.") Toward the close of section II there is a direct derivation of the basic expressions for welfare cost from a general utility function. This is very similar to that appearing in equations (1.1) to (1.5') in Chapter 1, but there are differences. Basically the derivation in Chapter 2 uses the linear resource constraint to eliminate problems connected with possible changes in the marginal utility of income, whereas the derivation in Chapter 1 works without making any assumptions regarding resource constraints and contains a more sophisticated handling of possible changes in the marginal utility of income. It is important to note, however, that for the problems treated in the following chapter, both derivations come to the same result.

Subsequent sections deal with the theoretical derivation of a measure of the welfare cost of income taxation, with an attempt to get a rough empirical estimate of the order of magnitude of this cost for the United States, with an assessment, in theoretical terms, of the comparative welfare costs of income and excise taxation, with explorations concerning the welfare costs related to the tax treatment of saving and with ruminations about the influence of taxation on economic growth.

Chapter 2

Taxation, Resource Allocation, and Welfare

I. INTRODUCTION[1]

During the past decade the traditional solution to the issue of direct vs. indirect taxation has been subjected to serious challenge. Whereas earlier the theoretical superiority of direct over indirect taxation was accepted as virtually axiomatic, now it must be regarded as something that cannot be "proved," and that in principle has to be investigated for each particular case. The traditional case for direct taxation rested on its alleged "neutrality" among the alternatives open to consumers. Whereas an indirect tax on one item of consumption made that item artificially expensive to consumers, relative to other goods, and thus consumers were faced with relative prices that did not reflect the relative marginal costs of production of different goods, an income tax was generally held to be free of this defect. The income tax, it was held, was similar to a system of excise taxes striking all commodities with an equal percentage tax rate. Whatever might be the ratios between the marginal costs of producing different goods, the same ratios would (under competition) apply to the prices facing consumers. Marginal rates of substitution in consumption (given by the ratios

[1] This introductory section is meant to serve, in addition to the usual functions of an introduction, as a guide to readers who might otherwise be put off by the amount of mathematics that appears in the main body of the paper. The principal motivation for and conclusions from each section are set out here in nonmathematical terms, so that readers may skip any offending section of the main text without substantial loss of continuity. For the further guidance of readers, let me here point out that section IV contains the most mathematical manipulation, and can be skipped with the aid of the summary in the introduction without serious loss. Section II, on the other hand, develops the fundamental framework that is used throughout the paper. Skipping this section therefore entails substantial loss of content. I have tried, in section II, to develop the basic argument with the aid of graphical analysis, so as to ease the burden on less mathematically oriented readers, and I hope, accordingly, that most readers will be able to work through the derivations presented there. In comparison with sections II and IV, the remaining sections contain only a modest amount of mathematical manipulation.

Reprinted by permission of the National Bureau of Economic Research, Arnold C. Harberger, "Taxation, Resource Allocation, and Welfare," in *The Role of Direct and Indirect Taxes in the Federal Reserve System*, Princeton University Press for the National Bureau of Economic Research and the Brookings Institution, Princeton, 1964.

of gross-of-tax prices between pairs of goods) would therefore be equal to marginal rates of substitution in production (given by the corresponding ratios of net-of-tax prices).

Many economists realized, long before 1951, that this proposition would have to be modified in a situation in which the supply of labor was other than completely inelastic. But the extent of the required modification was not appreciated. In point of fact, the required modification is so great that it destroys any theoretical presumption of the superiority of direct over indirect taxation. This was pointed out by Little in his fundamental paper written in 1951.[2] He presented a simple example in which labor was the only factor of production and in which there were only three "goods": say, bread, wine, and leisure. In this case, an excise tax on wine would distort the choices between wine and bread and between wine and leisure, but would leave the choice between bread and leisure undistorted. Similarly, an excise tax on bread would distort the choices between bread and wine and between bread and leisure, but would leave the choice between wine and leisure undistorted. However, an income tax (interpreted as an equal-rate excise tax on both bread and wine) would distort the choices between bread and leisure and between wine and leisure, leaving the choice between bread and wine undistorted. Each of the three cases distorts two of the three possible choices, while leaving the third choice undistorted. There is thus no qualitative difference between the nature of the effect of direct as against indirect taxation. Any preference for direct taxation over indirect must therefore be based on quantitative rather than qualitative comparisons, or else on grounds (like equity or political feasibility) that are not strictly economic.

This challenge to the traditional preference for direct taxation provides the focus for most of the present paper. Once Little's argument is appreciated, we can no longer resolve the issue by saying that distortions are present in the indirect-tax case but absent in the direct-tax case. We must recognize that distortions are present in both cases, obtain relevant measures of their effects, and then compare these measures. The relevant measure, in this case, is the cost to the economy of the inefficiencies resulting from tax-induced distortions of choices. This cost, which I like to call the welfare cost of a tax system, has traditionally been labeled the "excess burden" of taxation.

Section II of the paper is an attempt to expound the principles of measuring the welfare costs of a set of taxes in a case where all goods are produced at constant cost. The case chosen is a particularly simple one, because, with the simplification of constant costs, the argument can be carried out in diagrammatic terms.[3] From this exercise a general expression is derived, from which we can determine the welfare cost of any given pattern of taxes on final goods and services when production is governed by constant costs, when distortions other than taxes are absent, and when the amount of labor supplied by each individual to the market does not vary as a consequence of changes in tax rates.

[2] I. M. D. Little, "Direct Versus Indirect Taxes," *Economic Journal*, September 1951, pp. 577–584.
[3] For a more general mathematical treatment, see my paper, "The Measurement of Waste," *American Economic Review*, May 1964. [This volume, Chapter 3.]

In section III we generalize the result of section II, incorporating the possibility of tax-induced changes in the supply of labor. Thus we face up directly to the problem posed by Little, for the formulation of section III shows how it is possible to measure the welfare cost of an income tax and to compare this with the welfare costs induced by alternative patterns of indirect taxation. To emphasize the possibility of extracting useful numerical results from analyses of this type, an attempt is made at the conclusion of section III to estimate the welfare cost of the U.S. personal income tax. It should be borne in mind that this exercise is intended mainly as an example of how the job might be done, and not as a definitive analysis of the U.S. income tax. Among other things, the measurement effort of section III takes account only of the costs of the personal income tax arising from the labor-leisure choice, and not those that affect occupational choice, investment decisions, etc. Moreover, the measurement is based on crude and scanty evidence of a highly aggregative nature, whereas a more complete analysis would take into account the differential responses of different classes of labor supply to tax incentives (e.g., distinguishing between the effects of taxation on labor-force participation rates of women and men). Finally, the measurement in section III (as distinct from the theory presented) is based on the assumption that the income tax is the only tax present in the system, or, perhaps more plausibly, on the assumption that the welfare costs of the personal income tax are not altered by the many other taxes that are present in the U.S. system.

In spite of these qualifications, however, I feel that the exercise of section III provides us with some useful insights. The estimated welfare cost of the U.S. personal income tax is about $1 billion per year — hardly a negligible figure. Yet the simplifying assumptions just alluded to probably have the effect of understating the true cost. It is hard indeed, in the light of this result, to hold to the traditional position that the personal income tax is truly neutral.

In section IV we attempt a direct comparison of the welfare costs of income and excise taxation. This entails nothing more than a straightforward application of the general formulation derived in section III, but some relevant insights are obtained by carrying out the steps. As the first step in section IV, we try to find the "best" way of raising a given amount of revenue by commodity taxation. We find, as others[4] have previously shown, that an income tax (i.e., a tax striking all goods and services other than leisure at an equal rate) will be the "best" way only in very unusual circumstances. If, as seems to be the case in the real world, we cannot tax leisure as such, then the "best" tax system we can achieve under this constraint is one that strikes at higher-than-average rates those goods that are complements to or poorer-than-average substitutes for leisure, and that strikes at lower-than-average rates those goods that are better-than-average substitutes for leisure. An income tax is "best," given the constraint that leisure cannot be taxed, only if all goods are equally

[4] See Little in *Economic Journal*, September 1951; W. J. Corlett and D. C. Hague, "Complementarity and the Excess Burden of Taxation," *Review of Economic Studies*, No. 54, 1953–54, pp. 21–30; J. E. Meade, *Trade and Welfare*, Vol. II, Mathematical Supplement, London, 1955; R. G. Lipsey and K. Lancaster, "The General Theory of Second Best," *Review of Economic Studies*, No. 63, 1956–57, pp. 11–32.

good substitutes for leisure (i.e., only if a tax on leisure would lead to an equi-proportional change in the consumption of each and every good and service).

This conclusion could indeed be shattering to the principle of direct taxation if it meant that the welfare costs of taxation could be greatly lowered by having widely different rates of taxation on different goods and services as against the equal rates implied by income taxation. It does not appear, however, that this is the case. One way of determining the answer to the question just posed is to compare the welfare cost of a particular indirect tax with the welfare cost of an income tax yielding equal revenue. This is the second step taken in section IV. It recognizes that the relevant substitute for an indirect tax is not "no tax at all" but rather some other manner of obtaining the same yield, and it considers the particular alternative represented by income taxation. The result of this exercise is that, as long as the excise tax in question is not itself a very general tax (striking a large fraction of all goods and thus approaching an income tax in coverage), and as long as the elasticity of demand for the commodity or commodities subject to excise tax is not very small, the substitution of an income tax for the excise tax in question will very likely result in a reduction of welfare cost.

The third step in section IV attempts to make the preceding comparison a bit more realistic. One of the key propositions that emerges from the study of welfare costs in a general-equilibrium framework (such as that taken in this paper) is that the effects of a particular tax depend not only on that tax itself but on the other taxes that are present along with it. The comparison made in step two of section IV considers an excise tax that is being used as the sole tax in the system, and is replaced by and compared with an income tax of equal yield. In step three of section IV we alter this comparison, and instead consider an excise tax which, when present, stands side by side with an income tax of a given size. We compare this setup with an alternative one in which the excise tax is taken off and replaced by a sufficient rise in the rate of income tax to produce the same total yield as was previously obtained from the excise and income taxes combined. This comparison is slightly more complicated than that undertaken in step two, but does not greatly alter the conclusion. Broadly speaking, there is still a strong presumption in favor of replacing excise taxation with income taxation, as long as the excise taxation itself is not very general and as long as the taxed commodities do not have very low elasticities of demand. When one comes to consider excise taxes that have very low rates and/or very broad bases, however, the result is no longer so clear. In these cases, considerations of the complementarity (or low substitutability) of an excise-taxed commodity with leisure might weigh the final judgment in favor of retaining the excise tax rather than replacing it by an adjustment of income tax rates. One might say, in short, that the theoretical case in favor of direct taxation has been forced into full retreat by the considerations raised by Little and others in recent years; but that the practical case remains comparatively unscathed, particularly where the excise taxes in question have relatively high rates and do not strike a very high proportion of consumer expenditures.

In section V the effects of taxation on saving are considered. The treatment, far briefer than the subject deserves, focuses on the nonneutrality of ordinary income taxation with respect to the saving decision, and on the measurement of the welfare costs engendered by this nonneutrality. It is shown that income taxation has the effect of reducing the rate of saving, when the alternative to the income tax is a consumption tax yielding the same amount each year. A simple formula for estimating the welfare costs of the distortions introduced by income taxation through its influence upon the savings decision is then presented. In terms of this formula, a very rough judgment is reached on the possible order of magnitude of this class of welfare costs in the U.S. economy. Finally, it is suggested that the welfare costs stemming from the differential tax treatment of different kinds of income from capital in the United States are likely to be substantially greater than the welfare costs arising from the influence of taxation on the saving decision as such. That is to say, the U.S. economy very likely suffers greater costs from tax-induced misallocations of its given capital stock than from the influence of taxation on the over-all size of that capital stock.

Finally, in section VI, an effort is made to draw some conclusions from the preceding analysis on the influence of taxation on economic growth. Since previous sections of this paper are concerned mainly with the labor-leisure choice and with the saving decision, the discussion of taxation and growth is focused in these terms. The conclusion is reached that the effects of taxation on the labor-leisure choice have a truly negligible effect on the economy's rate of growth, but that the effect of taxation on the saving decision may reduce the economy's annual rate of growth by as much as one-tenth or two-tenths of a percentage point. For those who are surprised by the small effect of taxation via the saving decision, section VI reviews the evidence supporting this result.

To set the stage for the treatment which follows, I should first like to discuss certain key assumptions that will be used throughout this paper.

1. It is assumed that, under any two situations being compared, the economy's productive resources are fully employed. This assumption is the conventional one in studies of the allocative effects of taxation. The resource-allocation question can be framed as "how will our resources be used?" as distinct from the alternative income-and-employment question of "will some of our resources be idle?" The effect of this assumption, for the problems treated in this paper, is to restrict the set of possible resource allocations to that determined by the production frontier of the economy. Thus in Figure 2.1, the alternative bundles of goods X_1 and X_2 produced in any of the cases to be compared will lie somewhere along the production frontier AB. A production point like C, indicating that the economy is not producing up to its potential, is ruled out by assumption.

2. It is assumed that, under any two alternative taxes to be compared, the government will obtain just that amount of purchasing power needed to buy a given bundle of goods. One need not belabor the point that if we are to discuss the effects of a given tax on resource allocation, we must implicitly or explicitly compare the situation in which that tax exists with some alternative situation. Once this is recognized, we have a variety of choices. We can compare the "tax situation" with a "no-tax situation" or with any possible combination of alternative taxes. But this is not the worst of it. If the total

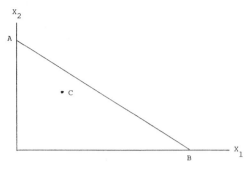

FIGURE 2.1

revenues of the government have different purchasing power in the cases being compared, we must either have differing amounts of deficit or surplus in the two cases, or differing amounts of government expenditure. If surpluses or deficits differ, deflationary or inflationary forces are set in motion by the tax change, and we are taken from the realm of allocative theory into that of income-and-employment analysis. If government expenditures differ in the two cases, we must inquire into how the government spends its added revenue or reduces its prior expenditures. This opens a Pandora's box of possibilities in an analysis of resource-allocation effects, for there are an infinity of ways in which the government could allocate any increase or reduction in expenditures. To avoid having to guess what the government would do with its money, we simply assume that the government would do the same thing in both the situations being compared. This, together with the previous assumption, enables us to conceive of a "consumption frontier" or, perhaps better, a private-sector expenditures frontier, obtained by deducting the fixed pattern of government purchases from the economy's production frontier. Thus, in Figure 2.2, every point on the "consumption frontier" CD is obtained by deducting the fixed amounts of government purchases G_1 and G_2 from the corresponding point on the production frontier AB. As long as the government is getting the bundle (G_1, G_2) of X_1 and X_2, and as long as the economy is operating on the production frontier, production will take place somewhere within the segment

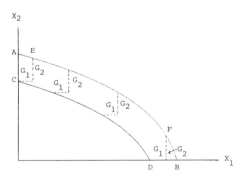

FIGURE 2.2

30

EF of *AB*, and the "consumption" of the private sector must lie somewhere along *CD* in any two cases being compared.

3. It is assumed that the changes in output dictated by the changes in tax policy being considered are accomplished at (approximately) constant unit cost. Taken strictly, this assumption requires that the production frontier be linear within the relevant range. Taken less strictly, it requires only that the production frontier be reasonably well approximated by a linear function within the relevant range. I am prepared to argue that this is likely to be the case for the changes in output which would be induced by plausible changes in the taxes now in force in the United States. But I must confess that this assumption is mainly dictated by considerations of convenience. The mathematical parts of subsequent sections of this paper would be greatly complicated if the assumption of constant costs were abandoned, and yet the principal qualitative conclusions of the analysis would be unaffected.

4. It is assumed that, where "welfare costs" are being measured, the tax setup being considered has as its alternative a tax system of similar overall incidence. The alternatives being compared are assumed to have similar overall incidence in order to isolate the allocative effects of taxation from its redistributive effects. For example, if we are concerned with the effects of eliminating a tax on jewelry, whose incidence among income brackets is as indicated in column 1 of Table 2.1, we might so adjust income-tax rates as to increase income-tax collections from each bracket by approximately these same amounts. Thus if income-tax collections, by bracket, were originally as given by column 2 of Table 2.1, we would consider an income tax collecting the amounts given in column 3 to be an appropriate alternative to the tax setup given by columns 1 and 2.

TABLE 2.1

Tax Collections by Income Bracket, per Taxpayer

	Alternative 1		Alternative 2
Income brackets	Excise tax on jewelry (1)	Income tax (2)	Income tax (3)
1	20	50	70
2	30	100	130
3	40	200	240
4	50	400	450
5	60	1,000	1,060

This is not to say that the real alternatives faced by policy-makers are likely to be as neatly comparable as those in Table 2.1. But if the practical alternative (say, 3) to alternative 1 is an income tax which is different in its incidence from alternative 2, we would simply analyze the move from 1 to 3 as the sum of a move from 1 to 2, which we would evaluate using purely allocative criteria,[5] plus a move from 2 to 3, which we would evaluate using purely distributive criteria.

II. MEASURING THE WELFARE COST OF EXCISE TAXES

In this section, we begin by outlining the "textbook" treatment of welfare cost in the simplest terms, and proceed to extend the analysis to more complicated cases. The textbook case is illustrated in Figure 2.3.

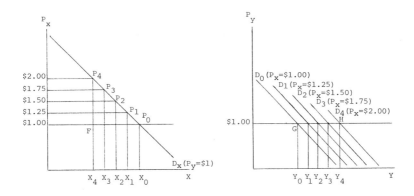

FIGURE 2.3

We are to compare a situation in which there is an excise tax of $1 per unit of X ($X = X_4$; $P_x = \$2.00$) with a situation in which this tax does not exist, but in which the government is raising equivalent revenue by an income tax ($X = X_0$; $P_x = \$1$). It is important to recognize at the outset that D_x is defined as holding government revenues constant. Thus at P_4 we have government revenues equal to ($\$1)(X_4)$, all obtained from the excise tax on X. As we move to P_3, the excise tax must be lowered to $\$.75$, and government revenues from the excise tax alone are only ($\$.75)(X_3)$. However, since government revenues must be constant all along the curve, there must be, at point P_3, income taxation to yield ($\$1)(X_4) - (\$.75)(X_3)$. At P_2 income taxes must yield ($\$1)(X_4) - (\$.50)(X_2)$; at P_1 they must yield ($\$1)(X_4) - (\$.25)(X_1)$; and at P_0 they must yield ($\$1)(X_4)$.

[5] Strictly speaking, one can eliminate distributive criteria in evaluating the move from 1 to 2 only when each and every individual bears the same burden of tax in both cases. Actually, the move from 1 to 2 as described above would entail some redistribution of income in favor of jewelry purchasers and away from those who do not purchase jewelry or purchase only small amounts relative to the average of their income bracket. But this redistribution is entirely within income brackets, and thus is not likely in itself to significantly alter the pattern of demand. Moreover, if the equal treatment of equals is accepted as a goal of tax policy, one would have to regard the move from 1 to 2 as having beneficial effects on distribution (differing tastes of people with similar incomes should not make these people "unequal"). Thus, as long as there would be an allocative gain on this move, we can consider it as being slightly reinforced by distributive considerations.

The simplest exposition of the measurement of the welfare cost of excise taxation can be made by looking only at the left-hand diagram in Figure 2.3. As between the situation (X_0, P_0) and the situation (X_4, P_4), consumers have given up $(X_0 - X_4)$ units of the good X. The value placed by them on the first unit given up was \$1, but subsequent units had higher values. If we think of the tax being gradually raised from zero to \$1, this is clearly evident. When the tax is raised from zero to \$.01, the units of X given up have values between \$1 and \$1.01; when the tax is raised from \$.01 to \$.02, the units of X given up have values between \$1.01 and \$1.02. Finally, when the tax is raised from \$.99 to \$1.00, consumers value the units of X given up at between \$1.99 and \$2.00. The sum total of the value placed by consumers on all the X they have given up in the process of raising the tax from zero to \$1 can be measured by the area $X_0 P_0 P_4 X_4$.

But in the process of demanding less X as a consequence of the tax, consumers have released resources from industry X and increased their demand for other goods (Y). The measure $X_0 P_0 P_4 X_4$ therefore overstates their real loss; from it we have to deduct the value of the extra Y they consume in the excise-tax case. Where there is no tax (or other divergence between the value placed by consumers on the marginal product of productive factors and the rewards received by those factors) on Y, the value to consumers of the extra Y they have in case (X_4, P_4) compared to case (X_0, P_0) can simply be measured by the area $X_0 P_0 F X_4$. This represents the amount which was originally paid in industry X to the factors transferred to Y as a result of the tax. Deducting $X_0 P_0 F X_4$ from $X_0 P_0 P_4 X_4$ leaves the triangle $P_0 P_4 F$ as the measure of the welfare cost or "excess burden" of a \$1 per unit excise tax on X.

The right-hand diagram in Figure 2.3 may help readers to verify that $X_0 P_0 F X_4$ does in fact measure the value to consumers of the extra Y they demand as a consequence of the tax on X. Again, considering a sequence in which the tax on X is gradually raised from zero to \$1, we have first a slight displacement of the demand curve for Y as the price of X is raised from \$1.00 to \$1.01, and a little extra Y is bought at the price of \$1.00. As the price of X is raised from \$1.01 to \$1.02, another slight displacement of the demand curve for Y occurs, and again a little extra Y is bought at the price of \$1. Summing up the values to consumers of the successive increments to Y generated by raising P_x all the way to \$2.00, we obtain the area $Y_0 G H Y_4$, which is equal to the area $X_0 P_0 F X_4$ in the left-hand diagram.

There is no contribution to welfare cost (corresponding to the triangle $P_0 P_4 F$) coming from the market for Y because, by assumption, no distortions are present in that market. The resource cost of an extra unit of Y is \$1.00, and the moment consumers find that it is worth \$1 to buy an extra unit of Y, they can freely do so. Thus the value to consumers of each extra unit of Y they take is equal to the price they pay for it.

To summarize the result obtained so far, when a tax on X of T_x per unit is the only distortion present, the welfare cost of that tax can be measured by $-1/2\ T_x\ \Delta X$, where ΔX is the change in the consumption of X induced by the tax. If we define $t_x (= T_x/P_{x0})$ as the percentage rate of tax, we can note that (with constant costs) it also represents the percentage change in the price of X. We then can derive $\Delta X = \eta_{xx} X t_x$, where η_{xx} is the own-price elasticity of demand for X. Substituting this expression for ΔX, and $P_{x0} t_x$ for T_x in the cost measure $(-1/2\ T_x\ \Delta X)$, we obtain as an alternative expression for the welfare cost of an excise tax $-1/2\ XP_{x0}\eta_{xx} t_x{}^2$. This expresses the welfare cost of a tax in terms of (XP_{x0}), the total net-of-tax receipts from sales of the product in question; η_{xx}, the own-price elasticity of demand for the product (a negative number); and t_x, the effective percentage rate of tax. Since the total tax yield, R_x, can be expressed as $XP_{x0} t_x$, we can also express the welfare cost of the tax as $-1/2\ R_x \eta_{xx} t_x$. Since data on R_x and t_x are usually available for any existing tax, only η_{xx} need be estimated to obtain a measure of the welfare cost of such a tax.

In the course of this paper we shall show that this simple textbook measure of welfare cost is not a bad approximation in the cases of most existing taxes. But in order to reach this conclusion, we must modify the above analysis to take account of the main ways in which the real-world situation diverges from that depicted in Figure 2.3.

By far the most disquieting assumption underlying Figure 2.3 and the analysis of it is the assumption that no excise taxes or other distortions exist in the "rest" of the economy (industry Y). It is possible, however, to modify the analysis so as to avoid making this assumption.

Figure 2.4 differs from Figure 2.3 only in that the initial price of Y is taken to be $1.50, consisting of a unit cost of $1 plus a tax of $.50 per unit. Once again, as we envision the tax on X being raised in small steps from 0 to $1.00 per unit, we obtain the area $X_0 P_0 P_4 X_4$ as measuring the value to consumers of the $(X_0 - X_4)$ units of X that they are induced to forego as a consequence of the tax.

The difference between this and the earlier case appears in the right-hand diagram of Figure 2.4. Whereas, in Figure 2.3, consumers were initially paying $1 per unit of Y, and continued paying that price after the tax was imposed on X, now, in Figure 2.4, consumers are initially paying $1.50 per unit of Y, and continue to pay that price throughout the exercise. Hence the value to consumers of the extra Y that they are induced to consume by the tax on X is

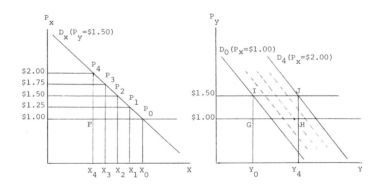

FIGURE 2.4

34

$Y_0 IJY_4$, rather than $Y_0 GHY_4$. In the present case, therefore, the net change in the welfare of consumers as a result of the tax on X is measured by the difference between a loss of $X_0 P_0 P_4 X_4$ (on account of $[X_0 - X_4]$ units of X being foregone), and a gain of $Y_0 IJY_4$ (on account of $[Y_4 - Y_0]$ more units of Y being consumed). Since the areas $X_0 P_0 FX_4$ and $Y_0 GHY_4$ are equal as before (the cost of production of the addition to Y is the same as the reduction in production costs of X), the net loss in the welfare of consumers can be measured by $P_0 P_4 F$ minus $GIJH$. Since $GIJH = (t_y) \times (Y_0 GHY_4)$, and $Y_0 GHY_4 = X_0 P_0 FX_4$, we can express $GIJH = (t_y) \times (X_0 P_0 FX_4) = t_y P_{x0} \Delta X$. This, in turn, can be expressed as $GIJH = t_y XP_{x0} \eta_{xx} t_x$. Now $P_0 P_4 F = -1/2 \, XP_{x0} \eta_{xx} t_x{}^2$, so that the net loss in welfare from placing a tax of t_x on X in the presence of an already existing tax of t_y on Y can be expressed as

$$-\tfrac{1}{2} XP_{x0} t_x \eta_{xx}[t_x - 2t_y] = -\tfrac{1}{2} R_x \eta_{xx}[t_x - 2t_y].$$

From this it can be seen that there is a clear gain from placing a tax on X equal to the pre-existing tax on Y. The expression $-1/2 \, R_x \eta_{xx}$ is always positive, and the expression $t_x - 2t_y$ is negative when $t_x = t_y$. Therefore the "cost" of moving t_x from zero to t_y is negative, indicating a gain in welfare.

In the example chosen for Figure 2.4, t_x was set at twice t_y. Thus the expression above indicates that there is no gain or loss in welfare. This can be verified by looking at Figure 2.4. The loss measured by the triangle $P_0 P_4 F$ is just counterbalanced by the gain measured by the rectangle $GIJH$.[6]

The extension of this result to the case of three or more commodities is self-evident. In Figure 2.5, we assume that a tax of $\$.50$ per unit on X_2, and one of $\$.25$ per unit on X_3 were already in existence before a tax of $\$1.00$ per unit was levied on X_1. The reduction in welfare of consumers as a consequence of the tax on X_1 is measured by the area ABC minus the sum of the areas $DEFG$ and $HIJK$.

We can now turn to the derivation of a general expression for the welfare cost of a set of excise taxes. Assume there are three commodities, X_1, X_2, X_3, all of which are taxed. The welfare cost of the whole set of taxes can be measured by taking first the welfare cost of a tax on X_1, with no other taxes in existence;

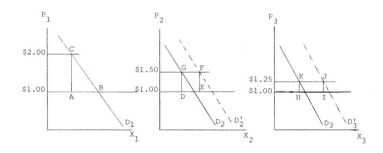

FIGURE 2.5

---

[6] Both the rectangle and the triangle have equal bases, but the height of the triangle is just twice that of the rectangle.

35

adding to this the addition to the welfare cost obtained by imposing a tax on X_2, given that the tax on X_1 already exists; and finally adding the increment to the welfare cost incurred by imposing a tax on X_3, given that the taxes on X_1 and X_2 already exist.

Since the effects of the taxes will be analyzed in three steps, let us denote by Δ_1 those changes taking place in the first step (when a tax is imposed on X_1), and by Δ_2 and Δ_3, respectively, those changes taking place in the second and third steps.

When a tax of T_1 is imposed on X_1, with no taxes on X_2 and X_3, the welfare cost is simply

(a) $$-\tfrac{1}{2}T_1\,\Delta_1 X_1,$$

i.e., the triangle P_0P_4F in Figure 2.3. When a tax of T_2 is imposed on X_2 in the presence of a tax of T_1 on X_1, the addition to welfare cost is

(b) $$-\tfrac{1}{2}T_2\,\Delta_2 X_2 - T_1\,\Delta_2 X_1.$$

The first component is the triangle under the demand curve for X_2 (corresponding to ABC in Figure 2.5), and the second is the offset (corresponding to $DEFG$ in Figure 2.5) arising from the fact that a tax on X_1 already exists. (There is no offset corresponding to $HIJK$ in Figure 2.5, because at this step we have not yet imposed any tax on X_3.)

When a tax of T_3 is imposed on X_3 in the presence of taxes of T_1 and T_2 on X_1 and X_2, the addition to welfare cost is

(c) $$-\tfrac{1}{2}T_3\,\Delta_3 X_3 - T_1\,\Delta_3 X_1 - T_2\,\Delta_3 X_2.$$

The sum of (a) + (b) + (c) gives us the welfare cost of the set of taxes (T_1, T_2, T_3) taken together. Let me here introduce S_{ij} as a general notation for $\partial X_i/\partial P_j$, defined to include just the substitution effect. We can then write:

$$\Delta_1 X_1 = \frac{\partial X_1}{\partial P_1}T_1 = S_{11}T_1$$

$$\Delta_2 X_1 = \frac{\partial X_1}{\partial P_2}T_2 = S_{12}T_2$$

$$\Delta_3 X_1 = \frac{\partial X_1}{\partial P_3}T_3 = S_{13}T_3$$

$$\Delta_2 X_2 = \frac{\partial X_2}{\partial P_2}T_2 = S_{22}T_2$$

$$\Delta_3 X_2 = \frac{\partial X_2}{\partial P_3}T_3 = S_{23}T_3$$

$$\Delta_3 X_3 = \frac{\partial X_3}{\partial P_3}T_3 = S_{33}T_3.$$

Substituting into (a), (b), and (c), and summing, we obtain as the expression for the welfare cost of the set of taxes

$$-\tfrac{1}{2}S_{11}T_1^2 - \tfrac{1}{2}S_{22}T_2^2 - \tfrac{1}{2}S_{33}T_3^2 - S_{12}T_1T_2 - S_{13}T_1T_3 - S_{23}T_2T_3,$$

or alternatively,

$$-\tfrac{1}{2}[S_{11}T_1^2 + S_{22}T_2^2 + S_{33}T_3^2 + 2S_{12}T_1T_2 + 2S_{13}T_1T_3 + 2S_{23}T_2T_3].$$

Recognizing that $S_{ij} = S_{ji}$,[7] we can express this as

$$-\tfrac{1}{2}\sum_i \sum_j S_{ij}T_iT_j.$$

This is one of three fundamental forms in which the welfare cost of a set of taxes may be written. The second fundamental form may be derived by breaking up (a) + (b) + (c) into expressions reflecting changes in the quantity of each commodity. Thus we have, from commodity 1,

$$-\tfrac{1}{2}T_1\,\Delta_1 X_1 - T_1\,\Delta_2 X_1 - T_1\,\Delta_3 X_1.$$

Denoting the total change in X_1 by $\Delta X_1 = \Delta_1 X_1 + \Delta_2 X_1 + \Delta_3 X_1$, we may express this as

(a') $$-\tfrac{1}{2}T_1\,\Delta X_1 - \tfrac{1}{2}T_1\,\Delta_2 X_1 - \tfrac{1}{2}T_1\,\Delta_3 X_1.$$

Likewise, we have for commodity 2,

$$-\tfrac{1}{2}T_2\,\Delta_2 X_2 - T_2\,\Delta_3 X_2,$$

which we can express as

(b') $$-\tfrac{1}{2}T_2\,\Delta X_2 - \tfrac{1}{2}T_2\,\Delta_3 X_2 + \tfrac{1}{2}T_2\,\Delta_1 X_2.$$

Finally, we have for commodity 3,

$$-\tfrac{1}{2}T_3\,\Delta_3 X_3,$$

which can be expressed as

(c') $$-\tfrac{1}{2}T_3\,\Delta X_3 + \tfrac{1}{2}T_3\,\Delta_1 X_3 + \tfrac{1}{2}T_3\,\Delta_2 X_3.$$

The sum of (a') + (b') + (c') will give us the welfare cost of the set of taxes under consideration. But six of the nine terms in the sum cancel each other out. Consider the two terms $-1/2\ T_1\,\Delta_2 X_1 + 1/2\ T_2\,\Delta_1 X_2$. We know that $\Delta_2 X_1 = S_{12}T_2$, and $\Delta_1 X_2 = S_{21}T_1$. Thus these terms can be expressed as

$$-\tfrac{1}{2}T_1 T_2 S_{12} + \tfrac{1}{2}T_2 T_1 S_{21},$$

[7] The equality of $\partial X_i/\partial P_j$ with $\partial X_j/\partial P_i$ is one of the fundamental properties of demand relationships reflecting the substitution effect only. See John R. Hicks, *Value and Capital*, p. 311. Hicks uses the notation X_{ij} to refer to what we have called S_{ij}. It is not easy to give an intuitive interpretation of why S_{ij} should equal S_{ji}. The best I can do is as follows: If the prices of both X_1 and X_2 rise by 1 percent, no substitution effects will take place between them. This means that the substitution effect between X_1 and X_2 which takes place because of a rise of 1 percent in P_1 is annulled by the substitution effect taking place as a result of a 1 percent rise in P_2. Now the transfer of purchasing power from X_1 to X_2 taking place as a result of a 1 percent rise in the price of X_1 is given by $P_2(\partial X_2/\partial P_1)P_1$. And the transfer of purchasing power from X_2 to X_1 resulting from a 1 percent rise in the price of X_2 is equal to $P_1(\partial X_1/\partial P_2)P_2$. In order for the second effect to annul the first, $(\partial X_1/\partial P_1)$ must equal $(\partial X_1/\partial P_2)$, or $S_{21} = S_{12}$.

which must equal zero since $S_{12} = S_{21}$. By the same token, each of the pairs of terms $(-1/2\ T_1\ \Delta_3 X_1 + 1/2\ T_3\ \Delta_1 X_3)$ and $(-1/2\ T_2\ \Delta_3 X_2 + 1/2\ T_3\ \Delta_2 X_3)$ must equal zero. Thus the second fundamental expression for welfare cost reduces to

$$-\tfrac{1}{2}T_1\ \Delta X_1 - \tfrac{1}{2}T_2\ \Delta X_2 - \tfrac{1}{2}T_3\ \Delta X_3 = -\tfrac{1}{2}\sum_i T_i\ \Delta X_i.$$

To derive the third form of the expression for welfare cost, consider the expression (first form), letting $C_i =$ unit cost of commodity i, t_i the percentage rate of tax on commodity i, and $C_i t_i = T_i$, the unit tax on i,

$$-\tfrac{1}{2}[C_1{}^2 S_{11} t_1{}^2 + C_2{}^2 S_{22} t_2{}^2 + C_3{}^2 S_{33} t_3{}^2$$
$$+ 2C_1 C_2 S_{12} t_1 t_2 + 2C_1 C_3 S_{13} t_1 t_3 + 2C_2 C_3 S_{23} t_2 t_3].$$

Now we make use of the well-known relationship among the S_{ij}, $\sum_i C_i S_{ij} = \sum_j C_j S_{ji} = 0.$[8]

$$C_1{}^2 S_{11} t_1{}^2 = -C_1 C_2 S_{12} t_1{}^2 - C_1 C_3 S_{13} t_1{}^2$$
$$C_2{}^2 S_{22} t_2{}^2 = -C_1 C_2 S_{12} t_2{}^2 - C_2 C_3 S_{23} t_2{}^2$$
$$C_3{}^2 S_{33} t_3{}^2 = -C_1 C_3 S_{13} t_3{}^2 - C_2 C_3 S_{23} t_3{}^2$$
$$2C_1 C_3 S_{13} t_1 t_3 = 2C_1 C_3 S_{13} t_1 t_3$$
$$2C_2 C_3 S_{23} t_2 t_3 = 2C_2 C_3 S_{23} t_2 t_3$$
$$2C_1 C_2 S_{12} t_1 t_2 = 2C_1 C_2 S_{12} t_1 t_2.$$

On the left-hand side of the equalities in the six equations above, we have the terms appearing within the bracket in the expression for welfare cost (first form). On the right-hand side, we have the expressions which will be used in deriving the third form. To do so, we simply collect terms in S_{12}, S_{13}, and S_{23}, yielding

$$-S_{12} C_1 C_2 [t_1{}^2 - 2t_1 t_2 + t_2{}^2] = -S_{12} C_1 C_2 (t_1 - t_2)^2$$
$$-S_{13} C_1 C_3 [t_1{}^2 - 2t_1 t_3 + t_3{}^2] = -S_{13} C_1 C_3 (t_1 - t_3)^2$$
$$-S_{23} C_2 C_3 [t_2{}^2 - 2t_2 t_3 + t_3{}^2] = -S_{23} C_2 C_3 (t_2 - t_3)^2.$$

[8] This relationship can be interpreted intuitively in two ways. First, when there is a linear constraint of the form $\sum_i C_i X_i = K$, then, as long as the constraint is satisfied, $\sum_i C_i (\partial X_i)/(\partial z) = 0$, for any definition of z. Thus setting $z = P_j$, we have $\sum C_i (\partial X_i)/(\partial P_j) = 0$, or $\sum_i C_i S_{ij} = 0$. Alternatively, we may start from the general property of substitution effects that "only relative prices count." This says that the effect on X_i of a 1 percent rise in its price would be annulled by a 1 percent rise in all other prices. The effect on X_i of a 1 percent rise in its own price is given by

$$\frac{\partial X_i}{\partial P_i} P_i = S_{ii} P_i.$$

The effect on X_i of a 1 percent rise in the price of X_j is $(\partial X_i)/(\partial P_j)P_j = S_{ij}P_j$. The effect on X_i of a 1 percent rise in all other prices is $\sum_{j \neq i} S_{ij} P_j$. In order for the first effect, $S_{ii} P_i$, to be offset by the second, we must have

$$S_{ii} P_i + \sum_{j \neq i} S_{ij} P_j = 0, \quad \text{or} \quad \sum_j S_{ij} P_j = 0.$$

Now if, as we do when measuring the total welfare cost of a set of distortions, we are measuring this cost as against an undistorted initial situation, we can characterize the undistorted situation as one in which, for all j, $P_j = kC_j$; that is, prices bear the same relationship to unit costs for all commodities. Thus we have $\sum_j S_{ij} kC_j = 0$, or $\sum_j S_{ij} C_j = 0$. [See Hicks, *Value and Capital*, pp. 310–311.]

Summing the three terms to the right of the equalities, we have an expression equivalent to that in brackets in the first form measure of the welfare cost. Since the bracket is multiplied by $(-1/2)$, we have for our third fundamental form of the measure for the welfare cost:

$$\tfrac{1}{2} \sum_j \sum_{i<j} S_{ij}(t_i - t_j)^2 C_i C_j.$$

The expression for the welfare cost of a set of taxes can be derived directly from utility functions as follows.

$$(2.1) \qquad\qquad U = U(X_1, X_2, \ldots, X_n)$$

Taking a Taylor expansion up to quadratic terms, we have

$$(2.2) \quad \Delta U = \sum_i U_i \Delta X_i + \tfrac{1}{2} \sum_i \sum_j U_{ij} \Delta X_i \Delta X_j, \quad \text{where} \quad U_i = \frac{\partial U}{\partial X_i} \quad \text{and}$$

$$U_{ij} = \frac{\partial^2 U}{\partial X_i \, \partial X_j}.$$

Now U_i is itself a function of the X_j, so

$$(2.3) \qquad\qquad U_i = U_i(X_1, X_2, \ldots, X_n), \quad \text{and}$$

$$(2.4) \qquad\qquad \Delta U_i = \sum_j U_{ij} \Delta X_j.$$

Thus we can rewrite (2.2) as

$$(2.5) \qquad\qquad \Delta U = \sum_i U_i \Delta X_i + \tfrac{1}{2} \sum_i \Delta U_i \Delta X_i.$$

If consumers maximize utility subject to their money income and the prices facing them in any situation, we have, as a first-order condition of maximum, that

$$(2.6) \qquad\qquad U_i = \lambda P_i,$$

where λ is a Lagrange multiplier representing the marginal utility of money. Obviously, from (2.6)

$$(2.7) \qquad\qquad \Delta U_i = \lambda \, \Delta P_i + P_i \, \Delta\lambda.$$

Substituting (2.6) and (2.7) into (2.5), we have

$$(2.8) \qquad \Delta U = \lambda \sum_i P_i \Delta X_i + \tfrac{1}{2}\lambda \sum_i \Delta P_i \Delta X_i + \tfrac{1}{2}(\Delta\lambda) \sum_i P_i \Delta X_i.$$

Interpreting the P_i's in (2.8) as representing the prices in an undistorted situation (i.e., as being proportional to unit costs), we have $\sum_i P_i \Delta X_i = \sum_i kC_i \Delta X_i$, which must equal zero under our assumption of constant costs (linear transformation functions). Thus (2.8) reduces to

$$(2.9) \qquad\qquad \Delta U = \tfrac{1}{2}\lambda \sum_i \Delta P_i \Delta X_i.$$

To translate ΔU from utility terms into money terms, we must divide by the marginal utility of money. Thus money value of change in utility equals

$$(2.10) \qquad\qquad \frac{\Delta U}{\lambda} = \tfrac{1}{2} \sum_i \Delta P_i \Delta X_i,$$

39

which expressed as a cost is $-1/2 \sum_i \Delta P_i \Delta X_i$. When the only disturbances between the two situations being compared are taxes, we have $\Delta P_i = T_i$. Thus from (2.10) we can derive $-1/2 \sum_i T_i \Delta X_i$ as the measure of the welfare cost of a set of taxes $(T_1, \ldots, T_n)$. Moreover, since we require that changes in the X_i all take place along a linear constraint, without first-order income effects, we can express $\Delta X_i = \sum_j S_{ij} \Delta P_j = \sum_j S_{ij} T_j$. Substituting this into $-1/2 \sum_i T_i \Delta X_i$, we obtain

$$-\tfrac{1}{2} \sum_i \sum_j S_{ij} T_i T_j,$$

as an alternative (equivalent) measure of welfare cost. This derivation is essentially the same as that given by H. Hotelling.[9] Hicks derives the expression $1/2 \sum_i \sum_j S_{ij} T_i T_j$ (in his notation $1/2 \sum_r \sum_s X_{rs} dP_r dP_s$) by a somewhat different route.[10]

III. MEASURING THE WELFARE COST OF INCOME TAXATION

In this section we apply the apparatus derived in the previous section to the problem of direct taxation with particular reference to the choice between labor and leisure. We shall disregard problems connected with the choice between consumption and saving, which will be dealt with separately below, and shall accordingly assume that all goods are direct consumption goods, and that all income is spent on such goods. The income tax will be represented as a flat-rate excise tax striking all goods (other than leisure) at the same percentage rate.

To begin, let us briefly review the traditional case for preferring direct to indirect taxation. Here leisure is not considered as a good, and the supply of work is assumed to be unaffected by alterations in the pattern of taxation. The third fundamental form of the expression for welfare cost, i.e.,

$$\tfrac{1}{2} \sum_j \sum_{i<j} S_{ij}(t_i - t_j)^2 C_i C_j,$$

shows that an income tax has no welfare cost under the assumptions stated above. Since, under an income tax (with no concomitant excise taxes) $t_i = t_j$, for all i and j, every term in the summation is equal to zero.

On the other hand, no pattern of taxes on individual commodities can have a negative welfare cost, since by definition the welfare cost of a total set of taxes is measured against a neutral alternative.[11] The best one could do, then, with unequal taxation of different goods, would be to have a zero welfare cost (such as would be the case if all goods but one were taxed equally, and the last good — taxed at a different rate — had a zero own-price elasticity of demand). But except in such curious and unrealistic cases, the welfare cost of a system of unequal excise taxes will be positive.

[9] "The General Welfare in Relation to Problems of Taxation and of Railway and Utility Rates," *Econometrica*, July 1938.
[10] *Value and Capital*, p. 331.
[11] Formally, the expression $1/2 \sum_i \sum_j S_{ij} T_i T_j$ is negative or zero for any values of the T's. So $-1/2 \sum_i \sum_j S_{ij} T_i T_j$ must be positive or zero. See Hicks, *Value and Capital*, p. 311.

When leisure is introduced as a separate good, however, these statements no longer hold. Now an income tax must be interpreted as an equal-rate tax on all goods except leisure. Hence the income tax is no longer a truly general tax, and cannot be presumed to have a zero welfare cost. As Little [1951] has pointed out, in a world of three goods, X_1, X_2, and X_3, where X_3 is leisure, an equal percentage tax on X_1 and X_2 at the rate of $t_1 = t_2$ leaves undistorted consumers' choices between X_1 and X_2, but distorts choices between X_1 and X_3 and between X_2 and X_3. On the other hand, taxing only X_1 distorts the choices between X_1 and X_2 and between X_1 and X_3, while leaving undistorted the choice between X_2 and X_3. Similarly, a tax on X_2 introduces distortions between X_2 and X_1, and between X_2 and X_3, but leaves choices between X_1 and X_3 undistorted.[12] In each case a distortion is introduced into choices in two pairs of goods, and choice in the third pair is left undistorted. In this sense, therefore, an income tax is on a par with an excise tax. Any preference for income taxation, from a welfare point of view, must be based on empirical considerations, not on a clear qualitative superiority of income taxation in all conceivable circumstances. We now turn, therefore, to the development of some propositions which will be of help in evaluating alternative patterns of taxation when the labor-leisure choice is explicitly taken into account.

First, considering the case in which there are three goods, of which the third is leisure, we may inquire into the effect of an income tax (i.e., a tax on X_1 and X_2 at the percentage rate t). For convenience, let us introduce at this juncture a harmless convention — we choose our units of commodities in such a way that their unit cost, C_i, is unity for every commodity. Thus we may say that the unit of leisure, for a given individual, is that amount of time in which he would earn a dollar, if working. The units of X_1 and X_2 are amounts which sell for a dollar net of taxes. This enables us to leave out the C in our expressions for welfare cost. The welfare cost of a tax at the rate t on X_1 and X_2 is therefore

$$\tfrac{1}{2}[S_{12}(t-t)^2 + S_{13}(t-0)^2 + S_{23}(t-0)^2] = \tfrac{1}{2}[S_{13}t^2 + S_{23}t^2].$$

When the C's are equal to 1, the restriction on the S_{ij}'s is simply $\sum_i S_{ij} = \sum_j S_{ij} = 0$. Thus $S_{13} + S_{23} = -S_{33}$, and the welfare cost of a proportional income tax at the rate t can be expressed as $-1/2 S_{33}t^2$. This expression is directly analogous to that for an excise tax on a single commodity. An excise tax on X_1 alone has a welfare cost of $-1/2 S_{11}t_1^2$, and one on X_2 alone has a welfare cost of $-1/2 S_{22}t_2^2$. This symmetry exists because a proportional income tax has the same effect on relative prices as a subsidy to leisure, and the expression $-1/2 S_{33}t^2$ is the same for a given absolute value of t, regardless of whether t is negative (subsidy) or positive (tax).

In the above formula, taxes are expressed as percentages of the net prices (unit costs) of the corresponding commodities. Income-tax rates, however, are normally expressed as percentages of income before tax. It is worthwhile to establish at an early stage the relationships involved in the comparison of income taxes with "equivalent" excise taxes, so as to avoid confusion later on.

---

[12] I. M. D. Little, "Direct Versus Indirect Taxes," *Economic Journal*, September 1951, pp. 577–584.

A proportional income tax of r percent has as its counterpart an excise tax on the net prices of all goods other than leisure of $r/(1-r)$ percent. That is, a 20 percent income tax corresponds to an excise tax of 25 percent on X_1 and X_2, for this creates a situation in which the gross prices of X_1 and X_2 exceed their net prices by 20 percent of the gross price. Correspondingly, an income tax has the same effect on the allocation of resources as a subsidy at the rate of $r/(1-r)$ percent on the net price of leisure. (Recall here that in this entire analysis we are holding the purchasing power of government receipts constant, so that if leisure were in fact to be subsidized directly there would have to exist a neutral — say, lump-sum — tax side by side with the subsidy on leisure so as to produce the required level of government receipts.) But a subsidy at the rate of $r/(1-r)$ percent on the net price of leisure is equal to a subsidy of r percent on the gross price of leisure. Using P_n and P_g to represent net and gross price, respectively, we have

$$P_n\left(1 + \frac{r}{1-r}\right) = P_g; \qquad P_n\left(\frac{1}{1-r}\right) = P_g.$$

This yields $P_g(1-r) = P_n$.

We can now render in diagrammatic form the expression $-1/2\, S_{33}t^2$ (Figure 2.6). Let LL be the supply curve of labor (defined so as to contain the substitution effect only). Let w be the prevailing wage, gross of income tax. Then, where r is the tax rate on gross income, $rw(=AC)$ is the amount of tax per unit of labor and DA is the net-of-tax income per unit of labor. Now S_{33} is the derivative of the demand function for leisure with respect to the wage rate, so the derivative of the supply function of labor with respect to the wage rate will be $-S_{33}$. Hence the reduction in the amount of labor performed as a consequence of an income tax at the rate r will be $-S_{33}rw(=BC)$. The over-all reduction in gross money income to the worker will be $DEBC$. But the worker will have gained leisure valued at $DEBA$. This leaves as the net welfare cost of the tax the triangle ABC, or $-1/2\, S_{33}(rw)^2$. Recalling that $-S_{33} = \partial L/\partial w$, this expression for welfare cost can be written

$$\frac{1}{2}\frac{\partial L}{\partial w}(rw)^2 = \frac{1}{2}\left(\frac{w}{L}\frac{\partial L}{\partial w}\right)r^2 wL = \tfrac{1}{2}er^2 wL,$$

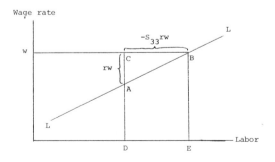

FIGURE 2.6

where e is the elasticity of supply of labour (expressing the substitution effect only), wL represents the earnings of labor gross of income tax, and r represents the rate of income tax expressed in the usual way as a percentage of gross income.

In order to apply this result to the United States case, we must first obtain an estimate of e, and then take account of the progressivity of the actual U.S. income tax. As far as e is concerned, we have fairly reliable estimates on the secular pattern of response of hours worked to changes in real wages. Broadly speaking, a 1 percent rise in real wages per hour has been associated with a reduction of .25 percent in average hours worked.[13] Unfortunately for our purposes, this historical relationship reflects both the income effect and the substitution effect of wage increases. The problem is illustrated in Figure 2.7. In response to a rise in real wages, we observe an increase in the amount of leisure taken equal to $A'C'$. But this is composed of an income effect $A'B'$ (such as would arise if the lower wage rate remained in effect and the worker inherited an annuity providing him with GE of income per period) plus a substitution effect $B'C'$ (such as would take place if simultaneously the worker's annuity were canceled and the wage rate rose as depicted). Our problem is to guess at the possible magnitude of the income effect so as to be able to conclude something about the size of the substitution effect.

[13] Wages per hour of work in the manufacturing industry rose from \$.502 in 1900 to \$2.24 in 1957, expressed in 1957 prices (Albert Rees, "Patterns of Wages, Prices, and Productivity," in Charles Myers, ed., *Wages, Prices, Profits, and Productivity*, New York, 1957, pp. 15–16). Average hours of work per week fell from 55 to 37.8 during the same period.

	Log Hours Worked	Log Real Wages per Hour
1900	1.74036	9.70070–10
1957	1.58771	0.35025
Difference	0.15265	0.64955

The elasticity of hours with respect to real hourly wages derived from these data is $-.235$. The elasticities obtained from the regression of annual data on these two variables for the period 1900–1957 (excluding the depression and war years) were $-.26$ for manufacturing, $-.26$ for railroads, $-.19$ for bituminous coal, and $-.21$ for anthracite coal. (See Ethel B. Jones, "Hours of Work in the United States, 1900–1957," unpublished Ph.D. dissertation, University of Chicago, 1961, p. 44.)

Obviously, using these figures to measure the elasticity of labor supply implicitly assumes that average hours tended to be those "desired" by workers, i.e., that workers were in some sense "on" their labor supply function. One need not labor the point that individual workers are constrained to some extent by the norms adopted in the particular places they work, so that a worker who desired to work only 30 hours a week would either have to find a job requiring this amount of work or be "off" his labor supply function. But it seems reasonable to suppose that the main force behind the historical downward trend in hours was the desire for additional leisure on the part of the typical worker. Unions would probably not have negotiated, and employers would probably not have conceded, reductions in normal hours of work if these reductions were not desired by the workers themselves. By the same token, there can be little doubt that wage rises were the principal force motivating the desire for greater leisure on the part of workers. Certainly, legislative changes do not account for a significant part of the reduction in hours. Laws imposing maximum hours affected only 4.1 percent of workers in manufacturing by 1929 (*ibid.*, p. 56). Jones concludes that only the Fair Labor Standards Act of 1938 is likely to have had a significant independent effect on hours worked in manufacturing, but finds that by the postwar period, actual hours in manufacturing were slightly above those which would be predicted by the pre-1929 relationships between average hours and real wage rates (*ibid.*, p. 70). Actually, the major reductions in hours in the postwar period have come through increases in vacation and holiday time, which are unaffected by legislation and which seem to be a highly plausible form for workers to take increases in their "desired" leisure time.

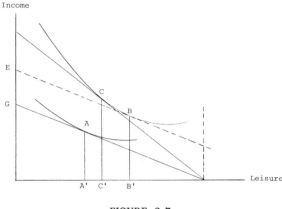

FIGURE 2.7

To put the problem in terms of the elasticity of supply of labor directly, let us define $\delta L/\delta w$ as the partial derivative of labor supply with respect to the wage rate, when the income effect is included, and $\partial L/\partial w$ as the corresponding partial derivative when the income effect is excluded. Let $\partial L/\partial y$ be the response of labor supply to a change in income (such as would come with the receipt of an annuity), holding the wage rate constant. Then we can write:

$$\frac{\delta L}{\delta w} = \frac{\partial L}{\partial w} + \frac{\partial L}{\partial y}\frac{\partial y}{\partial w}.$$

Now with no other changes taking place, income will change by the number of hours worked times the change in the wage rate (i.e., $\Delta Y = L \Delta w$) so we can set $(\partial y/\partial w) = L$. Hence $(w/L)(\delta L/\delta w) = (w/L)(\partial L/\partial w) + w(\partial L/\partial y)$ or $e' = e + w(\partial L/\partial y)$, where e' represents the elasticity of supply of labor including income and substitution effects and e represents the elasticity of supply of labor including the substitution effect only. $w(\partial L/\partial y)$ is simply the negative of the fraction of an increase in nonlabor income which is taken out in the form of leisure. Thus if, for example, a worker on receiving an annuity of $1,000 a year would reduce his labor earnings by $250 a year, $w(\partial L/\partial y)$ would for him be $-.25$. If he would reduce his labor earnings by $500 a year, $w(\partial L/\partial y)$ would for him be $-.50$.

Now, from historical observations, we take e' to be $-.25$. Hence if $w(\partial L/\partial y)$ equaled $-.25$, e must equal zero, and if $w(\partial L/\partial y) = -.50$, e must equal $+.25$. Since e cannot be negative, and the available evidence indicates that e' is about $-.25$, we cannot "guess" that $w(\partial L/\partial y)$ is less in absolute magnitude than $.25$. We can guess, however, that it is substantially less than $.5$ in absolute value. In order to have a specific number to play with, I shall assume that $w(\partial L/\partial y) = -.375$, indicating that a typical worker inheriting an annuity of $1,000 will tend to reduce his labor earnings by $375. Readers need not take this guess too seriously, however, for the results that will be obtained using it can easily be adjusted for alternative assumptions.

When measuring the welfare cost of a proportional income tax, we can use

44

TABLE 2.2

Welfare Cost per Dollar of Labor Income, by Adjusted Gross
Income Class

Adjusted gross income class (thousands)	Total adjusted gross income in class (millions) (1)	Taxable income per return with adjusted gross income in class (2)	Marginal tax rate in class (m_i) (3)	Implied reduction in labor supply within class (em_i) $(e = .125)$ (4)	Welfare cost per dollar of labor income in class $(\frac{1}{2}em_i{}^2)$ (5)
Less than $5	$84,278	$887	20%	2.50%	$.0025
$5– $10	144,984	3,750	20	2.50	.0025
10– 15	48,553	7,865	22	2.75	.0030
15– 20	15,151	12,400	30	3.75	.0056
20– 25	7,738	16,906	34	4.25	.0072
25– 50	16,594	26,496	43	5.38	.0116
50– 100	7,268	53,659	62	7.75	.0240
100– 150	2,015	96,775	72	9.00	.0324
150– 200	936	136,488	78	9.75	.0380
200– 500	1,750	223,392	89	11.13	.0495
500– 1,000	663	528,092	91	11.38	.0518
Over 1,000	806	1,480,450	91	11.38	.0518
Total	330,936				

Source: [U.S. Treasury Department, Internal Revenue Service] *Statistics of Income: Individual Income Tax Returns for 1961* [Washington, D.C.: Government Printing Office, 1963], pp. 14–16.

the expression $1/2\ er^2wL$ without further ado. But when the tax system is progressive, we must recognize that the choices of an individual at the margin are governed by his marginal tax rate, which we can call m. Letting m_i be the marginal tax rate in the ith tax bracket, and $W_i = w_iL_i$ be the total wage income earned by people in the ith tax bracket, we may express the total welfare cost of the personal income tax as $1/2\ \sum_i e_i m_i{}^2 W_i$. This is what is done in Tables 2.2 and 2.3. It is assumed that e_i is equal to .125 for all tax brackets, on the basis of the value of $-.375$ for $w(\partial L/\partial y)$ selected above. Column 1 of Table 2.2 is merely for the information of the reader. The $331 billion of reported income on returns with adjusted gross income compares with $427 billion reported as total personal income in the national accounts for 1961. Column 2 of Table 2.2 presents the average adjusted gross income per return with adjusted gross income in each class. This figure was used to determine the marginal tax rate that would be assumed for each class in the calculations to follow. In obtaining the marginal tax rate from the tax table, the rates applying to joint returns were used. Thus a downward bias was introduced into the calculations of welfare cost. Column 4 of Table 2.2 presents the percentage reduction in labor effort within each class which is implied by the assumptions of this analysis. It is meant to be a check on the plausibility of the results. As can be seen, the implied reductions in labor effort range from 2.5 percent in the 20 percent bracket to around 11.4 percent in the 91 percent bracket. This says, in effect, that if it were possible to extract out of each income class the same tax as was in fact

TABLE 2.3
Welfare Cost on Wages and Salaries and Business and Professional Income, by Adjusted Gross Income Class

Adjusted gross income class (thousands)	Welfare cost per dollar of labor income in class Table 2, col. 5) (1)	Wage and salary income in taxable returns in class (millions) (2)	Welfare cost on wage and salary income (cols. 1 × 2) (millions) (3)	Business and professional income on taxable returns in class (millions) (4)	Potential welfare cost on business and professional income in class (cols. 1 × 4) (millions) (5)
Less than $5	$.0025	$58,418	$146	$4,371	$11
$5– $10	.0025	129,695	324	6,630	17
10– 15	.0030	40,448	121	3,434	10
15– 20	.0056	9,837	55	2,166	12
20– 25	.0072	4,145	30	1,468	11
25– 50	.0116	6,864	80	3,338	39
50– 100	.0240	2,452	59	991	24
100– 150	.0324	546	18	115	4
150– 200	.0380	185	7	33	1
200– 500	.0495	234	12	30	1
500– 1,000	.0518	39	2	6	—
Over 1,000	.0518	19	1	5	—
Total		252,882	855	22,587	130

Source: [U.S. Treasury Department, Internal Revenue Service] *Statistics of Income: Individual Income Tax Returns for 1961* [Washington, D.C.: Government Printing Office, 1963], pp. 14–16.

obtained, but in such a way that tax incentives did not distort the choice between labor and leisure at the margin, we would get 11.4 percent more work out of our top income brackets and 2.5 percent more work out of people presently in the lowest range of taxable income. These figures do not imply that top-bracket people work less than low-bracket people, but only that they work 11 or so percent less than they would in the absence of the income-tax incentive for leisure.

Much work has still to be done to enrich the theory underlying this analysis and to check its implications in detail. However, I would suggest the following principal sources of the reduction in labor effort, particularly in the higher brackets:

1. Longer vacations (winters in Florida, etc.).
2. A higher incidence of early retirement.
3. Less labor force participation of women.
4. Less supplemental labor income from sources other than main employment.

And I find it quite plausible that these factors might account for a 5 percent reduction in labor effort in the $25,000–$50,000 bracket, and for an 11 percent reduction in the highest brackets, as against what it would be in the absence of tax incentives at the margin, but in the presence of the existing total weight of tax. Needless to say, I do not expect everybody to agree with this judgment,

46

but shall proceed on this basis in the absence of any alternative that seems clearly better to me.

Column 5 of Table 2.2 (reproduced as column 1 of Table 2.3) gives the estimated welfare cost per dollar of labor income in each class. In column 2 of Table 2.3 we have the amount of wage and salary income (by far the major category of labor income) declared on taxable returns in each class, and in column 3 the estimated welfare cost associated with the tax incentive to wage and salary earners. In column 4 we have the amount of business and professional income declared on taxable returns in each class. Obviously not all of this income comes from labor effort, but the estimates of welfare cost in column 5 are based on the extreme assumption that business and professional income is all labor income. Since the welfare costs estimated in column 5 are not large compared with those in column 3, I elected not to attempt an adjustment to exclude that fraction of business and professional income which might be attributable to property.

The results emerging from Table 2.3 suggest that the welfare costs associated with the distortion of the labor-leisure choice by the personal income tax may be of the order of $1 billion per year. My own reaction to this is twofold. First of all, $1 billion is not a very large amount in comparison to the $42 billion per year raised by the personal income tax in 1961. If this were a necessary cost to obtain the kind of progression that the personal income tax contributes to our tax system, I would judge it to be a worthwhile cost. But the roughly $1 billion per year cost estimated in Table 2.3 is clearly not a necessary cost to obtain the existing degree of progression in the personal income tax structure. Actually, the average tax rate (income-tax adjusted-gross-income) does not reach 45 percent even for the highest brackets, and for most brackets is only about half the marginal tax rate.[14] This means that there are real possibilities for obtaining about as much revenue from each class as at present, but with lower marginal rates. This can be done by broadening the tax base (reducing exemptions and deductions, eliminating or modifying a host of special provisions such as percentage depletion and capital gains, etc.). Most tax experts have advocated such a reform of our tax system, and the present analysis simply adds support to the proposal. If, for example, the marginal rate in each class of adjusted gross income could be reduced to seven-tenths of its present value, the welfare cost estimated above would be cut about in half. And it is likely that this could be done without loss of either revenue or effective progressivity.

IV. COMPARISON OF THE WELFARE COSTS OF DIRECT AND INDIRECT TAXATION

In this section we attempt to assess the relative merits of direct and indirect taxation taking explicit account of the issues raised by the labor-leisure choice. Throughout this section we shall set aside the problem of progressivity and

---

[14] The average tax rates in 1961 by bracket are: 7.2 percent for 0–$5,000; 11.0 percent for $5,000–10,000; 14.3 percent for $10,000–15,000; 17.0 percent for $15,000–20,000; 19.5 percent for $20,000–25,000; 24.5 percent for $25,000–50,000; 34.2 percent for $50,000–100,000; 40.1 percent for $100,000–150,000; 42.4 percent for $150,000–200,000; 43.7 percent for $200,000–500,000; 44.8 percent for $500,000–1,000,000; and 42.4 percent for over $1,000,000.

consider the income tax as a proportional tax, and as equivalent to a set of excise taxes striking all goods other than leisure at the same percentage rate. The first question we ask is: Granted that the income tax has a certain welfare cost, under what circumstances does it have a smaller welfare cost than a set of excise taxes at unequal rates which yields the same revenue? Second, we turn to the theoretical question of how to measure the difference in welfare costs between an excise tax and an income tax yielding the same revenue. Third, we turn to the more interesting question of how we would measure the change in welfare costs resulting from eliminating an existing excise tax and substituting for it an increment to an already existing income tax.

To answer our first question, let us again postulate a three-commodity world, in which the third good is leisure. We are allowed to tax only goods 1 and 2, and we are required to raise a given amount of revenue. The expression for welfare cost, when commodity units are chosen so that unit costs equal 1, is

$$-\tfrac{1}{2}[S_{11}t_1{}^2 + S_{22}t_2{}^2 + S_{33}t_3{}^2 + 2S_{12}t_1t_2 + 2S_{13}t_1t_3 + 2S_{23}t_2t_3].$$

Because our problem restricts t_3 to be zero, this reduces to

$$-\tfrac{1}{2}[S_{11}t_1{}^2 + S_{22}t_2{}^2 + 2S_{12}t_1t_2].$$

We seek to minimize this expression by our choice of t_1 and t_2, subject to the constraint that $t_1X_1 + t_2X_2 = K$, i.e., that a given amount of total revenue, K, is obtained. Minimizing

$$W = -\tfrac{1}{2}[S_{11}t_1{}^2 + S_{22}t_2{}^2 + 2S_{12}t_1t_2] + \lambda[t_1X_1 + t_2X_2 - K],$$

we obtain

$$\frac{\partial W}{\partial t_1} = -S_{11}t_1 - S_{12}t_2 + \lambda X_1 + \lambda t_1\frac{\partial X_1}{\partial t_1} + \lambda t_2\frac{\partial X_2}{\partial t_1} = 0.$$

Since

$$\frac{\partial X_1}{\partial t_1} = S_{11} \quad \text{and} \quad \frac{\partial X_2}{\partial t_1} = S_{21} = S_{12},$$

the above simplifies to

$$\frac{\partial W}{\partial t_1} = -S_{11}(1 - \lambda)t_1 - S_{12}(1 - \lambda)t_2 + \lambda X_1 = 0.$$

Similarly,

$$\frac{\partial W}{\partial t_2} = -S_{12}(1 - \lambda)t_1 - S_{22}(1 - \lambda)t_2 + \lambda X_2 = 0.$$

If we set $\mu = \lambda/(1 - \lambda)$, we obtain

$$\frac{\partial W}{\partial t_1} = -S_{11}t_1 - S_{12}t_2 + \mu X_1 = 0$$

$$\frac{\partial W}{\partial t_2} = -S_{22}t_2 - S_{12}t_1 + \mu X_2 = 0.$$

The solution for t_1 and t_2 for minimum welfare cost is

$$\hat{t}_1 = \frac{\begin{vmatrix} \mu X_1 & S_{12} \\ \mu X_2 & S_{22} \end{vmatrix}}{\begin{vmatrix} S_{11} & S_{12} \\ S_{12} & S_{22} \end{vmatrix}}; \qquad \hat{t}_2 = \frac{\begin{vmatrix} S_{11} & \mu X_1 \\ S_{12} & \mu X_2 \end{vmatrix}}{\begin{vmatrix} S_{11} & S_{12} \\ S_{12} & S_{22} \end{vmatrix}}.$$

Obviously, $\hat{t}_1$ will equal $\hat{t}_2$ when the numerators of the above expressions are equal, i.e., when

$$X_1 S_{22} - X_2 S_{12} = X_2 S_{11} - X_1 S_{12}.$$

Using the fact that, when unit costs $= 1$, $S_{11} = -S_{12} - S_{13}$; $S_{22} = -S_{12} - S_{23}$, this equality can be rewritten

$$-X_1 S_{12} - X_2 S_{12} - X_1 S_{23} = -X_2 S_{12} - X_1 S_{12} - X_2 S_{13}.$$

Hence the equality requires that $X_1 S_{23}$ be equal to $X_2 S_{13}$, or that $S_{13}/X_1 = S_{23}/X_2$. But $S_{13} = \partial X_1/\partial P_3$; and with $P_3 = 1$, η_{13}, the cross elasticity of demand for commodity 1 with respect to the price of leisure can be written $(1/X_1)(\partial X_1/\partial P_3) = (S_{13}/X_1)$. Likewise, $S_{23}/X_2 = \eta_{23}$. Hence the condition for equal excise taxation of both goods being the best pattern of excise taxation by which to raise a given sum of money is that both goods have the same cross elasticity of demand with respect to the price of leisure.

To see under what circumstances a minimum welfare cost is obtained with a lower (or a higher) tax on X_1 than X_2, we can express the ratio $\hat{t}_1/\hat{t}_2$ as

$$\frac{\hat{t}_1}{\hat{t}_2} = \frac{X_1 S_{12} + X_2 S_{12} + X_1 S_{23}}{X_1 S_{12} + X_2 S_{12} + X_2 S_{13}}.$$

Obviously, when $X_1 S_{23}$ is smaller than $X_2 S_{13}$, $\hat{t}_1$ is less than $\hat{t}_2$. This can happen when S_{23} is negative, i.e., when X_2 is complementary to leisure, or when, S_{23} and S_{13} both being positive, $X_1 S_{23} < X_2 S_{13}$. This last inequality is equivalent to $\eta_{23} < \eta_{13}$. Thus the tax on X_1 "should" be lower than the tax on X_2 whenever X_2 is less substitutable for leisure than is X_1.[15]

This result should not be taken to suggest, however, that it is likely that minimum-welfare-cost patterns of excise taxation are likely to have very different rates. Dividing both numerator and denominator in the above expression by $X_1 X_2$, and recalling that $S_{12} = S_{21}$, we obtain

$$\frac{\hat{t}_1}{\hat{t}_2} = \frac{\eta_{21} + \eta_{12} + \eta_{23}}{\eta_{21} + \eta_{12} + \eta_{13}}.$$

If, as is likely, the cross elasticity of both goods with respect to the price of leisure is low in comparison to the cross elasticities of the goods with respect to each other's prices, the ratio of $\hat{t}_1$ to $\hat{t}_2$ will not be "very" different from unity.

---

[15] For an early analysis arriving at essentially the same conclusion, though by a somewhat more complicated argument, see W. J. Corlett and D. C. Hague, "Complementarity and the Excess Burden of Taxation," *Review of Economic Studies*, 1953–54, pp. 21–30.

We now turn to the second question mentioned at the beginning of this section — measuring the difference in welfare cost between an excise tax and an income tax of equal yield. The welfare cost of an excise tax at the rate t_1 is simply

$$C_1 = -\tfrac{1}{2}S_{11}t_1^2.$$

A proportional income tax at the rate t^* will have equal yield when $t^*(X_1 + X_2) = t_1 X_1$, i.e., where $t^* = t_1 X_1/(X_1 + X_2)$. The welfare cost of this income tax will be

$$C_2 = -\tfrac{1}{2}S_{33}(t^*)^2.$$

Hence we may write

$$C_1 - C_2 = -\tfrac{1}{2}[S_{11}t_1^2 - S_{33}(t^*)^2], \quad \text{or}$$

$$C_1 - C_2 = -\frac{1}{2}\,S_{11}t_1^2\left[1 - \frac{S_{33}}{S_{11}}\left(\frac{t^*}{t_1}\right)^2\right].$$

This equation expresses the difference in welfare cost between an excise tax and an equal-yield income tax as the welfare cost of the excise tax taken by itself times one minus a "correction factor" $[(S_{33}/S_{11})(t^*/t_1)^2]$. Now t^*/t_1 is simply $X_1/(X_1 + X_2)$, or the fraction of money income accounted for by the taxed commodity. Calling this measure a_1, we may express the correction factor as $[S_{33}/(X_1 + X_2)][X_1/S_{11}]a_1$. Now X_1/S_{11} is simply $1/\eta_{11}$. Now, as indicated in the preceding section $-S_{33}$ is equal to the derivative of the supply of labor with respect to the wage (P_3). Where all income is produced by labor, and all prices are unity, $(X_1 + X_2)$ represents the quantity of labor supplied. Therefore $-S_{33}/(X_1 + X_2)$ is equal to e, the elasticity of supply of labor. Hence $[(S_{33}/S_{11})/(t^*/t_1)^2]$ can be expressed as $-a_1 e/\eta_{11}$. Since η_{11} is necessarily negative, the correction factor is positive. What is more important, however, is the fact that the correction factor is likely to be very small, as long as the excise tax is not so general as to be nearly an income tax itself. In the preceding section we judged a plausible value for e to be .125. Suppose we consider t_1 to be an excise tax which strikes 20 percent of all goods and services other than leisure, i.e., $.2 = X_1/(X_1 + X_2) = a_1$. The correction factor will then be equal to $-(.2)(.125)/\eta_{11}$, or $-.025/\eta_{11}$. Thus if the own-price elasticity of demand for the taxed good were as small in absolute value as .25, the correction factor would only be .1; and if the elasticity were in the range between $-.5$ and -1.0, the correction factor could, for all practical purposes, be neglected. Only when the elasticity of demand for the excise-taxed commodity is very small indeed would the correction factor become of sizable magnitude. And this elasticity would have to be virtually zero (in our example, less than .025) in order for the correction factor to exceed unity, and thus for the excise tax to have lower welfare cost than an equal-yield income tax.

The result just obtained is heartening to those who felt all along that direct taxation is better than indirect taxation. But the case just covered is one in which the excise tax and the income tax are strictly alternatives, and as such it is far removed from reality. We shall now modify the preceding example to allow for an income tax already in existence, and shall inquire about the size of the difference between the increments to welfare cost incurred by either adding a given amount to total revenue by way of an excise tax on X_1, or adding the same amount to total revenue by increasing the rate of income tax.

Let t_0 be the existing rate of income tax, and, as before t_1 and t^* be the alternative increments to tax rates. The situations we are comparing then are

	Tax Rate on X_1	Tax Rate on X_2
Situation 1	$t_0 + t_1$	t_0
Situation 2	$t_0 + t^*$	$t_0 + t^*$,

where, as before, $t^* = a_1 t_1$.

The expressions for the welfare cost are in this case most conveniently expressed in terms of the third fundamental form $1/2 \sum_j \sum_{i<j} S_{ij}(t_i - t_j)^2$.

$$C_1 = \tfrac{1}{2}[S_{12}t_1^2 + S_{13}(t_0 + t_1)^2 + S_{23}t_0^2]$$
$$C_2 = \tfrac{1}{2}[S_{13}(t_0 + t^*)^2 + S_{23}(t_0 + t^*)^2].$$

Expanding, we have

$$C_1 = \tfrac{1}{2}[S_{12}t_1^2 + S_{13}t_0^2 + 2S_{13}t_0t_1 + S_{13}t_1^2 + S_{23}t_0^2]$$
$$C_2 = \tfrac{1}{2}[S_{13}t_0^2 + 2S_{13}t_0t^* + S_{13}(t^*)^2 + S_{23}t_0^2 + 2S_{23}t_0t^* + S_{23}(t^*)^2].$$

Subtracting, we obtain

$$C_1 - C_2 = \tfrac{1}{2}[S_{12}t_1^2 + 2S_{13}t_0t_1 + S_{13}t_1^2 - 2S_{13}t_0t^* - S_{13}(t^*)^2$$
$$- 2S_{23}t_0t^* - S_{23}(t^*)^2].$$

Since $S_{12} + S_{13} = -S_{11}$, and $-S_{13} - S_{23} = S_{33}$, this reduces to

$$C_1 - C_2 = \tfrac{1}{2}[-S_{11}t_1^2 + S_{33}(t^*)^2 + 2S_{13}t_0t_1 - 2S_{13}t_0t^* - 2S_{23}t_0t^*].$$

Substituting $a_1 t_1$ for t^* in the last two terms, we have

$$C_1 - C_2 = \tfrac{1}{2}[-S_{11}t_1^2 + S_{33}(t^*)^2 + 2(1 - a_1)S_{13}t_0t_1 - 2a_1S_{23}t_0t_1].$$
$$C_1 - C_2 = -\frac{1}{2}S_{11}t_1^2\left[1 - \frac{S_{33}}{S_{11}}\left(\frac{t^*}{t_1}\right)^2 - 2\frac{(1 - a_1)S_{13}t_0 - a_1S_{23}t_0}{S_{11}t_1}\right].$$

Once again we are expressing the difference in the welfare cost of an excise tax and (in this case) an increment to the income tax rate as being equal to the welfare cost of the excise tax by itself times one minus a correction factor. For simplicity, let us say one minus two correction factors. The first of these, $(S_{33}/S_{11})(t^*/t_1)^2$, has already been shown to be equal to $-a_1e/\eta_{11}$, and likely to be small.

We therefore turn to an evaluation of the second correction factor, $2.\{[(1 - a_1)S_{13} - a_1S_{23}]/S_{11}\}(t_0/t_1)$. First let us convert this relationship into elasticity form, using $S_{13} = X_1\eta_{13}$; $S_{23} = X_2\eta_{23}$ and $S_{11} = X_1\eta_{11}$. This yields

$$2 \cdot \frac{(1 - a_1) X_1\eta_{13} - a_1 X_2\eta_{23}}{X_1\eta_{11}}\left(\frac{t_0}{t_1}\right).$$

Now let us define $a_2 = X_2/(X_1 + X_2) = (1 - a_1)$. Dividing numerator and denominator by $(X_1 + X_2)$, we obtain

$$2 \cdot \frac{a_2(\eta_{13} - \eta_{23})}{\eta_{11}} \left(\frac{t_0}{t_1}\right).$$

The correction factor will be positive if the taxed commodity (X_1) is complementary with leisure $(\eta_{13} < 0)$, or if, both goods being substitutes for leisure, the taxed commodity is the poorer substitute $(0 < \eta_{13} < \eta_{23})$. This simply reflects the fact that the minimum-welfare-cost pattern of taxing X_1 and X_2 calls for higher taxation of the poorer substitute for leisure. But it is to be emphasized that the sign of the second correction factor could be either positive or negative, and that neither sign is more likely than the other. The sign depends only on whether the commodity chosen for excise taxation happens to be a better-than-average or a worse-than-average substitute for leisure.

It is to be presumed that in most cases the second adjustment factor will be of small magnitude, at least where the tax rate t_1 is not very small in relation to the existing income tax rate, t_0, and where the own-price elasticity of demand for X_1 is not itself very small.

Another way of expressing the second correction factor is

$$2 \cdot \left[a_2 \left(\frac{S_{13}}{S_{33}}\right) - a_1 \left(\frac{S_{23}}{S_{33}}\right)\right] \left(\frac{S_{33}}{S_{11}} \cdot \frac{t_0}{t_1}\right).$$

Since $S_{13} + S_{23} = -S_{33}$, (S_{13}/S_{33}) and (S_{23}/S_{33}) must add up to -1. In the normal case where X_1 and X_2 are both substitutes for leisure, S_{13}/S_{33} and S_{23}/S_{33} will both be negative fractions. Calling them f_1 and f_2, respectively, the second correction factor can be rewritten as

$$2 \cdot (a_2 f_1 - a_1 f_2) \frac{S_{33} t_0}{S_{11} t_1}.$$

$(S_{33}t_0/S_{11}t_1)$ is simply the ratio of the welfare cost per dollar of tax receipts of the existing income tax to the welfare cost per dollar of tax receipts of the excise tax under consideration, divided by a_1, the share of the taxed commodity in total income. The welfare cost of the income tax is $-1/2\, S_{33} t_0^2 = 1/2$ $(X_1 + X_2) e t_0^2$. The revenue from the income tax is $(X_1 + X_2) t_0$, as the welfare cost per dollar of revenue is $1/2\, e t_0$. The welfare cost of the excise tax on X_1, in turn, is $-1/2\, S_{11} t_1^2 = -1/2\, X_1 \eta_{11} t_1^2$. It yields $X_1 t_1$ in revenue, so the welfare cost per dollar of tax is $-1/2\, \eta_{11} t_1$. Hence if we call h_0 and h_1 the welfare costs per dollar of revenue of the existing income tax and the excise tax under consideration, respectively, we can write $(S_{33}t_0/S_{11}t_1) = h_0/a_1 h_1$. Hence the correction factor is equal to

$$2([a_2 f_1/a_1] - f_2)(h_0/h_1).$$

Where the welfare cost per dollar of revenue is significantly higher for the excise tax than for the existing income tax, the correction factor is likely to be small. When $e = .125$, the welfare cost of an income tax, per dollar of revenue, will range between $.0125 and $.0250 for tax rates between .2 and .4, for example. When $\eta_{11} = -1$, on the other hand, the welfare cost of an excise tax of 20 percent will be $.10 per dollar of tax revenue. Thus where an excise tax is likely to look bad (i.e., to have a high welfare cost per dollar of tax revenue) when taken by itself, it is also likely to look bad in comparison with the alternative of adding to an existing income tax. When, on the other hand, an excise tax is contemplated which does not look bad by itself, we cannot be confident that an increase in income tax designed to produce an equal increment of revenue would be a preferable alternative.

The conclusion that I draw from this exercise is, therefore, that by and large the traditional preference for direct over indirect taxation is justified, and that the simple textbook measure of welfare cost (the triangle under the demand curve) yields a good first approximation in most cases.

V. TAXATION AND THE INCENTIVE TO SAVE

We now turn to a consideration of how taxation influences welfare through its effect on saving. Here we have another area where income taxation is non-neutral. The private incentives to save are governed by the after-tax yield on the sums involved, but the social rate of return is given by the before-tax yield. Clearly, in order to make the tax system neutral with respect to savings decisions, one would require a consumption tax of the type that Kaldor has proposed, rather than an income tax of the conventional type.

Having recognized the nonneutrality of income taxation with respect to savings, we now turn to the measurement of the welfare costs that it entails. The solution to this problem is not as clear-cut as that of labor-leisure choice. The difficulty arises because the introduction of savings into the picture injects a dynamic element into what would otherwise be a comparative static model. This can be handled neatly if the time path of savings is independent of the changes in tax policy under consideration, but in such a case income taxation would have no welfare cost arising from interference with the savings decision, and our problem would disappear. As long as we take our problem seriously, we must face up to a possible effect of taxation on the volume of savings and investment, and thus the problem of incorporating a dynamic element in what would otherwise be a static model must be faced.

I shall discuss here two alternative ways of dealing with the above problem, the first of which inquires into the purpose for which the saving in question is undertaken, and the second of which does not. The first approach starts by taking a particular time-horizon for a given act of saving — say, ten years. If $1 is saved now, and if its full social yield (at the rate ρ) is reinvested, it will produce, ten years from now, a sum equal to $1(1 + \rho)^{10}$. If, however, the yield of this saving is annually taxed at the rate t, its private value ten years from now will be $1(1 + r)^{10}$, if $r = \rho(1 - t)$ is the private rate of return on savings. The marginal rate of substitution in consumption between present goods and goods ten years in the future will therefore be $1 : (1 + r)^{10}$, while the social marginal rate of transformation will be $1 : (1 + \rho)^{10}$. The percentage excess of $(1 + \rho)^{10}$ over $(1 + r)^{10}$ plays the same role as would a tax of this percentage on savings made for the purpose of accumulation for ten years and for consumption at the end of the period. Similarly, the percentage excess of $(1 + \rho)^n$ over $(1 + r)^n$ plays the same role as a corresponding tax on savings made for the purpose of accumulation for n years and then for consumption. Since in the real world savings are not made for purposes as clearly specified as these, one may regard the effects of income taxation as being equivalent to a tax on savings at a rate equal to a weighted average of the expressions $[(1 + \rho)^n/(1 + r)^n - 1]$, the weights reflecting the probabilities attaching to the savings being used in particular future time periods.

The approach just outlined has the advantage of emphasizing the way in which the effects of tax incentives upon saving depend on what might be called the savings strategy of the affected individuals. The marginal rate of substitution between this year's goods and next year's goods is not likely to be much affected even by very heavy income taxation; while the marginal rate of substitution between this year's goods and goods a quarter century from now will be substantially affected, even by comparatively moderate income taxation. For example, taxing away 50 percent of the income from capital, in a case where ρ, the social marginal productivity of capital, is 6 percent, changes the marginal rate of substitution between present and future goods from 1.06 to 1.03 for one-year savings decisions, from 1.34 to 1.16 for five-year savings decisions, from 1.79 to 1.34 for ten-year savings decisions, and from 3.21 to 1.81 for twenty-year savings decisions. But by the same token, this approach runs into the difficulty of having to specify the savers' strategies with respect to reinvestment and consumption out of capital.

The second approach is simpler, neater, and more conventional. It simply regards each dollar saved as purchasing a perpetual income stream in the amount of $\$\rho$ per year for the society as a whole, and of $\$\rho(1 - t)$, or $\$r$ per year for the individual saver. The present value of this income stream to the saver, evaluated at the rate r, is \$1. But the present value to society is $\$\rho/r$. The social value of a marginal dollar of saving thus exceeds the private value by the percentage $t/(1 - t)$. If the elimination of this distortion would produce a change in savings equal to ΔS dollars, then we can assign as the welfare cost of the distortion of the savings decision the amount $1/2\,(\Delta S) \times [t/(1 - t)]$.

I must confess that I have labored for some time under a prejudice against this second approach, mainly because the idea of persons considering saving only in terms of perpetuities did not seem particularly realistic. However, further reflection has led me to conclude that my original objection was not a serious one. The essential difference between the two approaches lies in their treatment of decisions taken at different times. The first approach tries to deal simultaneously with the saving that takes place now, with the reinvestment of the earnings of that saving for some period in the future, and with the disinvestment of the accumulated value at the end of the period. The second approach deals only with the savings decisions taken at a given period in time. This year's savings are considered when the analysis focuses on this year's actions; next year's savings are taken into account when the analysis focuses on next year's actions, etc. In particular, the second approach does not ask what will be done next year with the earnings on this year's savings; it simply treats those earnings as part of the total income accruing next year, in terms of which the individual will reach a decision as to how much to save. Nor does the second approach treat the realization of the proceeds of a given investment as an act of dissaving; it looks instead at the total movement in the capital stock of an individual in a given year. If this capital stock has increased, the individual has saved, net, regardless of how many previous investments may have been liquidated during the year. It seems to me, therefore, that the second approach, in addition to being simpler and more convenient to handle in the analysis of welfare costs, also looks at the savings decision in a scientifically more sophisticated way.

Before leaving the subject of the effects of taxation on the rate of saving, we should inquire whether the distortions introduced by income taxation can lead to an increase in the rate of saving. It is well known that where changes in the rate of return on savings include an income effect, a reduction in the rate of return can produce an increase in the volume of savings. Does this possibility emerge in the case under discussion? The answer, I believe, is clearly negative. Income effects are kept out of the picture, in this analysis, by the requirement that the govenment be able, year by year, to buy the same bundles of goods under any alternative patterns of taxation being compared. If we were to consider the effects of reducing the rate of income taxation, without imposing any alternative tax to make up for the lost revenue, then an income effect would be present, and a decrease in saving could conceivably result. However, if we require that the government make up for the lost revenue, say, by increasing the rate of consumption taxation, then no first-order income effect will be present, and the change in the rate of savings must be in the same direction as the change in the net-of-tax rate of return.

Consumers in their role as savers see their future income reduced because of the tax that they have to pay on the return to capital under an income tax. But if the shift were made to a pure consumption tax, they would see their future income reduced because of the higher tax they would have to pay on their future consumption expenditures.[16] Consumers will in fact get more future income under a consumption-tax setup than under an equal-yield income tax, but they will do so only because they save more as a consequence of the higher return they perceive on their capital. If they save exactly the same amounts under the two setups, the extra future income they get from their capital will be just counterbalanced by the extra future taxes they have to pay on their consumption when they face a consumption rather than an income tax.

In spite of a clear presumption that the taxation of income from property will reduce the rate of savings as against what it would be under neutral taxation of equal yield, it is very hard to build an empirical case for the proposition that the taxation of property income has significantly affected the savings rate. But one must recognize that it would not require a phenomenal responsiveness of savings to the net rate of return in order to generate a fairly significant welfare cost as a consequence of the distortion of the savings-consumption decision. If

---

[16] See Martin J. Bailey, *National Income and the Price Level*, New York, 1962, pp. 180–182.

net savings, for example, were only 1 percent of the national income less than they would be under straight consumption taxation, the welfare cost of taxes striking the income from capital at a 33 1/3 percent rate would be roughly 1/2 (.01)(.50) times the national income. This is .25 percent of national income, or a sum of over $1 billion per year at present levels.

What rankles me much more than the possible effect of our tax system on the total volume of savings, however, is the way in which our taxes influence the uses to which our savings are put. The heavy weight of taxes on income from capital can be justified on equity grounds in a number of ways, but the grossly unequal tax treatment of different types of income from capital cannot be seriously defended by appeals to equity considerations. Most risky corporate investments, which have little chance to be financed by debt capital, have the worst of it, while oil wells are powerfully subsidized to produce petroleum at real cost far above what it would take to obtain the oil from abroad. Income is freely transmuted into capital gains in a variety of activities (lumber, coal mining, rental housing, cattle feeding), inducing an excessive flow of resources into these fields. Perhaps the most blatant case is that of owner-occupied housing which is allowed to generate no taxable income, just tax deductions. The stimuli given by the tax treatment of owner-occupied housing are virtually nil for the needy, and increase directly with the opulence of the taxpayer. It is easy to establish that these tax incentives give rise to a substantial misallocation of investible funds, with a consequent cost to consumers throughout the economy. Elsewhere[17] I have tried to establish the order of magnitude of the losses involved due to tax-induced misallocations of our capital stock. Roughly speaking, $1 billion per year (say, between $.5 and $1.5 billion) seems to be the right order of magnitude for the distortions caused by the corporation income tax. Percentage depletion and related provisions appear to cost the economy between $.5 and $1.0 billion per year. David Laidler, in a study currently nearing completion, estimates the cost to the economy of the inefficiencies introduced by the special treatment of owner-occupied housing to be in the order of $.5 to $1.0 billion per year. Taking all these costs together, and recognizing that there are a number of important tax incentives to the allocation of investment which are not accounted for above, I think that a clear case can be made for rationalizing our manner of taxing income from capital so as not to discriminate so severely among different allocations of capital resources.

VI. TAXATION AND GROWTH

It is likely that the feature which best distinguishes the economic thinking (both professional and popular) of the postwar period from earlier decades is the emphasis placed upon economic growth — as a phenomenon to be explained, as a criterion of economic performance, and as an objective of policy. In

[17] Arnold C. Harberger, "The Taxation of Mineral Industries," in *Federal Tax Policy for Economic Growth and Stability*, Washington, Joint Committee on the Economic Report, 1955, pp. 439–449 [this volume, Chapter 11], and "The Corporation Income Tax: An Empirical Appraisal," in *Tax Revision Compendium*, U.S. House of Representatives, Ways and Means Committee, Washington, 1959.

today's environment it is quite natural, therefore, to inquire into the likely effects of alternative policies upon the rate of growth. In the terms of reference of this conference, and of my paper, this boils down to the question of how significantly the rate of growth could be influenced by plausible changes in the mix of direct and indirect taxation. I think that the answer is not very much.

The modern approach to the empirical analysis of economic growth (used, with only slight variations, by Abramovitz, Denison, Fabricant, Kendrick, Schultz, and Solow, among others) is to split up observed growth into a part attributed to the increase in labor inputs, a part attributed to the increase in capital inputs, and a residual not explained by these factors. The part assigned to labor is this year's growth in man-hours times last year's average wage; this procedure uses last year's average wage as a measure of what the marginal product of the added labor would be in the absence of technical progress and of changes in the quality of labor. The part assigned to capital is this year's net investment times last year's average before-tax rate of return to capital; once again last year's observed rate of return is used as a measure of what added capital would contribute to national income in the absence of technical advance and other forces not taken directly into account. The breakdown of the change in output from one period (year) to the next can be summarized as

$$\Delta Y_t = w_{t-1}\,\Delta L_t + \rho_{t-1}I_t + T_t, \quad \text{where}$$

ΔY_t = change of national income (or net national product) between period $t-1$ and period t (expressed in dollars of $t-1$).

ΔL_t = change in labor input (man-hours) between period $t-1$ and period t.

w_{t-1} = average wage per man-hour in period $t-1$.

ρ_{t-1} = average (gross-of-tax) rate of productivity of capital (net of depreciation) in period $t-1$.

I_t = net investment in period t.

T_t = the amount of growth of national income between $t-1$ and t which is unexplained by changes in labor and capital inputs (expressed in dollars of $t-1$).

The formula above can be divided by Y_{t-1} so as to express the dependency of the rate of growth of income on various factors:

$$y_t = S_{t-1}l_t + \rho_{t-1}i_t + r_t, \quad \text{where}$$

$y_t = \Delta Y_t/Y_{t-1}$ = rate of growth of income in year t.

$S_{t-1} = w_{t-1}L_{t-1}/Y_{t-1}$ = share of labor in the national income in year $t-1$.

$l_t = \Delta L_t/L_{t-1}$ = rate of growth of labor input in year t.

$i_t = I_t/Y_{t-1}$ = net investment in year t as a fraction of Y_{t-1}.

$r_t = T_t/Y_{t-1}$ = percentage increase in income in year t which is unexplained by changes in labor and capital inputs.

The earlier sections of this paper were devoted to the possible effects of direct and indirect taxation on the supply of labor and on the volume of savings. There is a clear presumption that greater resort to indirect taxation would increase the supply of labor, though the magnitude of the increase would not be very great. The rough guesses of column 4 of Table 2.2 suggest that approximately a

3 percent increase in the supply of labor could be obtained by eliminating the inducements to leisure implied by our present marginal personal income-tax rates. But to get to this result in practice would require constructing a tax system in which there were no inducements favoring leisure over labor *at the margin*. The more likely alternatives to our present income-tax structure, such as greater reliance on broad-based indirect taxes, would not go this far; they would only reduce, not eliminate, the incentives toward leisure at the margin. Thus we should probably think of plausible shifts toward more indirect taxation as leading to a substantially less than 3 percent increase in the supply of labor, under given conditions. This change in the supply of labor would increase the measured national output (assuming full employment), but would not necessarily contribute to the normal rate of growth of output. Any contribution of decreased leisure to the rate of growth of output would have to come from its influence either on the rate of growth of the labor supply or on the share of labor in total income. I see no reason to expect any significant change in either of these magnitudes as a consequence of shifting the mix of direct and indirect taxation;[18] hence I would put down as negligible the possible contribution of such shifts to the overall rate of growth.

As distinct from their influence on growth via the labor-leisure choice, there are more significant possibilities for shifts between direct and indirect taxation to alter the rate of growth via their effects on saving. These can be conveniently represented if we make the assumption that, through time, the marginal rate of productivity of capital remains constant. If this rate is 10 percent, and net investment ($=$ net savings) increases from 8 to 9 percent of the national income, the rate of growth of output should on that account change by .10 percent per annum $(.10) \times (.01)$. Increasing the rate of net saving from 8 to 10 percent of the national income will, in these circumstances, add .20 percent per annum to the rate of growth.

Influencing the rate of growth by .10 or .20 of a percentage point may seem small, but it is not negligible in the sense that I have labeled the impact on growth via the labor-leisure choice as negligible. In discussing the effects on growth via savings, I shall first consider what kinds of effects on savings we might plausibly expect to come even from drastic changes in tax policy, and then proceed to deal with the possibility that the formulation of the growth process presented above might understate the contribution of added savings.

Although there has been some debate as to the degree to which the marginal propensity to save increases with income, I believe that there can be little doubt that it does increase. Existing studies of saving by income class do not include accruing capital gains either as part of income or as part of saving, yet in principle they should do both. Thus studies measuring income and savings on the conventional basis can yield what purports to be a constant marginal propensity

---

[18] It is clearly possible to influence the long-run rate of growth of the labor force by tax measures explicitly aimed at this objective. I have no doubt, for example, that the birth rate could be influenced by changes in income-tax exemption policy, or by indirect taxes on goods specific to child-raising. And any change in the birth rate would in the long run have its effect on the normal rate of growth of the labor force. But I do not believe that any of us considers specific measures aimed at influencing population growth to be within the terms of reference of this conference, and accordingly will not pursue the matter further.

to save, or only a mildly increasing one, and yet a correctly measured marginal propensity to save might be a significantly increasing function of income.

As far as I know, no study exists which incorporates accruing capital gains in both income and savings; hence I cannot bring evidence to bear on this subject. But making extreme assumptions often allows one to get an idea of the possibilities. Suppose, for example, that the marginal propensity to save were 50 percent for all incomes above $20,000 per year, and 10 percent for all incomes below $20,000. Suppose, moreover, that in a drastic tax revolution all incomes above $20,000 were entirely relieved of income tax, and that the entire income-tax burden now borne by them were placed (via direct or indirect taxation) on income brackets below $20,000. What would be the effect on savings? In 1961, adjusted gross incomes above $20,000 paid less than $11 billion of income tax. If these groups were relieved of this burden altogether, they would, on our absurd assumptions, save $5.5 billion more. And if lower brackets were required to bear $11 billion more of tax, they would, on our assumptions, save $1.1 billion less. There would be a net increase in savings of $4.4 billion, or just about 1 percent of the 1961 national income.

Now I cannot imagine that plausible redistributions in the tax burden would be nearly so drastic as that assumed above. Nor do I find it plausible that differences in marginal propensities to consume are as sharp as those assumed above. Hence I conclude that the redistributive effects associated with plausible tax changes are not likely to increase saving by more than, say, .50 percent of the national income.

The evidence we have on the substitution effects of taxation upon saving is even less secure than that on the redistributive effects. Here, appeal is often made to the observed secular constancy of the ratio of savings to income, and the conclusion is drawn, in the face of fairly substantial changes in the perceived rate of return, that the substitution effects in question are small. I adhere in general to this position, though it must be recognized that income effects were also present in the situations producing the observed data. Until we can isolate the magnitude of the income effects that were at work, we should not conclude that the substitution effects which operated to roughly offset the income effects were minor in importance. Having said this, however, let me add that I would be surprised if plausible tax changes (e.g., a shift from income to expenditures as the base of our major progressive tax) would increase national savings by more than 1, 1.5, or 2 percent of the national income.

If these rough judgments can be accepted, we must face the fact that tax changes are unlikely to increase the rate of growth of national income by more than .10 or .20 of a percentage point — unless the model set out at the beginning of this section has a serious flaw.

The flaw which would be the most likely to change the growth-rate implications of the preceding analysis would be an underestimation of the social marginal productivity of investment (= savings). If investment carries with it positive external effects on output, the average perceived gross-of-tax rate of return would understate the contribution of investment to the growth of national income, and our imputation would understate the part of observed growth due to capital accumulation.

Solow, in a highly original paper, has attempted to cope with this possibility by requiring that technical advances be "embodied" in capital equipment before they produce increases in output.[19] His method was to assume that the capital equipment produced in year t was 100λ percent "better" (i.e., more productive) than that produced in year $t - 1$. Working with this assumption, Solow reconstituted existing data making gross investment in year t "equivalent" to that of the base year by taking $I_t' = I_t(1 + \lambda)^t$, where I_t is the conventional measure of gross investment (in constant dollars) and I_t' is the measure incorporating the improved productivity of investment in year t over the same constant-dollar volume of investment in year 0. Proceeding on this basis, Solow builds up a time series on capital stock from the adjusted gross investment data, together with retirement estimates based on Terborgh's figures. He estimates separate capital stocks for plant and equipment, introducing the possibility of separate λ's for these two categories of capital. He ends up with one series for capital stock associated with λ's of .02 for both plant and equipment; another associated with λ's of .03 for both plant and equipment, and three more for other combinations (.02, .03), (.02, .04), (.03, .04) of λ's for plant and equipment. He then introduces these alternative measures of capital stock along with variables measuring labor input and unemployment, into a production function of the Cobb-Douglas type (modified to incorporate the unemployment variables). His results improve as he moves from capital stock estimates based on lower values for λ to those based on higher values.

Solow's device appears to yield some mileage, as far as the effect of investment on growth is concerned. Whereas on our assumption of a 10 percent rate of productivity on capital, it takes a 10 percentage point increase in the fraction of income invested to produce a 1 percentage point change in the growth rate, Solow achieves the same effect by an increase of 2.5 percentage points in the fraction of income invested.

However, Solow's results depend critically on his assumption that there are no independent forces producing economic growth. Eitan Berglas has followed Solow's procedure for calculating capital stock, but has allowed for the production function to shift with time as a result of independent forces as well.[20] Berglas finds that the best explanation of observed changes in output, under this hypothesis, emerges when the λ's for plant and equipment are both set at zero — i.e., when the conventional measure of capital stock is used. More important, as long as a trend shift of production functions is allowed for, the effect of investment on output is no greater when λ is high than when it is zero. That is, adjusting the capital stock to incorporate assumed rates of technical improvement does not add to the estimated effect of investment on economic growth — *regardless* of what positive values of λ are chosen.

It seems to me that Berglas' reformulation of Solow's procedure must be preferred to the original. In the first place, we know that there are forces which have had a trend influence on total factor productivity in the economy that

---

[19] R. M. Solow, "Technical Progress, Capital Formation, and Economic Growth," *American Economic Review*, May 1962, pp. 76–86.
[20] Eitan Berglas, "Stimulating Investment: Costs and Effects," unpublished Ph.D. dissertation, University of Chicago, 1963, Chapter 5.

are not directly associated with the volume of investment — improvements in the quality of the labor force and advances in the art of management are two cases in point. This knowledge should dictate a procedure which would allow for a trend shift of production functions as one of the explanatory factors of changes in output. If, when trend shifts were allowed for, they proved to have an insignificant explanatory power, we could conclude that they have been unimportant. But this is not the result that emerges. In fact, the trend variables introduced by Berglas are highly significant statistically (with t ratios lying between 8 and 15 for various assumptions regarding λ). Moreover, they lead to plausible coefficients for the capital input in the Cobb-Douglas production function (around .25 for $\lambda = 0$, as opposed to 1.31 for $\lambda = 0$ when trend is not taken into account, and .52 for $\lambda = .03$ when trend is not taken into account). I want to emphasize that, though Berglas' study suggests that $\lambda = 0$ is the best hypothesis for explaining observed changes in output in the presence of a trend shift in production functions, this is not the real lesson to be learned from his experiments. For $\lambda = .03$, when trend is allowed for, Berglas explains 99.31 percent of variations in output per man-hour over the period 1929–1960; while for $\lambda = 0$ he explains 99.46 percent of the same variations. There is thus not much basis for choice among different plausible values of λ. The important result emerging from Berglas' study is that higher values of λ do not mean that investment has a greater influence on economic growth than is obtained when λ is assumed to be zero. In short, Berglas' work has put us back into the situation where an extra percentage point of national income devoted to investment will affect the rate of growth by around .10 of a percentage point.

Berglas' conclusions are fortified by additional experiments. In the first, an effort was made to see whether the rate of growth depended significantly on the "newness" of the capital stock. To test this hypothesis, the cumulated gross investment of a period, expressed as a percentage of initial capital stock, is used to explain changes in total factor productivity over the same period in different industries. This was done for thirteen two-digit industries, for the periods 1948–1957, 1948–1953, and 1953–1957. In none of these cases did a significant correlation appear, and in two of the three (1948–1957 and 1953–1957) the correlation was mildly negative. Similar results emerged when cumulated investment for 1948–1953, expressed as a fraction of capital stock, was used to explain changes in total factor productivity between 1953 and 1957. This last effort was an attempt to allow for a possible lag between investment and subsequent improvement in total factor productivity.

The limited power of added investment to improve the growth rate should not really be surprising. It does not deny that, each year, technical advances make particular investments highly productive. Nor does it imply that the allocations presented at the beginning of this section are correct. I suspect, in fact, that there is a substantial degree of "embodiment" of technical advances in particular types of capital goods with high prospective marginal productivity. Each year, I think, technical improvements create prospects of very high rates of return in certain investments, say, 30, 25, or 20 percent. The contribution of these investments to economic growth is greater than ρ, the average observed rate of return to capital. If we ranked investments according to prospective rates of return, forming a function $I = f(\rho)$ where $f'(\rho) < 0$, we could state the contribution of investment to economic growth as $I\rho_0 + \int_{\rho_0}^{\infty} f(\rho) \, d\rho$, which would exceed the amount assigned to investment by the expression $I\rho_{t-1}$ if we set $\rho_0 = \rho_{t-1}$. The difference would be that inframarginal investments would then be assigned a greater contribution to economic progress. But, when we are talking about increasing the growth rate by adding to investment, we are not concerned with inframarginal investments, but about those beyond what would otherwise be the cut-off rate of return. There is nothing inconsistent between the following three statements:

1. Each year some investments are undertaken which promise to yield, at prevailing prices, very high rates of return.
2. Each year significant amounts of investment are undertaken which promise yields in the neighborhood of the observed past rate of return.
3. Additional investments above and beyond those actually undertaken would likely produce rates of return which are at best equal to the observed past average rate of return.

According to the point of view just expressed, "embodiment" of technical changes takes place principally in inframarginal investments. This sort of phenomenon could easily produce the results observed by Berglas, with the marginal effect of investment being approximated by the observed past average rate of return, but with a substantial time trend in the ratio of output to total input. It is also consistent with the observation that, across industries or time periods, there is relatively little relationship between the rate of increase in capital stock and the movements in total factor productivity.

This is not the place for a very detailed discussion of these points, so I will leave the matter here. I hope that I have been able to provide some support for my view that we cannot expect great changes in the growth rate from plausible changes in the mix of direct and indirect taxation.

I feel impelled, however, to point out that in our recent preoccupation with the rate of growth, we, as a profession, may have lost sight of some old and fundamental truths. We should distinguish between the rate of growth of income, the level of income, and the level of welfare as possible goals of economic policy. Concentration on the rate of growth as an objective can lead one to minimize the value of having, say, x percent more income each year as a result of a policy change — simply because income would not grow any faster except during a transitional period. On the other hand, concentration on the level of real income (as conventionally measured) can lead one to neglect the costs of bringing about changes in that level. If, by tax changes, we increase labor and reduce leisure, or if we increase saving and reduce consumption, we should, I think, not just look at the pluses and neglect the minuses. When we try to take both pluses and minuses into account, we come to grips with the measurement of the effects of policy changes on welfare, which was the subject of the earlier sections of this paper.

III

The next chapter, which was presented at the annual meeting of the American Economic Association in December, 1963, and published the following year in *The American Economic Review*, is substantially more sophisticated than "Taxation, Resource Allocation and Welfare," but to a considerable extent this gain was bought (given space limitations) at the expense of the slower-paced, more didactic presentation of that earlier effort. To help compensate the cryptic nature of the exposition, I take this opportunity to indicate what I consider to be its main points.

In the first place, expressions (3.4) and (3.5), which measure in terms of coefficients R_{ij} the change in welfare induced by a set of distortions, though they look exactly like their counterparts in Chapter 2, which express welfare change in terms of coefficients S_{ij}, are really quite different. On the assumptions laid out in Chapter 2, the coefficients S_{ij} could be interpreted as simply compensated demand coefficients, and the whole analysis could be handled in straightforward demand-theory language. The R_{ij} are no such simple animals — they are really reduced-form coefficients showing how the equilibrium levels of various activities $X_1, X_2, \ldots, X_n$ depend on the degrees of distortion $T_1, T_2, \ldots, T_n$ to which each of the activities is subject.

To explore a bit the nature of the R_{ij}, expressed in terms of more familiar supply and demand parameters, consider first the simplest of textbook cases:

(3A) $$X_1 = \underbrace{a_1 + b_1(P_1 + T_1)}_{\text{Demand}} = \underbrace{e_1 + f_1 P_1}_{\text{Supply}}.$$

The solution for P_1 is

(3B) $$P_1 = \frac{a_1 - e_1 + b_1 T_1}{f_1 - b_1}, \quad \text{and that for } X_1 \text{ is}$$

(3C) $$X_1 = \frac{f_1 a_1 - b_1 e_1 + f_1 b_1 T_1}{f_1 - b_1}.$$

The coefficient R_{11} is therefore given by

$$(3D) \qquad R_{11} = \frac{f_1 b_1}{f_1 - b_1},$$

which perhaps looks straightforward enough. Now, however, let us try just a slightly more complicated setup with demand and supply for two goods.

$$(3E) \qquad \begin{cases} X_1 = a_1 + b_1(P_1 + T_1) + C_1(P_2 + T_2) \\ \quad = e_1 + f_1 P_1 + g_1 P_2 \\ X_2 = a_2 + b_2(P_2 + T_2) + C_2(P_1 + T_1) \\ \quad = e_2 + f_2 P_2 + g_2 P_1 \end{cases} .$$

Solving this, we find

$$(3F) \qquad \begin{cases} P_1 = \dfrac{[a_1 - e_1 + b_1 T_1 + c_1 T_2](f_2 - b_2) - [a_2 - e_2 + b_2 T_2 + c_2 T_1](g_1 - c_1)}{\Delta} \\[2em] P_2 = \dfrac{[a_2 - e_2 + b_2 T_2 + c_2 T_1](f_1 - b_1) - [a_1 - e_1 + b_1 T_1 + c_1 T_2](g_2 - c_2)}{\Delta} \end{cases},$$

where $\Delta = (f_1 - b_1)(f_2 - b_2) - (g_2 - c_2)(g_1 - c_1)$. Using these equations we can solve explicitly for, say, G_{11}

$$(3G) \qquad G_{11} = \frac{f_1 b_1(f_2 - b_2) - f_1 c_2(g_1 - c_1) + g_1 c_2(f_1 - b_1) - g_1 b_1(g_2 - c_2)}{(f_1 - b_1)(f_2 - b_2) - (g_2 - c_2)(g_1 - c_1)}.$$

Now (3.7) can already be described as a reasonably messy expression, but imagine what G_{11} would be like when the system had three or four or five interdependent demand and supply equations, let alone an arbitrarily large N!

How lucky we are, then, to find that the G_{ij} behave just like Slutsky-Hicks compensated demand coefficients, so that we can transfer all our accumulated understanding and intuition about demand phenomena to this much more complicated world. Or, to put it another way, is it not nice to know that if one works out a problem in the comparatively simple constant-cost framework of Chapter 2, the solution thus found will carry over completely to a world of interdependent demands and supplies for all commodities, simply by replacing the demand-defined S_{ij}'s by the reduced-form R_{ij}'s, which have the same simple and useful properties in spite of the massive amount of clockwork that each of them represents? And finally, even more so, is it not useful to know that similar well-behavedness prevails among the four sets of reduced-form coefficients which show how the amount of capital or labor in activity i responds to the degree of distortion applying to the use of labor or to that of capital in activity j? In short, this way of being able to set out what would otherwise be enormously complex problems in simple, potentially manageable terms is to my mind probably the most important result of the "Measurement of Waste."

But there is at least one other range of issues that might merit comment. It is connected (a) with the consolidation of a whole set of taxes into an equivalent set striking with different rates at the incomes from labor and capital in different activities, and (b) with the question of when is a tax or tax system neutral, and when is it not. With respect to consolidation, I point out that it is not likely to be always possible to find a set of factor taxes on the incomes from labor and capital in an activity that will be equivalent to a given tax on the product of that activity. Before one can even approach this equivalence, two assumptions must be made — that the relationship of material inputs to output is fixed, at least in the sense that it is not influenced by which of the two allegedly "equivalent" tax packages is chosen, and that the pattern of economic depreciation of the assets of an activity is similarly uninfluenced.

Table 3A starts in column (1) with an ordinary excise tax of 20 percent on a given product. In column (2) the consequences of a 20 percent tax on all components of costs are shown. Taxes paid at any given stage are shown in parentheses. The equivalence between tax patterns (1) and (2) is obvious; taxing all components at a given rate (col. 2), or taxing the sum of the components at the same rate (col. 1) must produce the same result. As we pass from column (2) to column (3), however, the assumption of fixed proportions between material inputs and final product is crucial. If substitution were possible between materials and final products, the shift from (2) to (3) would induce a substitution toward a more material-intensive method of production, with less use of labor and capital, but with fixed proportions the material-intensiveness of production cannot change. Under this assumption, putting the tax of 20 on gross value added (col. 3) rather than on all inputs (col. 2) is like imposing a tax of $1 per shoe on all left shoes in place of a tax of $1 per pair. As long as shoes are always sold in pairs, there can be no difference whatsoever between the two alternatives.

Now suppose that the tax setup were that indicated in column (4) — a 25 percent tax on wage payments together

TABLE 3A

Components of cost and price	20% tax on final product (1)	20% tax on all inputs (2)	25% tax on gross value added (3)	25% tax on wages; 41 2/3% tax on capital's net earnings (4)	33 1/3% tax on net value added (5)
Market price of final product	120	120	120	120	120
Cost of final product	100(+20)[a]	120	120	120	120
Depreciation	20	20(+4)[a]	20(+5)[a]	20	20
Capital	30	30(+6)	30(+7.5)	30(+12.5)[a]	30(+10)[a]
Labor	30	30(+6)	30(+7.5)	30(+7.5)	30(+10)
Materials	20	20(+4)	20	20	20

[a] Figures in parentheses in each case represent the tax to be added to the cost item in question.

with a 41 2/3 percent tax on the net earnings of capital. This, too, would be equivalent to the other three systems, so long as the shift from system (3) to system (4) did not alter choices in regard to length of asset life (i.e., so long as the depreciation component of costs remained invariant under the tax shift). Finally, consider the tax setup shown in column (5) — a tax raising the same amount, but on the basis of equal taxation of net value added by capital and labor. Clearly, the systems given by columns (4) and (5) would be equivalent only if there were no possibilities of substitution between labor and capital, as the relative weight of taxation on these two factors is altered as one moves from one tax scheme to the other.

The above establishes that a tax on gross value added (col. 4) is different in its effects from a tax on net value added (col. 5). What now can be said about the circumstances under which *general* taxes of these types will be neutral with respect to resource allocation? Obviously neutrality will not exist if the labor-leisure or the consumption-savings choice is affected, so this analysis will be carried out on the assumption of fixed supplies of labor and capital, or in the dynamic case on the assumption that the time paths of these supplies are independently determined and therefore unaffected by the tax changes being analyzed. Once this assumption is made, it is self-evident that a uniform tax on all labor earnings will be totally neutral in an allocative sense since the tax will affect only the economic rent earned by labor and not the wage paid by users of labor services. Similarly, a uniform tax taking a certain amount per year per dollar of capital, or (what amounts to the same thing when the net-of-depreciation rate of return to capital is equalized across uses) a uniform tax on the net-of-depreciation yield from all capital assets will reduce the net rate of return received by owners of capital but will not affect the net-of-depreciation cost of capital to its users.

Since a uniform tax on gross value added is definitionally equivalent to a uniform tax on all labor earnings plus a uniform tax on all net earnings of capital plus a uniform tax on all depreciation of capital assets, the issue of whether the gross-value-added tax is neutral boils down to whether a uniform tax on capital consumption (depreciation) would be neutral. The user cost of a capital asset can be represented by $(r + \delta)V$, where r is the net-of-depreciation rate of return, δ is the annual percentage rate of depreciation, and V is the value of the asset. If r, which we presume will tend to be equalized across uses, is 6 percent, the user cost of a building with a depreciation rate of 2 percent per year will be 8 percent of its value, while that of a machine depreciating at 10 percent per year will be 16 percent of its value. Thus taxing depreciation on all forms of capital at, say, 20 percent will raise the user cost of buildings from 8 to 8.4 percent of their value, but will raise the user cost of machines from 16 to 18 percent of theirs. The effect on user cost is obviously not uniform and the depreciation tax is therefore distorting, except in the totally theoretical extreme case where δ is the same for all types of capital assets. By the same token, a uniform tax on gross value added (or its equivalent, a uniform tax on the market value of all final products) will be nonneutral, even with fixed supplies of capital and labor, except in the extreme case just cited.

Chapter 3

The Measurement of Waste

I

The subject of this paper might be called "The Economics of the nth Best." This would distinguish the approach taken here from that taken by Lipsey and Lancaster in their fine article, "The General Theory of Second Best" [7], as well as from the conventional concern of economic analysis with the characteristics of fully optimal situations. To state the differences briefly, the conventional approach is concerned with how to get to a Pareto-optimal position, the Lipsey-Lancaster approach is concerned with how to make the best of a bad situation (i.e., how to get to a position which is optimal subject to one or more constraints which themselves violate the conditions of a full optimum), while this paper is concerned with measuring the deadweight loss associated with the economy's being in any given nonoptimal position.

The measurement of deadweight losses is not new to economics by any means. It goes back at least as far as Dupuit; and more recently Hotelling [4], Hicks [3], Debreu [2], Meade [10], and H. Johnson [5, 6] have made important contributions. Nonetheless I feel that the profession as a whole has not given to the area the attention that I think it deserves. We do not live on the Pareto frontier, and we are not going to do so in the future. Yet policy decisions are constantly being made which can move us either toward or away from that frontier. What could be more relevant to a choice between policy A and policy B than a statement that policy A will move us toward the Pareto frontier in such a way as to gain for the economy as a whole, say, approximately $200 million per year, while policy B will produce a gain of, say, about $30 million per year? What could be more useful to us as a guide to priorities in tax reform than the knowledge that the deadweight losses stemming from the tax loopholes (percentage depletion and capital gains) open to explorers for oil and gas are probably greater in total magnitude than the deadweight losses associated

Reprinted with permission from Arnold C. Harberger, "The Measurement of Waste," *The American Economic Review* (May, 1964), pp. 58–76.

with all the other inefficiencies induced by the corporation income tax? What could be more tantalizing than the possibility (which I believe to be a real one) that the U.S. tariff, whose indirect effect is to restrict the equilibrium value of U.S. exports, produces by this route a gain for the U.S. from a partial exploitation of U.S. monopoly power in world markets which nearly offsets (or perhaps fully or more than fully offsets) the efficiency-losses produced by tariff-induced substitution of more expensive domestic products for cheaper imports? These and similar questions seem to me so interesting, so relevant, so central to our understanding of the economy we live in, that I find it hard to explain why the measurement of deadweight losses should be the province of only a handful of economists rather than at least the occasional hobby of a much larger group. Let me simply suggest four possible reasons for the apparent unpopularity of the loss-measurement game:

1. Even the simplest attempts to measure the deadweight loss (or, as I prefer to call it, the welfare cost) associated with particular distortions involve the use of numerical values for certain key parameters (elasticities of demand, of substitution, etc.), which may be impossible to obtain at all, or which may be estimated but with substantial error. Workers in this field must be ready to content themselves with results that may be wrong by a factor of 2 or 3 in many cases. But, on the other hand, it is a field in which our professional judgment is so poorly developed that the pinning down of an answer to within a factor of 2 can be very helpful. Be that as it may, one cannot expect the field to attract colleagues who prefer their results to be meticulously exact.

2. While it is relatively easy to measure the welfare costs of a particular distortion when one assumes other distortions to be absent, it is much more difficult to carry through the measurement in a way which takes account of the presence of other distortions. One of the profound lessons taught us by earlier workers in this field (Hotelling [4], Viner [11], Lipsey and Lancaster [7], Corlett and Hague [1], Little [8], and others) is that an action (i.e., imposing a tax of T_1 per unit on good X_1) which would take us away from a Pareto optimum if we were starting from that position can actually bring us toward such an optimum if we start from an initially distorted situation. Crude measures can thus mislead us, while correct measures are hard to come by.

3. Many people find it difficult to isolate the measurement of efficiency losses due to particular distortions from the changes in the distribution of income that they conceive would ensue if the distortions were actually removed. Of these, some are undoubtedly not willing to make the kind of assumptions they have to make in order to compare the changes in welfare of different individuals or groups.

4. Consumer surplus, in spite of its successive rehabilitations, is still looked upon with suspicion by many economists. In spite of the fact that it is possible to formulate measures of welfare cost which do not directly involve the use of the consumer surplus concept, the most convenient and most frequently cited measures of welfare cost do involve this concept. Thus, I venture to guess, another group of potential workers (or at least tasters) in the vineyard do not venture to enter.

70

The main purpose of this paper is to explore a variety of possible ways of formulating measures of deadweight losses. All the ways considered are members of a single family. This section begins by expounding a widely accepted approach to the problem and then proceeds to extend this approach to what I believe are new areas.

Let us begin by assuming that the only distortions present in the economy are taxes. Monopoly elements, externalities, and other market imperfections will be introduced at a later stage. We shall assume that the economy will seek and find a unique full employment equilibrium once its basic resource endowments, the distribution of income, the quantities of goods purchased by the government, and the set of distortions (taxes) are known. Letting X represent the vector of equilibrium quantities, D be a vector representing the proportion of total income received by each spending unit, G be a vector representing the quantities of the different goods and services purchased by government, and T be a vector representing the tax levied per unit of the different goods and services produced in the economy, we have $X = f(D, G, T)$.

Now to isolate the efficiency effects of distortions, we must hold D and G constant. Thus, with respect to D, we conceive of the possibility of keeping the percentage share of each spending unit in the total national income constant by means of neutral taxes and transfers. With respect to G, we assume that, in any pair of situations being compared, the government buys the same bundle of goods and services. Even though the comparison of two actual situations might be between $X = f(D, G, T)$ and $X' = f(D', G', T')$, we split up the move from X to X' into a minimum of two steps. The first step is from $X = f(D, G, T)$ to $X^* = f(D, G, T')$. This step isolates the efficiency aspects of the change. The move from X^* to X' entails no change in the distortions affecting the economy, and involves only shifts in the distribution of income and in the level of government expenditures. To the extent that the tax yield produced by the vector T is insufficient or more than sufficient to finance the expenditure vector G, we assume that neutral taxes or transfers will be called upon to make up the difference. (Should fiscal policy measures be necessary to provide full employment, neutral taxes and transfers would be the instruments used to bring the total tax take to the required level. Government expenditures, on our assumptions, would be held fixed.)

The above assumptions have the effect of setting first-order income effects (whether caused by redistributions or changes in the size of government purchases) to one side so as to isolate the efficiency effects of alternative tax patterns. They put us in a world of substitution effects and of relative prices. When dealing with relative price phenomena, it is customary to treat a single product as the numeraire. This procedure is, however, not essential. One could normalize by holding any desired index of prices constant, or in a variety of different ways. For our purposes, it is convenient to normalize by holding the money national income constant as among all possible situations being compared. We could alternatively hold constant money net national product, gross national product, gross national product less excise taxes, or any of a variety of other possible aggregates. But, as will be seen, holding money national income constant is exceedingly convenient for the problems with which we shall deal.

Let us consider first a case that has been frequently dealt with in the literature. Assume that the production function of the economy is linear and that only one factor of production, in fixed supply, is involved in production.

The fact that the only distortions present in our system are per unit excise taxes assures us that when the vector $T = 0$, we are at a Pareto optimum. (In this case the government is raising all its revenue by taxes that are by definition neutral; e.g., head taxes.) Thus if we set up an index of welfare W as a function of the tax vector T, we have that $W_{\max} = W(0)$. We can take money national income, $\bar{Y}$, as the measure of $W(0)$. We can, therefore, indicate the level of welfare associated with any tax vector T by $\bar{Y}$ plus a deviation ΔW, depending on T and expressed in the same units as Y. The relevant expression for ΔW, in a wide class of cases, is

(3.1)
$$\Delta W = \sum_{i=1}^{n} \int_0^{T_i} \sum_{j \leq i} T_j \frac{\partial X_j}{\partial T_i} \, dT_i.$$

Two basic rules underlie this expression.

First, if as a result of an increment dT_i in the unit tax on X_i, there is an increment or decrement dX_j in the equilibrium quantity of a good X_j in the market for which no distortion exists, the change dX_j carries with it no direct contribution to the measure of ΔW. For each successive minute increment of X_j, demand price is equal to marginal cost, and the gain to demanders of having more of X_j is just offset by the costs of producing the extra amount.

Second, if as a result of an increment dT_i in the unit tax on X_i there is an increment dX_j in the equilibrium quantity of good X_j, in the market for which a distortion T_j already exists, there is a social gain associated with the change dX_j equal to $T_j \, dX_j$. Here demand price exceeds marginal cost, on each unit increment of X_j, by the amount T_j. Likewise if dX_j is negative, there is a social loss involved equal in magnitude to $T_j \, dX_j$.[1]

Obviously, the second rule given above contains the first, but I have set them out as two rules to emphasize the neutrality of changes taking place in undistorted sectors. Once this fact is appreciated, the rest of the road is easy.

Let me emphasize at this point that up to now there is nothing new in what has been said. Expression (3.1), and the rules behind it, say only that

(3.2)
$$\frac{\partial W}{\partial T_i} = \sum_j T_j \frac{\partial X_j}{\partial T_i}.$$

[1] Another way of looking at this problem is to consider that consumers, in transferring their demand to X_j are indifferent between what they get and what they give up for each marginal unit of purchasing power transferred; and that suppliers of factor services are likewise, for each marginal unit of services transferred, on the borderline of indifference. But if X_j goes up by dX_j, the government will obtain an increase in tax receipts of $T_j \, dX_j$, which (under our assumptions) will permit either a corresponding reduction in associated lump-sum taxes or a corresponding increase in lump-sum transfers. In short, "the people" gain to the tune of $T_j \, dX_j$.

This expression pops up in one form or another all through the literature on the measurement of welfare costs, the economics of second best, the theory of customs unions, etc. It appears, or can be derived from what appears, in Corlett and Hague [1], Hotelling [4], H. Johnson [5, 6], Meade [10], and Lipsey and Lancaster [7], among others.

Let us now linearize expression (3.1) by setting

$$\frac{\partial X_j}{\partial T_i} = R_{ji}.$$

With this substitution, (3.1) evaluates at

(3.3) $$\Delta W = \frac{1}{2} \sum_{i=1}^{n} R_{ii} T_i^2 + \sum_{i}^{n} \sum_{j<1} R_{ji} T_j T_i.$$

Expression (3.3) can be simplified, however, using the integrability condition

$$\frac{\partial X_i}{\partial T_j} = \frac{\partial X_j}{\partial T_i},$$

which translates in the linearized form into $R_{ij} = R_{ji}$. In economic terms, this same condition derives from the fact that the welfare cost of a set of taxes should not, in a comparative static framework such as this, depend on the order in which those taxes are conceived to be imposed. Thus if we impose T_1 first and follow it by T_2, we have $\Delta W = 1/2\, R_{11} T_1^2 + 1/2\, R_{22} T_2^2 + R_{12} T_1 T_2$. If on the other hand we impose T_2 first and follow it by T_1, we have $\Delta W = 1/2\, R_{22} T_2^2 + 1/2\, R_{11} T_1^2 + R_{21} T_2 T_1$. Hence if the linearized expression (3.3) is to be invariant with respect to order of imposition of taxes, R_{12} must equal R_{21}, and in general R_{ij} must equal R_{ji}. This enables (3.3) to be simplified to

(3.4) $$\Delta W = \frac{1}{2} \sum_i \sum_j R_{ij} T_i T_j.$$

For each $R_{ji}(j < i)$ appearing in (3.3), we simply substitute $1/2\, R_{ji} + 1/2\, R_{ij}$, to obtain (3.4).

A further condition on the R_{ij} can be established by noting that a set of taxes with some $T_i \neq 0$ can at best produce an equal level of welfare as an undistorted situation. This yields

(3.5) $$\Delta W = \frac{1}{2} \sum_i \sum_j R_{ij} T_i T_j \leq 0 \qquad \text{for all possible values of } T_i,\, T_j.$$

As a special case of (3.5) we have

(3.6) $$R_{ii} \leq 0 \qquad \text{for all } i.$$

This is obtained when $T_i \neq 0$, while $T_j = 0$ for all $j \neq i$.

We are by now quite close to establishing the Hicksian substitution conditions by the back door, so to speak. What we need to finish the job is the adding-up property. Suppose it to be true that a proportional tax at the rate t on all the X_i would indeed be a neutral tax. We can define $T_i = t_i c_i$, where $c_i =$ marginal cost, and t_i = percentage rate of tax on X_i, to obtain

$$(3.7) \qquad \Delta W = \frac{1}{2} \sum_i \sum_j c_i c_j R_{ij} t_i t_j.$$

If an equal percentage tax on all commodities is neutral, we have

$$(3.8) \qquad \sum_i \sum_j c_i c_j R_{ij} = 0.$$

But we actually have much more than this. If a proportional tax at the rate t is truly neutral, then, given our assumptions about the constancy of income distribution and of government purchases, it simply substitutes for the head tax that would have to exist if all the T_i were zero. It must produce the same equilibrium quantity for each and every commodity. Thus we have that

$$(3.10) \qquad \frac{\partial X_i}{\partial t} = \sum_j c_j R_{ij} = 0 \qquad \text{for all } i.$$

This is the counterpart of the Hicksian adding-up property.

However, a tax at the rate t on all X_i will be neutral only in certain cases.

Case A: Suppose that, as was assumed above, the production frontier of the economy is linear —

$$\sum_i c_i X_i = \text{a constant.}$$

This means that total production is in inelastic supply, and therefore that a tax which strikes the value of all production at a constant rate will be neutral. In this case all the X_i must be final products; the R_{ij} here turn out to be precisely the Hicksian substitution terms.

Case B: Suppose that all the X_i are final products, and that the production frontier of the economy is convex from above. Suppose, moreover, that all basic factors of production are fixed in total supply. So long as a tax at the rate t on final products is in effect a tax at a fixed rate on the net earnings of all factors of production, it will be neutral, and condition (3.10) will hold. In this case, the R_{ij}, while obeying the properties of the Hicksian substitution terms, are actually quite different from them. Here the R_{ij} are really the "reduced form" coefficients showing how the equilibrium value of X_i (with supply and demand equal for all commodities) depends on T_j.

Case B presents no problem when capital is not among the basic factors of production, or when the relation between gross and net earnings of capital is the same in all uses. However, when capital is among the basic factors and when the relationship between gross and net earnings does (because of different depreciation patterns) differ among uses, then an equal tax on all final products will not be neutral, even though capital and other factors of production are fixed in total supply. This is because increases in the rate of proportional tax, t, will create incentives which would relatively favor the longer-lived applications of capital. An equal tax on value added in all industries, however, would be neutral in these circumstances, because we assume the net rate of return on capital to be equalized among all uses of capital. (This, of course, assumes that

74

the stock of capital and the supplies of other basic factors of production are fixed.)

Problems quite similar to those presented by different depreciation patterns in different applications of capital arise when the possibility of taxing intermediate products is introduced. As McKenzie [9] has forcefully pointed out, an equal percentage tax on all products will generally be nonneutral if any of the products in question are intermediate or primary products not in fixed supply. A tax at an equal percentage rate on value added in every activity will, on the other hand, be neutral so long as the basic factors of production are in fixed supply.

Case C: When considering taxes on value added we let X_i represent the volume of final product of industry (or activity) i, v_i represent value added per unit of the product of activity i, and T_i represent the tax per unit of final product in industry i. (Although the tax is levied on value added, T_i is here expressed per unit of product.) Once again letting $R_{ij} = \partial X_i / \partial T_j$, we have (3.5) as the expression for ΔW. To reflect the neutrality of an equal percentage tax on value added everywhere, we require that the response of any X_i to such a tax be zero; i.e., that

$$\sum_j v_j R_{ij} t_j = 0 \quad \text{when} \quad t_j = t \quad \text{for all } j.$$

Here v_j = value added per unit of the product X_j, t_j = percentage rate of tax on value added in industry j, $v_j t_j = T_j$. Hence we have

$$\sum_j v_j R_{ij} = 0; \quad R_{ij} = R_{ji}; \quad \sum_i \sum_j R_{ij} T_i T_j \leq 0 \text{ for all } T_i, T_j; \quad R_{ii} \leq 0 \text{ for all } i$$

as before.

Case C deals rather neatly with problems of differential depreciation and taxes on nonfinal products. However, case C assumes that indirect taxes are levied on value added, whereas most frequently in the real world they are levied on the final product.

Fortunately, it is possible to translate product taxes into value-added taxes, and still stay within the framework of case C so long as inputs other than labor and capital enter their respective products in fixed proportions. The reason for this is obvious. All the effects of a tax at the rate t_i on product i can be replicated by a tax at the same rate on all factor shares (including materials input) entering into the production of product i. These are simply two ways of imposing the same tax. Suppose that with a tax of 10 percent on all factor shares in the ith industry an equilibrium is reached in which materials inputs account for half the value of product and labor and capital the other half. So long as materials inputs must be used in fixed proportions per unit of product, a shift from a 10 percent tax on all factor shares in the ith industry to a 20 percent tax on value added in the ith industry would introduce no incentive to change the equilibrium reached with a 10 percent tax on all factor shares. Purchasers could pay the same price for the product; labor, capital, and materials sellers could get the same net reward; and the government could get the same tax take. Moreover, since the taxes on labor and capital shares would still be at equal percentage rates, there would be no inducement for substitution between them. In short, so long as materials are used in fixed proportions to output, we can translate any given tax on output into a tax on value added that is equivalent in all respects relevant for this analysis.

We now turn to a broader set of problems — all of which take into account the possibility of different rates of tax on the return to capital and to labor in any given activity. Consider first the set of possible taxes B_i per unit of capital in activity i. The change in welfare associated with such taxes can be written, assuming no other nonneutral taxes in the system, as

(3.11)
$$\Delta W = \frac{1}{2} \sum_i \sum_j G_{ij} B_i B_j,^2$$

where

$$G_{ij} = \frac{\partial K_i}{\partial B_j},$$

and K_i represents the number of units of capital employed in activity i. Correspondingly, if we consider the set of possible taxes E_i per unit of labor in activity i, and assume no other nonneutral taxes, we can write:

(3.12)
$$\Delta W = \frac{1}{2} \sum_i \sum_j M_{ij} E_i E_j,$$

where

$$M_{ij} = \frac{\partial L_i}{\partial E_j},$$

and L_i represents the number of units of labor employed in activity i. The G_{ij} and the M_{ij} will obey the following properties:

$$G_{ij} = G_{ji}; \qquad \sum_i \sum_j G_{ij} B_i B_j \leq 0 \text{ for all } B_i, B_j; \qquad G_{ii} \leq 0 \text{ for all } i$$

$$M_{ij} = M_{ji}; \qquad \sum_i \sum_j M_{ij} E_i E_j \leq 0 \text{ for all } E_i, E_j; \qquad M_{ii} \leq 0 \text{ for all } i.$$

Moreover, with fixed supplies of capital and labor we have

$$\sum_i G_{ij} = 0, \qquad \sum_i M_{ij} = 0.$$

When nonneutral taxes are levied only on capital in different activities, (3.11) measures the cost of the distortions involved; when only labor is affected by nonneutral taxes, (3.12) is the relevant measure. But when nonneutral taxes are levied on both labor and capital in different activities, the interaction

---

[2] We could here have explicitly set out an equation corresponding to (3.1); i.e.,

$$\Delta W = \sum_{i=1}^{n} \int_0^{B_i} \sum_{j \leq i} B_j \frac{\partial X_j}{\partial B_i} dB_i,$$

linearized this expression as in (3.3), and then used the symmetry property to obtain (3.11) or its counterpart. These steps are not presented explicitly in this and the other cases treated in this section.

between them must be taken into account. Let us define

$$H_{ij} = \frac{\partial K_i}{\partial E_j} \quad \text{and} \quad N_{ij} = \frac{\partial N_i}{\partial B_j}.$$

Here symmetry exists between H_{ij} and N_{ji}. Suppose for example, we impose first a tax of B_1 and then one of E_2. We obtain $1/2\, G_{11}B_1{}^2 + M_{22}E_2{}^2 + H_{12}B_1E_2$ as our measure of ΔW. If we conceive of E_2 being imposed first, and then B_1, we obtain $1/2\, M_{22}E_2{}^2 + 1/2\, G_{11}B_1{}^2 + N_{21}E_2B_1$. If we think of imposing a set of taxes B_i first and then a set of taxes E_i, we have

$$(3.13) \qquad \Delta W = \frac{1}{2}\sum_i\sum_j G_{ij}B_iB_j + \frac{1}{2}\sum_i\sum_j M_{ij}E_iE_j + \sum_i\sum_j H_{ij}B_iE_j.$$

If we think of it the other way around, we have

$$(3.14) \qquad \Delta W = \frac{1}{2}\sum_i\sum_j M_{ij}E_iE_j + \frac{1}{2}\sum_i\sum_j G_{ij}B_iB_j + \sum_j\sum_i N_{ji}E_jB_i.$$

For a reason that will be apparent later, it is most convenient to write:

$$\Delta W = \frac{1}{2}\sum_j\sum_i M_{ji}E_jE_i + \frac{1}{2}\sum_j\sum_i N_{ji}E_jB_i + \frac{1}{2}\sum_i\sum_j G_{ij}B_iB_j$$

$$(3.15)$$

$$+ \frac{1}{2}\sum_i\sum_j H_{ij}B_iE_j.$$

Now, when labor is in fixed supply, a tax on capital in industry i can only redistribute the existing amount of labor. Hence

$$\sum_j N_{ji} = 0.$$

Likewise, when capital is in fixed supply, a tax on labor in industry j can only redistribute the available capital, so that

$$\sum_i H_{ij} = 0.$$

The interaction terms disappear for neutral taxes because in this case $E_i = \bar{E}$ for all i, $B_i = \bar{B}$ for all i. (Since the wage is assumed to be equalized in all uses of labor and since the net rate of return is assumed to be equalized in all uses of capital, an equal tax per unit of labor is also an equal percentage tax on value added by labor in different activities, and likewise for capital.)

Thus we have:

Case D: When labor and capital are in fixed supply, expression (3.15) measures the change in welfare due to any pattern of taxes on labor and capital in different activities. The M_{ji} and the G_{ij} obey the Hicksian conditions, with the adding-up property in this case

$$\sum_j M_{ij} = 0 = \sum_i G_{ij}.$$

All terms vanish for taxes on labor that are equal in all uses together with taxes on capital that are equal in all uses. The interaction terms can in general be positive or negative, but the whole expression (3.15) must always be ≤ 0. In this case the coefficients reflect not only conditions of final demand and supply but also conditions of factor substitution.

We now attempt to allow for the fact that the supply of labor in the market may itself be a function of the pattern of taxation. This question has been dealt with in the literature of second-best by Little, Corlett, and Hague, Lipsey and Lancaster, and Meade, among others. The key to at least the last three of these treatments is the substitution of the assumption (!) that the number of hours in the year is fixed for the assumption that the number of man-hours offered in the market is fixed. We can do this simply by adding another activity for labor — labeled "leisure" or "nonmarket activity." If there are n market activities, we add an $n + 1$st, and have

$$\sum_{j=1}^{n+1} L_j = L.$$

This does not change the form of equation (3.12) but it does alter the definition of a neutral tax. Now an equal tax on all labor in market activities is not neutral, because it neglects the $n + 1$st activity. However, a tax that struck all hours equally (including leisure hours) would be neutral. Hence we have

$$\sum_{j=1}^{n+1} M_{ji} = 0 = \sum_{i=1}^{n+1} M_{ij}.$$

To measure the welfare cost of an equal tax of $\bar{E}$ on all activities except leisure we take

(3.16)
$$\Delta W = \frac{1}{2} \sum_{j=1}^{n} \sum_{i=1}^{n} M_{ji} \bar{E}^2$$

but

$$\sum_{i=1}^{n+1} M_{ji} = 0, \quad \text{so} \quad \sum_{i=1}^{n} M_{ji} = -M_{j,n+1}.$$

Hence (3.16) reduces to

(3.17)
$$\Delta W = -\frac{1}{2} \sum_{j=1}^{n} M_{j,n+1} \bar{E}^2.$$

But

$$\sum_{j=1}^{n+1} M_{j,n+1} = 0, \quad \text{so that} \quad \sum_{j=1}^{n} M_{j,n+1} = -M_{n+1,n+1}.$$

Thus (3.17) reduces to

(3.18)
$$\Delta W = \tfrac{1}{2} M_{n+1,n+1} \bar{E}^2,$$

where $M_{n+1,n+1}$ represents the responsiveness of leisure to a change in the tax rate on leisure (or to the negative of a change in the tax rate on work). This exercise illustrates, I think, the usefulness of properties of the kind that we have been establishing in the various cases examined. (3.16) taken by itself looks hard to interpret; with the aid of the adding-up properties, however, it can be reduced to (3.18), which is easy to interpret and perhaps even to measure.

The general expression for ΔW, for a fixed capital stock and for a fixed amount of labor-plus-leisure, is

$$\Delta W = \frac{1}{2} \sum_{j=1}^{n+1} \sum_{i=1}^{n+1} M_{ji} E_j E_i + \frac{1}{2} \sum_{j=1}^{n+1} \sum_{i=1}^{n} N_{ji} E_j B_i + \frac{1}{2} \sum_{i=1}^{n} \sum_{i=1}^{n} G_{ij} B_i B_j$$

$$(3.19) \qquad + \frac{1}{2} \sum_{i=1}^{n} \sum_{j=1}^{n+1} H_{ij} B_i E_j.$$

Its properties are basically the same as those of (3.15), modified only to take account of the fact that labor has $n + 1$ activities available to it while capital has only n. Thus, in the interaction terms we have

$$\sum_{j=1}^{n+1} N_{ji} = 0; \qquad \sum_{i=1}^{n} H_{ij} = 0.$$

Hence we have

Case E: Where capital is in fixed supply to market activities, but labor is in fixed supply only to market-plus-nonmarket activities, and where taxes are considered which strike labor and capital differentially in different activities, (3.19) measures the change in welfare stemming from any set of such taxes. Neutral taxes in this case are taxes striking each unit of capital (or each dollar of net return from capital) equally, and taxes striking each hour of a worker's day equally. This last set of taxes could equivalently be called head taxes, but, as was shown above, convenient results can be obtained using properties derived from the neutrality of an equal tax per hour.

The formulation of case E is quite versatile. It can deal with proportional income taxation (equal percentage taxes on the income from labor and capital), and can recognize the nonneutrality of ordinary income taxation as regards the choice between labor and leisure. It can also cope with progressive income taxation, simply by using the effective marginal rate of tax to apply to income from labor and capital (here one has to assume that each individual's supply of capital is constant). It can cope with indirect taxes on intermediate as well as final products, provided that one is prepared to make the assumption that materials inputs bear fixed relationships to final products. And, most important of all, it can cope with property and corporation income taxes, which have widely differing burdens on the income from capital in different industries. Finally, it is possible to deal with situations in which all the above-mentioned taxes are simultaneously present, amalgamating those taxes (including allocations of excise tax receipts) falling on income from capital in each activity, and those falling on income from labor.

III

This section consists of three "appended notes" to the earlier analysis. The first (A) reduces the expressions derived in section II to a common simplified form. The second (B) discusses how distortions other than taxes can be incorporated in the analysis. The third (C) discusses the problems that arise when one eliminates the assumption of a constant capital stock.

A. The cases dealt with in the preceding section all have in common a simple property. Since, in (3.4)

$$\sum_j R_{ij}T_j \text{ can be expressed as } \Delta X_i,$$

(3.4) itself can be rewritten:

(3.4')
$$\Delta W = \tfrac{1}{2} \sum_i T_i \Delta X_i.$$

For cases A and B, T_i refers to taxes on final products only, and the X_i's are final products. For case C, (3.4') might better be written

(3.4'')
$$\Delta W = \tfrac{1}{2} \sum_i v_i t_i \Delta X_i,$$

where the X_i are now final or intermediate products, the v_i represent value added per unit of product in activity i, and the t_i are percentage taxes on value added in activity i. Since

$$\sum_j G_{ij}B_j \text{ can be expressed as } \Delta K_i,$$

(3.11) can be written:

(3.11')
$$\Delta W = \tfrac{1}{2} \sum_i B_i \Delta K_i.$$

Similarly, (3.12) can be written:

(3.12')
$$\Delta W = \tfrac{1}{2} \sum_i E_i \Delta L_i.$$

In (3.15),

$$\sum_i M_{ji}E_i + \sum_i N_{ji}B$$

can be expressed as ΔL_j, while

$$\sum_j G_{ij}B_j + \sum_j H_{ij}E_j$$

can be expressed as ΔK_i, so that (3.15) can be written:

(3.15')
$$\Delta W = \tfrac{1}{2} \sum_j E_j \Delta L_j + \tfrac{1}{2} \sum_i B_i \Delta K_i.$$

(3.15') also serves as an alternative form for (3.19), with the index j going from 1 to $n + 1$ and the index i going from 1 to n. Thus all of the cases discussed here are extensions of the "triangle-under-the-demand-curve" that emerges in textbook discussions of the excess burden of taxation. But I believe that for actual work the simplified forms presented above are not as useful as those presented in section II of this paper, in which explicit account is taken of how the reaction coefficients R_{ij}, G_{ij}, H_{ij}, M_{ij} and N_{ij} enter into the determination of the result. One can conceive, at least hypothetically, of measuring these reaction coefficients by experimental movements in individual tax rates. Once measured, they will enable us to estimate the changes in welfare associated with any arbitrary combination of taxes.

In practice one cannot expect to measure all the relevant reaction coefficients, but one can place reasonable bounds on their orders of magnitude and thus get estimates of the order of magnitude of the welfare costs of a given set of taxes, or of particular changes in the existing tax structure. In dealing with practical problems, the presumptive dominance of the diagonal elements in the matrices of reaction coefficients can be put to good use. Consider, for example, the case of a tax of T_1 on X_1, in case A or B of section II. If there are no other taxes present in the system, the change in welfare associated with this tax will be $\Delta W = 1/2\, R_{11} T_1{}^2$. If there are other taxes already present in the system, the effect on welfare of adding a tax of T_1 on X_1 will be

$$(3.20) \qquad \frac{\partial W}{\partial T_1}\, T_1 = \tfrac{1}{2} R_{11} T_1{}^2 + \sum_{i=2}^{n} R_{i1} T_i T_1, \quad \text{or}$$

$$(3.20') \qquad \frac{\partial W}{\partial T_1}\, T_1 = \tfrac{1}{2} c_1{}^2 R_{11} t_1{}^2 + \sum_{i=2}^{n} c_1 c_i R_{i1} t_i t_1.$$

Since

$$\sum_{i=2}^{n} c_i R_{i1} = -c_1 R_{11},$$

$(3.20')$ can be rewritten as

$$(3.21) \qquad \frac{\partial W}{\partial T_1}\, T_1 = \tfrac{1}{2} c_1{}^2 R_{11} t_1 \left[t_1 - 2 \sum_{i=2}^{n} (c_i R_{i1}/-c_1 R_{11}) t_i \right].$$

Thus, t_1 has to be compared with a weighted average of the tax rates on other commodities. Even though we cannot measure the R_{i1}, so as to know the precise weights to apply, in many cases it is possible to set reasonable limits within which the true weighting pattern is likely to lie. We are likely to have a good idea of which, if any, of goods X_2 to X_n are very close substitutes or complements to good X_1. After making allowance for the plausible degree of substitution or complementarity here, we are not likely to go far wrong if we assume that the remaining commodities are remote, "general" substitutes for X_1. Thus the procedure would be first to estimate $-c_1 R_{11}$; then to estimate $c_2 R_{21}$ and $c_3 R_{31}$, say, if goods 2 and 3 were particularly close substitutes or complements to good one; and finally to distribute the remaining total weights $(-c_1 R_{11} - c_2 R_{21} - c_3 R_{31})$ to commodities X_4 to X_n, say, in proportion to their relative importance in the national income. Obviously this procedure is not exact, but it is unlikely to lead to a result that is of an erroneous order of magnitude.

B. We now attempt to take account of distortions other than taxes. These can be treated as "autonomous" taxes or subsidies. If a monopoly is present in industry i, which prices its products at 20 percent above marginal cost, it is as if a 20 percent tax existed on the product of industry i, or, perhaps, a 40 percent tax on the value added by labor and by capital in industry i. If activity j has positive external effects, leading to an excess of 10 percent of social benefit over marginal cost (at the margin) it is once again as if a tax of 10 percent existed on the value produced in industry j, or of an appropriately greater percentage on the value added in industry j. Correspondingly, if an industry's product has negative external effects, it is as if a subsidy existed on the value produced or the value added in that industry (i.e., the economy, by itself, tends to produce too much of that industry's product).

To see how these other distortions would be taken into account, assume that a monopoly exists in industry 1, such that price is $(1 + m_1)$ times marginal cost. Suppose, moreover, that a tax of t_1' percent exists (or is contemplated) on this product. To take account of the combined effect of the monopoly and the tax, we would simply set $t_1 = [(1 + m_1)/(1 - t_1')] - 1$, and then use this value for t_1 in (3.7).

It seems to me that most distortions other than taxes can be taken into account in the way just indicated. There is no intrinsic difficulty, however, in dealing with more complicated cases in which the percentage excess of social value over marginal cost is a function of output rather than a constant. Cases in which the external effects of an industry or activity are independent of its output or level, and depend only on the existence of the industry, need not be dealt with within the framework of this analysis. If the industry or activity is to exist in all situations being compared, external effects of this sort will be equal in all such situations. If, on the other hand, one contemplates eliminating an industry with a given negative external effect, one can calculate by an analysis of the type used in this paper what would be the efficiency-cost of a tax which was just barely prohibitive of the activities of the industry, and see whether this cost outweighed the negative external effect or not.

C. We now turn to a problem which was consciously avoided in section II. There we maintained the assumption that the capital stock was given. Now we must investigate the possibilities of eliminating this restrictive assumption.

In the first place, we can recognize that, for the analysis of section II, we do not need to assume that the capital stock remains fixed through time. Both population and capital stock can change through time, and the analysis of section II can be modified to take account of these changes, so long as the changes (in population and in capital stock) are not dependent on tax rates and other distortions. The difficulties appear when we try to allow for the effects of changes in tax rates, etc., on the level of capital stock (and/or population).

Particularly since I have no really satisfactory solution to the problem posed, I am inclined to defend the assumption that the level of capital stock is reasonably independent of tax rate changes (at least of the sorts of tax rate changes that we have observed in the past). Here I rely on the secular constancy of the rate of net saving in the United States, in the face of substantial swings in the rate of return and in the face of significant alterations in the tax structure. I would not expect, given this historical experience, that the neglect of an effect of taxation upon savings would introduce large errors into the measures derived in section II.

Obviously, however, this answer, though perhaps adequate for many practical applications, really begs the fundamental question. As I see it, there are three main roads to a solution.

1. One could attempt to extend the "models" of section II to many time periods, building in all of the relevant dynamics. This, I think, would be scientifically the most satisfying approach to take. However, I am afraid that this approach is likely to complicate the analysis to the point where it will be hard to apply it to real-world problems. Nonetheless, I feel that this is a line worth pursuing.

2. One could attempt to separate the "comparative static" from the "dynamic" costs of alternative tax set-ups. Suppose that changing from tax vector T to tax vector T' leads to a change in the rate of saving from s to s'. We could measure the change in welfare due to the change in taxes first on the assumption that the rate of saving was unaffected, and then attempt to measure the additional cost or benefit associated with the change in the rate of saving. This approach has a particular appeal because, given the assumption that the net rate of return to capital is equalized in all uses, it is reasonable to assume the rate of saving depends only on the level of real income and the net rate of return.

One can go quite some distance with this approach without greatly complicating the analysis. The present value to the saver of a dollar of saving at the margin is $\$1.00 = \rho(1 - t)/r$, where ρ is the social rate of marginal net productivity of capital and r (which at least in uncomplicated situations should equal $\rho(1 - t)$) is the after-tax rate of discount which the individual uses to obtain present values, and t is the expected future rate of tax on income from saving. The present value of the social yield of capital is simply ρ/r, so that a dollar's worth of savings should have a social value of $\$1.00/(1 - t)$. The change in welfare due to the difference in this year's savings stemming from a tax rate of t rather than a tax rate of zero would then be $1/2\ t\Delta s/(1 - t)$, where Δs is the tax-induced change in the amount of this year's savings. If we call this expression $\Delta_2 W$, and expression (3.19), say, $\Delta_1 W$, we can express ΔW as $\Delta_1 W + \Delta_2 W$. $\Delta_1 W$ expresses the cost this year of misallocating the resources that would be present this year if the rate of savings were unaffected by tax changes. $\Delta_2 W$ measures the present value of the future benefit foregone because the economy — for tax reasons — did not save "enough" this year. One could correspondingly estimate the ΔW stemming from a particular tax structure for a series of future years, and estimate the present value of the future stream of welfare costs associated with that tax structure.

The principal difficulty with approach number 2 is, I believe, that it requires the assumption that ρ will remain constant in the future. The approach could of course be modified so as to impose a particular nonconstant time-path for ρ in the future, but the basic difficulty remains that the model does not itself tell us what that time-path should be. As a practical matter, however, I believe that changes in the marginal net productivity of capital are likely to be sufficiently slow so that the assumption of constancy will not introduce serious errors in the estimation of ΔW.

83

3. One could attempt to incorporate tax-induced changes in capital stock directly into the analysis. This approach requires two changes in the analysis of cases D and E of section II. First the assumptions that

$$\sum_i G_{ij} = 0 \quad \text{and} \quad \sum_i H_{ij} = 0$$

must be abandoned; and second, we must eliminate the assumption of the neutrality of any tax striking equally the income from capital in all uses. In effect this means that the only neutral tax treatment of the income from capital would be not to tax it all.[3] These two adjustments could easily be incorporated into the framework developed in section II. One additional step would also be necessary. Since the savings-effects of a tax change are likely to go on indefinitely, one would have to decide on the specific time period over which one was measuring the effect of tax changes on the capital stock. This would enable one in principle to deal with specific values for

$$\sum_i G_{ij} \quad \text{and} \quad \sum_i H_{ij},$$

whereas otherwise these values could be almost anything, depending on the time period over which the reactions were being measured. This last requirement — of measurement over a specific time period — is to my mind the most serious disadvantage of approach number 3.

I shall not go into more detail here on the possible merits and disadvantages of the three approaches to the savings problem that I have suggested. This problem is, as I have indicated, the most serious "open end" in the analysis of section II, and I hope that further work in the field, following one or more of the approaches outlined above, will help close this important gap.

REFERENCES

1. Corlett, W. J. and D. C. Hague. "Complementarity and the Excess Burden of Taxation," *Rev. of Econ. Studies*, 1953, pp. 21–30.
2. Debreu, Gerard. "The Coefficient of Resource Utilization," *Econometrica*, July 1951, pp. 273–292.
3. Hicks, J. R. *Value and Capital* (2d ed.; Oxford: Clarendon Press, 1946), esp. pp. 330–333.
4. Hotelling, Harold. "The General Welfare in Relation to Problems of Taxation and of Railway and Utility Rates," *Econometrica*, July 1938.
5. Johnson, Harry G. "The Cost of Protection and the Scientific Tariff," *J.P.E.*, August 1960, pp. 327 ff.
6. ———. "The Economic Theory of Customs Unions," in *Money*,

[3] Though I find the nontaxation of income from capital repugnant as a policy prescription, there is no doubt that even proportional income taxation is nonneutral in respect of the decision to save. The social yield of saving is the gross of tax return to capital, while the private yield is net of tax.

Trade and Economic Growth (London: George Allen and Unwin, 1962), pp. 48 ff.

7. Lipsey, R. G., and K. Lancaster. "The General Theory of Second Best," *Rev. of Econ. Studies*, XXIV, No. 63. (1956–57), pp. 11–32.

8. Little, I. M. D. "Direct versus Indirect Taxes," *Econ. J.*, September 1951.

9. McKenzie, L. W. "Ideal Output and the Interdependence of Firms," *Econ. J.*, December 1951, pp. 785–803.

10. Meade, J. E. *Trade and Welfare*, Vol. II (Mathematical Supplement [London: Oxford Univ. Press, 1955]).

11. Viner, Jacob. *The Customs Union Issue* (Carnegie Endowment for Int. Peace, 1950).

IV

Although I had maintained an active interest in applied welfare economics since graduate-school days, the following article, which appeared in *The American Economic Review* in 1954, was my first published piece on the subject. In many respects it sets the format for my subsequent work in this area, especially in terms of its adherence to a general-equilibrium, multisectoral approach. My debt to Harold Hotelling's pioneering article in the area of welfare cost measurement, which is reiterated in each of my subsequent writings on the subject, is stated in footnote 2. I must confess, however, that at the time of its writing, my appreciation of the nature and power of the analytical apparatus being used was somewhat rudimentary and intuitive.

As is pointed out in Chapters 1, 2, and 3, when one thinks of introducing distortions sequentially into an economy, the change in welfare induced by each added distortion (T_i^*) will consist of a triangle $1/2 \ T_i^* \Delta X_i$ plus a series of rectangles $\sum_{j<i} T_j^* \Delta X_j$, where $\Delta X_j = \int_{T_i=0}^{T_i^*} (\partial X_j)/(\partial T_i) \ dT_i$. Yet my formulation in "Monopoly and Resource Allocation," as well as Hotelling's famous $1/2 \sum dp_i \ dq_i$, consists just of a set of triangles.

What happened to the rectangles? The answer is that they are still there (in the sense that the areas they represent are not being neglected), but recognizing this fact also affects the interpretation of the results. In Figure 4A1 is presented the standard triangle-rectangle analysis of a pair of distortions in a two-sector economy with constant unit costs. The introduction of the first distortion T_1^* generates a welfare cost equal to the triangle *ABC*, while the introduction of T_2^* in the presence of T_1^* generates an addition to welfare cost equal to the triangle *GHJ* plus the rectangle *BCDE*. On the other hand, the Hotelling measure that I employed would

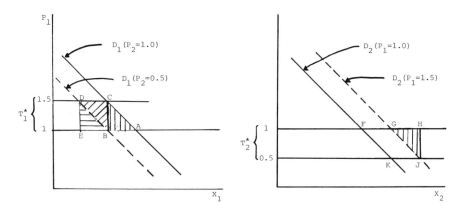

FIGURE 4A1

take triangles *ADE* plus *FHJ* of Figure 4A2 as the measure of welfare loss. But it is easy to see that base *AE* of *ADE* is equal to the sum *AB* plus *CD* of the bases of triangles *ABC* and *BCD*. Since the heights of all three triangles are the same, we have that the areas of *ABC* and *BCD* sum to that of *ADE*. Less easy to see, perhaps, is the fact that the areas *GHJ* plus *BDE* add up to that of *FHJ*. But *FG* is equal to $[\partial X_2/\partial T_1] \cdot T_1{}^*$, and *EB* is equal to $[\partial X_1/\partial T_1] \cdot T_1{}^*$. And given the linear production constraint here assumed, this means that *FG* is equal to *BE*. Since, moreover, the height *HJ* equals *DE* by construction in this example, we conclude that *BDE* plus *GHJ* equals *FHJ*.[1]

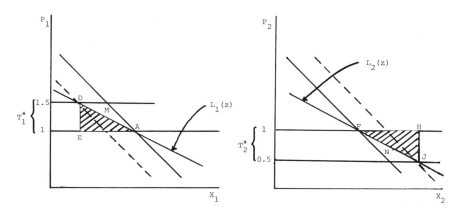

FIGURE 4A2

[1] When the two distortions are not equal in magnitude one has to use the symmetry property $\partial X_1/\partial T_2 = \partial X_2/\partial T_1$ to complete the geometric proof. *BDE* is equal to $(\partial X_1/\partial T_2) \cdot T_2{}^*T_1{}^*$. But *FGK* is equal to $(\partial X_2/\partial T_1) \cdot T_1{}^*T_2{}^*$. Given the symmetry property $\partial X_1/\partial T_2 = \partial X_2/\partial T_1$, *BDE* must

Thus the functions that are relevant for measuring welfare costs of a set of two or more distortions "without rectangles" are different from ordinary demand functions. They are instead loci [in this case $L_1(z)$ and $L_2(z)$] of potential equilibrium points, generated in principle by the package of distortions $[zT_1{}^*, zT_2{}^*, \ldots, zT_n{}^*]$, as one varies z. At points A and F, z is equal to zero; at points D and J, it is equal to one. The points M (the midpoint of AD) and N (the midpoint of FJ) are simultaneously generated by the distortion pattern $T_1 = 0.25 = 1/2\ T_1{}^*$; $\ T_2 = -0.25 = 1/2\ T_2{}^*$. It is important to note that one value of z generates points on both L_1 and L_2 in our example and on these plus $L_3, L_4, \ldots, L_n$ in the general case.

Turning now, perhaps belatedly, to the substantive conclusion to which all this leads, it is that if, as I state in "Monopoly and Resource Allocation," the elasticities of *demand* for the various products are unity, then the estimates there presented are on this ground understatements. Viewed conversely, the estimates presented there would be approximately right for a typical elasticity of demand somewhat less than unity.

It is difficult to estimate precisely the adjustment that would be necessary to take into account unit-elastic *demand* functions as against unit-elastic *loci*, L_i, but I believe one can say with some assurance that the actual adjustment is unlikely to be nearly as high as the factor of two suggested in the diagram.

A heuristic "proof" follows. Suppose there were in the economy depicted an additional substitute commodity X_3, with no distortion in its market. How would that change the picture? First, the rightward shift FG caused by the imposition of $T_1{}^*$ would be smaller, because part of the reduction AB of demand for X_1 would go to X_3. Similarly the leftward shift BE in X_1, caused by the introduction of the negative distortion $T_2{}^*$ would be smaller. Hence the rectangle $BCED$ — which we have shown to be the source of the differences between ABC and ADE on the one hand and between GHJ and FHJ on the other — is reduced in size relative to the "demand-curve triangles" ABC and GHJ.

Alternatively, consider a rectangular distribution of distortions among sets of commodities, each having equal weight. Then let $T_N{}^* = -T_1{}^*$, $T_{N-1}{}^* = -T_2{}^*$, etc., with $T_1{}^* > T_2{}^* > \cdots > T_{N-1}{}^* > T_N{}^*$. Consider now putting on the distortions in a specified order — first $T_1{}^*$ and $T_N{}^*$,

---

equal FGK. For further discussion of this and similar matters see Chapter 2, section II and Chapter 3, sections II and III.

next $T_2{}^*$ and $T_{N-1}{}^*$, etc., always pairing each positive distortion with its "opposite number" negative distortion. When $T_1{}^*$ and $T_N{}^*$ were imposed, something like what is depicted in Figure 4A1 would happen, except that now BE would be very small relative to the movement in X_N corresponding to GH, for most of the substitution into X_N would come from commodities $X_2, \ldots, X_{N-1}$. Now take the next step and impose $T_2{}^*$ and $T_{N-1}{}^*$. Now if X_1 responds in essentially the same way to changes in P_2 and in P_{N-1}, the simultaneous imposition of $T_2{}^*$ (a positive distortion on X_2) and $T_{N-1}{}^*$ (a negative distortion on X_{N-1}) will have offsetting effects, and no additional rectangle corresponding to $BCDE$ will be produced in the market for X_1. There would, however, be such a rectangle (once again small) in the market for X_2 as a consequence of the introduction of $T_{N-1}{}^*$. Proceeding in this fashion, and recalling that we cannot get "rectangles" of the type we are speaking until a market is distorted, one finds that there would be $N/2$ rectangles, each associated with the reaction of a positively distorted market to the imposition of its "partner" distortion. And the order of magnitude of each of these rectangles would be $1/N - 1$ times the distortion cost calculated from the two "partner" triangles.

Viewed in this light, the differences between the demand schedules and the L_i loci are probably negligible in the case of the calculations in "Monopoly and Resource Allocation," considering the large number of sectors in the breakdown that was used. I have entered into this material not so much to point out a possible minor new bias, but to call attention to an important conceptual distinction (that between demand curves and $L_i(z)$) that is relevant not only to the problem of measuring the welfare costs of monopoly but to many other problems in applied welfare economics as well.

It is curious to note that in the plethora of discussion about this article, whether in published form, in correspondence, or in conversation, the above distinction has to my knowledge not been recognized. At the opposite extreme in terms of frequency is one comment that I cannot refrain from responding to here. "How can you assume a demand elasticity of unity when that implies a marginal revenue of zero?" The important distinction here is that between the firm and the industry. If the elasticity of demand for a product is -1.25, and it is produced at constant costs by a full monopolist, its selling price would be five times cost. Yet few if any products sell at prices five times cost, and if so probably not for long. There are actual competitors (not in the sense of the textbook version of perfect competition, but in the sense of other firms producing similar products) as well as potential competitors in the form of new entrants (often through diversification). A firm's pricing policy must be geared to the threats entailed in both actual and potential competition, both from within and without the nation's boundaries. While responding to or anticipating these threats, firms may well still be able to charge prices in excess of costs including a normal return to capital. In that sense they are exercising monopoly power. But it would be the rarest of cases in which an individual firm would find it in its interest to take the industry-demand curve as the relevant demand curve facing it. Yet for purposes of welfare-cost measurement it is the industry demand curve which is relevant, for it is along that demand curve that market clearing takes place. Thus, I hope, the paradox of a 10 or 20 percent "monopoly markup" coexisting with an assumed unit elasticity of industry demand has been explained.

Chapter 4

Monopoly and Resource Allocation

One of the first things we learn when we begin to study price theory is that the main effects of monopoly are to misallocate resources, to reduce aggregate welfare, and to redistribute income in favor of monopolists. In the light of this fact, it is a little curious that our empirical efforts at studying monopoly have so largely concentrated on other things. We have studied particular industries and have come up with a formidable list of monopolistic practices: identical pricing, price leadership, market sharing, patent suppression, basing points, and so on. And we have also studied the whole economy, using the concentration of production in the hands of a small number of firms as the measure of monopoly. On this basis we have obtained the impression that some 20 or 30 or 40 percent of our economy is effectively monopolized.

In this paper I propose to look at the American economy, and in particular at American manufacturing industry, and try to get some quantitative notion of the allocative and welfare effects of monopoly. It should be clear from the outset that this is not the kind of job one can do with great precision. The best we can hope for is to get a feeling for the general orders of magnitude that are involved.

I take it as an operating hypothesis that, in the long run, resources can be allocated among our manufacturing industries in such a way as to yield roughly constant returns. That is, long-run average costs are close to constant in the relevant range, for both the firm and the industry. This hypothesis gives us the wedge we need to get something from the data. For as is well known, the malallocative effects of monopoly stem from the difference between marginal cost and price, and marginal costs are at first glance terribly difficult to pin down empirically for a wide range of firms and industries. But once we are ready to proceed on the basis of constant average costs, we can utilize the fact that under such circumstances marginal and average costs are the same, and we can easily get some idea of average costs.

Reprinted with permission from Arnold C. Harberger, "Monopoly and Resource Allocation," *The American Economic Review* (May, 1954), pp. 77–87. Footnotes are renumbered.

But that does not solve all the problems, for cost and profit to the economist are not the same things as cost and profit to the accountant, and the accountants make our data. To move into this question, I should like to conjure up an idealized picture of an economy in equilibrium. In this picture all firms are operating on their long-run cost curves, the cost curves are so defined as to yield each firm an equal return on its invested capital, and markets are cleared. I think it is fair to say that this is a picture of optimal resource allocation. Now, we never see this idyllic picture in the real world, but if long-run costs are in fact close to constant and markets are cleared, we can pick out the places where resources are misallocated by looking at the rates of return on capital. Those industries which are returning higher than average rates have too few resources; and those yielding lower than average rates have too many resources. To get an idea of how big a shift of resources it would take to equalize profit rates in all industries, we have to know something about the elasticities of demand for the goods in question. In Figure 4.1, I illustrate a hypothetical case. The industry in question is earning 20 percent on a capital of 10 million dollars, while the average return to capital is only 10 percent. We therefore build a 10 percent return into the cost curve, which leaves the industry with 1 million in excess profits. If the elasticity of demand for the industry's product is unity, it will take a shift of 1 million in resources in order to expand supply enough to wipe out the excess profits.

The above argument gives a general picture of what I have done empirically. The first empirical job was to find a period which met two conditions. First, it had to be reasonably close to a long-run equilibrium period; that is, no

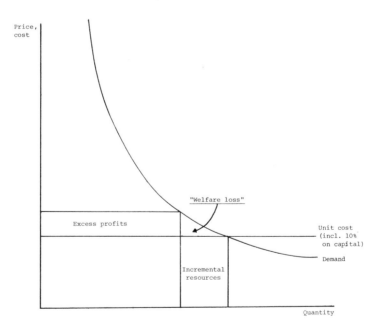

FIGURE 4.1

violent shifts in demand or economic structure were to be in process. And second, it had to be a period for which accounting values of capital could be supposed to be pretty close to actual values. In particular, because of the disastrous effect of inflation and deflation on book values of capital, it had to be a period of fairly stable prices, which in turn had been preceded by a period of stable prices. It seemed to me that the late twenties came as close as one could hope to meeting both these requirements.

The late twenties had an additional advantage for me — because my choice of this period enabled me to use Professor Ralph C. Epstein's excellent study, *Industrial Profits in the United States* (National Bureau of Economic Research, 1934), as a source of data. Professor Epstein there gives, for the years 1924–1928, the rates of total profit to total capital for seventy-three manufacturing industries, with total capital defined as book capital plus bonded indebtedness and total profit defined as book profit plus interest on the indebtedness. To get rid of factors producing short-period variations in these rates of return, I average the rates, for each industry, for the five-year period. The results are given in column 1 of Table 4.1. The differences among these profit rates, as between industries, give a broad indication of the extent of resource malallocation in American manufacturing in the late-twenties.

Column 2 presents the amount by which the profits in each industry diverged from what that industry would have obtained if it had gotten the average rate of profit for all manufacturing industry. In column 3, these excesses and shortages of profit are expressed as a percent of sales in the industry. By analogy with Figure 4.1, you can see that this column really tells by what percentage prices in each industry were "too high" or "too low" when compared with those that would generate an optimal resource allocation.

Now suppose we ask how much reallocation of resources it would take to eliminate the observed divergences in profit rates. This depends, as you can see in Figure 4.1, on the demand elasticities confronting the industries in question. How high are these elasticities? It seems to me that one need only look at the list of industries in Table 4.1 in order to get the feeling that the elasticities in question are probably quite low. The presumption of low elasticity is further strengthened by the fact that what we envisage is not the substitution of one industry's product against all other products, but rather the substitution of one great aggregate of products (those yielding high rates of return) for another aggregate (those yielding low rates of return). In the light of these considerations, I think an elasticity of unity is about as high as one can reasonably allow for, though a somewhat higher elasticity would not seriously affect the general tenor of my results.

Returning again to Figure 4.1, we can see that once the assumption of unit elasticity is made the amount of excess profit measures the amount of resources that must be called into an industry in order to bring its profit rate into line. When I say resources here I mean the services of labor and capital plus the materials bought by the industry from other industries. In many ways it seems preferable to define resources as simply the services of labor and capital. This

TABLE 4.1

Industry	Rate of profit on capital (1924–1928) (1)	Amount by which profits diverged from "average" (millions) (2)	Column (2) as percent of sales (3)	Welfare cost of divergence in column (2) (millions) (4)
Bakery products	17.5%	$17	5.3%	$.452
Flour	11.9	1	0.4	.002
Confectionery	17.0	7	6.1	.215
Package foods	17.9	7	3.3	.116
Dairying	11.8	3	0.7	.010
Canned goods	12.4	1	0.6	.003
Meat packing	4.4	−69	−1.7	.596
Beverages	5.8	−2	−4.0	.080
Tobacco	14.1	27	0.3	.373
Miscellaneous foods	8.1	−13	−2.4	.164
Cotton spinning	10.0	−0	0	0
Cotton converting	8.0	−1	−0.6	.008
Cotton weaving	4.7	−15	−5.5	.415
Weaving woolens	2.6	−16	−9.5	.762
Silk weaving	7.9	−3	−2.3	.035
Carpets	9.8	−1	−1.3	.006
Men's clothing	11.4	1	0.5	.002
Knit goods	12.9	3	1.9	.028
Miscellaneous clothing	13.1	1	1.1	.006
Miscellaneous textiles	9.2	−2	−0.9	.008
Boots and shoes	15.8	9	3.8	.172
Miscellaneous leather products	7.7	−3	−2.1	.032
Rubber	7.6	−23	−2.5	.283
Lumber manufacturing	7.8	−6	−3.9	.118
Planing mills	13.1	1	3.2	.016
Millwork	7.3	−1	−2.9	.014
Furniture	13.4	2	2.2	.022
Miscellaneous lumber	12.9	4	1.7	.034
Blank paper	6.6	−17	−6.2	.524
Cardboard boxes	13.6	2	3.1	.031
Stationery	7.5	−2	−3.0	.030
Miscellaneous paper	9.3	−1	−1.1	.005
Newspapers	20.1	37	8.5	1.570
Books and music	14.6	2	4.3	.042
Miscellaneous printing and publishing	18.6	1	5.6	.028
Crude chemicals	10.2	−0	0	0
Paints	14.6	5	3.3	.082
Petroleum refining	8.4	−114	−3.6	2.032
Proprietary preparations	20.9	25	11.7	1.460
Toilet preparations	30.4	3	15.0	.225
Cleaning preparations	20.8	15	5.5	.413

could be done by applying to the value added in the industry the percentage of excess profits to sales. The trouble here is that adding to the output of industry X calls resources not only into that industry but also into the industries that supply it. And by the time we take all the increments in value added of all these supplying industries that would be generated by the initial increase in output of industry X, we come pretty close to the incremental value of sales in industry X. Of course, the movement to an optimal resource allocation entails some industries expanding their output, like X, and others, say Y, contracting their output. If we really traced through the increments to value added which are required in their supplying industries, say Z, we would often find that there was some cancellation of the required changes in the output of

TABLE 4.1 *continued*

Industry	Rate of profit on capital (1924–1928) (1)	Amount by which profits diverged from "average" (millions) (2)	Column (2) as percent of sales (3)	Welfare cost of divergence in column (2) (millions) (4)
Miscellaneous chemicals	15.6%	$45	8.8%	$.197
Ceramics	10.8	1	1.0	.005
Glass	13.5	4	2.6	.052
Portland cement	14.3	10	8.4	.420
Miscellaneous clay and stone	17.6	14	8.0	.560
Castings and forgings	5.6	−234	−7.7	8.994
Sheet metal	10.5	0	0	0
Wire and nails	11.6	1	1.2	.006
Heating machinery	13.3	3	1.6	.024
Electrical machinery	15.7	48	5.3	1.281
Textile machinery	13.6	3	6.1	.092
Printing machinery	9.7	−0	0	0
Road machinery	17.3	10	6.8	.374
Engines	13.7	2	5.9	.059
Mining machinery	11.0	1	0.7	.004
Factory machinery	11.7	33	3.0	.045
Office machinery	16.1	7	5.6	.194
Railway equipment	6.0	−24	−9.6	1.148
Motor vehicles	18.5	161	4.4	3.878
Firearms	12.9	1	2.0	.010
Hardware	12.8	8	2.3	.092
Tools	11.6	1	1.1	.006
Bolts and nuts	15.4	1	3.1	.016
Miscellaneous machinery	12.6	3	2.2	.032
Nonferrous metals	11.9	15	1.4	.106
Jewelry	10.6	0	0	0
Miscellaneous metals	12.5	14	2.0	.140
Scientific instruments	21.2	20	11.6	1.163
Toys	15.0	1	3.2	.016
Pianos	9.9	−0	0	0
Miscellaneous special manufacturing	12.0	4	1.4	.027
Job printing	13.8	4	2.2	.044

Col. (1) — from Ralph C. Epstein, *Industrial Profits in the United States* (N.B.E.R., 1934), Tables 43D through 53D. Entries in column (1) are the arithmetic means of the annual entries in the source tables.
Col. (2) — divergences in the profit rates given in column (1) from their mean (10.4) are here applied to the 1928 volume of capital in each industry. Total capital is the sum of book capital (Epstein, Appendix Table 6C) plus bonded debt (Epstein, Appendix Table 6D).
Col. (3) — 1928 figures were used for sales (Epstein, Appendix Table 6A).
Col. (4) — measures the amount by which consumer "welfare" fell short of the level it would have attained if resources had been so allocated as to give each industry an equal return on capital. It assumes that the elasticity of demand for the products of each industry is unity and approximates the area designated as "welfare loss" in Figure 4.1.

Z. Hence by using sales rather than value added as our measure of resource transfer, we rather overstate the necessary movement.

Keeping this in mind, let us return to the data. If we add up all the pluses and all the minuses in column 2, we find that to obtain equilibrium we would have to transfer about 550 million dollars in resources from low-profit to high-profit industries. But this is not the end. Those of you who are familiar with Epstein's study are aware that it is based on a sample of 2046 corporations, which account for some 45 percent of the sales and capital in manufacturing industry. Pending a discussion of possible biases in the sample a little later, we can proceed to blow up our 550 million figure to cover total manufacturing. The result is 1.2 billion. Hence we tentatively conclude that the misallocations of resources which existed in United States manufacturing in the period

1924–1928 could have been eliminated by a net transfer of roughly 4 percent of the resources in manufacturing industry, or 1 1/2 percent of the total resources of the economy.

Now let us suppose that somehow we effected these desired resource transfers. By how much would people be better off? This general question was answered in 1938 for an analogous problem by Harold Hotelling.[1] His general formula would be strictly applicable here if all our industries were producing products for direct consumption. The question thus arises, how to treat industries producing intermediate products. If we neglect them altogether, we would be overlooking the fact that their resource shifts and price changes do ultimately change the prices and amounts of consumer goods. If, on the other hand, we pretend that these intermediate industries face the consumer directly and thus directly affect consumer welfare, we neglect the fact that some of the resource shifts in the intermediate sector will have opposing influences on the prices and quantities of consumer goods. Obviously, this second possibility is the safer of the two, in the sense that it can only overestimate, not underestimate, the improvement in welfare that will take place. We can therefore follow this course in applying the Hotelling formula to our data. The results are shown in column 4 of Table 4.1. This gives, opposite each industry, the amount by which consumer welfare would increase if that industry either acquired or divested itself of the appropriate amount of resources. The total improvement in consumer welfare which might come from our sample of firms thus turns out to be about 26.5 million dollars. Blowing up this figure to cover the whole economy, we get what we really want: an estimate of by how much consumer welfare would have improved if resources had been optimally allocated throughout American manufacturing in the late twenties. The answer is 59 million dollars — less than one-tenth of 1 percent of the national income. Translated into today's national income and today's prices, this comes out to 225 million dollars, or less than $1.50 for every man, woman, and child in the United States.

---

[1] Harold Hotelling, "The General Welfare in Relation to Problems of Taxation and of Railway and Utility Rates," *Econometrica*, July, 1938, pp. 242–269. The applicability of Hotelling's proof to the present problem can be seen by referring to pp. 252 ff. He there indicates that he hypothecates a transformation locus which is a hyperplane. This is given us by our assumption of constant costs. He then inquires what will be the loss in moving from a point Q on the hyperplane, at which the marginal conditions of competitive equilibrium are met, to a point Q' at which these conditions of competitive equilibrium are not met. At Q' a nonoptimal set of prices P' prevails. These are, in our example, actual prices, while the equilibrium price-vector P is given by costs, defined to include normal profits. Hotelling's expression for the welfare loss in shifting from Q to Q' is $1/2 \Sigma dp_i \, dq_i$ where p_i and q_i are the price and quantity of the ith commodity. We obtain this by defining our units so that the cost of each commodity is $1.00. The equilibrium quantity of each commodity under the assumption of unit elasticities is then equal to the value of sales of that commodity. If we call r_i the percentage divergence of actual price from cost, we may write the total welfare loss due to monopoly as $1/2 \Sigma r_i^2 q_i$ if the elasticities of demand are unity, and as $1/2 \Sigma r_i^2 q_i k_i$, if the elasticities of demand are k_i. In column 4 of Table 4.1, I attribute to each commodity a welfare loss equal to $1/2 \, r_i^2 q_i$. This measure of the welfare loss due to monopoly abstracts from distributional considerations. Essentially it assumes that the marginal utility of money is the same for all individuals. Alternatively, it may be viewed as measuring the welfare gain which would occur if resources were shifted from producing Q' to producing Q, and at the same time the necessary fiscal adjustments were made to keep everybody's money income the same.

Before drawing any lessons from this, I should like to spend a little time evaluating the estimate. First let us look at the basic assumption that long-run costs are constant. My belief is that this is a good assumption, but that if it is wrong, costs in all probability tend to be increasing rather than decreasing in American industry. And the presence of increasing costs would result in a lowering of both our estimates. Less resources would have to be transferred in order to equalize profit rates, and the increase in consumer welfare resulting from the transfer would be correspondingly less.

Industry	Adjusted profit rate*	Adjusted rate of excess profit	Adjusted amount of excess profits (millions)	Adjusted welfare loss (millions)
Confectionery	21.1%	10.7%	$11	$.530
Tobacco	19.0	8.6	66	2.225
Men's clothing	14.9	4.5	5	.068
Stationery	8.8	—	—	—
Newspaper publishing	27.9	17.5	67	5.148
Proprietary preparations	27.8	17.4	42	4.121
Toilet preparations	50.8	40.4	6	1.400
Printing machinery	12.9	2.5	2	.064
			199	13.556
Less previous amount of excess profit or welfare loss			−100	−3.845
Net adjustment			99	9.711

* Epstein, *op. cit.*, p. 530.

On the other hand, flaws in the data probably operate to make our estimate of the welfare loss too low. Take for example the question of patents and good will. To the extent that these items are assigned a value on the books of a corporation, monopoly profits are capitalized, and the profit rate which we have used is an understatement of the actual profit rate on real capital. Fortunately for us, Professor Epstein has gone into this question in his study. He finds that excluding intangibles from the capital figures makes a significant difference in the earnings rates of only eight of the seventy-three industries. I have accordingly recomputed my figures for these eight industries.[2] As a result, the estimated amount of resource transfer goes up from about 1 1/2 percent to about 1 3/4 percent of the national total. And the welfare loss due to resource misallocations gets raised to about 81 million dollars, just over a tenth of 1 percent of the national income.

There is also another problem arising out of the data. Epstein's sample of firms had an average profit rate of 10.4 percent during the period I investigated, while in manufacturing as a whole the rate of return was 8 percent. The reason for this divergence seems to be an overweighting of high-profit industries in Epstein's sample. It can be shown, however, that a correct weighting procedure

[2] Following is a breakdown of the adjustment for the eight industries in question.

97

would raise our estimate of the welfare cost of equalizing profit rates in all industries by no more than 10 million dollars.[3]

Finally, there is a problem associated with the aggregation of manufacturing into seventy-three industries. My analysis assumes high substitutability among the products produced by different firms within any industry and relatively low substitutability among the products of different industries. Yet Epstein's industrial classification undoubtedly lumps together in particular industries products which are only remote substitutes and which are produced by quite distinct groups of firms. In short, Epstein's industries are in some instances aggregates of subindustries, and for our purposes it would have been appropriate to deal with the subindustries directly. It can be shown that the use of aggregates in such cases biases our estimate of the welfare loss downward, but experiments with hypothetical examples reveal that the probable extent of the bias is small.[4]

Thus we come to our final conclusion. Elimination of resource misallocations in American manufacturing in the late twenties would bring with it an improvement in consumer welfare of just a little more than a tenth of a percent. In present values, this welfare gain would amount to about $2.00 per capita.

Now we can stop to ask what resource misallocations we have measured. We actually have included in the measurement not only monopoly misallocations but also misallocations coming out of the dynamics of economic growth and development and all the other elements which would cause divergent profit rates to persist for some time even in an effectively competitive economy. I know of no way to get at the precise share of the total welfare loss

[3] Epstein's results in samples from small corporations (not included in his main sample) indicate that their earnings rates tend to be quite close, industry by industry, to the earnings rates of the large corporations in the main sample. This suggests that the average rate of profit in the main sample (10.4 percent) was higher than the average for all industry (8 percent) because high-profit industries were overweighted in the sample rather than because the sampled firms tended to be the high-profit firms within each industry. The overweighting of high-profit industries affects our estimate of the welfare cost of resource misallocations in two ways. First, quite obviously, it tends to overstate the cost by pretending that the high-profit industries account for a larger share of the aggregate product of the economy than they actually do. Second, and perhaps not so obviously, it tends to understate the cost by overstating the average rate of profit in all manufacturing, and hence overstating the amount of profit which is "built in" to the cost curves in the present analysis. The estimated adjustment of 10 million dollars presented in the text corrects only for this second effect of overweighting and is obtained by imputing as the normal return to capital in the Epstein sample only 8 percent rather than 10.4 percent and recomputing the welfare costs of resource misallocations by the method followed in Table 4.1. It takes no account of the first effect of overweighting, mentioned above, and thus results in an overstatement of the actual amount of welfare cost.

[4] The extent of the bias is proportional to the difference between the average of the squares of a set of numbers and the square of the average, the numbers in question being the rates of excess profit in the subindustries. Consider an industry composed of three subindustries, each of equal weight. Assume, for an extreme example, that the rates of excess profit (excess profit expressed as a percent of sales) are 10 percent, 20 percent, and 30 percent in the three subindustries. The average rate of excess profit of the aggregate industry would then be 20 percent, and, by our procedure, the estimate of the welfare loss due to that industry would be 2 percent of its sales. If we had been able to deal with the hypothetical subindustry data directly, we would have estimated the welfare loss associated with them at 2 1/3 percent of the aggregate sales.

that is due to monopoly, but I do think I have a reasonable way of pinning our estimate down just a little more tightly. My argument here is based on two props. First of all, I think it only reasonable to roughly identify monopoly power with high rates of profit. And secondly, I think it quite implausible that more than a third of our manufacturing profits should be monopoly profits; that is, profits which are above and beyond the normal return to capital and are obtained by exercise of monopoly power. I doubt that this second premise needs any special defense. After all, we know that capital is a highly productive resource. On the first premise, identifying monopoly power with high profits, I think we need only run down the list of high-profit industries to verify its plausibility. Cosmetics are at the top, with a 30 percent return on capital. They are followed by scientific instruments, drugs, soaps, newspapers, automobiles, cereals, road machinery, bakery products, tobacco, and so on. But even apart from the fact that it makes sense in terms of other evidence to consider these industries monopolistic, there is a still stronger reason for making this assumption. For given the elasticity of demand for an industry's product, the welfare loss associated with that product increases as the square of its greater-than-normal profits. Thus, granted that we are prepared to say that no more than a third of manufacturing profits were monopoly profits, we get the biggest welfare effect by distributing this monopoly profit first to the highest profit industries, then to the next highest, and so on. When this is done, we come to the conclusion that monopoly misallocations entail a welfare loss of no more than a thirteenth of a percent of the national income. Or, in present values, no more than about $1.40 per capita.

Before going on, I should like to mention a couple of other possible ways in which this estimate might fail to reflect the actual cost of monopoly misallo- cations to the American consumer. First, there is the possibility that book capital might be overstated, not because of patents and good will, but as a result of mergers and acquisitions. In testing this possibility I had recourse to Professor J. Fred Weston's recent study of mergers. He found that mergers and acquisitions accounted for only a quarter of the growth of seventy-odd corpora- tions in the last half-century (*The Role of Mergers in the Growth of Large Firms*, pages 100–102). Even a quite substantial overstatement of the portion of their capital involved in the mergers would thus not seriously affect the profit rates. And furthermore, much of the merger growth that Weston found came in the very early years of the century; so that one can reasonably expect that most of the assets which may have been overvalued in these early mergers were off the books by the period that I investigated.

The second possibility concerns advertising expenditures. These are included as cost in accounting data, but it may be appropriate for our present purpose to include part of them as a sort of quasi-monopoly profit. I was unable to make any systematic adjustment of my data to account for this possibility, but I did make a cursory examination of some recent data on advertising ex- penditures. They suggest that advertising costs are well under 2 percent of sales for all of the industries in Table 4.1. Adjustment of our results to allow for a maximal distorting effect of advertising expenditures would accordingly make only a slight difference, perhaps raising our estimate of the welfare cost of monopoly in present values to $1.50 per capita, but not significantly higher.[5]

I should like now to review what has been done. In reaching our estimate of the welfare loss due to monopoly misallocations of resources we have assumed constant rather than increasing costs in manufacturing industry and have assumed elasticities of demand which are too high, I believe. On both counts we therefore tend to overstate the loss. Furthermore, we have treated intermediate products in such a way as to overstate the loss. Finally, we have attributed to monopoly an implausibly large share — 33 1/3 percent — of manufacturing profits, and have distributed this among industries in such a way as to get the biggest possible welfare loss consistent with the idea that monopolies tend to make high profits. In short, we have labored at each stage to get a big estimate of the welfare loss, and we have come out in the end with less than a tenth of a percent of the national income.

I must confess that I was amazed at this result. I never really tried to quantify my notions of what monopoly misallocations amounted to, and I doubt that many other people have. Still, it seems to me that our literature of the last twenty or so years reflects a general belief that monopoly distortions to our resources structure are much greater than they seem in fact to be.

Let me therefore state the beliefs to which the foregoing analysis has led me. First of all, I do not want to minimize the effects of monopoly. A tenth of a percent of the national income is still over 300 million dollars, so we dare not pooh-pooh the efforts of those — economists and others — who have dedicated themselves to reducing the losses due to monopoly. But it seems to me that the monopoly problem does take on a rather different perspective in the light of present study. Our economy emphatically does not seem to be monopoly capitalism in big red letters. We can neglect monopoly elements and still gain

[5] I was unable similarly to take account of selling costs other than advertising expenditures, even though some of such costs may be the price paid by firms to enhance market control or monopoly position. In principle, clearly, some share of selling costs should be taken into account, and it is a limitation of the present study that no adjustment for such costs was possible. Scrutinizing Table 4.1, however, I should suggest that such selling costs are important in only a few of the industries listed, and that an allowance for them would almost certainly not alter the general order of magnitude of the estimates here presented. It should be pointed out, also, that the general conclusions reached in this paper are not closely dependent on the precise data used. Suppose, for example, that we had observed the following situation: industries accounting for half the output of American manufacturing were charging prices which yielded them a 10 percent "monopoly profit" on sales, while the remainder of industries earned a constant rate of profit on capital (here called normal profit) but no more. If we were, in this situation, to reallocate resources so as to equalize profit rates in all industries, the prices of competitive products would rise and those of monopolistic products would fall. If demand for the product of each sector were assumed to be of unit elasticity, we would estimate the gain in welfare incident upon the reallocation of resources at .125 percent of total industrial sales. This would be just about a tenth of a percent of the national income if the ratio of manufacturing sales to national income approximated its 1924–1928 figure. The estimated welfare gain is obtained as follows: Under our elasticity assumption, prices would rise by 5 percent in the competitive sector and fall by 5 percent in the monopolistic sector, and quantities would change inversely by an equal percentage. Taking 100 as the aggregate sales of manufacturing, the change in output in each sector will be 2.5, and taking 1 as the index of initial prices in each sector, the change in price in each sector will be .05. According to the Hotelling formula, the welfare gain coming from each sector will be 1/2 (2.5) (.05), and when these gains are added together the aggregate gain turns out to be .125.

a very good understanding of how our economic process works and how our resources are allocated. When we are interested in the big picture of our manufacturing economy, we need not apologize for treating it as competitive, for in fact it is awfully close to being so. On the other hand, when we are interested in the doings of particular industries, it may often be wise to take monopoly elements into account. Even though monopoly elements in cosmetics are a drop in the bucket in the big picture of American manufacturing, they still mean a lot when we are studying the behavior of this particular industry.

Finally I should like to point out that I have discussed only the welfare effects of resource misallocations due to monopoly. I have not analyzed the redistributions of income that arise when monopoly is present. I originally planned to discuss this redistribution aspect as well, but finally decided against it. All I want to say here is that monopoly does not seem to affect aggregate welfare very seriously through its effect on resource allocation. What it does through its effect on income distribution I leave to my more metaphysically inclined colleagues to decide. I am impelled to add a final note in order to forestall misunderstandings arising out of matters of definition. Resource misallocations may clearly arise from causes other than those considered here: tariffs, excise taxes, subsidies, trade-union practices, and the devices of agricultural policy are some obvious examples. Some of these sources of misallocation will be discussed in a forthcoming paper. Suffice it to say here that the present paper is not concerned with them.

V

This next chapter, which originally appeared in *The American Economic Review* in 1959 is similar to "Monopoly and Resource Allocation" in trying in some sense to quantify the resource-allocation costs stemming from various distortions, in this case those operating to reduce the efficiency of the Chilean economy. It is different in the sense that it does not operate with a specific body of consistent data, but rather with impressions buttressed by piecemeal fragments of information. It is also different in the sense of focusing on distortions related to factor markets.

The need to use fragmentary and often unreliable data is one of the crosses that economists working on less-developed countries (along with economic historians looking far into the past for almost any country) have to bear. This places a high premium on finding the appropriate conceptual apparatus for dealing with a particular problem and then "filling in the boxes" with as plausible estimates of the relevant parameters and variables as one can find. The latter part of section I of the paper is one example of this kind of interplay. The initial observations or impressions were that distortions were very substantial in both the labor and capital markets and also among sectors in the product market. And the conceptual apparatus into which the observations were fed was a Cobb-Douglas utility function (as a homogeneous-of-degree-one measure of welfare) into which sectoral Cobb-Douglas production functions were grafted.

The end result, then, expressed welfare as a direct function of the amounts of labor and capital used in each sector. In this sense it foreshadowed, obliquely but still quite clearly, the development in "The Measurement of Waste" of the idea that for any given set of product taxes, general factor taxes, sectoral factor taxes, etc., one can find an equivalent system composed only of sectoral factor taxes. In the context of the model of Chapter 5, how else can a final-product tax on X_1 reduce the efficiency with which resources are used except by reducing the labor and capital resources devoted to producing X_1? Thus when assumptions were made as to how badly (in the extreme) labor and capital resources were misallocated in Chile, the effects of product-market distortions (of which monopoly is one type) as well as factor-market distortions were taken into account.

This chapter is also the only place in this volume where I make the distinction between price distortions and quantity distortions. It is obvious from simple supply-and-demand analysis that the welfare cost of a tax at a given percentage rate is higher, the higher are the underlying elasticities of supply and demand. On the other hand, the welfare cost of a quota which restricts consumption and production (say by sale of production licenses) to, say, 10 percent below what would otherwise be the equilibrium quantity will be greater, the smaller are the underlying elasticities of supply and demand. These distinct properties of "price distortions" and "quantity distortions" gave the exercise of section I a curious robustness. Making the typical elasticity of substitution higher than the 1.0 implied by the Cobb-Douglas exercise will have the effect of increasing our measure of welfare cost if we keep price distortions (represented by the differences among sectors in the "marginal productivity of labor" row of Table 5.1) the same, but consistency would then require us to increase the dispersion of quantity distortions. On the other hand, raising the same typical elasticity will reduce our measure of welfare costs if we keep quantity distortions (represented by the differences among sectors in the "quantity of labor" row of Table 5.1) the same, but then consistency would require us to reduce the degree of price distortions implied by the exercise. So we do not even know the direction in which a higher typical elasticity of substitution would take us; what's more, if the patterns of both price and quantity distortions given in Table 5.1 are accepted as plausible extremes of dispersion among sectors, then the effects of a change in the assumed elasticity of substitution could *only* be to lower the estimated welfare cost.

Section II discusses Chile's growth rate and its possible decomposition into sources, together with the sorts of contributions to increased growth that might be expected from each source. The treatment here is sketchy, but a later and more elaborate treatment of the same problem can be found in Arnold C. Harberger and Marcelo Selowsky, "Key Factors in the Economic Growth of Chile," in Arnold C. Harberger,

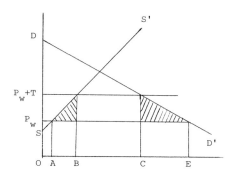

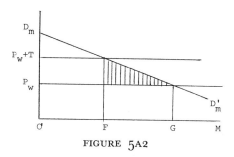

FIGURE 5A2

Papers in Economic Development (London: Macmillan, and Chicago: Markham, 1973).

There is one point on which I have had serious second thoughts since writing the following article: namely, my treatment of the distortions to international trade involved in the Chilean case. The approach I took was derived from the standard treatment of small countries in international trade theory. In Figure 5A1, the world price of a given import product, M, is denoted by P_w, and its tariff-inclusive price by $P_w + T$. SS' is the domestic supply curve of the good, and DD' its domestic demand curve. When no tariff protection exists, domestic production will be OA, total domestic demand OE, and imports AE. With protection, domestic production expands to OB, with domestic demand contracting to OC and imports to BC. The welfare cost of the tariff is then the sum of the two shaded triangles in Figure 5A1, the left-hand one representing the excess resource cost (production cost) of expanded production, and the right-hand one representing the loss in consumer surplus (consumption cost) stemming from the tariff-induced reduction in demand.

In Figure 5A2 the curve $D_m D_m'$ represents the demand function for imports, derived as the horizontal excess of DD' over SS'. The point D_m thus has the same ordinate as the intersection of the domestic demand and supply curves in Figure 5A1, and the lateral distances $O'G$ and $O'F$ correspond to AE and BC, respectively. By construction, then, the area of the shaded triangle in Figure 5A2 equals the sum of the two shaded areas in Figure 5A1.

My procedure of estimating the welfare loss due to trade restrictions was based on the assumptions that FG was less than or equal to $O'F$, i.e., that the reduction of trade resulting from trade restrictions was not greater in absolute amount than the amount of trade actually remaining, and, implicitly, that there would be some domestic production of each importable good in the absence of restrictions. My doubts mainly concern this latter assumption, for it does not adequately capture the phenomenon of high-cost "hothouse" industries that never would have come into existence in the absence of trade restrictions. This phenomenon remains to this day a significant one in most Latin American countries, and it certainly was present in Chile during the period when the paper was written.

Figure 5B illustrates two variants of this case. The curve QQ' represents the average cost of domestic production of the good in question, and once again OE represents the free-trade equilibrium, here with demand being fully met by imports. In Figure 5B1, it is assumed that a just barely prohibitive tariff is imposed, which raises price to the point (K) where the domestic average cost curve intersects the domestic demand curve. The welfare costs now consist of a triangle of consumption costs as before, but a substantial rectangle of production costs, in place of the left-hand triangle in Figure 5A1.

Figure 5B2 represents a case in which the costs are even greater. Here tariff protection is set so high as to enable the domestic producer to behave as a monopolist, restricting

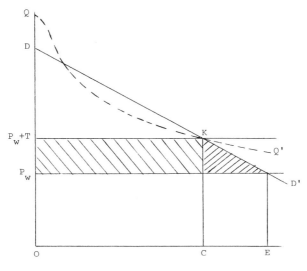

FIGURE 5B1

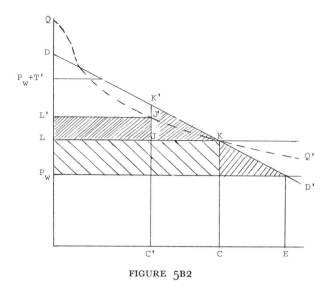

FIGURE 5B2

production to OC' and charging that price $C'K'$ which maximizes monopoly profits. The sum of the consumption-cost
triangle and the production-cost rectangle in this case exceeds
the total shaded area in Figure 5B1 by the amount JKK'
plus $LJJ'L'$.

The cases depicted in Figure 5B have relevance for the
estimation of the welfare cost of trade restrictions, especially
in the light of recent studies of effective protection, which
have revealed that not infrequently the rates of such protection rise above 100 and even 200 percent. For the sake of
illustration, let us assume that 10 percent of total national
production [i.e., value added at world prices] is thus protected,
divided evenly between effective rates of protection of 200,
150, 100, 75, and 50 percent. This would yield a total
production cost of protection equal to 11.5 [= (200 × .02) +
(150 × .02) + (100 × .02) + (75 × .02) + (50 × .02)] percent of national production [measured at world prices]. To this
would have to be added a consumption cost that could easily
be of similar magnitude, amounting to some 8 percent of the
national product in the case where the relevant domestic
demand schedules are unit-elastic.[1]

[1] Elimination of 200 percent protection would cause demand to expand
by 200 percent, or by 4 percent of the national income, generating a
triangle whose area equals 1/2 (.04) (200), or 4 percent of national income.
For the other categories the corresponding areas are [1/2 (.03)(150) =
2.25 percent], [1/2 (.02)(100) = 1 percent], [1/2 (.015)(.75) = 0.57
percent], and [1/2 (.01)(.50) = 0.25 percent]. [In this calculation we assume
that the rate of protection relevant to demanders (i.e., the nominal rate
applying to the final product) is equal to that used above (i.e., the
effective rate of protection of domestic value added) for measuring
production costs. Where this is not the case, the estimated consumption
costs should be reduced by the proportion which imported input costs
(valued at world prices) bear to the world price of the protected product.]

106

The example just presented, yielding a welfare cost of trade restrictions approaching 20 percent of the national income, stands in marked contrast to my original estimate of 2 1/2 percent of national income, and I want to emphasize that it probably substantially overstates that cost. One way to see this is to note that, in this example, elimination of restrictions on trade would automatically cause imports to rise by the amount of "hothouse" domestic production initially displaced, that is, by 10 percent of national production. In addition there would be a further rise in imports induced by the reduction of their prices to world-market levels. This, on the assumption of unit-elastic domestic demand schedules, would amount to an additional 11.5 $[= (.04) + (.03) + (.02) + (.015) + (.01)]$ percent of the national output. Exports, reflecting the country's comparative advantage, would have to be found to generate the additional revenue to buy all these added imports, and there can be no doubt but that these new exports would come only at increasing real cost. The full equilibrium of trade would thus doubtless be reached with a lower expansion of imports (and exports) than the 21.5 $(= 10.0 + 11.5)$ percent of national product implied by the example just given; and the resulting welfare cost would accordingly be lower than the nearly 20 percent of national product that the example implies.

Still, it is quite plausible that the welfare costs of protection in Chile and a number of other Latin American countries could be as high as 10 to 15 percent of national product, which is still a far cry from the 2 1/2 percent estimated in the following article. I take pains to point out this fact because it emphasizes the potential gains from the process of trade liberalization (and its corollary, export expansion) that has gained significant momentum in Latin America and in other less-developed parts of the world in recent years. If its end result were an increase in welfare of only 2 1/2 percent, this effort might not be thought worth the candle; with a potential gain of perhaps 10–15 percent, it surely is.

With this modification, my conclusion in section I that the elimination of distortions in resource allocation might raise national income by probably no more than 15 percent should now be changed to "by probably no more than 25 percent or so." The basic analysis of domestic distortions which occupies most of section I remains unaltered, as does the main message of section II, to the effect that the main key to improvement of welfare lies in accelerating the various forces (most particularly the speed of adoption of available technical knowledge) involved in the process of economic growth.

Chapter 5

Using the Resources at Hand More Effectively

In this paper I attempt to explore the possible results of eliminating mis-allocations of resources in economies like Chile, Brazil, and Argentina.[1] In section I, a static framework is adopted; the conclusion is reached that re-allocating existing resources, while maintaining the existing production functions in each line of activity, would raise national welfare by no more than 15 percent. Section II focuses on the rate of growth; here it is concluded that policies aimed at eliminating "distortions" in the price mechanism can raise the long-term rate of growth of national income, but not spectacularly. It is argued that spectacular advances in the growth rate will come, if at all, from improvement in the quality of the labor force and from an increased pace of technical advance.

I

The principal sources of misallocation in the countries in question are: (a) a rapid rate of inflation, (b) a rate of interest on bank loans below the rate of inflation and hence negative in real terms, (c) substantial barriers to foreign trade, through a number of different devices, (d) considerable monopoly, usually in protected industries, (e) a sluggish and disequilibrated labor market, in which "equivalent" labor may get as little as two-thirds or three-fourths the average wage in some sectors (e.g., agriculture), and as much as one and one-fourth or one and one-half times the average wage in others (e.g., the large foreign-owned enterprises), and (f) a system of taxes and tax evasion which in various ways draws resources into a pattern in which the value of marginal product of similar resources differs quite substantially among activities and sectors. To try to estimate precisely the welfare costs of each type of distortion would at the present stage be hopelessly difficult. I have contented myself with

[1] This paper summarizes the main lines of a more extensive study done at the Centro de Investigaciones Economicas of the Catholic University of Chile. Space limitations have made it necessary to eliminate much of the supporting argument at several points. The author will provide further information on request.

Reprinted with permission from Arnold C. Harberger, "Using the Re-sources at Hand More Effectively," *The American Economic Review* (May, 1959), pp. 134–146.

trying to overestimate the welfare costs of each of two broad categories of distortions: external and internal. I try to overestimate in the sense that at the many places where more-or-less arbitrary assumptions were necessary, I have leaned toward those leading to a higher rather than a lower estimate of welfare cost. I divide the internal from the external distortions because it is convenient to attempt to measure their costs in somewhat different ways.

To estimate the welfare costs of trade restrictions, I utilize the concept of an equivalent tariff. There must exist some rate of ad valorem duty on all imports which would restrict imports to their present overall level. I judge this rate to be around 50 percent in the case of Chile.[2] This judgment is based on the fact that most of the protected industries could maintain present levels of output with this amount of protection. A few industries would have to curtail output if given only 50 percent protection, but counterbalancing them would be a number of industries for which 50 percent protection would be more than they currently enjoy, and which would expand output at the expense of imports if given such protection.

Assuming, then, that a 50 percent tariff would restrict trade about as much as the present restrictions, we proceed to estimate the welfare costs of such a tariff. The foreign trade sector is sufficiently small (some 10 percent of national income) that we can employ Marshallian methods without serious error. Initially, I assume that Chile has no influence over the world price of either her exports or her imports. With a 50 percent tariff, the marginal dollar's worth of exports will buy import goods worth $1.50 internally; on the first dollar's worth of expanded exports, accordingly, the net gain is $.50. On the last unit of expanded trade following the elimination of the tariff, the net gain would be zero. Our measure of the welfare cost of a 50 percent tariff is thus a triangle whose altitude is $.50 and whose base is the number of dollars by which exports (and imports) under free trade would exceed their levels under the tariff. I assume that trade would not more than double as a result of the introduction of free trade. The base of the triangle in question is thus taken to be not more than the present dollar value of exports, which amounts, in the countries in question, to some 10 percent of the national income; and the area of the triangle, which is our measure of the welfare gain which would result from eliminating present restrictions, is estimated to be no more than 2 1/2 percent of the national income.

Why is it reasonable to suppose that trade would not more than double as a consequence of removing a 50 percent tariff? Let us consider an example in which the freeing of trade leads to a 20 percent rise in the relative price of the dollar. Internal prices of export-type goods thus rise 20 percent. Internal prices of import-type goods, which would have fallen from index 150 to index 100 as a result of the tariff repeal if the exchange rate had remained unchanged, actually end up at 120, having fallen in the net by 20 percent. In these circumstances a doubling of trade would reflect elasticities of import demand and

[2] My own experience has been largely with the Chilean economy. I have the feeling and several knowledgeable experts have assured me that the situations of Argentina and Brazil are roughly similar to Chile in the matters treated in this section.

export supply equal to 5. Neither a commodity-by-commodity approach, asking where one might expect additional imports or exports to appear as a result of price changes in, say, the Chilean economy, nor an examination of how imports and exports appear to have responded to price changes in the past suggests that the elasticities in question are as high as this.[3]

Two considerations would operate to modify our estimate that trade restrictions might cost the Chilean economy up to 2 1/2 percent of its national income. The first is that an across-the-board tariff at 50 percent for all commodities tends to have less welfare cost than a set of different tariffs whose average rate is 50 percent, since the welfare cost of a tariff varies with the square of the rate. This consideration, which would lead us to raise our estimate of the welfare costs of restrictions, is unlikely to be serious except in the cases of a few commodities (e.g., automobiles) on which the present restrictions operate with extreme severity, and which account for only a very small fraction of total trade. The second consideration is that to the extent that Chile has some monopoly power in the markets for its exports, the expansion of trade should optimally stop somewhat short of the free-trade point. This would lead us to lower our estimate, but again probably not to a serious extent. The only plausible instances of monopoly power are in copper and nitrates, and even here Chile's power to influence world market prices is probably quite small, especially in the longer run relevant to this discussion.

In estimating the welfare costs of "internal" distortions, I have chosen to focus on the basic resources: labor and capital. By comparing their actual distribution among sectors with that which would emerge in an optimum situation, we get an idea of the quantity distortions prevailing in the economy. Alternatively, by comparing the values of the marginal product produced by given resources in different sectors, we get an idea of the price distortions in the economy. This device is highly convenient for a problem as complicated as ours. A sector can have "too little" labor because of monopoly power of its producers, or because its output is subject to excise taxation, or because of an artificially high wage rate; yet the welfare costs of having a given amount less labor than the optimum are to a first approximation the same, regardless of the cause.

---

[3] A 20 percent fall in the internal prices of imports and a 20 percent rise in the internal prices of exports represent only one of the possible sets of price changes that might result from eliminating a 50 percent tariff. If the exchange rate rose by 35 percent, there would be a 35 percent rise in the internal price level of exports, but only a 10 percent fall in the internal price level of imports. In this case a doubling of trade would entail an elasticity of export supply of roughly 3, and an elasticity of import demand of 10. If the exchange rate rose only by 5 percent, there would be a 30 percent fall in import prices, and a 5 percent rise in export prices, requiring elasticities of around 3 for import demand and around 20 for export supply in order to produce a doubling of trade. In all of these cases at least one of the elasticities necessary for a doubling of trade is implausibly high. In arriving at my judgments as to the elasticity of import demand, I have in mind that the relevant elasticity is long run and should take into account the curtailment of domestic production of import-type goods following a reduction in their internal price. Suppose that at present the total demand for import-type goods is 100, and that it is supplied half by domestic production and half by imports. A doubling of imports could then emerge if domestic production were cut from 50 to 25, while total demand expanded from 100 to 125. I believe that it is pressing towards the limits of plausibility to assume that this result would come from a price change as small as 20 percent. It might quite plausibly result from a price reduction of a third, but then the rise in export prices would not be sufficient to generate the necessary doubling of the level of exports.

Viewed from the price distortion side, the story is the same. The welfare costs of a given sector's having a marginal productivity of capital 10 percent above the level which would equalize net rates of return in all sectors do not in the first instance depend on the reason why too little capital is used in the sector.

Needless to say, a focus as broad as ours requires a general-equilibrium approach. I have chosen to divide the economy into ten sectors producing equal values of product and to use initially as my measure of welfare a utility index of the Cobb-Douglas form:

$$U = X_1^{1/10} X_2^{1/10} X_3^{1/10} X_4^{1/10} X_5^{1/10} X_6^{1/10} X_7^{1/10} X_8^{1/10} X_9^{1/10} X_{10}^{1/10}.$$

This index has the property that it says people are y percent better off in any instance in which each of the goods and services they use has increased by y percent. It furthermore implies a unitary elasticity of demand for the product of each of the sectors; in the case given, 10 percent of the national income is spent on the product of each of the sectors regardless of the relative price structure. This assumption will be defended later, as will the arbitrary division into ten sectors.

Within each sector, I assume a production function of the form $X_i = L_i^{1/2} K_i^{1/2}$, where X_i is the output of the sector (measured in value-added terms), and L_i and K_i the quantities of labor and capital it uses. This function implies that if labor and capital were paid the value of their marginal product, half of the value added of each sector would go to each. These production functions can be substituted into the utility function to express utility directly as a function of the allocation of resources. Thus:

$$U = L_1^{1/20} K_1^{1/20} L_2^{1/20} K_2^{1/20} \cdots \quad \cdots \quad \cdots L_{10}^{1/20} K_{10}^{1/20}.$$

If labor in any sector were paid the value of its marginal product, it would receive 1/20 of the national income; thus in a competitive optimum situation labor would be equally distributed among the sectors. The same goes for capital. If we set the available amounts of labor and capital at 1000 each, we conclude that the optimal allocation would be 100 of each factor in each sector.

We are now in a position to impose a set of distortions on this model economy. Table 5.1 shows a possible allocation of labor, different from the optimum, together with indices of the value of marginal product of labor in each sector. In this case, sector 1 has only a third of the optimum quantity of labor, while sector 10 has two-thirds "too much." The marginal product of labor in sector 1 is five times that in sector 10, and that in sector 2 more than three times that

TABLE 5.1

Sector	1	2	3	4	5	6	7	8	9	10
Quantity of labor	33 1/3	50	75	90	100	100	110	125	150	166 2/3
Marginal productivity of labor	300	200	133 1/3	111	100	100	91	80	66 2/3	60

III

in sector 10. I feel quite confident that the situation depicted in Table 5.1 is substantially more distorted than that actually prevailing in the labor market in Chile. Wages for labor of equivalent quality there may differ by a factor of two, but probably not much more and not in a very large fraction of the total market. The example thus allows for substantial effects from other influences, such as monopoly and taxes, which would cause differences between wages and the value of marginal product, and might make for more variance among sectors in marginal productivity than there is in wages.[4]

Under the optimum distribution of labor and capital (100 units of each factor in each sector), our welfare index would be 100; if capital were allocated optimally but labor were distributed as in Table 5.1, the welfare index would be 95. If labor were distributed as in Table 5.1, and capital likewise, the welfare index would be 91.[5] I believe that this last case allows for distortions in both the labor and capital markets which are more extreme than any likely distortions in the actual Chilean economy. My conclusion is accordingly that eliminating the internal, intersectoral distortions in the Chilean economy would raise the level of welfare by probably no more than 10 percent.

I now turn to a brief defense of the assumptions underlying the above model, followed by an indication of how sensitive the result obtained is to changes in the assumptions.

The elasticity of demand for each sector's product was assumed to be unity. I take this to be a reasonable central value for the range of price elasticities that have been reliably estimated in demand studies. The price elasticity of demand for food appears to be about $-.4$, and this is almost surely at the low end of the scale; at the other extreme, price elasticities for housing and for refrigerators appear to be in the range between -1 and -2. Higher elasticities have been measured only in cases where the good in question has been so narrowly defined as to exclude an obvious close substitute.[6] I define my sectors as sets of products such that for no member of a set is there an obvious close

---

[4] The much-discussed case of zero marginal productivity of labor in agriculture does not exist in the economies of southern South America. The bulk of the agricultural labor force in these countries is voluntarily hired by entrepreneurs who are free to adjust the size of their labor force over time, in accordance with their notions of profit possibilities. It may indeed be possible in these countries to reduce the agricultural labor supply and at the same time maintain or increase output, but these possibilities entail either adding to the capital employed in agriculture and/or changing the production functions along which entrepreneurs are operating. This analysis takes the production functions currently "in use" as given, and measures the marginal product of any resource on the basis of given amounts of cooperating resources. I take sectors 9 and 10, where labor's marginal productivity is low relative to the rest of the economy, to represent agriculture in the Chilean case. Note that in our example these sectors account for almost a third of the labor force.

[5] I assume here not that the same sector will have one-third the optimum amount of capital as has one-third the optimum amount of labor, etc., but only that there be one sector with one-third the optimum amount of capital, another with one-half, etc. In our example, the result is invariant with respect to shifts in the location of distortions, so long as the percentages of the labor force and capital stock subject to given amounts of distortion remain unchanged.

[6] The elasticity for prime beef, holding the price of choice beef constant, or that for Fords, holding the price of Chevrolets constant, would surely be greater than 2, but the elasticities of beef of all types, and for automobiles as a group, appear from existing studies to be substantially less than 2. Likewise, there is evidence that elasticities of import demand are sometimes greater than 2, but not that elasticities of demand for import-type goods (imports and their domestic substitutes) are as high as 2.

substitute outside the set; thus guarding almost by definition against extremely high sector elasticities. On this definition there would be many more sectors than ten, but the sectors can then be reaggregated, putting those with similar resource distortions in one group.

The elasticity of substitution between labor and capital was assumed to be unity. In the absence of strong empirical evidence on this point, I defend my assumption by assuming alternatively very low (say .25) and very high (say 4.0) values for the elasticity of substitution. If capital were a very poor substitute for labor, the marginal product of capital would fall rapidly as extra capital was absorbed; we should have to conclude that Chile's capacity to absorb capital profitably was quite severely limited. On the other hand, if capital and labor were extremely good substitutes, the idea of Chile being seriously short of capital would make little sense. Labor, production-wise, could do practically the same jobs as capital would, and even adding greatly to the stock of capital relative to labor would have little effect on real wages. Even elasticities as low as .5 or as high as 2.0 appear to me to have implausible implications as to the consequences of a doubling of the capital stock in a country like Chile.[7]

The result obtained is only mildly sensitive to some of the assumptions made. It is, for example, not necessary that all the demand elasticities be unity, but only that they average to unity, in order to yield roughly the same result, provided that the sectoral demand elasticities are not highly correlated with the sectoral distortions. A similar situation prevails in the case of the sectoral elasticities of substitution between labor and capital. The result is quite insensitive to the division of the product of each sector between labor and capital; indeed it is mathematically invariant to changes in the exponents of the Cobb-Douglas function in the set of cases where the exponents are the same in all sectors.

The sensitivity to changes in the average demand elasticity and average substitution elasticity is a bit curious, because if we keep the price distortions the same as assumed earlier and reduce the amount of substitution in the model, the quantity distortions have to be reduced; while if we keep the quantity distortions the same as earlier and reduce the amount of substitution, the price distortions have to be increased. The welfare costs of a set of price distortions vary directly with the elasticities assumed, while the costs of a set of quantity distortions vary inversely with the elasticities. Thus, saying that the average demand elasticity and the average substitution elasticity "ought" to have been assumed to be 1/2 rather than unity does not get one very far; one must decide whether to maintain the old set of price distortions or the old set of quantity distortions in the new situation in order to know whether the

[7] Assuming that initially capital gets half the national income and has a marginal net productivity of 20 percent, a doubling of the capital stock while keeping the labor force constant would lead to a fall of capital's marginal productivity to 17 percent in the case of an elasticity of substitution of 2, to 14 percent if the elasticity were 1, and to 8 percent if the elasticity were one-half. Wages would rise only a little more than 20 percent in response to the doubled capital stock if the elasticity were 2; they would rise by 50 percent if the elasticity were 1, and by 90 percent if it were one-half. These calculations assume a perpetual capital stock; if depreciation is allowed for, the implied changes in the net marginal productivity become even more markedly different under the alternative elasticity assumptions. In the calculations, arc elasticities were evaluated at the midpoint of the range of each variable.

new elasticity assumption will cut our earlier estimate in half or double it. If, however, one is prepared to say that neither more extreme price distortions nor more extreme quantity distortions than those assumed are likely to prevail in the Chilean economy, then no changes in the assumed average elasticities can yield a higher estimate of welfare cost.

The principal sensitivity of the estimate is to the extreme distortions assumed. If, for sector 5 in Table 5.1, we had assumed the same quantity and price distortions as for sector 1, and if for sector 6 we had assumed the same quantity and price distortions as for sector 10, and if a similar augmentation of extreme distortions were made in the case of capital, our welfare index would have been 86 rather than 91. I feel reasonably confident that the assumed distortions are sufficiently extreme but indicate this sensitivity in the event that the judgments of others may differ.

Thus far we have not considered the possibility of distortions within sectors. Here I shall allow for 30 percent of the national income to be affected by such distortions. Within this 30 percent, I allow for one-half of each set of close substitutes to be priced 50 percent "too high" relative to the other half of the set, and I allow for the cross-elasticities of demand between the two halves of each set to be 5 (to my knowledge, no reliable estimate of this high a cross-elasticity has yet appeared). These extreme allowances lead to an estimate of the welfare cost of within-sector distortions equal to 3 percent of the national income. (The derivation of this result will be provided on request.)

In summary, I have estimated that the welfare costs of external distortions are less than 2 1/2 percent of the national income, the welfare costs of internal distortions among sectors less than 10 percent of the national income, and the welfare costs of within-sector distortions less than 3 percent of the national income. I reach the judgment that eliminating resource misallocations while maintaining existing production functions might raise the level of national welfare by some 15 percent, but probably not more.

II

Section I suggests that policies to improve resource allocation in economies like Chile may have effects which are substantial but would probably not lead to spectacular changes in the level of living. In this section we test the possibility that better allocation policies might lead to a substantial increase in the rate of growth of national income; thus having a spectacular dynamic effect on living standards.

The percentage rate of growth, g, of national income can be expressed as follows:

$$g = s_L l + im + r + q_L + t,$$

where s_L is the share of labor in the national income, l the percentage rate of growth of the (employed) labor force, i the fraction of national income devoted to net investment, m a weighted average of the net marginal productivities of capital in the various segments of the economy, r the contribution to the rate of income growth of reallocations of the resources of the economy, q_L the contribution of improvements in the quality of the labor force, and t

the contribution of technological advance. I shall consider each of the five components of the rate of growth in turn, defining it in more detail, indicating its possible order of magnitude, and attempting to judge its sensitivity to improved allocation policies.

The contribution of labor force growth to income growth is measured by $s_L l$. If the aggregate employed labor force grows at 2 percent per year, we estimate its potential contribution to national income by assuming that the new entrants have a similar quality distribution as the existing labor force and that they distribute themselves among industries and activities in the same proportions as the existing labor force. Taking the wage rate in each activity as our indicator of marginal productivity, we estimate the dollar contribution of this year's labor force growth to be 2 percent of last year's aggregate wage bill. Expressing this as a percentage of last year's national income yields $s_L l$. In Chile the labor force has grown at around 2 percent or slightly more per annum and the share of labor in the national income has been a little over one-half. Hence we reach the conclusion that labor force growth contributes slightly more than 1 percent per annum to the rate of income growth. Presumably neither the share of labor in the national income nor the rate of growth of the labor force would be affected by improved allocation policies.

The contribution of increased capital can be measured analogously with that of labor, yielding an expression $s_K k$, where s_K is the share of capital in the national income and k is the percentage rate of growth of the capital stock. Improved allocation policies would presumably not influence the share of capital but might influence the rate of growth of the capital stock through their effect on savings. Eliminating inflation would be the principal mechanism through which savings might be influenced; presumably voluntary savings would increase with less inflation, but "forced" savings would decline. To get an idea of the present magnitude of $s_K k$, it is convenient to express s_K as mK/Y, and k as I/K, where K is capital stock, I is net investment, and Y is national income. Thus $s_K k$ is equal to mI/Y, or im, which appeared in the formula given earlier. Net investment in Chile appears to have averaged somewhat less than 5 percent of the national income in recent years, and the marginal productivity of capital (in real terms) appears to be somewhere between 10 and 20 percent. The contribution of net investment to the rate of income growth thus probably lies between 1/2 and 1 percent per year. My judgment is that the low level of income of Chile would itself prevent net domestic investment from reaching a figure as high as 7 percent of the national income; hence I conclude that even in the event that the stopping of inflation leads to greater savings and investment, the resulting increase in the rate of income growth would be small, probably less than 1/2 percent per year.[8]

---

[8] Foreign investment does not help to raise the per capita income of the host country to the extent that the marginal product of the investment accrues to foreigners. The host country gains to the extent that part of the return on the foreign capital can be siphoned off, principally by taxes, and also through such technical advances as may be embodied in the foreign investment. Technical advance will be considered separately below. For the moment I shall write off as negligible the amount that could be siphoned off by the government out of the return on such extra foreign investment as might be made as a result of improved allocation policies.

In isolating the influence of increased labor and capital, we hypothetically held the distribution of each resource among industries and activities constant. The actual distribution will of course typically change over time, making for increases in national income if resources have moved from less productive to more productive uses, and for decreases in income if the opposite sort of movement has occurred. The potential increase of up to 15 percent in national welfare, which we estimated in section I might result from policies leading to improved resource allocation, would be reflected in r, the reallocation component of the growth rate. Since the job of reallocation clearly takes time, the whole gain would not be reflected in the income growth of a single year but would presumably be spread over several years, contributing, say, 1 or 2 percent to the annual growth rate for a series of years. Once this process of adjustment was completed, there would presumably be no further significant influence of improved policies on the reallocation component of the growth rate.[9]

Improved quality of labor makes a contribution q_L to the growth rate, which could be measured with reasonable accuracy if we had statistics on the distribution of the labor force by stable and well-defined quality categories. In the absence of such data, let me note (a) that policies to improve resource allocation would presumably have no direct effect on the improvement of labor quality; (b) that improvement in labor quality at present appears to contribute only a relatively small component to the rate of income growth in Chile; and (c) that additional expenditures on technical training and education in Chile might have substantial effects on the growth rate.[10]

The contribution of technical advance to the rate of growth of income works via changes in production functions which reduce unit costs (or improve quality for given cost). These changes can be organizational or technical, and may or may not entail additional net expenditures on capital equipment. We do not

[9] There is always some reallocation being called for, because of the changes in tastes and technology that steadily take place. However, the amount of reallocation newly called for in any given year would be only a small fraction of the total amount needed to move from the present highly distorted situation to an optimum. The normal contribution of r to the growth rate would thus probably be quite small once the transition toward an optimal allocation was substantially completed. This small contribution might be lower than the present normal contribution of r, because at present some of the reallocation which takes place is in response to price or wage disequilibria, which presumably would be smaller (or absent) in an optimal situation. On the other hand, some of the reallocation which now occurs may actually take resources from uses of higher to uses of lower marginal productivity (e.g., because of a subsidy on the latter uses). Such negative contributions to r would presumably not occur under a set of optimal policies.

[10] Statement (b) is based on the fact that over the last five or so years the rate of income growth has been at about the same rate as the rate of growth of population and can be largely explained on the basis of the incremental capital and labor that have been fed into the productive machine. There is thus little room for a substantial contribution from q_L. Because of Chile's high rate of population growth, relatively large expenditures on education and training are necessary in order to keep the average quality of the labor force constant, counteracting, so to speak, a potential decline in labor quality. Statement (c) is based on the fact that a year of technical training will raise an unskilled laborer's earning power by 50 percent or more, while four years of technical university training will about treble a high school graduate's earning capacity. The rate of return on investment in technical training is in the neighborhood of 20 percent per year, in real terms; this counts both foregone earnings and costs of providing instruction as components of the sum "invested."

have measures of the contribution of technical advance to the rate of economic growth in Chile, but, as in the case of improvement in the quality of labor, we infer from the low rate of per capita income growth that the contribution of technical advance has been small. I would not expect policies leading toward better resource allocation to have a substantial effect upon t, the contribution of technical advance to the growth rate. Incentives to reduce costs are just as strong in the present distorted price structure as they would be in an optimal one. Possibly, however, the elimination of inflation would produce a minor increment in t, because rapid inflation blurs people's perceptions of the relative price structure and may prevent them from being aware of some of the possibilities of reducing real costs.

I conclude from this evaluation of the possibilities of increase in the different components of the growth rate that policies aimed at improving resource allocation might help somewhat but would probably not provide the spectacular "take off" into economic development which most countries in Chile's position hope for. I would think of improved allocation policies as being an important component of any well-planned effort at achieving such a take off but not as the key factor. In the case of Chile, the potential gain of up to 15 percent in national income, indicated in section I as the static effect of improved resource allocation, would probably add a percent or two to the growth rate over a period of years. As the reallocation of resources neared completion, the contribution of r to the growth rate would fall back to its normal low level, but there might be some longer term influence of improved allocation policies on the growth rate via the increased saving and the increased precision of cost calculations which might result from stopping or greatly reducing inflation.

If there is any key factor at all for achieving rapid development, I believe it is technical advance. The possibilities of increasing the rate of saving are quite limited in poor countries, as are the possibilities of reducing the rate of population growth. The limited changes in these factors that seem plausible would not have a drastic effect on the growth rate of income. Technical advance, on the other hand, seems to be capable of contributing substantially to the growth rate for fairly long periods. According to Kendrick's estimates, technical advance (i.e., real cost reduction) in U.S. manufacturing went on at an average rate of over 3 percent per year from 1919 to 1929 and at an average rate of over 2 percent per year from 1929 to 1937.[11] Brazil, in spite of being poorer than Chile and in spite of having equally severe distortions in internal resource allocation, has enjoyed a growth rate of between 2 and 3 percent per year in per capita real income in recent years, as compared with Chile's rate of close to zero. I find the only plausible source of this difference to be a differential rate of technical progress.

---

[11] John W. Kendrick, "Productivity Trends: Capital and Labor," *Rev. of Econ. and Statis.*, Aug., 1956, p. 254. Kendrick's measure was essentially of $(q_L + t)$. He netted out of the observed growth the effects of added labor and capital, assuming that labor quality remained unchanged. Effects of reallocations were largely removed by his measuring growth rates for thirty-three industry groups separately. Kendrick's median measure for the 1919–29 period was 3.9 percent per year and for the 1929–37 period 2.6 percent per year. I use somewhat lower figures to make allowance for possible improvement in labor quality.

One way of viewing technical advance which may help rationalize its variations as among time periods and places is to treat it as a process of adaptation to possibilities. Let Z be the maximum income that could be produced with a country's existing resources if the best techniques possible with today's level of scientific knowledge were used. Define $G (= (Z - Y)/Y)$ as the percentage gap between today's income and its potential, Z. Let A be the coefficient of adaptation, telling the fraction of previously unutilized possibilities which are put to use in a year. If G were 50 percent, indicating a potentiality of raising income levels by 50 percent, and A were 2 percent, then technical advance would contribute 1 percent to the rate of income growth this year, the formula being $t = AG$.

Even the most casual observation suggests that the percentage gap between actual and potential use of existing resources is much greater in Chile than it has been in the United States — probably easily twice as big. If Chile were to achieve a coefficient of adaptation equal to that of the United States, she would thus probably obtain a level of t two or more times as high as prevails in the U.S. The long-term average level of t for the whole U.S. economy appears to have been somewhere between 1.0 and 1.5 percent per year.[12] We are thus suggesting that raising the Chilean coefficient of adaptation to the U.S. level might lead to a rate of technical advance of 2 or 3 percent per year. This would give Chile a rate of per capita income growth comparable to those which Brazil and Mexico appear to have had in recent years.

The disturbing thing about focusing on the rate of technical advance and on the coefficient of adaptation is the possibility that these key factors may be largely beyond the influence of policy decisions. An energetic and acquisitive society is likely to have a high coefficient of adaptation, but it is hard to see how public policy can create such a society. Furthermore, as Kendrick's work shows, even in a given society the rate of technical advance is subject to substantial fluctuations, for which no satisfactory explanation has yet appeared. Yet there are surely ways in which public policy can accelerate the rate at which available knowledge is applied to use resources more efficiently. This can be done in part by promoting the international flow of technical knowledge (e.g., fostering foreign direct investment or co-operative technical arrangements between domestic and foreign firms and technical training of nationals abroad) and in part by spreading knowledge internally.

In the Chilean case, I would emphasize the possibilities to be achieved from spreading technical knowledge internally. The rewards given by the market to engineers, technically trained managers, agronomists, and other technicians themselves justify the investment in their training at a rate of real return which compares favorably with the best returns on investment in physical capital equipment. Yet these are the very people who make it their business to reduce costs, and the benefits of cost reduction accrue largely to the general

---

[12] Kendrick, *op. cit.*, estimates $(r + q_L + t)$ for the U.S. private domestic economy to have averaged 1.7 percent per year from 1899 to 1953. A figure of about 1.6 percent is estimated by Abramovitz in "Resource and Output Trends in the United States since 1870," *A.E.A. Papers and Proceedings*, May, 1956, p. 8 (Table 1, Row 18). My lower figures attempt to make plausible allowance for the contributions of r and q_L.

public. Between the reward of these cost-reducers and their real social productivity we probably find divergences far more extreme than those which occur between private and social benefits in any other significant area of the economy. So long as the rate of private return on investment in technical training remains at or near the normal rate of return on capital, we have evidence that the social rate of return must be much higher, and an indication that public policy efforts to expand the supply of technically trained people have a high place on the list of policies to promote economic development.[13]

[13] Most of the physical investment projects which are justified on the basis of external economies have a private rate of return well below the normal rate; in addition, many of the external economies alleged to exist in these cases turn out on close examination to be questionable or of small magnitude. I feel that public investment in technical training represents a more advantageous use of public funds than a goodly fraction of the physical investments which have been carried out in Latin America either by the state or through direct or indirect subsidies.

In terms of the breakdown of the growth rate given earlier, the training of engineers, managers, etc., presents a problem. Should it be classified as contributing to q_L or to t? In principle the increment in quality of labor as measured by improvement in productivity along existing production functions belongs in q_L, while the effect of shifting production functions belongs in t. Faced with the need of making a practical choice, I would allocate the increment in market earning power of the people trained to q_L, and the excess of their total social productivity over their earnings to t. The issue is, however, in any case not substantive.

VI

The next three chapters, all of which deal with the corporation income tax, do not seem to need the introductory comment made for most of the others. In fact, Chapter 6, which was written well after Chapters 7 and 8 as my contribution to the *International Encyclopedia of the Social Sciences* (New York: Crowell Collier, 1968), serves that purpose, drawing together and highlighting the main conclusions of the following two chapters.

The element that perhaps best characterizes the approach taken in these chapters is the treatment of the corporation income tax as what has come to be called a partial factor tax, i.e., a tax on the earnings of a particular factor (in this case capital) in some but not all its uses. In the United States case at least, agriculture and housing (defined not as construction but as the activity providing the services out of existing housing facilities), plus miscellaneous repair services (plumbers, electricians, painters, etc.), constitute an overwhelmingly noncorporate sector. These activities pay a negligible percentage of their income in corporation tax as compared with the rest of the economy, which is predominantly corporate. The "gray area" between the two extremes is occupied only by wholesale and retail trade, where there is a genuine mixture of corporate and noncorporate businesses, and by oil and gas, where special tax provisions (treated in Chapters 11 and 12) operate to limit the force of the corporation income tax in important ways. These latter activities, however, pay in the form of corporation income tax several times the percentage of their income from capital that is paid by what is called above the noncorporate sector; hence in empirical applications I classify them as part of the corporate sector. Lest readers conclude that with only housing, agriculture, and miscellaneous repair services classified as noncorporate, practically the whole economy must be corporate, let me note that approximately half the capital of the United States economy is in fact in the noncorporate sector as I have delineated it. This point (which will be repeated later) is made here mainly to underscore the relevance of the treatment of the corporation income tax as a partial tax on the income from capital.

The two-sector model developed in Chapter 7 provides the theoretical structure for analyzing the incidence of a partial factor tax, under conditions in which the basic supplies of labor and capital are unaffected by the existence of the tax. The main "practical" conclusion that I draw from that exercise a decade after having written it is highlighted in Chapter 6: namely, that the idea of a partial factor tax (in this case a tax on the income from corporate-sector capital) being borne fully by the factor in question (in this case not just corporate-sector capital but all capital) does not represent an extreme case, but rather one that is quite "in the middle" of the range of plausible outcomes. Moreover, empirical evidence is presented in Chapter 7 that suggests it is likely, in the United States case, that "all capital" bears something close to (and perhaps even a little more than) the full burden of this partial factor tax.

The question of the efficiency effects of a partial tax on the income from capital is discussed in Chapter 6, and dealt with empirically for the United States case in Chapter 8. This analysis is basically an application of the theoretical structure built up in Chapters 1–3, and the empirical exercise suggests that the efficiency costs involved in differential taxation of the income from capital in different uses are substantial. This is especially so if one accepts the conclusion that the true burden of a partial tax on income from capital will in any case fall largely on capital generally. In this case a tax directly levied on all income from capital would have the same ultimate incidence as the present partial tax set-up, but the costs in terms of resource allocation would be greatly reduced — even absent if the stock of capital (i.e., the supply of savings) were inelastic with respect to the net rate of return.

Chapter 6

Corporation Income Taxes

The taxation of the income of corporations has come to be one of the major sources of fiscal revenue in most countries. According to the 1965 *Yearbook of National Accounts Statistics* of the United Nations, corporation tax receipts in 1962 equaled or exceeded 2 percent of the national income in 32 countries, and represented 10 percent or more of current government receipts in 19 countries. Of the major countries, Japan places the heaviest reliance upon the corporation income tax, receipts from this tax accounting for 22 percent of current revenues and amounting to 6 percent of the national income. Australia, Canada, New Zealand, the Republic of South Africa, and the United States all collect more than 15 percent of their current revenues from this source, the amounts in each case representing more than 5 percent of national income. In western Europe corporation income taxes typically represent 3–4 percent of national income and 6–10 percent of current government revenues. The corporation income tax tends to be less important, relative to national income and government revenues, in the developing countries than in the more advanced economies; but this is due mainly to the fact that the corporate sector itself is less important, rather than to a failure of the developing countries to levy the tax at all or to a tendency on their part to impose the tax at significantly lower rates than those applied by the more advanced countries.

This widespread and heavy reliance on the corporation income tax testifies to its administrative feasibility and political popularity. It is highly feasible administratively because the laws under which corporations are established generally require the maintenance of accounts on a standardized basis; thus the enforcement of the tax reduces to the problem of requiring honest and accurate accounts and of resolving a series of technical issues, such as the determination of which expenditures may be expensed and which must be capitalized, and the setting of allowable rates of depreciation for specific classes of assets. These problems have been handled in most countries by administrative

Reprinted from Arnold C. Harberger, "Corporation Income Taxes," from *International Encyclopedia of the Social Sciences* (New York: Crowell Collier, 1968), "Capital Taxation: Corporation Income Taxes." Vol. 15, Part III, pp. 538–545, with the permission of Macmillan Publishing Co., Inc. Copyright © 1968 by Macmillan Publishing Co., Inc.

decrees or regulations issued by the tax-collecting authority itself, operating under broad guidelines set out in the tax legislation.

The political appeal of the corporation income tax has two roots. First, the tax obviously conforms to popular conceptions of ability to pay, since the man in the street tends to view corporations as wealthy entities themselves and as being owned predominantly by wealthy stockholders. But second, and in many ways equally important as a source of political appeal, is the fact that the corporation income tax, by definition, cannot be a source of loss to a corporation. Those corporations which have no net income pay no corporation income tax; only "profitable" companies are required to bear this levy. By contrast, other forms of business taxation can themselves be responsible for converting what would otherwise be a net profit situation into one of net loss. Hence, even within the world of business, companies in a marginal or precarious financial situation are likely to prefer the taxation of corporate net income to other forms of business taxation, and the strong opponents of corporate income taxation are likely to be the more profitable companies with the most "ability to pay."

The administrative and political advantages of the corporation income tax do not, however, imply that it is a good tax from the economic point of view. Quite to the contrary, it is readily demonstrable that, of the major revenue sources, this tax is one of the least justifiable on economic grounds. It entails an essentially arbitrary discrimination among industries or activities, it tends to inhibit the growth of the more dynamic sectors of the economy, and it probably causes a reduction in the overall rate of capital formation.

EFFICIENCY EFFECTS

All the discriminatory features of the corporation income tax stem from the the fact that corporate net income is the tax base. By the definition of the tax, all unincorporated activities are exempt; and even within the corporate sector of the economy, the tax falls more heavily on activities with low ratios of debt to equity (because interest on debt is a deductible expense). The consequence of these discriminations is a distortion of the economic structure, favoring noncorporate over corporate activities and, within the corporate sector, a distortion favoring those activities which can readily be financed in large measure by debt capital over those which cannot. The tax may also discriminate within the corporate sector against capital-intensive activities and favor labor-intensive activities, but the existence of this effect depends on the incidence of the tax; it may be present but need not be.

The basis for these assertions is the fact that in all economies in the modern world there is a tendency toward the equalization of the rates of return that investors receive on capital in different industries or activities. This tendency can be frustrated by restrictions on the entry of capital into given areas, can be blunted by imperfect information, can be modified by considerations of differential risk or convenience among different investment outlets, and can be obscured by random year-to-year variations in earnings — but it is always present. Stigler [1963, p. 23] found, for example, that whereas the mean rate of return (after taxes) on invested capital in U.S. manufacturing industries averaged 7.6 percent in 1947–1954, the standard deviation of the rates of return by two-digit industries (about this mean) was only 1.6 percent. Moreover, he found no significant evidence of a risk premium (either positive or negative) when he related observed average rates of return in individual industries to the standard deviation of each industry's rate of return. Stigler's results accord well with that what one would expect a priori from a reasonably well-functioning capital market. If higher-than-average rates of return to capital exist and persist in a given activity, then one would expect investment in that activity to increase and so drive down the rate of return; if lower-than-average rates of return prevail, one would expect investment to fall off, inducing an increase in the rate of return.

The following analysis will, accordingly, be based on a tendency toward equalization of after-tax rates of return to capital in different investment uses. Given this tendency, it is clear that the corporation income tax will produce an equilibrium pattern of net rates of return among industries only through its differential impact's being reflected in differential gross rates of return. Thus, assuming that the net-of-tax rate of return on equity would, in a given capital-market situation, tend to stabilize at 6 percent, and assuming that the rate of return to capital in the noncorporate sector and the rate of interest on debt would also tend to stabilize at 6 percent, we have the following possible pattern of rates of return on capital, gross of a corporation income tax at a rate of 50 percent:

Noncorporate Industry	6%
Corporate Industry A: 2/3 debt	8%
Corporate Industry B: 1/3 debt	10%
Corporate Industry C: 100% equity	12%

The differentials in gross rates of return on capital induced by the corporation income tax have two kinds of effects: first, they are reflected in product prices and, consequently, in the levels of output of particular activities; second, they confront the different activities with different relative costs of labor and capital and, hence, induce decisions concerning the relative intensity of use of these resources which are uneconomic from the standpoint of the economy as a whole. For example, the net annual cost of $100,000 of capital, for a year, to Noncorporate Industry (see above), would be $6000, while that to Corporate Industry C would be $12,000. If labor of a given class is paid $6000 per year, Noncorporate Industry is induced to operate at a point where the marginal $100,000 of capital produces a yield equivalent to the marginal product of one man-year of labor, while Corporate Industry C will tend to operate at a point where $100,000 of capital will have a yield equivalent to the marginal product of two man-years of labor. Clearly, economic efficiency could be improved by a tax system which took an equal fraction of the income generated by capital in all lines of activity, regardless of whether they were corporate in structure or not, and regardless of their degree of access to debt financing.

Effect of Other Taxation. The foregoing sketch of the efficiency-effects of the corporation income tax implicitly viewed the tax as the only levy in the tax system that affected gross-of-tax rates of return differently in different activities. Actually, there are a variety of taxes and tax provisions in most countries which have such effects, and it is important in any analysis of real-world tax systems to consider the combined effect of all such provisions rather than attempt artificially to isolate one tax, such as the corporation income tax, from the overall structure of which it is a part.

Property taxes, for example, are often levied at different effective rates on real property of different types. More important, property taxes often are levied only on land and buildings. Thus machines, inventories, and such may escape the property tax; and corporate capital, in which machines and inventories play a larger role than in noncorporate capital, will then pay relatively less through property taxation than noncorporate capital. In this way the property tax may tend to offset somewhat the discrimination against the corporate sector that is implicit in the corporation income tax.

Similarly, in countries like the United States, where capital gains are taxed at rates lower than normal personal income tax rates, or in countries with no capital gains taxation at all, the effects of corporate income taxation as such are likely to be offset to some extent by the favored treatment of capital gains. This is so because the earnings of capital in unincorporated enterprises are taxed under the personal income tax as they are earned, at full personal income tax rates, while the personal income tax strikes only that portion of corporate earnings paid out in dividends at the full rate. Let D be the proportion of earnings paid out in dividends, t_c be the corporate tax rate, t_p, the personal tax rate, and t_g be the effective rate of tax on capital gains. Then $1 of corporate earnings will pay a total personal-plus-corporate tax bill equal to

$$t_c + (1 - t_c)Dt_p + (1 - t_c)(1 - D)t_g.$$

This can turn out to be lower than t_p, the total income tax paid on $1 of income of an unincorporated enterprise, provided that the rate of tax applicable to a marginal dollar of personal income is sufficiently higher than the corporate tax rate.

For example, assume that an individual is in the 70 percent bracket of the personal income tax and is contemplating investing some savings in either a specific corporation, C, or a specific unincorporated enterprise, U. Suppose that both investments are expected to have a gross-of-tax yield of 20 percent. The net-of-tax return from the investment in U will be 6 percent, while that from the investment in C will depend on t_c, D, and t_g. Suppose t_c is 40 percent, D is 33 1/3 percent, and t_g is 15 percent. Then, of $20 of earnings in C, $8 will be paid in corporation tax, and $2.80 in personal tax on dividends of $4. If the corporation's savings of $8 out of earnings of $20 ultimately are fully reflected in capital gains, and if these are taxed at an effective rate of 15 percent, then $1.20 will be paid in capital gains taxes. The total tax on $20 of income will be $12, and the net-of-tax rate of return from the investment in C will be 8 percent — higher by 2 points than that on the investment in U.

Obviously, the effective rate of corporate-cum-personal tax on an investment will vary from individual to individual (depending on their marginal tax rates) and from corporation to corporation (depending on their dividend policies and on the degree to which their corporate savings are reflected in capital gains). Moreover, the effective rate of tax on capital gains will itself vary from situation to situation, since individuals can postpone realization of capital gains, thus postponing payment of capital gains tax and shrinking the present value of the tax paid on capital gains account. For example, if a share bought for $100 today rises in value at 8 percent per year, capital gains tax payable upon sale r years in the future will be $t_g*[(1.08)^n - 1]$, where t_g* is the nominal rate of tax on capital gains, but the present value of this tax (evaluated at 8 percent) will be $t_g*[1 - (1/1.08)^n]$. This is what was meant above by the effective rate of tax on capital gains. It is clearly, from this example, a decreasing function of the length of time that the stock is held. In the United States, the effective rate of capital gains tax can in fact be zero, since assets held until the death of the owner pass to his heirs, who in turn are taxed only on increases in value that take place after they have inherited the property.

While the property tax and capital gains provisions tend somewhat to offset the distorting effects of the corporation income tax, the traditional treatment of income from owner-occupied housing works to reinforce the distortions implicit in the corporation income tax. Obviously, owner-occupied housing generates income in real terms, but traditionally this income has not been a part of the personal income tax base. As a consequence, this important part of the income generated by capital in the unincorporated sector of the economy pays neither corporate nor personal income tax, while the income generated in the corporate sector is subject to both.

Empirical Estimation.   Harberger [see Krzyzaniak 1966] has attempted to derive rough estimates of the cost to the U.S. economy of the pattern of distortions created by the differential taxation of capital in different uses. He incorporates into a single model, which distinguishes between the corporate sector and the noncorporate sector, the effects of corporate income taxation, property taxation, capital gains taxation, and the exemption from personal income taxation of the imputed income from owner-occupied housing. Making conservative assumptions about the elasticities of response of the economy to the various distortions involved, Harberger estimates the "efficiency cost" of the U.S. pattern of taxation of income from capital at approximately $2 billion per year. This estimate concerns *only* the costs associated with the misallocation of a given capital stock, costs which would be zero if all income from capital were to be taxed at a given constant rate. It does not take into account the possible effects of the taxation of income from capital upon the size of the capital stock itself (through the influence of taxation on the rate of saving), nor does it fully incorporate the effects of various special provisions (e.g., percentage depletion) affecting specific industries. Hence, it is a conservative estimate in this respect as well.

INCIDENCE

The incidence of the corporation income tax has long been the subject of debate among economists, a state of affairs which is likely to continue for some time. Underlying this debate are some genuine differences, both analytical (reflecting different assumptions about the behavior of firms) and empirical (reflecting differing views about, for example, the quantitative response of saving to the disturbances engendered by the imposition of the tax). However, expositions of the effects of the corporation income tax at times contain serious conceptual and analytical errors which should long since have been laid to rest.

Perhaps the main source of confusion has been the conception of the incidence of the tax as falling either (a) on stockholders, or (b) on consumers, or (c) on workers, or on some combination of these three. There are three errors involved in this traditional trichotomy. The first has to do with the use of the term "stockholders" rather than "owners of capital"; the second relates to the distinction between consumers and workers; and the third concerns the assumption, which is usually implicit when the trichotomy is stated, that none of the three groups will gain as a consequence of the tax.

The Distinction between Stockholders and Owners of Capital. The idea that the burden of the corporation income tax will fall on the stockholders of the affected corporations is a valid one within the confines of standard short-run equilibrium analysis. This is because in the short run, with the capital of each corporation considered as a fixed factor of production, the earnings of equity capital represent the residual share. This residual share is assumed, in traditional short-run models of competitive and of monopolistic behavior, to be maximized by the firm. So long as the demand and cost conditions facing the firm are unchanged — the conventional assumption — the output which generated maximum profit before the tax was imposed will also yield maximum profit in the presence of the tax.

Although the above analysis is correct for the short run, a major change occurs when longer-run adjustments are allowed for. Here the appropriate assumption is that the after-tax rate of return is equalized between the corporate and the noncorporate sectors. Any fall in the rate of return perceived by the owners of shares will therefore also be perceived by the holders of other kinds of titles to capital, and the isolation of *stockholders* as the relevant group when assessing the incidence of the tax is no longer correct. The relevant group becomes *owners of capital*, once attention is focused on the longer-run incidence of the tax.

The Distinction between Consumers and Workers. Once the above is recognized, the error implicit in the distinction between consumers and workers becomes apparent. Since all income-earners in the community are owners of either labor or capital resources or both, the reduction in real income implicit in the tax must reflect the sum of the reductions in the real incomes of these two groups. That is to say, a distribution of the burden of the tax between people in their role as owners of capital, on the one hand, and people in their role as sellers of labor services, on the other, is exhaustive, leaving no room for an additional burden to be borne by consumers.

This is not to say that, within each group, different individuals will not bear different burdens because of differences in their consumption patterns. In general, those, whether capitalists or workers, who consume a greater-than-average proportion of "corporate" products as against "noncorporate" products will be relatively harder hit as a consequence of the tax than those who have the opposite bias in their consumption pattern. But the extra benefits accruing to those consumers with relatively "noncorporate" consumption patterns must, because of the deviations of these patterns from the average, exactly offset the extra burden borne by those with relatively "corporate" consumption patterns. (This statement is precisely correct if only the first-order effects of the change in tax regime are taken into account. When second-order effects are considered, there emerges an "excess burden" of the tax, deriving from the distortion of consumption patterns and resource allocation which results from the tax. Excess burden, however, is conventionally left out of account in discussions of incidence, for otherwise the sum of all burdens allocated would exceed the yield of the tax; that is, incidence is conventionally defined as dealing only with first-order effects.)

There is, nevertheless, a way in which sense can be made out of a statement like "The tax is wholly passed on to consumers." For if analysis reveals that the real incomes accruing to labor and capital fall by equal percentages as a result of the tax, then it is equally convenient to describe the tax as being borne fully by people in their role as consumers. And if labor's real income falls by 10 percent as a consequence of the tax, while capital's falls by 20 percent, it is just as convenient to regard the tax burden as being a 10 percent reduction of the real income of consumers as such (the percentage point fall common to the two groups), plus an additional 10 percent reduction falling upon the owners of capital. But if this approach is taken, there is no burden to be allocated to labor in the example just cited, just as there would be none to allocate to capital if its real income fell by 10 percent and labor's by 20 percent. Thus the idea of a three-way division of the burden remains illogical even when a plausible device is found for ascribing some of it to consumers.

The "No-Gain" Fallacy. The third error involved in typical presentations of the trichotomy — the implicit assumption that no group will gain as a consequence of the imposition of a corporation income tax — is perhaps the most serious of all, since it leads to a gross misapprehension of the nature of its incidence. It is not at all true that the share of the total burden of the tax which falls on capital must lie between zero and 100 percent; a much more plausible range for capital's share runs from a_k to $1/b_c$ (where a_k is the proportion of the national income accruing to capital and b_c is the fraction of the capital stock which is occupied in the corporate sector), though even this range can easily be exceeded.

To demonstrate the plausibility of the suggested range, assume that, with fixed and fully employed stocks of labor and of capital and holding the wage rate constant as the *numéraire*, the net-of-tax return to capital remains unchanged as a consequence of the tax. The nominal income of both labor and capital is therefore unchanged, but the real income of both groups falls because the prices of products of the corporate sector must rise to accommodate the tax. Labor and capital must therefore suffer equiproportionally as a consequence of the tax, capital's fraction of the total burden being a_k, its share in the national income.

The other end of the range is generated when the gross-of-tax rate of return to capital remains unchanged as a consequence of the tax. The net-of-tax rate of return must therefore fall by the percentage rate of the tax imposed. But the equilibrium condition for the capital market assures that if the net-of-tax rate of return falls by this percentage in the corporate sector, it must fall by the same percentage in the noncorporate sector. Since the fall in the return to capital in the corporate sector just reflects the tax paid, the parallel fall in the non-corporate sector reflects that capital is bearing more than the full burden of the tax, the ratio of capital's loss to the full burden of the tax being the ratio of total capital to corporate capital, or $1/b_c$. In this case, therefore, labor gains an amount equal to the reduction in real income per unit of capital times the amount of capital in the noncorporate sector.

The "plausible limits" just outlined can be derived from a two-sector model with homogeneous (of first degree) production functions, on the assumption that the elasticity of substitution between labor and capital is infinite in one sector or the other. If this elasticity is infinite in the untaxed (noncorporate) sector, then so long as some production takes place in that sector in the post-tax equilibrium, the relationship between the return to a unit of capital and the wage received by a unit of labor must be the same as in the pretax equilibrium. Capital and labor therefore must bear the same percentage losses of real income as a result of the tax. When, on the other hand, the elasticity of substitution between labor and capital is infinite in the corporate sector, the post-tax gross-of-tax return per unit of capital must bear the same relationship to the wage of labor as prevailed before the tax was imposed. Hence the net-of-tax return per unit of capital must fall, in both sectors, relative to the wage of labor, by the percentage of the tax, and capital must accordingly bear $(1/b_c)$ times the full burden of the tax.

Strikingly, these same "plausible limits" come into play when the elasticity of substitution is zero in one of the two sectors and nonzero in the other. When the corporate sector has a zero elasticity of substitution between labor and capital, the reduction in its output resulting from the tax leads to the ejection of labor and capital from that sector in the fixed proportions given by its technical coefficients of production. Suppose that the corporate sector uses labor and capital in the ratio of 1:2; as it contracts, it must therefore eject the factors in these proportions. If, now, the noncorporate sector was, in the pretax equilibrium, using the two factors in just these proportions, it will be able to absorb the "rejects" from the corporate sector without any change in relative factor prices. And since factor prices in the noncorporate sector are already net-of-tax, this means that both factors must suffer in the same proportion as a consequence of the tax, just as in the case of an infinite elasticity of substitution in the noncorporate sector.

The above result occurs when labor and capital were initially used in the same proportions in the two sectors, and it must be modified when the initial proportions differ. If the corporate sector ejects labor and capital in the ratio of 1:2, while the noncorporate sector was initially using them in the ratio 1:1, the noncorporate sector (which is assumed to have a nonzero elasticity of substitution) must alter its factor proportions so as to absorb relatively more capital. Capital's return must therefore fall relative to labor's, in order for equilibrium to be restored; and capital will bear more than the fraction a_k of the total burden of the tax. Conversely, if the noncorporate sector were initially more capital-intensive than the corporate sector, using the factors, say, in the proportions $1:3$, the relative price of labor would have to fall so as to enable this sector to absorb the "rejects" from the corporate sector; and capital would end up bearing less than a_k of the total burden of the tax.

Thus, when the elasticity of substitution between labor and capital is zero in the corporate sector, capital will bear the fraction a_k of the total burden if the two sectors have equal factor intensities; will bear more than a_k when the corporate sector is the more capital-intensive of the two; and will bear less than a_k when the corporate sector is the more labor-intensive of the two. Exactly how much more or less than a_k capital will bear depends upon the extent of the difference in factor proportions between the two industries, on the elasticity of substitution between labor and capital in the noncorporate sector (which determines the ease with which it can absorb new factors in proportions different from those initially used), and on the elasticity of substitution on the demand side between corporate products and noncorporate products (the greater this elasticity, the sharper the decline in demand for corporate products as a consequence of the tax, the larger the ejection of resources by this industry, and therefore the greater the shift in relative factor prices required to restore equilibrium).

When, on the other hand, the elasticity of substitution between labor and capital is zero in the untaxed industry and nonzero in the taxed industry, capital tends to bear more than the full burden of the tax. In this case, when the initial factor proportions are the same in both industries, the fixity of proportions in the untaxed industry assures that they will remain the same even after the tax has worked out its full effects. The relative returns to labor and capital, being governed in this case by the proportions in which the factors are used in the taxed industry, will remain the same, gross-of-tax, as they were in the pretax equilibrium. Capital's return net-of-tax will fall by the amount of the tax, but, as in the case of infinite elasticity of substitution in the taxed industry, the reduction will occur for capital used in either industry. The total reduction in capital's earnings will be $(1/b_c)$ times the yield of the tax, reflecting a very substantial "overbearing" of the tax by owners of capital and a corresponding net gain to those whose income accrues principally from the sale of labor services.

The above result (for a zero elasticity of substitution in the untaxed industry) is modified when the initial factor proportions are different in the two sectors. If the corporate sector is initially more labor-intensive than the noncorporate sector, the ejection of capital and labor resources in the proportions in which the latter sector will absorb them will make the corporate sector still more labor-intensive. A readjustment of factor prices against labor and in favor of capital will have to occur, and capital will end up bearing less than $(1/b_c)$ times the observed yield of the tax. Conversely, if the corporate sector is initially more capital-intensive than the noncorporate sector (which is still being assumed to have a zero elasticity of substitution) factor proportions will have to alter to make the corporate sector still more capital-intensive, requiring a shift of the gross-of-tax ratio of factor prices against capital. Capital will then bear more than $(1/b_c)$ times the observed yield of the tax.

When Capital Bears 100 Percent of the Burden. Falling well within the "plausible limits" of incidence defined by a_k and $1/b_c$ is the case in which capital bears 100 percent of the burden of the tax. This result therefore cannot be regarded as being an extreme outcome, as the conventional use of the capital–labor–consumer trichotomy implies. Added insight into the plausibility of capital's bearing the full burden of the tax can be gained from an analysis of the case in which each industry is characterized by a Cobb-Douglas production function and in which the elasticity of substitution in demand between the products of the two sectors is unity. Letting X represent the quantity of the product of the corporate sector, Y the quantity of the product of the noncorporate sector, P_x and P_y their respective prices, and Z the national income, the unit elasticity of substitution between X and Y implies

$$(6.1) \qquad XP_x = \alpha Z; \qquad YP_y = (1 - \alpha)Z,$$

where α is the fraction of Z which is spent on X. Competitive behavior of producers of X and of Y, together with the Cobb-Douglas functions $X = K_x^\beta L_x^{(1-\beta)}$, $Y = K_y^\gamma L_y^{(1-\gamma)}$, where β and γ are constants, lead to the relations

$$(6.2) \qquad \begin{aligned} K_x P_{kx} &= \beta X P_x; & L_x P_L &= (1 - \beta) X P_x, \\ K_y P_k &= \gamma Y P_y; & L_y P_L &= (1 - \gamma) Y P_y. \end{aligned}$$

Here K_x and K_y represent the amounts of capital used in the X and Y industries, respectively, and L_x and L_y refer to the corresponding amounts of labor. The price of labor is denoted by P_L, this being the same in the two industries. The cost of the services of a unit of capital is denoted by P_{kx} for the corporate sector and by P_k for the noncorporate sector, the former including the corporation income tax and the latter, of course, not including it. If τ is the rate of corporation income tax applied to the earnings of capital in sector X, then $P_k = P_{kx}(1 - \tau)$, since the after-tax *earnings* (as distinct from the before-tax *cost*) of a unit of capital are assumed to be brought to equality in both industries through the workings of the capital market.

It can be seen from relations (6.1) and (6.2) that labor will always earn a constant fraction of the national income, regardless of whether a corporation income tax exists or not. This already guarantees that exactly the full burden of the corporation tax must in this case be borne by capital. The precise way in which the burden reaches all units of capital can be seen by analyzing the relations derived from (6.1) and (6.2):

$$(6.3) \qquad K_x P_{kx} = \beta \alpha Z; \qquad K_y P_k = \gamma (1 - \alpha)Z.$$

From these it results that $[(K_x P_{kx})/(K_y P_k)]$ is a constant equal to $\beta \alpha / [\gamma (1 - \alpha)]$. But since $P_k = P_{kx}(1 - \tau)$, this means that $K_x/[K_y(1 - \tau)]$ will also be a constant — that is, the ratio (K_x/K_y) will vary directly with $(1 - \tau)$. If, with no tax at all, there were 150 units of capital in each sector, a tax of 50 percent will eventually result in there being 100 units of capital in X and 200 in Y. The

200 units of capital in Y will earn the same fraction of national income as was previously earned by the 150 units of capital in Y; hence the net-of-tax return to capital will have been reduced by a quarter, say, from $1.00 to $.75 per unit. The 100 units of capital in X will *cost* entrepreneurs $1.50 per unit and will therefore have the same total cost as the 150 units employed in X at a unit cost of $1.00 before the tax was imposed. But the after-tax earnings of capital in X will, like those of capital in Y, have fallen from $1.00 to $.75 per unit. Overall, capital will have lost $75, represented by the reduction of $.25 per unit spread over all 300 units, and this amount will be precisely equal to the yield of the tax to the government.

The result obtained in the above example applies not only to all cases fulfilling relations (6.1) and (6.2), which are derived on the basis of unit elasticities of substitution in demand between the two products, and in production between the two factors in each industry. It has been shown elsewhere [see Harberger 1962] that the same result obtains so long as the three critical elasticities of substitution are equal, regardless of their magnitude.

The General-Equilibrium, Two-Sector Model. All the cases presented above are special cases of a general-equilibrium, two-sector model of the incidence of taxation, in which the incidence of the corporation income tax is shown to depend in a specific way on the three critical elasticities of substitution and on the relative factor intensities of the two sectors. This model, based on the assumptions that the supplies of capital and labor are not influenced by the presence or absence of the tax, that competition prevails in both the corporate and noncorporate sectors, and that per-unit net-of-tax earnings of each productive factor are equalized between sectors, was first presented by Harberger [1962] and further elaborated by Mieszkowski [1967]. They have adapted the model to explore the implications of various possible types of monopolistic and oligopolistic behavior in the corporate sector; the results of the original model have proved quite insensitive to plausible allowances for noncompetitive behavior.

The chief weakness of the model appears, at this writing, to be the assumption that the path of the capital stock through time is independent of the rate of corporate taxation. If, through a tax-induced reduction in the net rate of return on capital and/or through a tax-induced shift in the distribution of disposable income, the rate of saving is affected, the relative supplies of capital and labor will gradually diverge from the path they would have followed in the absence of a corporation income tax, with consequent effects on the distribution of income. The difficulties confronting attempts to resolve this issue are twofold. First, a dynamic rather than a comparative-static approach is required, which, while not a serious obstacle as such, involves additional parameters whose magnitudes are difficult to estimate and requires the specification of the precise nature of the dynamic structure of the economy. A great deal of further work is needed before our understanding of the economy's workings can advance to the point where these dynamic aspects can be treated with a degree of precision comparable to that with which problems of comparative statics·are handled today.

The second difficulty is conceptual rather than practical. In a comparative-static approach to incidence, excess-burden being neglected, the sum of the changes in real income of the separate groups of the economy is a global reduction in real income equal to the proceeds of the tax; this is no longer true when a dynamic framework is employed. If the rate of saving is reduced by the corporation income tax, the future incomes accruing to individuals are reduced not only because the tax has to be paid each year, but also because less has been saved in the years since the tax was introduced. But it would be wrong, in estimating the incidence of the tax, to count both (a) the full reduction of real income in the year the tax is paid and (b) the future reduction in real income stemming from the reduction in savings induced by the tax. If one counts (a), one has already accounted for the present value of the future reduction in real income. To take explicit account of the future effects of changes in the savings pattern, one would properly have to convert the entire calculation of incidence to a consumption rather than an income basis and count (c) the current reduction in consumption resulting from the tax paid today plus (d) the future reduction in consumption occasioned by the reduction in future incomes stemming from the current tax-induced reduction in the rate of saving.

When the above difficulties are considered, it appears that the current-income approach (i.e., counting only (a) as the measure of incidence) is preferable, on grounds of both clarity and convenience, to approaches attempting to introduce dynamic responses into the measurement of incidence. Nevertheless, the dynamic responses in question here are of substantial interest in their own right, even if they are not linked to the analysis of incidence. The study of this aspect of the effects of corporation income taxation has only recently begun, the most important early efforts being those of Krzyzaniak [1966] and Sato [1967].

REFERENCES

Goode, Richard B. 1951. *The Corporation Income Tax*. New York: Wiley.

Harberger, Arnold C. 1959. "The Corporation Income Tax: An Empirical Appraisal." Vol. 1, pp. 231–250 in U.S. Congress, House, Committee on Ways and Means, *Tax Revision Compendium*. Washington, D.C.: Government Printing Office.

Harberger, Arnold C. 1962. The Incidence of the Corporation Income Tax. *Journal of Political Economy* 70:215–240. [This volume, Chapter 7.]

Harberger, Arnold C., and Martin J. Bailey (editors). 1968. *The Taxation of Income From Capital*. Washington: Brookings Institution.

Krzyzaniak, Marian (editor). 1966. *Effects of the Corporation Income Tax: Papers Presented at the Symposium on Business Taxation*. Detroit, Mich.: Wayne State Univ. Press. See pp. 107–117, "Efficiency Effects of Taxes on Income from Capital," by Arnold C. Harberger.

Mieszkowski, Peter. 1967. "On the Theory of Tax Incidence." *Journal of Political Economy* 75:250–262.

Musgrave, Richard A. 1959. *The Theory of Public Finance: A Study in Public Economy*. New York: McGraw-Hill.

Musgrave, Richard A., and Marian Krzyzaniak. 1963. *The Shifting of the Corporation Income Tax: An Empirical Study of Its Short-run Effect Upon the Rate of Return*. Baltimore: Johns Hopkins Press.

Sato, Kazuo. 1967. "Long-run Shifting of the Corporation Income Tax." Unpublished manuscript.

Stigler, George J. 1963. *Capital and Rates of Return in Manufacturing Industries*. National Bureau of Economic Research, General Series, No. 78. Princeton Univ. Press.

Yearbook of National Accounts Statistics. Published by the United Nations since 1958. Contains detailed estimates of national income and related economic measures for some 76 countries.

Chapter 7

The Incidence of
the Corporation Income Tax

I. INTRODUCTION

This paper aims to provide a theoretical framework for the analysis of the effects of the corporation income tax and, also, to draw some inferences about the probable incidence of this tax in the United States. It is clear that a tax as important as the corporation income tax, and one with ramifications into so many sectors of the economy, should be analyzed in general-equilibrium terms rather than partial-equilibrium terms. The main characteristic of the theoretical framework that I present is its general-equilibrium nature. It was inspired by a long tradition of writings in the field of international trade, in which the names of Heckscher, Ohlin, Stolper, Samuelson, Metzler, and Meade are among the most prominent. These writers inquired into the effects of international trade, or of particular trade policies, on relative factor prices and the distribution of income. Here we shall examine the effects of the corporation income tax on these same variables.

Our model divides the economy into two industries or sectors, one corporate and the other noncorporate, each employing two factors of production, labor and capital. The corporation income tax is viewed as a tax which strikes the earnings of capital in the corporate sector, but not in the noncorporate sector. Both industries are assumed to be competitive, with production in each governed by a production function which is homogeneous of the first degree (embodying constant returns to scale). We do not inquire into the short-run effects of the imposition of the corporation tax, on the supposition that it is the long-run effects which are of greatest theoretical and practical interest. In the very short run, the tax will necessarily be borne out of the earnings of fixed capital equipment in the affected industry, so long as our assumption of competition applies. But this will entail a disequilibrium in the capital market, with the net rate of return to owners of capital in the taxed industry being less than the net rate of return received by owners of capital in the untaxed sector. A redistribution of the resources of the economy will result, moving toward a long-run equilibrium in which the net rates of return to capital are equal in

Reprinted with permission from Arnold C. Harberger, "The Incidence of the Corporation Income Tax," *Journal of Political Economy*, LXX (June, 1962), pp. 215–240. Copyright © 1962 by The University of Chicago.

both sectors. In this long-run equilibrium the wages of labor will also be equal in the two sectors, and the available quantities of labor and capital will be fully employed.

I also assume that the available quantities of labor and capital in the economy are not affected by the existence of the tax. This assumption is rather innocuous in the case of labor, but in the case of capital it is surely open to question. It is highly likely that as a result of the imposition of the corporation tax, the net rate of return received by owners of capital will be lower than it would be in the absence of this tax. This reduction in the return to capital can influence savings in two ways: first, because now the owners of capital have less total income, and second, because the rate of return facing them is lower. On the first, we must bear in mind that any alternative way of raising the same revenue would entail the same reduction in income in the private sector; the impact on saving of the corporation tax would thus differ from that, say, of a proportional income tax yielding the same revenue, only as a result of such differences as may exist among economic groups in their savings propensities. On the second, we must inquire into the elasticity of the supply of savings with respect to the rate of interest. If this elasticity is zero, the alteration in the net rate of interest facing savers will not influence the size of the capital stock at any given time, or the path along which the capital stock grows through time. In the United States, the fraction of national income saved has been reasonably constant, in periods of full employment, for nearly a century. Over this time span, income levels have increased greatly, and interest rates have fluctuated over a rather wide range. We have no clear evidence, from these data or from other sources, that variations in the rate of interest within the ranges observed in the United States exert a substantial influence on the level of savings out of any given level of income. We shall therefore proceed on the assumption that the level of the capital stock at any time is the same in the presence of the tax as it would be in its absence; but in the conclusion of this paper we shall briefly consider how the results based on this assumption might be altered if in fact the corporation income tax has influenced the total stock of capital.

The relevance of this approach for the analysis of real-world taxes might also be questioned on the ground that the economy cannot reasonably be divided into a set of industries which are overwhelmingly "corporate," and another set which is overwhelmingly noncorporate. This objection has little validity, at least in the case of the United States. In the period 1953–1955, for example, the total return to capital in the private sector of the United States economy averaged some $60 billion per year, $34 billion being corporate profits and $26 billion being other return to capital. Of the $26 billion which was not corporate profits, more than 80 percent accrued to two industries — agriculture and real estate, in which corporate profits were negligible. In all but seven industries in a forty-eight-industry classification, corporation taxes averaged more than 25 percent of the total return to capital, and one can, for all practical purposes, say that no industries except agriculture, real estate, and miscellaneous repair services paid less than 20 percent of their total return to capital in corporation taxes, while the three named industries all paid less than 4 percent of their income from capital as corporation taxes. Within the "corporate" sector, different industries paid different fractions of their total return to capital in corporation tax, owing partly to differences in their relative use of debt and equity capital, partly to the presence in some of these industries of a fringe of unincorporated enterprises, and partly to special situations such as loss-carryovers from prior years, failure of full use of current losses to obtain tax offsets, and so on. But these differences, in my view, are not large enough to affect seriously the validity of the main distinction made here between the corporate and the noncorporate sectors.[1]

The relevance of the approach taken in this paper might also be questioned on the ground that the capital market does not in fact work to equalize the net rates of return on capital in different industries. If this objection is based on the idea that the capital market might be poorly organized, or that participants in it might not be very adept at seeking the best available net return on their invested funds, I believe it must be rejected for the United States case, for in the United States the capital market is obviously highly organized, and the bulk of the funds involved are commanded by able and knowledgeable people. The objection may, however, be based on the idea that rates of return in different industries, and perhaps on different types of obligations, will differ even in equilibrium because of the risk premiums which investors demand for different kinds of investments. At this point we must make clear that the "equalization" which our theory postulates is equalization net of such risk premiums. So long as the pattern of risk differentials is not itself significantly altered by the presence of the corporation income tax, our theoretical results will be applicable without modification. And even if the pattern of risk premiums applying to different types of activities and obligations has changed substantially as a result of the tax, it is highly likely that the consequent modification of our results would be of the second order of importance.

II. OUTLINES OF THE INCIDENCE PROBLEM: THE COBB-DOUGLAS CASE

So long as the capital market works to equilibrate rates of return net of taxes and risk premiums, and so long as the imposition of a corporation income tax does not itself have a significant effect on the (pattern of) risk premiums associated with different types of activities, it is inevitable that in the long run the corporation tax will be included in the price of the product. That is, of two industries, one corporate and one noncorporate, each using the same combination of labor and capital to produce a unit of product, the equilibrium price of the corporate product will be higher than the equilibrium price of the noncorporate product by precisely the amount of corporation tax paid per

[1] For the data from which the above figures were derived, see my paper, "The Corporation Income Tax: An Empirical Appraisal," in United States House of Representatives, Ways and Means Committee, *Tax Revision Compendium* (Washington: Government Printing Office, November, 1959), I, 231–250, esp. Table 20. That paper also contains a brief statement of the problem of the incidence of the corporation income tax (pp. 241–243), which in some ways foreshadows the work presented here. It is, however, principally concerned with the resource allocation costs of the corporation income tax rather than its incidence.

unit of product. This result is taken by some people as evidence that the burden of the corporation tax is borne by consumers, that is, that the tax is shifted forward. Such an inference is far wide of the mark.

Perhaps the easier way of demonstrating the error of the above inference is to present a simple counterexample. Consider an economy producing only two products — product X, produced by firms in the corporate form, and product Y, produced by unincorporated enterprises. Let the demand characteristics of the economy be such that consumers always spend half of their disposable income on X and half on Y. Let the production functions in both industries be of the Cobb-Douglas type, with coefficients of $1/2$ for both labor and capital: that is, $X = L_x^{1/2}K_x^{1/2}$, $Y = L_y^{1/2}K_y^{1/2}$, where L_x and L_y represent the amounts of labor used in the X and Y industries, and K_x and K_y the corresponding amounts of capital. The total amounts of labor and capital available to the economy are assumed to be fixed, at levels L and K, respectively.

Under competitive conditions, production in each industry will be carried to the point where the value of the marginal product of each factor is just equal to the price paid by entrepreneurs for the services of the factor. Thus, in the absence of taxes, we have $L_x p_L = 1/2\ Xp_x$; $K_x p_k = 1/2\ Xp_x$; $L_y p_L = 1/2\ Yp_y$; $K_y p_k = 1/2\ Yp_y$. If the total income of the economy is $1200, equally divided between X and Y, then labor in industry X will be earning $300, labor in industry Y $300, capital in industry X $300, and capital in industry Y $300. It is clear that both the labor force and the capital stock will have to be equally divided between industries X and Y. Choosing our units of labor and capital so that in this equilibrium position $p_L = p_k = \$1.00$, we have the result that without any taxes there will be 300 units of labor in industry X and 300 in industry Y, and that the capital stock will be similarly distributed.

Suppose now that a tax of 50 percent is levied on the earnings of capital in industry X, and that the government, in spending the proceeds of the tax, also divides its expenditures equally between the two industries. Labor in industry X will once again earn $300, as will labor in industry Y. Since the price paid by entrepreneurs for labor is also the price received by the workers, and since equilibrium in the labor market is assumed, the equilibrium distribution of the labor force will be the same in this case as in the previous one, that is, 300 workers in each industry.

The situation is different, however, when we come to capital. The price paid by entrepreneurs for capital, multiplied by the amount of capital used, will again be $300 in each industry. But the price paid by entrepreneurs in industry X will include the tax, while that paid in industry Y will not. With a tax of 50 percent on the total amount paid, capital in industry X will be receiving, net of tax, only $150, while capital in industry Y will be getting $300. For equilibrium in the capital market to obtain, there must be twice as much capital in industry Y as in industry X. Thus, as a result of the tax, the distribution of capital changes: instead of having 300 units of capital in each industry, we now have 200 units in industry X and 400 units in industry Y.

Out of the total of $600 which entrepreneurs are paying for capital in both industries, one-half will go to capital in industry Y, on which no tax will be paid, one-quarter will go to capital in industry X, net of tax, and one-quarter will go to the government as a tax payment. The price of capital will fall from $1.00 to $0.75.

A crude calculation suffices to suggest the resulting tax incidence. Out of a national income of $1200, labor obtained $600 before the imposition of the tax and after it, but capital obtained (net of tax) only $450 after the tax was imposed as against $600 before the tax, the difference of $150 going to the government. Capital is clearly bearing the brunt of the tax, in spite of the fact that in the tax situation, the tax is included in what consumers are paying for commodity X.

Of course, this does not tell the whole story of the incidence of the tax. Since the price of commodity X rises, and the price of commodity Y falls, consumers with particularly strong preferences for one or the other of the two goods will be hurt or benefited in their role as consumers, in addition to whatever benefit they obtain or burden they bear in their role as owners of productive factors. It is important to realize, however, that the price of Y does fall, and that this brings to consumers as a group a benefit which counterbalances the burden they bear as a result of the rise in the price of X.[2]

I would sum up the analysis of the incidence of the assumed tax on capital in industry X as follows: capitalists as a group lose in income earned an aggregate amount equal to the amount received by the government. This reduction in the income from capital is spread over all capital, whether employed in industry X or in industry Y, as soon as the capital market is once again brought into equilibrium after imposition of the tax. Insofar as individual consumers have the same expenditure pattern as the average of all consumers, they neither gain nor lose in their role as consumers. Insofar as individual consumers differ from the average, they gain if they spend a larger fraction of their budget on Y than the average, and lose if they spend a larger fraction of their budget on X than the average. The gains of those consumers who prefer Y, however, are counterbalanced by the losses of those who prefer X. If we are prepared to accept this canceling of gains and losses as the basis for a statement that consumers as a group do not suffer as a consequence of the tax, then we can conclude that capital bears the tax. Otherwise, we must be content to note that the gross transfers from individuals as capitalists and consumers of X

---

[2] The counterbalancing is not precise owing to the fact that the corporation income tax carries an "excess burden." In the post-tax equilibrium, the value of the marginal product of capital in industry X exceeds that in industry Y by the amount of the tax, whereas efficient allocation of capital would require these two values to be equal. Moreover, the pattern of consumption in the economy is also rendered "inefficient" by the tax, because the marginal rate of substitution of X for Y in consumption (which is given by the ratios of their prices gross of tax) is different from the marginal rate of substitution of X for Y in production (which is given by the ratio of their prices net of tax). The result of this twofold inefficiency is that the same resources, even though fully employed, produce less national income in the presence of the tax than in its absence. If, as is customary in discussions of incidence, we neglect "excess burden," we can treat the effects of changes in the prices of X and Y as having exactly offsetting influences on consumer welfare and can determine the incidence of the tax by observing what happens to the prices of labor and capital. This approach does not preclude the full burden of the tax being borne by consumers, for in cases in which the prices (net of tax) of labor and capital move in the same proportions as a result of the tax, it is just as correct to say that the tax is borne by consumers as it is to say that the tax burden is shared by labor and capital in proportion to their initial contributions to the national income; examples of such cases are given below.

exceed the yield of the tax by an amount equal to the gross transfer to consumers of Y.

The above example is representative of the entire class of cases in which
expenditures are divided among goods in given proportions, and production of
each good is determined by a Cobb-Douglas function. The exponents of the
Cobb-Douglas functions can differ from industry to industry, and even the tax
rates on the earnings of capital can be different in different taxed industries;
yet the conclusion that capital bears the tax, in the sense indicated above,
remains. It is easy to demonstrate the truth of the above assertion. Let A_i be
the fraction of the national income spent on the product of industry i, B_i be
the coefficient of the labor input in the ith industry (equal to the fraction of
the receipts of the ith industry which is paid in wages to labor), and C_i ($= 1 -
B_i$) be the coefficient of the capital input in the ith industry (equal to the
fraction of the receipts of the ith industry which is paid [gross of tax] to capital).
Then $\sum A_i B_i$ will be the fraction of national income going to labor, both in the
tax situation and in the case in which taxes are absent. Immediately one can
conclude that labor's share in the national income will remain the same in the
two cases. Moreover, the distribution of labor among industries will also
remain unchanged since each industry i will employ the fraction $A_i B_i / (\sum A_i B_i)$
of the labor force in both cases. Likewise, capital will receive a fixed fraction
of the national income (gross of tax) equal to $\sum A_i C_i$. When a tax is levied on
capital, capital will receive $\sum A_i C_i (1 - t_i)$ net of tax, and the government
will receive $\sum A_i C_i t_i$, where t_i is the percentage rate of tax applying to income
from capital in the ith industry. Thus capital as a whole will lose a fraction
of the national income exactly equal to that garnered by the government in
tax receipts. As in the case presented in the above example, the distribution of
capital among industries will change as a result of the imposition of the tax,
the fraction of the total capital stock in the ith industry being $A_i C_i / (\sum A_i C_i)$
in the absence of the tax and $A_i C_i (1 - t_i) / [\sum A_i C_i (1 - t_i)]$ in its presence.
Except when the tax rate on income from capital is equal in each industry,
there will be effects on relative prices, and transfers of income among consumers, of the same general nature as those outlined above for the simpler case.
But, as before, the gains of those consumers who do gain as a result of the
changes in relative prices will, to a first approximation, be offset by the losses
of those consumers who lose; thus, if we accept this offsetting as a canceling
of effects as far as people in their role as consumers are concerned, we can say
that capital bears the full burden of the tax.

III. THE CASE OF FIXED PROPORTIONS IN THE TAXED INDUSTRY

Returning now to an example in which there are only two industries, let us
assume that the taxed industry is not characterized by a Cobb-Douglas production function, but instead by a production function in which the factors
combine in strictly fixed proportions. Let us retain all of the other assumptions
of the preceding example — that expenditure is divided equally between the
two products, that production in industry Y is governed by the function

$Y = L_y^{1/2}K_y^{1/2}$, that there are 600 units of each factor, and that the prices of the two factors are initially each \$1.00. These assumptions determine that the initial, pre-tax equilibrium will be the same as before, with 300 units of each factor occupied in each industry. The fixed-proportions production function for industry X which is consistent with these assumptions is $X = \text{Min } (L_x, K_x)$.

What happens when a tax of 50 percent is imposed on the income from capital in industry X? It is clear that whatever reduction in output may occur in industry X, the two factors of production will be released to industry Y in equal amounts. Since industry Y is already using one unit of capital per unit of labor, it can absorb increments in these two factors in the same ratio without altering the marginal productivity of either factor in physical terms. The price of Y will have to fall, however, in order to create an increased demand for it. Whatever may be this fall in the price of Y, it will induce a proportionate fall in the price of each of the factors (since their marginal physical productivities are unchanged). We thus have the result that, in the final equilibrium after the tax, \$600 will be spent on the product of industry Y, with half going to capital and half to labor, and \$600 will be spent on the product of industry X, with \$200 going to labor, \$200 to capital (net of tax), and \$200 to the government. The price of labor will have fallen from \$1.00 to \$(5/6), and the price of capital will also have fallen from \$1.00 to \$(5/6). The tax will have fallen on capital and labor in proportion to their initial contributions to the national income.

It should be evident that the result just obtained, of labor and capital suffering the same percentage burden, depends critically on the fact that in the above example industry Y was in a position to absorb capital and labor in precisely the proportions in which they were ejected from industry X without a change in the relative prices of the two factors. If industry X had ejected two units of labor for each unit of capital, while industry Y had initially been using equal quantities of the two factors, the price of labor would have had to fall relative to the price of capital in order to induce the necessary increase in the proportion of labor to capital in industry Y. In such a case, labor would bear more tax, relative to its share in the national income, than capital. The following example will demonstrate that this is so.

Suppose that in the initial equilibrium 300 units of labor and 300 units of capital are engaged in the production of Y, and that the production function here is, as before, $Y = L_y^{1/2}K_y^{1/2}$. Suppose also, however, that 400 units of labor and 200 units of capital were initially dedicated to the production of X, with the production function for X requiring that labor and capital be used in these fixed proportions, that is, $X = \text{Min } [(L_x/2), K_x]$. Assume as before that the initial prices of labor and capital were \$1.00, and that national income remains unchanged at \$1200 after the imposition of the tax. Likewise retain the assumption that expenditure is divided equally between goods X and Y.

The post-tax equilibrium in this case will be one in which the price of labor is \$0.83916, the price of capital \$0.91255. Industry X will use 171.25 units of capital and 342.5 units of labor; capital in industry X will receive a net income of \$156.274, and the government, with a 50 percent tax on the gross earnings of capital in industry X, will get an equal amount; labor in industry X will receive $287.412. These three shares in the product of industry X add up (but for a small rounding error) to $600, the amount assumed to be spent on X. Industry Y will employ 328.75 ($= 500 - 171.25$) units of capital and 357.5 ($= 700 - 342.5$) units of labor, and the total receipts of each factor in industry Y will be, as before, $300.[3]

Since the price of capital has gone down from $1.00 to $0.91255, and the price of labor has gone down from $1.00 to $0.83916, it is clear that labor is roughly twice as heavily burdened by this tax (a tax on the earnings of *capital* in industry X!) than is capital, each factor's burden being taken relative to its initial share in the national income. The more labor-intensive is industry X, relative to the proportions in which the factors are initially used in industry Y, the heavier will be the relative burden of the tax upon labor. For example, if initially industry X had used 500 units of labor and 100 units of capital, while industry Y again used 300 of each with the same production function as before, the end result of a tax of 50 percent of the earnings of capital in industry X would have been a fall in the price of capital from $1.00 to $0.9775, and in the price of labor from $1.00 to $0.8974. The burden on labor, relative to its initial share in the national income, would be more than five times that on capital.[4]

Whereas, in the Cobb-Douglas case discussed in section II, capital bore the whole tax regardless of the proportions in which capital and labor combined in the two industries, we find in the present case that the relative proportions are of critical importance. The fact is that once fixed proportions are assumed to prevail in the taxed industry, it matters little whether the tax is nominally placed on the earnings of capital in X, on the earnings of labor in X, or on the sales of industry X. A tax on any of these three bases will lead to the ejection of labor and capital from industry X precisely in the proportions in which they are there used. If industry Y is initially using the factors in just these proportions,

---

[3] Let W be the net earnings of capital in industry X. Our other assumptions require that capital in industry Y must receive $300. Therefore, in the post-tax equilibrium $[W/(\$300 + W)]$ (500) units of capital must be employed in industry X. Since $600 is the total amount spent on X, and since the government's take is equal to the net amount (W) received by capital in industry X, labor in X must receive, in the post-tax equilibrium, an amount equal to $600 - 2W$. Since labor in industry Y must receive, under our assumptions, $300, total labor earnings will be $900 - 2W$, and the number of units of labor in industry X must be $[(\$600 - 2W)/(\$900 - 2W)]$ (700). (Recall that in this example there are 500 units of capital and 700 units of labor in the economy.) The production function for X requires that the industry employ twice as many units of labor as of capital. Hence we have that $(2)[W/(\$300 + W)]$ (500) $= [(\$600 - 2W)/(\$900 - 2W)]$ (700) in the post-tax equilibrium. Solution of this quadratic for W permits us to calculate the proportion of the capital stock $[W/(\$300 + W)]$ used in industry X. Applying this proportion to the total capital stock (500 units), we obtain the number of units of capital used in X. Likewise, we obtain the proportion $[(\$600 - 2W)/(\$900 - 2W)]$ of the labor force used in X, and from it the number of workers employed in X. Once we have these, we calculate the number of units of labor and capital employed in Y, and using these results, together with the fact that labor and capital in Y each earn a total of $300, we calculate the prices of the two factors. (Although the quadratic in W that must be solved has two solutions, one of these is economically inadmissible.)

[4] The key equation for arriving at this solution is $(5)[W/(\$300 + W)]$ (400) $= [(\$600 - 2W)/(\$900 - 2W)]$ (800). The solution is $W = 91$, $K_x = 93.1$, $L_x = 465.7$, $K_y = 306.9$, $L_y = 334.3$. Capital in industry X gets, net of tax, $91, the government gets $91, and labor in industry X earns $418.

there will be no change in their relative prices, and they will bear the tax in proportion to their initial contributions to the national income. If industry Y is initially more capital-intensive than X, the price of labor must fall relative to that of capital in order to induce the absorption in Y of the factors released by X, and labor will bear a greater proportion of the tax than its initial share in the national income. If, on the other hand, industry Y is initially more labor-intensive than X, the opposite result will occur, and capital will bear a larger fraction of the tax burden than its initial share in national income.

IV. THE CASE OF FIXED PROPORTIONS IN THE UNTAXED INDUSTRY

When production in the taxed industry is governed by a Cobb-Douglas function, and fixed proportions prevail in the untaxed industry, the results of the tax are very different from those in the case just discussed. Now the normal result is for capital to bear more than the full burden of the tax, while labor enjoys an absolute increase in its real income. The degree of increase in labor's real income depends on the relative factor proportions in the two industries, but the fact that labor will get such an increase is not dependent on these proportions.

The reason for this apparently anomalous result is that, in order for the untaxed industry to absorb any capital at all from the taxed industry, it must also absorb some labor, for it uses the two factors in fixed proportions. However, since in our example the fraction of national income spent on the taxed industry is given, and since the Cobb-Douglas function determines that the share of this fraction going to labor is fixed, it follows that any reduction in the amount of labor used in the taxed industry will carry with it a rise in the wage of labor.

A few examples of the type presented in the preceding sector will serve both to clarify this general result and to show how the degree of labor's gain depends on the relative factor proportions in the two industries. Assume first that the initial proportions in which the factors are combined are the same in the two industries. Let the production function for X be $X = K_x^{1/2}L_x^{1/2}$, and that for Y be $Y = \text{Min}\ (K_y, L_y)$, and let there be initially 300 units of each factor in each industry, earning a price of \$1.00. Once again let total expenditures be divided equally between the two products. It follows that, after a tax of 50 percent is imposed on the earnings of capital in industry X, capital in X will be earning \$150 net of tax while labor in X will be getting \$300. Since there are just as many units of labor as of capital in the economy, and since industry Y uses one unit of labor per unit of capital, industry X must, in the final equilibrium, employ as many units of labor as of capital. Since the total earnings of labor in X must be twice the total after-tax earnings of capital in that industry, it follows that the unit price of labor must be twice the unit price of capital. Of the total national income of \$1200, the government will get \$150, capital will get \$350, and labor will get \$700. The price of capital will have fallen from \$1.00 to \$0.5833, and that of labor will have risen from \$1.00 to \$1.1667. Capital will have lost a total of \$250 in income, of which \$150 will have gone to the government in taxes and \$100 will have been gained by labor.

Now consider a case in which the taxed industry is more labor-intensive than the untaxed industry. Let industry Y use twice as many units of capital as of labor, and let Y's initial levels of factor use be 400 capital and 200 labor, otherwise keeping the same assumptions as before. In this case, as a result of a 50 percent tax on the earnings of capital in industry X, the price of capital will fall from $1.00 to $0.677855, and that of labor will rise from $1.00 to $1.15100. Capital will have lost a total of $225.5 in income, of which $75.5 will have been gained by labor.[5]

In a more extreme case, let industry Y use five times as many units of capital as of labor, and let Y's initial levels of factor use be 500 capital and 100 labor, again retaining our other assumptions. Now the price of capital falls from $1.00 to $0.774393, and that of labor rises from $1.00 to $1.076272. Capital loses a total of $180.5 in income from the pre-tax to the post-tax situation, of which $30.5 is gained by labor.[6]

It is clear that the more capital-intensive is the untaxed industry, the less is the percentage reduction in income that capital must sustain as a result of the tax. If the untaxed industry is more labor-intensive than the taxed industry, capital is made even worse off by the tax than in the case of initially equal factor proportions. Where the untaxed industry is twice as labor-intensive as the taxed industry, for example, the price of capital falls from $1.00 to $0.528 as a result of the tax, capital losing some $236 in total income, of which $86 is gained by labor.[7]

V. A GENERAL MODEL OF THE INCIDENCE OF THE CORPORATION TAX

Although the examples presented in the three preceding sections give some insight into the nature of the incidence problem and into the factors which are likely to govern the incidence of the corporation income tax, they suffer from the defect of being based on particular restrictive assumptions about the nature of demand and production functions. In this section I shall present a model of substantially greater generality.

---

[5] Let Z stand for the (as yet unknown) total earnings of capital in industry Y in the new equilibrium. Our other assumptions determine that capital in X will be earning $150 net of tax. Therefore the fraction of the capital stock employed in Y will be $Z/(\$150 + Z)$, and the number of units of capital in Y will be this fraction times 700, the total amount of capital in the economy. Labor in Y, in the final equilibrium, will be getting ($600 − Z$), and labor in X $300. Therefore the fraction of the labor force occupied in Y will be ($600 − Z)/(\$900 − Z$), and the number of units of labor in Y will be this fraction times 500. Since the number of units of capital in Y must be twice the number of units of labor, we have as a necessary condition of equilibrium $[Z/(\$150 + Z)](700) = (2)[(\$600 − Z)/(\$900 − Z)](500)$. Z turns out to be $324.5, $K_y = 478.714$, $L_y = 239.357$. K_x is, therefore, 221.286, and p_k is $150 divided by this number. Likewise p_l is $300 divided by 260.643, the number of units of labor in X.
[6] The key equation in this case is $[Z/(\$150 + Z)](800) = (5)[(\$600 − Z)/(\$900 − Z)](400)$.
[7] This assumes that initially there were 400 units of labor and 200 units of capital occupied in industry Y. The key equation is $(2)[Z/(\$150 + Z)](500) = [(\$600 − Z)/(\$900 − Z)](700)$. Though the amount of the induced transfer from capital to labor is in this case less in total than it was in the case of equal factor proportions ($86 vs. $100), the transfer amounts to a greater fraction of capital's initial income, which in this case is $500 as against $600 in the equal-proportions case treated earlier.

Let there be two products in the economy, X and Y, with their units of quantity so chosen that their prices are initially equal to unity. Demand for each product will depend on its relative price and on the level of income of demanders. The incomes of consumers will naturally fall as a result of the imposition of the tax, and through the consequent restriction of their demand for goods, command over resources will be released to the government. The ultimate demand position will depend on how consumers react to the change in their income and to whatever price change takes place, and on how the government chooses to spend the proceeds of the tax. Assume for the sake of simplicity that the way in which the government would spend the tax proceeds, if the initial prices continued to prevail, would just counterbalance the reductions in private expenditures on the two goods. This assumption, plus the additional assumption that redistributions of income among consumers do not change the pattern of demand, enable us to treat changes in demand as a function of changes in relative prices alone. Since full employment is also assumed, the demand functions for X and Y are not independent; once the level of demand for X is known, for given prices and full employment income, the level of demand for Y can be derived from the available information. We may therefore summarize conditions of demand in our model by an equation in which the quantity of X demanded depends on (p_x/p_y). Differentiating this function we obtain

(7.1) $$\frac{dX}{X} = E\frac{d(p_x/p_y)}{(p_x/p_y)} = E(dp_x - dp_y) \qquad \text{(Demand for } X),$$

where E is the price elasticity of demand for X, and where the assumption that initial prices were unity is used to obtain the final expression.

Assume next that the production function for X is homogeneous of the first degree. This enables us to write

(7.2) $$\frac{dX}{X} = f_L\frac{dL_x}{L_x} + f_K\frac{dK_x}{K_x} \qquad \text{(Supply of } X),$$

where f_L and f_K are the initial shares of labor and capital, respectively, in the total costs of producing X.

In an industry characterized by competition and by a homogeneous production function, the percentage change in the ratio in which two factors of production are used will equal the elasticity of substitution (S) between those factors times the percentage change in the ratio of their prices. Thus we have, for industry Y,

(7.3) $$\frac{d(K_y/L_y)}{(K_y/L_y)} = S_y\frac{d(p_k/p_L)}{(p_k/p_L)}.$$

If we choose units of labor and capital so that their initial prices are equal to unity, this can be simplified to

(7.3') $$\frac{dK_y}{K_y} - \frac{dL_y}{L_y} = S_y(dp_k - dp_L) \qquad \text{(Factor response in } Y).$$

(Note at this point that the elasticity of substitution, like the elasticity of demand, is here defined so as to make its presumptive sign negative.)

We may follow an analogous procedure to obtain an equation for factor response in industry X, but we must realize here that the return to capital is being subjected to a tax in X, but not in Y. If (dp_k) is the change in the price of capital relevant for production decisions in industry Y, it is clearly the change in the price of capital net of tax. The change in the price of capital including the tax will be $(dp_k + T)$, where T is the amount of tax per unit of capital. The factor response equation for X will therefore be

$$(7.4) \qquad \frac{dK_x}{K_x} - \frac{dL_x}{L_x} = S_x(dp_k + T - dp_L) \qquad \text{(Factor response in } X\text{)},$$

where S_x is the elasticity of substitution between labor and capital in industry X.[8]

The four equations, (7.1), (7.2), (7.3′), and (7.4), contain the following nine unknowns: dX, dp_x, dp_y, dL_x, dL_y, dK_x, dK_y, dp_L, and dp_k. These can be reduced to four by the use of the following five additional equations:

$$(7.5) \qquad\qquad dK_y = -dK_x$$

$$(7.6) \qquad\qquad dL_y = -dL_x$$

$$(7.7) \qquad\qquad dp_x = f_L\, dp_L + f_k(dp_k + T)$$

$$(7.8) \qquad\qquad dp_y = g_L\, dp_L + g_K\, dp_k$$

$$(7.9) \qquad\qquad dp_L = 0.$$

Equations (7.5) and (7.6) come from the assumption of fixed factor supplies: the amount of any factor released by one of the two industries must be absorbed by the other. Equations (7.7) and (7.8) come from the assumptions of homogeneous production functions in both industries, and of competition. These assumptions assure that factor payments exhaust the total receipts in each industry. Thus, for industry Y, we have $p_y\, dY + Y\, dp_y = p_L\, dL_y + L_y\, dp_L + p_k\, dK_y + K_y\, dp_k$, to a first-order approximation. Since the marginal product of labor in Y is (p_L/p_y), and that of capital (p_k/p_y), we have, also to a first-order approximation, $p_y\, dY = p_L\, dL_y + p_k\, dK_y$. Subtracting, we obtain $Y\, dp_y = L_y\, dp_L + K_y\, dp_k$, which, dividing through by Y and recalling that the initial prices of both factors and products are assumed to be unity, we find to be equivalent to (7.8), where g_L and g_k represent the initial shares of labor and capital, respectively, in the product of industry Y. An exactly analogous procedure applied to industry X yields equation (7.7); here, however, it must be borne in mind that the change in the price of capital as seen by entrepreneurs in industry X is not dp_k but $(dp_k + T)$.

Equation (7.9) is of a different variety than the others. The equations of the model contain absolute price changes as variables, while in the underlying

---

[8] It is convenient in this exercise to treat the tax on capital as a fixed tax per unit of capital employed in X. The analysis, however, is equally applicable to a tax expressed in percentage terms. If t is the percentage rate of tax on the gross income from capital, then in the post-tax equilibrium the absolute tax T can be obtained from the equation $t = T/(1 + dp_k + T)$. Thus a case in which the tax is expressed in percentage terms can be analyzed by substituting for T in equation (7.4) the expression $[t(1 + dp_k)/(1 - t)]$.

economic theory it is only relative prices that matter. We have need of some sort of *numeraire*, a price in terms of which the other prices are expressed, and equation (7.9) chooses the price of labor as that *numeraire*. This choice places no restriction on the generality of our results. The government invariably will gain $K_x T$ in tax revenue. If the price of capital, net of tax, falls by $TK_x/(K_x + K_y)$ as a result of the tax, we can conclude that capital bears the entire tax. The change in national income, measured in units of the price of labor, is $K_x T + (K_x + K_y) dp_k$, so the result assumed above would leave labor's share of the national income unchanged, while capital's share would fall by just the amount gained by the government. If the solution of our equations told us that dp_k was zero, on the other hand, we would have to conclude that labor and capital were bearing the tax in proportion to their initial contributions to the national income. The relative prices of labor and capital (net of tax) would remain the same as before, hence both factors would have suffered the same percentage decline in real income as a result of the tax. The case where labor bears the entire burden of the tax emerges when the percentage change in the net price of capital (measured in wage units) is equal to the percentage change in the national income (also measured in wage units). Since dp_k is already in percentage terms because the initial price of capital is unity, this condition can be written $dp_k = [K_x T + (K_x + K_y) dp_k]/(L_x + L_y + K_x + K_y)$, which in turn reduces to $dp_k = K_x T/(L_x + L_y)$. Thus the choice of the price of labor as the *numeraire* by no means predestines labor to bear none of the burden of the tax, as might at first be supposed; in fact this assumption in no way restricts the solution of the incidence problem.

Substituting equations (7.5)–(7.9) into equations (7.1), (7.2), (7.3′), and (7.4), we obtain:

(7.1′)
$$\frac{dX}{X} = E[f_k(dp_k + T) - g_k \, dp_k]$$

(7.2)
$$\frac{dX}{X} = f_L \frac{dL_x}{L_x} + f_k \frac{dK_x}{K_x}$$

(7.3″)
$$\frac{K_x(-dK_x)}{K_y K_x} - \frac{L_x(-dL_x)}{L_y L_x} = S_y \, dp_k$$

(7.4′)
$$\frac{dK_x}{K_x} - \frac{dL_x}{L_x} = S_x(dp_k + T).$$

Equating dX/X in equations (7.1′) and (7.2), and rearranging terms, we have the following system of three equations:

(7.10)
$$Ef_k T = E(g_k - f_k) \, dp_k + f_L \frac{dL_x}{L_x} + f_k \frac{dK_x}{K_x}$$

(7.3″)
$$0 = S_y \, dp_k - \frac{L_x}{L_y} \frac{dL_x}{L_x} + \frac{K_x}{K_y} \frac{dK_x}{K_x}$$

(7.4′)
$$S_x T = -S_x \, dp_k - \frac{dL_x}{L_x} + \frac{dK_x}{K_x}.$$

The solution for dp_k, which gives us the answer to the incidence question, is

$$(7.11) \qquad dp_k = \frac{\begin{vmatrix} Ef_k & f_L & f_k \\ 0 & \dfrac{-L_x}{L_y} & \dfrac{K_x}{K_y} \\ S_x & -1 & 1 \end{vmatrix}}{\begin{vmatrix} E(g_k - f_k) & f_L & f_k \\ S_y & \dfrac{-L_x}{L_y} & \dfrac{K_x}{K_y} \\ -S_x & -1 & 1 \end{vmatrix}} \cdot T.$$

Alternatively, (7.11) can be written:

$$(7.12) \qquad \frac{Ef_k\left(\dfrac{K_x}{K_y} - \dfrac{L_x}{L_y}\right) + S_x\left(\dfrac{f_L K_x}{K_y} + \dfrac{f_k L_x}{L_y}\right)}{E(g_k - f_k)\left(\dfrac{K_x}{K_y} - \dfrac{L_x}{L_y}\right) - S_y - S_x\left(\dfrac{f_L K_x}{K_y} + \dfrac{f_k L_x}{L_y}\right)} \cdot T = dp_k.$$

In solving the determinant in the denominator of (7.11) to obtain the expression in the denominator of (7.12), use is made of the fact that $(f_L + f_k) = 1$.

Before turning to an examination of some of the economic implications of this solution, let us establish the fact that the denominator of (7.12), or of (7.11) is necessarily positive. S_x is necessarily negative; the expression in brackets which it multiplies in the denominator of (7.12) is necessarily positive; and S_x is preceded by a minus sign; therefore, the whole third term in the denominator of (7.12) is positive. $(-S_y)$ is also positive. In the first term, E is negative, so that if it can be shown that $(g_k - f_k)[(K_x/K_y) - (L_x/L_y)]$ is negative or zero, it will be established that the whole denominator is positive (or, in the limiting case, zero). If g_k is greater than f_k, industry Y is more capital-intensive than industry X and therefore $[(K_x/K_y) - (L_x/L_y)]$ must be negative; therefore, the indicated product must be negative. Likewise, if $(g_k - f_k)$ is negative, industry X will be the more capital-intensive of the two industries, and $[(K_x/K_y) - (L_x/L_y)]$ will be positive. The whole first term in the denominator of (7.12) is therefore positive, and the denominator also.

VI. DETAILED EXAMINATION OF THE GENERAL SOLUTION

In this section, I shall set out certain general conclusions which can be drawn on the basis of the solution given in (7.12).

1. *Only if the taxed industry is relatively labor-intensive can labor bear more of the tax, in proportion to its initial share in the national income, than capital.* Recall that when dp_k is zero, labor and capital bear the tax precisely in proportion to their initial shares in the national income. For labor to bear more than this, dp_k must be positive. Since the denominator of (7.12) is positive, the sign of dp_k will be determined by the sign of the numerator of (7.12). The second term

in the numerator is necessarily negative, so dp_k can be positive only if the first term is positive and greater in absolute magnitude than the second term. Since E is negative, the first term can be positive only if $[(K_x/K_y) - (L_x/L_y)]$ is negative, and this can occur only if industry X is relatively more labor-intensive than industry Y. Q.E.D.

2. *If the elasticity of substitution between labor and capital in the taxed industry is as great or greater in absolute value than the elasticity of demand for the product of the taxed industry, capital must bear more of the tax than labor, relative to their initial income shares.* In this case the term $Ef_k(-L_x/L_y)$, which is the only term which can give the numerator of (7.12) a positive sign, is dominated by the term $S_x f_k(L_x/L_y)$.

3. *If the elasticity of substitution between labor and capital in the taxed industry is as great in absolute value as the elasticity of substitution between the two final products, capital must bear more of the tax than labor, relative to their initial income shares.* This holds a fortiori from the above, since the elasticity of substitution between X and Y must be greater in absolute value than the elasticity of demand for X. The formula relating the elasticity of substitution between X and Y, which I shall denote by V, and the elasticity of demand for X, E, is $E = V[Y/(X + Y)]$.[9]

4. *The higher is the elasticity of substitution between labor and capital in the untaxed industry, the greater will be the tendency for labor and capital to bear the tax in proportion to their initial income shares.* This elasticity, S_y, appears only in the denominator of (7.12). It changes not the sign but the magnitude of the expression for dp_k. The larger is S_y in absolute value, the smaller will be the absolute value of dp_k. In the limit, where S_y is infinite, dp_k must be zero: in this case the relative prices of labor and capital are determined in the untaxed industry; the tax cannot affect them.

5. *The higher the elasticity of substitution between labor and capital in the taxed industry, the closer, other things equal, will be the post-tax rate of return on capital to the initial rate of return less the unit tax applied to capital in industry* X. This elasticity, S_x, appears in the numerator and the denominator of (7.12) with equal coefficients but with opposite signs. When S_x is infinite, and the other elasticities finite, the expression for dp_k is equal to $-T$. The price of capital in the taxed industry, gross of tax, must in this case bear the same relationship to the price of labor as existed in the pre-tax situation. The net price of capital must therefore fall by the amount of the tax per unit of capital in X. Since this fall in price applies to capital employed in Y as well as in X, the reduction in the income of capital must exceed the amount of revenue garnered by the government; labor's real income must therefore rise. When S_x is not infinite, its contribution is to move the value of dp_k toward $-T$, from whatever level would be indicated by the other terms in (7.12) taken alone.

---

[9] One of the many places in which the derivation of this relationship is presented is my paper, "Some Evidence on the International Price Mechanism," *Journal of Political Economy*, LXVI (December, 1957), 514. The relationship applies when the relevant elasticity of demand is one which excludes first-order income effects. This is the concept relevant for the present analysis, because we are treating government demand for goods on a par with consumer demand. The presentation of this relationship at this point may seem a bit out of context; I bring it in because it will be used later.

6. *When factor proportions are initially the same in both industries, capital will bear the full burden of the tax if the elasticities of substitution between labor and capital are the same in both industries, will bear less than the full burden of the tax if the elasticity of substitution between labor and capital is greater in the untaxed than in the taxed industry, and will bear more than the full burden of the tax if the elasticity of substitution is greater in the taxed industry.* When $(K_x/K_y) = (L_x/L_y)$, the first terms in both the numerator and denominator of (7.12) vanish, and the expression simplifies to $dp_k = -TS_x K_x/(S_y K_y + S_x K_x)$. When, additionally, $S_x = S_y$, this reduces to $-TK_x/(K_y + K_x)$, which was indicated earlier to be the condition for capital's bearing exactly the full burden of the tax. When S_x is greater than S_y, capital's burden will be greater than in the case where the two elasticities are equal, and conversely.

7. *When the elasticity of demand for the taxed commodity is zero, the results are somewhat similar to those just reached. In this case, however, capital does not necessarily bear precisely the full burden of the tax even when the elasticities of substitution are equal in the two industries. It bears somewhat more if the taxed industry is labor-intensive and somewhat less if the taxed industry is capital-intensive.* When E is zero, the first terms in both the numerator and denominator of (7.12) again vanish, but now the expression for dp_k reduces to $-Tf_L K_x S_x/(g_L K_y S_y + f_L K_x S_x)$.[10] It is clear that, even when $S_x = S_y$, this is equal to $-TK_x/(K_y + K_x)$ only when $f_L = g_L$, that is, when the two industries are initially equally labor-intensive. The fall in the price of capital will be greater or less than this according as f_L is greater than or less than g_L.

8. *When the elasticity of substitution between labor and capital is zero in both industries, the incidence of the tax will depend solely on the relative proportions in which the factors are used in the two industries, labor bearing the tax more than in proportion to its initial contribution to national income when the taxed industry is relatively labor-intensive, and vice versa.* In this case (7.12) simplifies to $dp_k = f_k T/(g_k - f_k)$, which will be positive when g_k is greater than f_k (taxed industry relatively labor-intensive) and negative when f_k is greater than g_k (taxed industry relatively capital-intensive). A somewhat anomalous aspect of this solution is that the absolute value of dp_k varies inversely with the difference in factor proportions in the two industries. When f_k is $1/4$ and g_k is $1/2$, $dp_k = T$; but when f_k is $1/4$ and g_k is $3/4$, dp_k is only $1/2\ T$. To see the reason for this, it is useful first to recognize that when there are only two industries, each of which uses the two factors in different proportions, there is only one set of outputs of X and Y which will provide full employment. So long as the full-employment condition is not violated, demand conditions require that the relative prices of the two products must remain unchanged. In our notation, $dp_x - dp_y$ must be zero. Since $dp_x = f_k(dp_k + T)$, and $dp_y = g_k dp_k$, it is clear that this condition on the relative prices of final products is sufficient to give the solution $dp_k = f_k T/(g_k - f_k)$. If, for example, capital initially accounts for one-tenth of the value of output in X and one-half in Y, a rise in the price of capital by $0.25\ T$ will

---

[10] Since $f_L = L_x/(L_x + K_x)$ and $f_k = K_x/(L_x + K_x)$, it is clear that $f_L K_x = f_k L_x$. The coefficient of S_x in the numerator of (7.12) can therefore be written $f_L K_x[(1/K_y) + (1/L_y)] = f_L K_x[(L_y + K_y)/(L_y K_y)] = f_L K_x/g_L K_y$. Setting $E = 0$ in (7.12), and multiplying numerator and denominator by $g_L K_y$, one obtains the expression given above for dp_k.

permit relative product prices to remain unchanged. Recalling that the price of labor is the *numeraire*, and therefore is assumed to remain unchanged, one can see that the rise in the price of X would be $(0.1)(0.25T + T) = 0.125T$, while the rise in the price of Y would be $(0.5)(0.25T)$, also equal to $0.125T$. Suppose, however, that capital initially accounts for four-tenths of the value of product in X, and one-half in Y. Then the price of capital will have to rise by $4T$ in order to yield the equilibrium ratio of product prices. The rise in the price of X would then be $(0.4)(4T + T) = 2T$, and the rise in the price of Y would be $(0.5)(4T)$, which is also equal to $2T$. In the limit, where the factor proportions are the same in both industries, and where the production functions are such that these proportions cannot be altered, the model does not give sufficient information to determine the prices of capital and labor, either in the pre-tax or in the post-tax equilibrium.

9. *Where the elasticity of substitution in demand between goods* X *and* Y *is equal to* -1, *and the elasticities of substitution between labor and capital in the two industries are also equal to* -1, *capital will bear precisely the full burden of the tax*. This is the Cobb-Douglas case treated in section II above. The easiest way to demonstrate this proposition is to substitute the solution for dp_k, dL_x/L_x, and dK_x/K_x directly into equations (7.10), (7.3''), and (7.4'). Since the determinant of this system of equations is nonzero, we know that there can be only one solution; thus, if we find one that works, we know we have the right one. The correct solution is $dp_k = -TK_x/(K_x + K_y)$; $(dL_x/L_x) = 0$; and $(dK_x/K_x) = -TK_y/(K_x + K_y)$. Substituting this solution, and $S_x = -1$, into (7.4'), we obtain $-T = [-TK_x/(K_x + K_y)] + [-TK_y/(K_x + K_y)]$. Equation (7.4') is therefore satisfied. Substituting into (7.3''), with S_y set equal to -1, we obtain $[K_xT/(K_x + K_y)] + [-K_xT/(K_x + K_y)] = 0$. Equation (7.3'') is therefore satisfied. Recalling that when the elasticity of substitution between X and Y is -1, the elasticity of demand for X will be $-Y/(X + Y)$, we substitute this value for E in (7.10), together with the solution values for the three unknowns, obtaining

$$\frac{-f_k YT}{X + Y} = \frac{YK_x g_k T}{(X + Y)(K_x + K_y)} - \frac{YK_x f_k T}{(X + Y)(K_x + K_y)} - \frac{f_k K_y T}{K_x + K_y}.$$

First, add $YK_x f_k T/(X + Y)(K_x + K_y)$ to both sides of the equation, to obtain

$$\frac{-f_k YK_y T}{(X + Y)(K_x + K_y)} = \frac{YK_x g_k T}{(X + Y)(K_x + K_y)} - \frac{f_x K_y T}{K_x + K_y};$$

here we use the fact that

$$\frac{K_x}{K_x + K_y} + \frac{K_y}{K_x + K_y} = 1.$$

Now add $f_k K_y T/(K_x + K_y)$ to both sides of the equation, to get

$$\frac{f_k XK_y T}{(X + Y)(K_x + K_y)} = \frac{YK_x g_k T}{(X + Y)(K_x + K_y)};$$

here we use the fact that $[X/(X + Y)] + [Y/(X + Y)] = 1$. Now, noting that $f_k = K_x/X$ and $g_k = K_y/Y$ under our assumption that all prices are initially equal to unity, we make the corresponding substitutions to obtain

$$\frac{K_x K_y T}{(X + Y)(K_x + K_y)} = \frac{K_x K_y T}{(X + Y)(K_x + K_y)}.$$

Equation (7.10) is therefore satisfied, and the solution has been verified to be the correct one.

10. *In any case in which the three elasticities of substitution are equal (and nonzero), capital will bear precisely the full burden of the tax.* We have shown that when $S_x = S_y = V = -1$, the solution for dp_k is $-KT_x/(K_x + K_y)$, which is what is required for capital to lose precisely what the government gains. Recalling that $E = VY/(X + Y)$, we see from (7.12) that multiplying S_x, S_y, and V by any positive constant would change the numerator and denominator of (7.12) in the same proportion, leaving the solution for dp_k unchanged.

VII. APPLICATION TO THE UNITED STATES CASE

If we divide the United States economy into two broad sectors, one corporate and the other noncorporate, the most plausible broad division is between agriculture, real estate, and miscellaneous repair services on the noncorporate side, and the remainder of United States industries on the other. As was indicated in the introduction, the industries here classified as corporate all paid some 20 percent or more of their total income from capital in corporation tax; and one may add at this point that two thirds of them paid corporation taxes amounting to more than 40 percent of their return to capital.[11]

On this classification, the corporate sector, in 1953–1955, earned roughly $40 billion in return to capital, and paid roughly $20 billion in corporation income taxes. Its wage bill averaged around $200 billion per year. The noncorporate sector, on the other hand, contributed some $40 billion per year to the national income, of which some $20 billion was return to capital and $20 billion return to labor; this sector paid practically no corporation income taxes (less than $500 million).[12] These data are sufficient to enable us to estimate some of the key elements in formula (7.12).

---

[11] In making the computations that follow, I have eliminated from consideration the government and rest-of-the-world sectors, together with the financial intermediaries (banking, brokers, finance, insurance), and certain of the services (private households, commercial and trade schools, medical, health, legal, engineering, educational, and other professional services, and nonprofit membership organizations). The industrial classification used was that given in the official statistics on national income by industry. Because net interest and income of unincorporated enterprises are not given in so detailed an industrial breakdown as national income, corporate profits, corporate profits taxes, and so forth, it was necessary to estimate the industrial breakdown for them independently. The methods used, and the tests applied to check the consistency of the resulting figures with official data available for broader aggregates, are given in the appendix to my earlier paper, "The Corporation Income Tax: An Empirical Appraisal," *op. cit.*

[12] Readers of my earlier paper may recall that I reported there on a set of calculations in which the national output was divided into two sectors, and that the two sectors turned out to have roughly equal factor proportions. That division differs from the present one because it was based on the assumption that in each of the many industries considered, fixed factor proportions prevailed. In such a case, a tax on the earnings of capital in each industry is equivalent to an excise tax on the value added to that industry at a rate equal to the ratio of corporation

If the corporation income tax were of small magnitude, the pre-tax values of (L_x/L_y), (K_x/K_y), f_L, f_k, and g_k would all be very close to their post-tax values, and the post-tax values could be inserted into equation (7.12) without fear of significant error. However, the tax is in fact substantial in the United States. I have accordingly decided to use two alternative sets of values for these elements in the formula: Set I is derived from the observed values in the period 1953–1955, and Set II represents the values that would have emerged in 1953–1955 in the absence of the tax if each sector were characterized by a Cobb-Douglas production function and if the elasticity of substitution between the products of the two sectors were unity. In both cases $(L_x/L_y) = 10$. This is the ratio of the wage bill in the taxed sector to the wage bill in the untaxed sector that was observed in 1953–1955, and it will be recalled from the analysis of the Cobb-Douglas case in section II that the pre-tax and post-tax distributions of the labor force are the same. Likewise, $g_k = 0.5$ in both cases, this being the share of capital in the untaxed industry in 1953–1955; under Cobb-Douglas assumptions this fraction also is invariant between the pre-tax and post-tax situation. The observed value of (K_x/K_y) is 1, the after-tax receipts of capital being the same in the two sectors in 1953–1955. The hypothetical initial value, however, is 2 under Cobb-Douglas assumptions, for these assumptions imply that in the absence of the tax the capital stock would be distributed between the industries in the same proportions as the gross-of-tax earnings of capital in the two industries after the tax had been imposed. Since under Cobb-Douglas assumptions the shares of the gross earnings of the factors in the total product of the industry are constant, we have for this case $f_k = (1/6)$ and $f_L = (5/6)$. For our alternative assumptions (Set I) we shall take the observed net-of-tax ratios in 1953–1955: $f_k = (1/11)$ and $f_L = (10/11)$. The assumed initial values for these magnitudes are summarized below:

	(K_x/K_y)	(L_x/L_y)	f_k	f_L	g_k
Set I	1	10	1/11	10/11	0.5
Set II	2	10	1/6	5/6	0.5

Substituting these figures into equation (7.12), we obtain expressions for dp_k in which the incidence of the corporation tax is expressed directly in terms

---

tax receipts to value added. In my example I compared the results of such a pattern of excises with the results of a flat-rate excise tax on the value added of all industries, the rate being so chosen as to yield the same revenue as the present corporation tax. I then divided industries into two groups according to whether their ratios of corporation tax payments to value added were greater or less than this calculated flat rate. Under the assumption of no substitutability between capital and labor, those industries whose actual rate was higher than the flat rate would presumably contract, as a result of substituting the flat-rate excise for the present tax. Those that would contract would eject labor and capital, and the others would expand their use of both factors. The calculation I made was of the total amounts that would be demanded by the expanding industries, assuming unit elasticities of substitution among final products and also that relative factor prices did not change as a result of the alteration in tax provisions. It turned out that the expanding industries would demand new labor and capital in almost precisely the same amounts as contracting industries would eject them and that therefore the relative prices of the factors would remain substantially unchanged. I note this merely to explain the difference in concept between my earlier calculation of factor proportions and the present one. In the earlier case, the ratio of corporate tax payments to value added was the basic variable considered; here the basic variable is the ratio of corporate tax payments to total income from capital.

of the elasticities of substitution and of demand:

$$(7.13) \qquad dp_k = \frac{T[-9E + 20S_x]}{-40.5E - 11S_y - 20S_x} \qquad \text{(based on Set I)};$$

$$(7.14) \qquad dp_k = \frac{T[-8E + 20S_x]}{-16E - 6S_y - 20S_x} \qquad \text{(based on Set II)}.$$

We have evidence which I believe permits us to estimate the order of magnitude of E reasonably well, albeit by an indirect route. The untaxed sector, Y consists overwhelmingly of two industries — agriculture and real estate — and the activity of the latter is principally the provision of residential housing services. We know that the elasticity of demand for agricultural products lies well below unity, and recent evidence suggests strongly that the price elasticity of demand for residential housing in the United States is somewhere in the neighborhood of unity, perhaps a bit above it.[13] It is thus highly unlikely that the price elasticity of demand for the products of our noncorporate sector (which would be a weighted average of the price elasticities of the component commodities, adjusted downward to eliminate the contribution of substitutability among the products in the group) would exceed unity in absolute value; in all likelihood it is somewhat below this figure. This evidence permits us to use unity as a reasonable upper bound for the elasticity of substitution between X and Y. A value of unity for this elasticity of substitution implies a value of $-6/7$ for the elasticity of demand for the products of the noncorporate sector, and a value of $-1/7$ for the elasticity of demand for the products of the corporate sector.[14] Only if one feels that the elasticity of demand for the noncorporate sector's product is higher than 6/7 in absolute value can he place a higher value than 1/7 on the elasticity of demand for the corporate sector's product.

Evidence on the elasticity of substitution (S_x) between labor and capital in the corporate sector is both more meager and less reliable than the evidence on elasticities of demand. However, two recent studies, one by Solow and the other by Minasian, suggest rather strongly that the elasticity of substitution between labor and capital in manufacturing industries in the United States tends to be near unity. Of nineteen elasticities of substitution measured by Solow for two-digit manufacturing industries, ten were greater than and nine less than unity. Of fourteen elasticities of substitution measured by Minasian for two-digit industries, six were greater than and eight less than unity. Of forty-six elasticities measured by Minasian for three-digit and four-digit industries, twenty-two were greater and twenty-four less than unity. Only in a small fraction of the cases were the differences between the estimated elasticities and unity statistically significant; and the majority of the estimated elasticities for which this difference was significant were greater than unity.[15]

---

[13] See Richard F. Muth, "The Demand for Nonfarm Housing," in A. C. Harberger (ed.), *The Demand for Durable Goods* (Chicago: University of Chicago Press, 1960), pp. 29–96.
[14] Recall that V, the elasticity of substitution between X and Y, is related to the own-price elasticities of demand for those commodities by the formulas: $E_x = V[Y/(X + Y)]$, and $E_y = V[X/(X + Y)]$. In our 1953–1955 data $[X/(X + Y)] = \$240/\$280$, and $[Y/(X + Y)] = \$40/\$280$.
[15] See R. M. Solow, "Capital, Labor, and Income in Manufacturing" (paper presented at the Conference on Income and Wealth, April, 1961, sponsored by the National Bureau of Economic

We can be still less sure about the elasticity of substitution, S_y, between labor and capital in the untaxed sector. We may recognize the relative success that agriculture economists have had in fitting Cobb-Douglas production functions to data for different components of agriculture and perhaps tentatively accept an elasticity of substitution of unity as applying there. However, close to half the contribution of the noncorporate sector to national income comes from real estate and not from agriculture. It is difficult to see how the elasticity of substitution between labor and capital in the provision of housing services could be very great. Very little labor is in fact used in this industry (compensation of employees is only one-tenth of the value added in the industry), and it is hard to imagine that even fairly substantial changes in relative prices would bring about a much greater relative use of labor. Taking the noncorporate sector as a whole, I think it is fair to assume that the elasticity of substitution between labor and capital in this sector is below, and probably quite substantially below, that in the corporate sector.

We may now attempt to assess the burden of the corporation income tax in the United States. Let us take as a first approximation the Cobb-Douglas case, in which all three elasticities of substitution are unity. We have seen that this case implies that capital will bear precisely the full burden of the tax. This means, using Set I of initial conditions, that $dp_k = -1/2\ T$, and using Set II that $dp_k = -2/3\ T$. Inserting the values $E = -1/7$; $S_x = S_y = -1$ in equations (7.13) and (7.14), we find that, under Set I, $dp_k = -0.509\,T$, while under Set II $dp_k = -2/3\ T$.[16]

The most plausible alteration to make in the above assumptions is to reduce the value of S_y. This will clearly operate to increase the burden on capital. To see how sensitive is the incidence of the tax to a reduction in S_y, let us assume $E = -1/7$; $S_x = -1$; $S_y = -1/2$. Here we find that under Set I $dp_k = -0.598\,T$, while under Set II $dp_k = -0.746\,T$. Comparing these results with the level of dp_k which would mean capital's just bearing the tax, we find that in this case capital's burden is 120 percent of the tax under Set I and 112 percent under Set II.

The results are even less sensitive to changes in the assumed demand elasticity than to changes in S_y. If we assume the elasticity of substitution between X and Y to be only $-1/2$ (which is implausibly low, since it implies an elasticity of demand for the noncorporate sector's product of only -0.42, even though we have strong evidence that this magnitude is much higher), while the elasticities of substitution in production are both -1, capital turns out to bear 114 percent

Research [to be published]), and Jora R. Minasian, "Elasticities of Substitution and Constant-Output Demand Curves for Labor," *Journal of Political Economy*, LXIX, June, 1961), 261–270. Both of these studies were based on cross-section data, Solow's data being classified by regions and Minasian's by states. Though the overall statistical significance of the conclusion that the substitution elasticity between labor and capital in most manufacturing industries is not far from unity is good, there is the possibility of bias toward unity in the results due to errors of measurement or to differences in the quality of labor among states or regions. It is on this ground that I regard these results as less firm than those on elasticities of demand.

[16] Set I does not yield exact results because the assumed initial conditions are inconsistent with the assumed values of the three elasticities. However, the error is so small as to be negligible for practical purposes.

of the burden of the tax under Set I and 107 percent under Set II of initial values. Raising the elasticity of substitution between X and Y to -1.5 (implying an elasticity of demand for the noncorporate sector's product of around -1.25), we obtain the result that capital bears 91 percent of the tax under Set I and 93 percent under Set II.

Raising S_x to -1.2 (which is perhaps a rather high value in the light of the Solow-Minasian evidence), and leaving the other elasticities of substitution at unity, gives the result that capital bears 111 percent of the tax under Set I and 106 percent under Set II of initial conditions. If we set S_x at $-.8$, we find that capital bears 90 percent of the burden of the tax under Set I, and 92 percent under Set II.

To reduce S_x below unity while not reducing S_y appears unrealistic, since our evidence suggests that S_x is near -1, while evidence and presumption suggest that S_y is lower. Let us accordingly test the consequences of a substantial reduction of S_x and S_y simultaneously, say, to $-2/3$, while leaving the elasticity of substitution between X and Y at -1. This gives the same relationship among the elasticities as existed when we assumed the elasticity of substitution between X and Y to be -1.5, and the elasticities of substitution in production to be -1; again we find that capital bears 91 percent of the tax under Set I and 93 percent under Set II of initial conditions.

It is hard to avoid the conclusion that plausible alternative sets of assumptions about the relevant elasticities all yield results in which capital bears very close to 100 percent of the tax burden.[17] The most plausible assumptions imply that capital bears more than the full burden of the tax.

Let us now consider how this result would be modified if, as a result of the existence of the tax, the rate of saving was less than it would have been in the absence of this particular tax. I shall assume that, in the absence of the corporation income tax, the government would have raised the same amount of revenue by other means, and hence that there is no "income effect" of the tax on the volume of saving. However, our analysis implies that the net rate of return on capital is lowered as a result of the tax, and this would have an effect on capital accumulation if the elasticity of savings with respect to the rate of interest were not zero. Let the capital stock that we now observe be called K_1, and the capital stock that we would have had at the present time in the absence of the corporation tax be K_2. Let R be the percentage excess of K_2 over K_1. An increase in the capital stock from K_1 to K_2 would have caused an increase in output of $h_k R$ percent, where h_k is the fraction of the national

[17] Actually, the method used to estimate the percentages of the tax borne by capital in the above examples is biased away from this conclusion. The method was to divide the estimated value of dp_k by the value that dp_k would have if capital bore the whole tax. This method would tell us that capital bore none of the tax if the estimated dp_k were zero; yet we know that when $dp_k = 0$ the tax is shared by labor and capital in proportion to their initial contributions to total income. The method is precise only when $dp_k = -K_x T/(K_x + K_y)$. If p_k falls more than this, with the price of labor constant, the general price level will fall somewhat; capital will not suffer in real terms by as much as our approximation indicates. If p_k falls by less than this, the general price level will rise, and capital will suffer a greater burden (will come closer to bearing the full weight of the tax) than our approximation indicates. Correcting the above percentages for this bias would accordingly strengthen the conclusion stated above. The corrections would, however, be minor in the cases presented in the text.

income earned by capital. If, as is probably true, Cobb-Douglas assumptions apply, the shares of capital and labor in the national income will remain constant. Therefore, of the increase in output stemming from the increase in capital stock, a fraction h_L would accrue to labor, where h_L is the share of labor in the national income. Thus in the absence of the tax there would have occurred a transfer of $h_L h_k R$ percent of the national income to labor. This transfer does not take place because of the existence of the tax; hence in a sense it may be said that the potential amount of this unrealized transfer is a burden imposed on labor by the tax.

How large is the amount of the potential transfer relative to the burden of the tax itself? Using our 1953–1955 data, we find that h_k is about 0.22 and h_L is about 0.78, while the tax represents 1/14 of the total income produced in the two sectors considered. In order for $(0.22)(0.78) R$ to equal 1/14 of the national income, R would have to be about 0.42. That is to say, the capital stock that would have existed in the absence of the corporation tax would have had to be some 42 percent greater than the capital stock we now have.

It is quite implausible that the influence of the corporation tax on the capital stock could have been this great. If the tax did not influence the capital stock at all, it would have reduced the net rate of return on capital by a third; to the extent that it did influence the capital stock, the reduction in the net rate of return would have been less than this. K_2 is made different from K_1 by the influence of the reduction in the rate of return upon the rate of saving. If there is such an influence, its effect increases through time. In the first few years after the tax is imposed, only small differences between K_2 and K_1 can emerge. As time goes on, and the capital stock comes to consist more and more of capital accumulated after the imposition of the tax, the difference becomes larger. The percentage excess of K_2 over K_1 can, however, never be greater than the percentage excess of the savings rate that would have existed in the absence of the tax over the savings rate in the presence of the tax. Thus, if one thinks that in the absence of the corporation tax the net savings rate in the United States might be 20 percent higher than it is now, he may set the maximum value for R at 0.2. This would mean that a maximum of half the burden of the corporation tax would be "shifted" to labor. If one thinks that the savings rate in the absence of the tax would be no more than 10 percent higher than at present, a maximum of one-quarter of the burden of the tax would be "shifted" to labor. The observed constancy of the savings rate in the United States in the face of rather wide variations in the rate of return on capital suggests that the effect of the tax on the rate of saving is probably small. Moreover, no more than half of the present capital stock of the United States is the result of accumulations made after corporation tax rates became substantial in the mid-thirties. Thus even if savings in this period would have been 20 percent greater in the absence of the tax, the current capital stock would be only 10 percent less than it would have been in the absence of the tax. And if the effect of the tax was to reduce savings by 10 percent, the current value of R would be only 5 percent.

I conclude from this exercise that even allowing for a rather substantial effect of the corporation income tax on the rate of saving leads to only a minor modification of my overall conclusion that capital probably bears close to the full burden of the tax. The savings effect here considered might well outweigh the presumption that capital bears more than the full burden of the tax, but it surely is not sufficiently large to give support to the frequently heard allegations that large fractions of the corporation income tax burden fall on laborers or consumers or both.

At the presentation of this paper at the 1961 meetings of the International Association for Research in Income and Wealth, and in other discussions of its content, some questions have been raised that clearly merit treatment, yet that do not quite fit as integral parts of, or as footnotes to, particular statements in the main text. These notes discuss two of these points.

1. *Other Special Tax Provisions Relating to Capital.* In this paper I have tried to get at what might be called the partial or particular effects of the corporation income tax. In the simple models presented, the corporation income tax was the only tax in the system, but the analysis can easily be adapted to cases where other taxes exist. In such cases the effects of adding the corporation income tax to a set of preexisting taxes will be essentially the same as those derived in this paper for the case where there were no preexisting taxes. Differences of detail in formulas such as equation (7.12) may appear as one considers different patterns of pre-existing taxes, but the basic roles played by relative factor proportions, by substitutability between corporate and non-corporate products in demand, and by the relative degrees of substitutability between labor and capital in producing the two classes of products will remain the same.

One may, however, accept the approach presented in the text as appropriate for analyzing the effects of the corporation income tax and may have no quarrel with the empirical exercise of section VII as indicating the particular effect of the corporation income tax in the United States, and yet may doubt that capital is as heavily discriminated against in the corporate sector, or that capital as a whole bears as heavy a weight of "special" taxation, as is indicated in section VII. Such doubts have been expressed to me on several occasions, the argument being that other "special" provisions of our tax laws operate to offset, to some extent, the particular effects of the corporation income tax.

The capital gains provisions of the personal income tax are a case in point. Capital gains in the United States are taxed only upon realization, and then (except for short-term gains) at a preferential rate that cannot exceed 25 percent. Accrued gains that have not been realized before the death of the owner escape capital gains tax altogether and are subject only to the estate tax. These provisions operate to make the tax load on owners of capital lighter than it would be in their absence. They also operate to attract capital to the corporate sector, for it is here that capital gains can be expected to accrue in the normal course of events (as a result of corporate saving), whereas in the noncorporate sector capital gains come mainly from less normal causes such as general price inflation or relative price changes.

To get an idea of how taking capital gains provisions into account would alter the results of section VII, let us assume that corporate saving of a given amount tends to generate an equal amount of capital gains, and that no capital gains normally accrue in the noncorporate sector. Let us, moreover, assume that the special provisions regarding capital gains lead to a reduction in personal income-tax liabilities (as against a situation in which capital gains would be taxed as ordinary income) equal to half the amount of the gains themselves. This last assumption implies a "typical" marginal income-tax rate for corporate shareholders somewhere between 50 percent (what it would be if no capital gains tax were in fact paid on the gains generated in the corporate sector) and 75 percent (what it would be if the maximum long-term capital gains tax of 25 percent were actually paid on all the gains generated in the corporate sector). These assumptions are meant to be extreme rather than realistic, so that we may see how large the possible offsetting effects of the capital gains provisions may be.

In the period 1953–1955, from which the data used in section VII were taken, corporate savings averaged slightly less than $10 billion per year. The assumptions above imply a personal tax offset, due to the capital gains provisions, of about $5 billion per year. Thus, in analyzing corporation-tax-cum-capital-gains-provisions we would set up an example in which corporate capital paid $15 billion in special taxes and noncorporate capital nothing, as compared with the $20 billion and nothing, respectively, used in the example of section VII. The argument would run along precisely the same lines, and we would come to the conclusion that the $15 billion in special taxes was borne predominantly by capital.

Two other special tax provisions relating to income from capital deserve notice here. One consists of the property taxes levied by state and local governments. These averaged about $10 billion per year during 1953–1955, with about three-quarters of this amount falling upon residences and farms, and about one-quarter falling on commercial and industrial property.[18] The other provision is the exclusion from personal income subject to tax of the imputed net rent on owner-occupied dwellings. The official national income statistics of the United States estimate the value of this net rent to have been slightly over $5 billion per year in the period 1953–1955.[19] We may estimate that at least $1 billion of potential tax yield is foregone by the government as a result of the failure to tax imputed rent.

Taking all four special provisions together, we may estimate that noncorporate capital is liable in the first instance to no more than $6.5 billion ($7.5 billion of property taxes minus at least $1 billion of tax forgiveness on net rent) of special taxes. Corporate capital, on the other hand, is liable to at least $17.5 billion ($20 billion of corporation income tax plus $2.5 billion of property taxes minus at most $5 billion in personal tax offsets due to the capital gains provisions). Since there are roughly equal amounts of capital in each of the two sectors, it is clear that corporate capital is taxed substantially more heavily than noncorporate capital. To get at the incidence of the roughly

[18] United States Bureau of the Census, *Statistical Abstract of the United States*, 1960 (Washington: Government Printing Office, 1960), p. 417.
[19] United States Department of Commerce, *U.S. Income and Output* (Washington: Government Printing Office, 1958), p. 229.

$24 billion accruing to the government on account of all four special provisions taken together, we can break up the problem into two parts. The $6.5 billion paid by noncorporate capital together with the first $6.5 billion paid by corporate capital function in roughly the same way as would a flat-rate, across-the-board tax on all capital. So long as the total supply of capital is not sensitive to changes in the net rate of return in the relevant range, capital will bear the full burden of this $13 billion. The remaining $11 billion paid by corporate capital is not matched by any corresponding tax on noncorporate capital. This can be treated as a special levy on corporate capital, over and above the flat-rate levy on all capital represented by the $6.5 billion figure above. The analysis of the incidence of this special levy would follow exactly the same lines as my analysis in the main body of this paper of the incidence of the corporation income tax. This leads to the conclusion that the bulk of the $11 billion is probably also borne by capital.

To sum up this survey of the impact of other tax provisions relating to capital we can say that no more than a quarter of the burden of the corporation income tax is offset as a result of the capital gains provisions. The fact that property taxes strike noncorporate capital more heavily than corporate capital mitigates, to a limited extent, the tendency induced by the corporation tax for capital to be driven out of the corporate sector. This fact also, however, practically assures us that half or more (represented by the $13 billion figure above) of the total burden resulting from all four provisions taken together is solidly borne by capital. There remains a substantial amount of corporation tax (represented by the $11 billion figure above) that is neither offset by the capital gains provisions nor matched by the higher property taxes on noncorporate capital. It is to study the incidence of this residual amount of corporation tax that the methods outlined in this paper would apply, and I want to emphasize that the amount is substantial even when possible offsets are taken into account. In all likelihood, the proper figure would be greater than $11 billion, for I have consciously overstated the offsetting effect of the capital gains provisions and understated the amount by which the imputed rent provisions reduce the tax burden on noncorporate capital. Adjusting either of these in the appropriate direction would raise the amount of "special" taxation striking corporate capital above $11 billion. I would therefore claim that the analysis presented in the text is relevant not only for estimating the incidence of the corporation income tax itself, but also for understanding the effects of the combination of special provisions with regard to income from capital that prevails in the United States.

2. *Monopoly Elements in the Corporate Sector.* Several readers of the original draft of this paper have been disturbed by the assumption of competition in the corporate sector. Rather than attempt to argue for the applicability of this assumption, I propose here to outline how the analysis of the paper can be adjusted to accommodate the presence of monopoly elements in the corporate sector. I shall leave untouched as much of the basic model as possible: production functions, demand functions, the equalization of returns to labor and to capital in the two sectors all remain as before. Monopoly elements are

introduced by means of a "monopoly markup," M, which represents the percentage by which the price charged by the monopoly firm exceeds unit cost including the equilibrium return on capital.

It is important to realize at this point that I am not treating the entire corporate sector as one huge monopoly firm. If it were such, it could surely extract a huge monopoly markup from consumers in the economy, to say nothing of the gains it could achieve through the monopsony power that such a great aggregate could wield in the markets for labor and capital. M is kept down to modest size by the existence of many independent firms within the corporate sector; by the availability, elsewhere in the corporate sector, of reasonably close substitutes for the products of any one firm; and by the perennial threat of new entry into any field in which the monopoly markup is large. The strength of these forces, which determine what M will be, is not likely to be altered by the imposition or removal of a corporation income tax. Thus M is assumed to be the same in the pre-tax and the post-tax situations.

The effects of introducing monopoly elements can be seen quite clearly in a simple example similar to that of section II above. Suppose that consumers always spend 50 percent of their income on X, the corporate product, and 50 percent on Y, the noncorporate product, and that production of both X and Y is governed by Cobb-Douglas production functions in which the exponents applying to labor and capital are each one-half. Suppose, moreover, that the monopoly markup in X is 25 percent. These assumptions dictate that 50 percent of the national income is spent on Y, of which half goes to labor and half to capital; and that 50 percent of the national income is spent on X, of which 2/5 goes to labor, 2/5 to capital, and 1/5 is monopoly profit.

Imposing a corporation income tax of 50 percent on the profits of industry X (including the monopoly profits, of course), will not alter the fractions of the national income spent on X and Y, nor the shares earned by labor in X and Y, and by capital in Y. It will also not alter the gross earnings of capital in X, or the gross amount of monopoly profit. But net earnings on capital in industry X will be reduced by the tax from 20 percent to 10 percent of the national income, and net monopoly profits will be reduced by the tax from 10 percent to 5 percent of the national income. The distribution of capital between the two industries will change so as to equalize net returns. Whereas before the tax 4/9 of the capital stock was located in industry X, after the tax only 2/7 of the capital stock would be occupied there.

The only difference between this example and that of section II is that here the tax bites into monopoly profits as well as into the return on capital as such. It is no longer quite proper to say that the tax is exclusively borne by capital, but it is proper to say that the tax is exclusively borne by profits (in the broad sense of the term which includes interest, rent, return on equities, and monopoly profits).

It is also quite straightforward to incorporate the monopoly markup into the more general model of section V. Of the basic equations (7.1) through (7.9), only (7.7) is altered. It becomes:

(7.7')
$$dp_x = [f_L \, dp_L + f_k(dp_k + T)](1 + M).$$

In the reduction of the system to equations (7.10), (7.3″) and (7.4′), only (7.10) is altered. It becomes:

(7.10′)
$$Ef_k(1 + M)T = E[g_k - f_k(1 + M)]\, dp_k + f_L \frac{dL_x}{L_x} + f_k \frac{dK_x}{K_x}.$$

Finally, the solution for dp_k, given in equation (7.12), now becomes:

(7.12′)
$$dp_k = \frac{Ef_k(1 + M)\left(\dfrac{K_x}{K_y} - \dfrac{L_x}{L_y}\right) + S_x\left(f_L \dfrac{K_x}{K_y} + f_k \dfrac{L_x}{L_y}\right)}{E[g_k - f_k(1 + M)]\left(\dfrac{K_x}{K_y} - \dfrac{L_x}{L_y}\right) - S_y - S_x\left(f_L \dfrac{K_x}{K_y} + f_k \dfrac{L_x}{L_y}\right)} \cdot T.$$

Comparison of (7.12′) with (7.12) reveals that the determinants of the incidence of the corporation income tax play essentially the same roles in the "monopoly" case as they did in the competitive case treated in the text. And for plausible values of the key parameters and ratios, the magnitude of dp_k/T is not likely to be very sensitive to a change in the value of M from zero to something like 0.05 or 0.1 or 0.2.

A word should be said, however, about the interpretation of T in the monopoly case. Recall that the basic model treats T as a specific tax per unit of capital. If such a tax were in fact levied, it would not strike monopoly profits as such. If, however, a tax of a given percentage, t, is levied on all profits in the corporate sector, it will strike monopoly profits as well as the normal return to capital. Its total yield will be $t(MXp_x + K_x p_k')$, where the magnitudes in parentheses are measured in the post-tax situation, and p_k' represents the gross-of-tax price of capital in industry X. To fit such a tax into our model, it is convenient to view it as two different taxes: one, a direct tax taking a percentage t of all monopoly profits, and the other, a specific tax at the rate $T = tp_k'$ per unit of capital in industry X. The incidence of the first tax is purely upon monopoly profits. Equation (7.12′) gives us the answer to the incidence of the second tax.

We may summarize the results of this note as follows: the main effect of introducing monopoly elements in the corporate sector is that now a corporation income tax of the usual type will fall on monopoly profits as well as on the ordinary return to capital. The part that falls on monopoly profits will be borne by them. The part, however, that falls on the ordinary return to capital in the corporate sector will introduce a disequilibrium in the capital market. To restore a full equilibrium in factor and product markets, the distribution of factors of production between the corporate and noncorporate sectors, the relative quantities of the two classes of products, and the relative prices of factors and products will all typically change. The ultimate resting place of the part of the burden of the tax that is not directly borne by monopoly profits will be determined by a mechanism that differs only in minute detail from that which determines the incidence of the corporation income tax in the competitive case.

Chapter 8

Efficiency Effects
of Taxes on Income from Capital

NATURE OF THE EFFICIENCY COST OF TAXES ON
INCOME FROM CAPITAL

The effects of the taxation of income from capital can be conveniently classified into (a) those affecting the distribution of income, and (b) those affecting economic efficiency. The first class of effects concerns the question of incidence, about which no general consensus of professional opinion has yet emerged. Although this paper is concerned with the second class of effects, I should like to emphasize at the outset the distinction between the issues that arise in the two classes of problems. This can perhaps best be seen within the confines of the simple model developed in my paper, "The Incidence of the Corporation Income Tax" [1], where it was shown that, so long as the elasticity of substitution between labor and capital is the same in both the taxed sector X and the untaxed sector Y and so long as the elasticity of substitution between the final products of X and Y is the same as the elasticities of substitution between factors of production within the two sectors, then the burden of a tax on income from capital in sector X (the corporate sector) falls exclusively on capital as a factor of production [1, p. 230]. Thus, regardless of whether the three elasticities of substitution in question are all equal to -1, or all equal to -4, or all equal to $-1/4$, the answer to the incidence problem will be the same. However, the efficiency costs of the tax in question will vary greatly, according as the elasticities of substitution are large or small.

To demonstrate the measurement of efficiency costs graphically, Figure 8.1a represents the schedule of the rate of marginal productivity of capital (net of depreciation but gross of tax) in the corporate sector, while Figure 8.1b represents the corresponding schedule for the noncorporate sector. In the absence of any tax, the equilibrium rate of return would be $\bar{r}$, equal in both sectors. However, when a tax is imposed on the income from capital in sector X, the rate of return gross of tax rises there to r_g, while the rate of return net of tax falls in both industries to r_n. The quantity of capital employed in sector X falls from K_{x0} to K_{x1}, while the quantity of capital employed in sector Y

Reprinted from Arnold C. Harberger, "Efficiency Effects of Taxes on Income from Capital," in *Effects of Corporation Income Tax* by M. Krzyzaniak, ed., by permission of the Wayne State University Press.

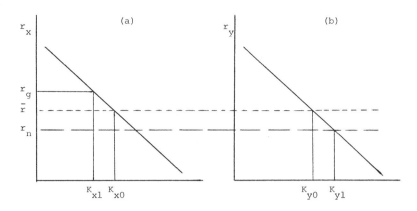

FIGURE 8.1

rises by an equal amount, from K_{y0} to K_{y1}. The economy thus transfers capital from high productivity applications in the taxed sector to low productivity applications in the untaxed sector, with a consequent loss in overall economic efficiency equal to the sum of the two shaded triangles in Figures 8.1a and 8.1b. That this loss equals $1/2 \, (r_g - r_n)(K_{x0} - K_{x1})$ can easily be seen once it is recognized that $(K_{y1} - K_{y0}) = (K_{x0} - K_{x1})$. In shorthand form the loss can be written as $-1/2 \, T_x \, \Delta K_x$, where $T_x (= [r_g - r_n])$ is the amount of tax per unit of capital employed in sector X, and ΔK_x is simply $(K_{x1} - K_{x0})$, the tax-induced change in employment of capital in industry X.

This measure of the loss in efficiency stemming from a tax on capital in industry X is an application of a more general formulation of the efficiency losses arising from a general set of differential taxes on income from capital in various industries in the economy. This more general formulation is

$$-1/2 \sum_i T_i \, \Delta K_i,$$

where T_i is the tax per unit of capital in the ith industry and ΔK_i is the change in the amount of capital in the ith industry arising as a result of the whole set of taxes $(T_1, T_2, \ldots, T_n)$. The derivation of this formula can be found in my paper, "The Measurement of Waste" [2], especially section IIIA.

Now the size of the loss depicted in Figures 8.1a and 8.1b obviously depends on the slopes of the marginal productivity schedules. For a given tax T_x, the size of the loss will be proportional to ΔK_x, and it can be shown, for the case in question, that ΔK_x will be proportional to the elasticity of substitution. When the three critical elasticities of substitution are all the same, the expression for ΔK_x is $\Delta K_x = S_x(K_x K_y/[K_x + K_y]) T_x$. Thus, for given initial conditions $(K_x K_y/[K_x + K_y])$, and for a given amount of tax per unit of capital in the corporate sector, the size of ΔK_x, and therefore the size of the efficiency cost of the tax, will be proportional to S_x. The general expression for efficiency cost in this class of cases is $-1/2 \, S_x(K_x K_y/[K_x + K_y]) T_x^2$. It will clearly be 4 times as great for an elasticity of substitution of -1 as for one of $-1/4$, and 16 times as great for an elasticity of -4 as for one of $-1/4$. Since the incidence of the corporation income tax is identical for the whole class of cases here treated, there can obviously be no close linkage between the effects of the tax in terms of incidence and its effects in terms of economic efficiency. The formulas for efficiency cost, $-1/2\ T_x\ \Delta K_x$ for a tax in capital in a single sector and

$$-1/2 \sum T_i\ \Delta K_i$$

for a set of differential taxes on capital in a variety of sectors, are valid regardless of the incidence of taxes in question. They depend only on three assumptions: (a) a fixed supply of capital to the economy as a whole; (b) equilibrium in the capital market, in the sense that net rates of return are equalized in all uses of capital; and (c) absence of distortions of types other than taxes on capital (or on the income from capital) in different uses. Even these assumptions can be relaxed, but only at a cost of complicating the formulas in question (see [2]).

DISTRIBUTION OF THE TAX BURDEN ON INCOME FROM CAPITAL BY MAJOR SECTORS

This section of my paper develops a rough measure for the efficiency costs of an assumed pattern of taxation on income from capital. The basic data are drawn from the U.S. economy in the period 1953–1959, but the results should be taken as merely suggesting the possible orders of magnitude for the efficiency costs involved, because the values of the relevant elasticities represent plausible assumptions rather than exact estimates. Table 8.1 presents the basic data.

TABLE 8.1

Taxes on Income from Capital, by Major Sectors (annual averages, 1953–1959, in millions of dollars)

	Total income from capital	Property and corp. income taxes	Other tax adjustments	Total tax on income from capital	Net income from capital
"Noncorporate" sector	$26,873	$6,639	$1,724	$8,363	$18,510
Agriculture	7,481	1,302	927[a]	2,229	5,252
Housing	18,429	5,140	797[b]	5,937	12,492
Crude oil and gas	963	197	—[c]	197	766
"Corporate" sector	52,399	22,907	9,945[d]	32,852	19,547
Total	79,272	29,546	11,669	41,215	38,057

[a] Fifteen percent of (1) minus (2). Assumes a typical effective tax rate of 15 percent on farm income.

[b] Assumes 70 percent of (1) generated by owner-occupied housing, on which income no personal tax liability is incurred. Assumes 30 percent of (1) and (2) generated by rental housing, with personal tax of 20 percent paid on the excess of income over property taxes. Thus (3) = 6 percent of the difference between (1) and (2).

[c] Assumes personal tax offsets on account of depletion; expensing and similar privileges counterbalance personal taxes on dividends and capital gains arising out of crude petroleum and natural gas operations.

[d] Twenty percent of (1)–(2). Assumes a 50 percent dividend distribution rate, and a "typical" effective tax rate of 40 percent on dividend income.

Source: For cols. 1 and 2, Leonard G. Rosenberg, "Taxation of Income from Capital by Non-Financial Industry Groups" (unpublished Ph.D. Dissertation, University of Chicago, 1963), Table 14.

The terms "Corporate" sector and "Noncorporate" sector are really mis-nomers: it might perhaps be better to call them the "Heavy-Tax" sector and the "Light-Tax" sector. Agriculture and Housing (i.e., the industry that provides residential housing services) are relatively lightly taxed and also predominantly unincorporated, but the Crude Oil and Gas Industry, although it is largely incorporated, is nonetheless favored by special tax treatment. Likewise, one finds within what I have called the "Corporate" sector a few industries (e.g., personal and business services and wholesale and retail trade) that are not overwhelmingly corporate in structure. These are, however, heavily enough taxed that, even without allowing for taxes on their dividends, approximately 30 percent of the income from capital generated by them is taken in the form of taxes. For the great bulk of the industries in the "Corporate" sector, corporation and property taxes together take 45 or more percent of the total income from capital. Thus no great damage is done by lumping together all nonfinancial industries other than Agriculture, Housing, and Crude Oil and Gas into a single "Corporate" sector for the purposes of this analysis.

The second aspect of Table 8.1 that requires emphasis is that, to my knowl-edge, it is the first attempt to approximate the total weight of taxation on the income from capital in various sectors. Leonard Rosenberg, from whose work the basic data in columns 1 and 2 are taken, has made a painstaking effort to allocate property tax receipts among industries. His complete results, which cover some fifty separate industries, will be made available in a forthcoming Brookings Institution volume. Here I have aggregated his data into the two broad sectors previously defined. In addition to Rosenberg's allocations, I have attempted to take into account the personal income tax burdens (or offsets) attaching to the income from capital generated in the sectors considered. In making the adjustments in column 3, I have tried consciously to err on the side of being conservative. Thus I have tried not to overstate the personal tax burden arising out of the corporate sector, both by assuming a comparatively low (for dividend recipients) effective tax rate on dividends and by neglecting capital gains taxes altogether. Capital gains themselves are indirectly taken into account by the fact that retained earnings are counted as part of the income from capital generated in the corporate sector, but no tax liability whatsoever is imputed to them. Similarly, I have attempted not to understate the personal tax liabilities nor to overstate the personal tax offsets arising in the noncorporate sector. For example, the effective tax rate on farm income is probably not as high as the 15 percent figure assumed in Table 8.1. Similarly, it is conservative, in the case of Oil and Gas, to assume that the personal tax payments due on the dividends, etc., arising out of Crude Oil and Gas operations are just barely counterbalanced by the personal tax offsets (depletion, expensing, etc.) generated by this set of activities — in fact the personal tax offsets prob-ably far outweigh the personal tax liabilities arising from Oil and Gas.

From columns 4 and 5 of Table 8.1, it can be seen that total taxes on income from capital in the "Noncorporate" sector amounted to $8.36 billion, on the average, in 1953–1959, or approximately 45 percent of the annual average net income from capital generated in this sector during the period. On the other hand, in the "Corporate" sector, total taxes on income from capital averaged some $32.8 billion per year during the same period, which amounted to some 168 percent of the annual average net income from capital here. (The figures are not so shocking when taxes are expressed as percentages of gross income — 31.0 percent for the noncorporate and 62.7 percent for the corporate sector — but convenience in applying the formula for efficiency cost dictates the use of taxes expressed as a percentage of net income.) The taxation of income from capital in the United States can therefore be very roughly approximated by a general tax of 45 percent on all net income from capital plus a surtax equal to some 85 percent of the net income from capital generated in the corporate sector ($1.45 \times 1.85 = 2.68$).

If we treat a general tax on all income from capital as neutral, as the analysis underlying the first section of this paper implies, we can approximate the efficiency costs of the existing tax system by measuring the efficiency losses associated with a tax of 85 percent of net-of-tax income from capital in the corporate sector. To do this let us take as our unit of capital that amount which generated, in the period considered, $1 of annual net income. Then $K_x = \$19,547$ million, and $K_y = \$18,510$ million. Applying these figures, plus $T_x = .85$ and $S_x = -1$, to the formula $-1/2\, S_x(K_x K_y/[K_x + K_y])\, T_x^2$, we obtain a measure of efficiency cost of the system of taxes on income from capital equal to approximately $3.5 billion per year. If, on the other hand, $S_x = -.5$, the efficiency cost of the same system would be around $1.75 billion per year.

To check on the plausibility of these results, we can examine the sorts of changes that would be implied by a shift to "neutral" taxation of income from capital, within the context of the model being used. Recall that in the first section, an alternative (equivalent) expression for the efficiency cost of a non-neutral tax on capital in a single sector was $-1/2\, T_x\, \Delta K_x$. Thus our results for an elasticity of substitution equal to unity imply a ΔK_x of approximately -8 billion units, while for an elasticity of substitution of $-.5$ they imply a ΔK_x of approximately -4 billion units. The alternative allocations of capital resources are summarized in Table 8.2.

TABLE 8.2
Alternative Allocations of Capital

	Corporate sector	Noncorporate sector
Existing tax system	19.5	18.5
Neutral taxes ($S_x = -1$)	27.5	10.5
Neutral taxes ($S_x = -.5$)	23.5	14.5

My own judgment is that the results for $S_x = -.5$ appear quite plausible while those for $S_x = -1$ appear rather extreme. Nonetheless, it should be recalled that there is some evidence in favor of the proposition that the elasticity of substitution between labor and capital, in manufacturing industry at least, may be in the neighborhood of unity (see Solow [4], and Minasian [3]).

Rather than elaborating the results of Table 8.2, which are built on the assumption that the elasticity of substitution (S_x) between labor and capital in the production of X, the elasticity of substitution (S_y) between labor and capital in the production of Y, and the elasticity of substitution (V) between the final products of X and Y are all the same. In this section, I attempt to derive a general expression for the efficiency cost of non-neutral taxation of income from capital in a two-sector model.

The basic model is that developed in my paper on incidence (8.1), and the notation used here will be the same as in that paper. The expression for $\Delta K_x / K_x$ obtained by solving that model is:

$$(8.1) \quad \frac{\Delta K_x}{K_x} = T \cdot \frac{-V r_y \left[g_k S_x \dfrac{L_x}{L_y} + f_k S_y \right] - S_x S_y f_L}{V r_y (g_k - f_k) \left(\dfrac{K_x}{K_y} - \dfrac{L_x}{L_y} \right) - S_y - S_x \left(\dfrac{f_L K_x}{K_y} + \dfrac{f_k L_x}{L_y} \right)}.$$

where

$V =$ elasticity of substitution between products X and Y (defined as a negative number).

$S_x =$ elasticity of substitution between labor and capital in X (also negative).

$S_y =$ elasticity of substitution between labor and capital in Y (also negative).

$r_y =$ share of national income spent on Y.

$V r_y =$ price elasticity of demand for X (defined as a negative number).

$f_k, f_L =$ shares of capital and labor, respectively, in the value added of industry X.

$g_k, g_L =$ shares of capital and labor, respectively, in the value added of industry Y.

$L_x, L_y =$ amounts of labor used in industries X and Y, respectively.

$K_x, K_y =$ amounts of capital used in industries X and Y, respectively.

The sign of ΔK_x is unambiguously negative.

The wages bill of what is here defined as the corporate sector averaged approximately $200 billion per year in the 1953–1959 period, while that for the noncorporate sector averaged about $20 billion per year. Thus we shall use 10 as the figure to be inserted for (L_x / L_y) in equation 8.1. The return to capital, net of tax, was about $20 billion on both sectors; thus we shall use 1 as the figure for (K_x / K_y) in equation 8.1. The gross-of-tax return to capital in the corporate sector was slightly over $50 billion out of a total value of product of $250 billion; hence we shall set $f_k = .2$ and $f_L = .8$. In the non-corporate sector the gross-of-tax return to capital was about $27 billion out of a total value of product of about $50 billion; hence we set $g_k = .54$. The non-corporate sector accounted for some $50 billion out of a total value of product of some $300 billion for the two sectors combined, so we set $r_y = .17$.

Substituting these values in equation 8.1 we obtain:

$$(8.2) \qquad \frac{\Delta K_x}{K_x} = T \frac{-.17V[5.4S_x + .2S_y] - .8S_xS_y}{-.52V - S_y - 2.8S_x},$$

and for $K_x = \$20$ billion, and $T = .85$ we have:

$$(8.3) \qquad \Delta K_x = \frac{-15.6S_xV - .58S_yV - 13.6S_xS_y}{-.52V - S_y - 2.8S_x}.$$

Using this expression, Table 8.3 was derived.

TABLE 8.3

Estimates of Efficiency Cost of Existing Taxes on Income from Capital in the United States

S_x (1)	S_y (2)	V (3)	ΔK_x (billions of units) (4)	$-1/2\, T_x\, \Delta K_x$ (billions) (5)
−1	−1	−1	−6.9	$2.9
−0.5	−0.5	−0.5	−3.5	1.5
−1	−1	−0.5	−5.3	2.3
−1	−0.5	−1	−5.9	2.5
−0.5	−1	−1	−5.2	2.2
−1	−0.5	−0.5	−4.2	1.8
−0.5	−1	−0.5	−4.1	1.7
−0.5	−0.5	−1	−4.8	2.0
−1	0	−1	−4.7	2.0
−0.5	0	−0.5	−2.4	1.0
−1	0	−0.5	−5.0	2.1
−0.5	0	−1	−3.9	1.7

Table 8.3 explores the plausible ranges for the elasticities of substitution in question. For S_x and V, the plausible range is from −.5 to −1. In the case of S_y, because of the importance of the Housing Industry and the Crude Oil and Gas Industry in this sector, the possibility of a zero elasticity of substitution is also explored. In both of these industries — recalling again that the Housing Industry refers to the provision of the services of housing rather than the construction of buildings — there is probably little possibility of substituting labor for capital. Nonetheless, an elasticity of zero is not very plausible for the noncorporate sector taken as a whole because of the demonstrated possibilities of substitution between labor and capital in agriculture.

The general idea emerging from Table 8.3 is that the present pattern of taxes on income from capital in the United States probably has reduced the capital stock in the corporate sector by between 1/6 and 1/3. According to these calculations, the present capital stock of $20 billion (measured in units of net income from capital) would lie between $23 billion and $27 billion if the income from capital were equally taxed in all uses. By the same calculations, the efficiency costs of the existing pattern of taxation lie somewhere between $1 billion and $3 billion, more probably between $1.5 billion to $2.5 billion per year.[1]

These are probably underestimates of the true efficiency costs involved because, in the process of aggregating industries into broad sectors, distortions induced by the tax system among the industries within each broad sector were ignored. Taking these distortions into account would surely add to the estimated efficiency costs. Moreover, the calculations assume that the taxes on income from capital do not introduce any substitution effect away from saving and toward consumption — that is, so far as the substitution effect alone is concerned, it is assumed that the elasticity of response of savings with respect to the net rate of return on capital is zero. If this substitution effect were not zero, there would be an additional efficiency cost stemming from the distortion of choices between consumption and saving. I do not wish to press this latter point too far, however, because in any taxation of the income from capital — even if such income in all industries and sectors is treated equally — some distortion of the consumption-savings choice is implicit. Only a consumption tax of the Kaldor type would avoid this distortion altogether. My main point in presenting the cost calculations of Table 8.3 is to show that we could substantially improve efficiency by simply rationalizing our existing pattern of taxes on income from capital so as to approach more equal tax treatment of the income generated by capital in the various industries and sectors of our economy.

REFERENCES

1. Harberger, A. C. "The Incidence of the Corporation Income Tax," *Journal of Political Economy*, LXX (June 1962), 215–240. [This volume, Chapter 7.]
2. ———. "The Measurement of Waste," *American Economic Review, Papers and Proceedings*, volume LIV (May 1964), pp. 58–76. [This volume, Chapter 3.]
3. Minasian, Jora R. "Elasticities of Substitution and Constant-Output Demand Curves for Labor," *Journal of Political Economy*, LXIX (June 1961), 261–270.
4. Solow, R. M. "Capital, Labor, and Income in Manufacturing," paper presented at National Bureau of Economic Research, Conference on Income and Wealth (April 1961).

[1] The results in Table 8.3 for the cases where $S_x = S_y = V$ are not the same as those emerging from the earlier calculations which were based on the algebraic solution of the system for this special case. The reason for the discrepancy is that the values chosen for (K_x/K_y), (L_x/L_y), f_k, etc., are derived from the tax situation rather than the pretax equilibrium. This is similar to the discrepancy one obtains in measuring demand elasticities over a very broad range, depending on whether one takes initial or terminal points as the basis on which percentage changes are computed.

VII

Chapter 9, which originally appeared in the *Journal of Political Economy* in 1967, is basically a critique of the empirical study of corporation tax incidence by Marian Krzyzaniak and Richard A. Musgrave (*The Shifting of the Corporation Income Tax* [Baltimore: Johns Hopkins Press, 1963]). This study attracted substantial attention among public finance experts and others upon its publication and subsequently. This attention has been sufficient to warrant including the critical analysis which I wrote jointly with John G. Cragg and Peter Mieszkowski. Further belaboring of my position on the Krzyzaniak-Musgrave study would be redundant in this introduction. Rather, with their permission, I have included as appendixes to Chapter 9 their published reply and our published rejoinder, which appeared in the *Journal of Political Economy* in 1970, so that readers will have access to the full debate.

Chapter 9

Empirical Evidence on the Incidence
of the Corporation Income Tax

John G. Cragg, Arnold C. Harberger, and Peter Mieszkowski

I

The incidence of the corporation income tax cannot easily be determined from empirical evidence for a variety of reasons. First, changes in the corporation tax rate are only one of many forces that operate secularly on the distribution of income; also operative are secular changes in the quality of labor and of capital equipment, secular changes in demand which may shift the pattern of production from relatively capital-intensive to relatively labor-intensive activities (or vice versa), secular changes in production functions themselves (reflecting, among other things, technical innovations which may be biased either in a labor-saving or capital-saving direction), plus, of course, non-tax-induced movements in labor supply and in the stock of capital in the economy. Second, and similarly, the cyclical movements of income distribution in the economy are the products of many forces other than corporation income tax changes — the complicated workings of the housing cycle, of inventory cycles, of investment and savings incentives for the economy as a whole, together with their interactions; plus the influences of monetary and fiscal policies (other than corporate tax rate changes themselves); plus the pressures and constraints imposed on the economy through its dealings with the rest of the world on both current and capital account — all these exert powerful influences on the short-term movements of both the level and distribution of income in the economy, above and beyond any impact that corporation income tax changes may themselves have. Third, and of serious importance in the case of the U.S. evidence, is the fact that movements in the corporation income tax rate

Reprinted with permission from John G. Cragg, Arnold C. Harberger, and Peter Mieszkowski, "Empirical Evidence on the Incidence of the Corporation Income Tax," *Journal of Political Economy* (December, 1967), pp. 811–822. Copyright © 1967 by The University of Chicago.

itself have come in stages, with the rate drifting upward in the 1930s, rising to a peak in the war years, falling off in the late forties, rising again in the Korean war years, and stabilizing finally during the late fifties. Given this type of movement, the different phases being associated with radically different types of economic environment, one runs the risk of mistaking association for causation in any empirical attempt to assess the impact of changes in the tax rate.

Undaunted by these difficulties, Krzyzaniak and Musgrave [1963] have made a bold attempt to extract empirical evidence on the incidence of the U.S. corporation income tax, using data from the years 1935–1942 and 1948–1959. Using widely accepted techniques of statistical analysis, they came to the striking conclusion that the corporation income tax is probably more than fully shifted — that is, that the owners of capital actually gain, in after-tax income, as a consequence of a rise in the corporation tax rate! Not only does this result run counter to most economists' judgments of plausibility, it also opens questions concerning the pricing behavior of corporations which have wide ramifications beyond the specific issue of corporation tax incidence. Indeed, it is certainly not far from the truth to say that if we accept the Krzyzaniak-Musgrave results at face value, we must also accept the task of rebuilding the foundations of the theory of the behavior of the firm.

The striking nature of the Krzyzaniak-Musgrave (hereafter K-M) results, and the profound implications that they would have if they were indeed true, have motivated us to devote this paper to a detailed examination of the procedures by which these results were reached, to an exploration of alternative statistical approaches to the same problem, and to a more careful study of the problem of interpreting the results of these exercises. It should be stated at the outset that we remain profoundly impressed by the difficulties outlined in the opening paragraph of this essay, which confront time-series analyses of the tax-incidence question. In particular, we do not in any way contend that our modifications of the K-M procedures and experiments adequately cope with the difficulties listed above. Our purpose, in fact, is the much more modest one of showing that making highly plausible and theoretically justified modifications in experiments of the K-M type leads to a reversal of the main conclusions apparently implied and that, therefore, at the very least, serious doubt is cast on the validity of K-M's conclusions.

II

Our principal objections to the K-M procedures stem from our conviction that there exists, in the time series for 1935–1942 and 1948–1959, a spurious correlation between the corporation tax rate and the gross-of-tax rate of return on corporate capital in manufacturing. Krzyzaniak and Musgrave take the latter variable, which they denominate Y_{gt}, as the dependent variable in their principal regression equations. Alongside other independent variables, they introduce two alternative tax variables to explain the variations in Y_{gt}. The first of these tax variables, which they call L_t, is the ratio of corporation income tax liabilities in year t to the total capital stock of the relevant group of corporations in the same year. The second tax variable, Z_t^*, is the effective tax rate in year t and is calculated by dividing total tax liabilities by the total profits of the relevant group of corporations in year t. On a few occasions, they introduce the nominal statutory tax rate, Z_t, as the tax variable, but they find no significant difference between the results obtained using Z_t and those emerging when Z_t^* is used. They group their experiments using L_t under what they call Model A, and those using Z_t^* or Z_t under Model B.

The observed simple correlations between Y_{gt} and $L_t (r^2 = .90)$ and between Y_{gt} and $Z_t^* (r^2 = .62)$ provide us with a convenient starting point for our discussion. We felt that it would be absurd to assert that these correlations represented causal relations proceeding from the tax variables to the profit rate. The five years of highest profit rates were 1941, 1942, 1948, 1950, and 1951. During these years, the average profit rate was 22.2 percent, while the average effective tax rate (Z^*) was 56.7 percent, and the average value of L_t was 11.7 percent. On the other side, the five years of lowest profits were 1935–1939, during which period profits averaged 7 percent of capital, the effective tax rate averaged 19.6 percent, and L_t averaged 1.1 percent. We simply cannot believe that the changes in either L_t or Z_t between these sets of years were the dominant causes of the variations in Y_{gt} between an average of 7 percent in the "low" years and an average of 22 percent in the "high" years. Other important forces were clearly at work influencing profit rates, these forces may, as in the cases of the World War II and Korean war years, have led to statutory tax rates being high under circumstances when profits were also high. There may indeed be a certain degree of causal connection running *from* profit rates *to* tax rates, in the sense that Congress would not be prone to raise corporation tax rates at times when profit rates themselves were low, or to make substantial cuts in tax rates at times when profit rates were very high.

We therefore approach the data with a strong suspicion that the observed simple correlations between tax variables and the profit rate do not reflect a strong causal connection in the tax-profits direction. We may now ask whether the additional explanatory variables which K-M introduced in their regressions may plausibly have represented the independent forces that caused profit rates to be low in the thirties, when tax rates were also low, and to be high in the war years, when tax rates were also high. The answer, we believe, is negative. These additional variables are:

$\Delta C_{t-1} =$ change from year $t - 2$ to year $t - 1$ in the ratio of consumption to GNP.

$V_{t-1} =$ ratio of inventories to sales in manufacturing in year $t - 1$.

$J_t =$ ratio of tax accruals (other than the corporation income tax) minus government transfers to GNP in year t.

$G_t =$ ratio of government purchases of goods and services to GNP in year t.

The failure of the additional variables introduced by K-M to correct adequately for the other forces indicated above is decisively shown in the following exercise. We take for granted, for the reasons indicated earlier, that the observed simple regression coefficient of Y_{gt} on L_t grossly exaggerates the effect of tax changes upon profit rates. This simple regression coefficient is 1.430; yet when all the additional variables are introduced, the partial regression co-efficient of Y_{gt} on L_t remains at approximately the same level.[1] Similarly, the simple regression coefficient of Y_{gt} on Z_t^* is 0.313, while after the addition of ΔC_{t-1}, V_{t-1}, J_t, and G_t as explanatory factors, the partial regression coefficient of Y_{gt} on Z^* is 0.481 (see below, regression [13.1]). Here the addition of the four extra variables has worked dramatically to exaggerate further what was already an exaggerated estimate of the power of the tax rate to influence profits. Obviously, K-M's additional variables have not corrected for the essentially spurious, noncausal connections between tax rates and profit rates which we pointed out in part I. Indeed, the additional variables they introduce make matters still worse!

We propose an attempt to correct for the deficiencies of the K-M model by introducing two additional variables: the employment rate $(= [1 - \text{the unemployment rate}] \times 100)$ and a dummy variable, W_t, for the mobilization and war years 1941, 1942, 1950, 1951, and 1952. The dummy variable is simply an attempt to correct for the fact that no one attributes the association between high profits and high taxes in these years to be principally due to the fact that tax rates were high; both profits and taxes were high due to the pressures of the mobilization and/or war situations. The employment rate, E_t, is introduced to provide a plausible explanation for the low profit rates of the thirties and of the dips in the profit rate during the recession years 1949, 1954, and 1958. Again, the low levels of profit rates achieved in these years cannot plausibly have been caused by changes in the tax rate or in the other explanatory variables introduced by K-M.

III

The use of a cyclical variable with the aim of correcting for some of the bias implicit in K-M's procedures was attempted by Richard Slitor [1966] and Richard Goode [1966] in papers criticizing K-M's work. In their reply to this criticism, K-M [1966] argue (a) that the cyclical variable (in Slitor's and Goode's case, the ratio of actual to potential GNP, and, in our case, the employment rate) "is itself a function of the corporate income tax. Hence if [such a] variable is included, the coefficient of the tax variable does not represent the isolated tax effect upon the rate of return, part of this effect being hidden in the coefficient of the [cyclical] variable" (p. 248). They also argue (b) that, when such a variable is included in the estimating equation for Y_{gt}, estimation by least squares yields biased and inconsistent coefficients (p. 249).

In this section, we propose to cope explicitly with both of these objections, in the context of a simplified model which we believe captures all the relevant

[1] K-M do not use direct least squares in obtaining the partial regression coefficient of Y_{gt} on L_t; in an attempt to correct for the positive bias implicit in the fact that $L_t = Y_{gt} \cdot Z_t^*$, they use Z_t^* as an instrumental variable for L_t; that is, where a direct application of least-squares regression would require taking moments with L_t, they instead take moments with Z_t^*. The simple regression coefficient of Y_{gt} on L_t, using Z^* as an instrumental variable for L_t, is $(M_{Z^*Y}/M_{Z^*L}) = 1.304$. When the additional variables are introduced, and Z_t^* is again used as an instrument for L_t, the resulting partial regression coefficient is 1.511 (see K-M, 1963, pp. 44–45, Table 6-1, regression 2). Thus, in this case, by including the additional variables, K-M further exaggerate what was already an implausibly high causal connection between tax rates and profit rates.

aspects of the problem. For simplicity, we eliminate ΔC_{t-1}, V_{t-1}, J_t, and G_t from consideration, and thus reduce the basic K-M regression to

(9.1) $$Y_{gt} = a_0 + a_1 L_t + U_t.$$

K-M object to expanding this equation to

(9.2) $$Y_{gt} = f_0 + f_1 L_t + f_2 E_t + V_t,$$

for the reasons given above. We do not assert that E_t is a truly exogenous variable, nor do we deny that f_2 may capture some of the effect upon Y_{gt} of movements in L_t. We thus accept from the outset the general framework adopted by K-M in their reply to Slitor and Goode.

We justify the use of E_t in (9.2) as a proxy for exogenous, cyclical forces that K-M have failed to capture in their regression. We thus postulate a true reduced-form equation for Y_{gt}:

(9.3) $$Y_{gt} = b_0 + b_1 L_t + b_2 R_t + \omega_t.$$

Here R_t is defined as a truly exogenous (though possibly unobservable) variable, summarizing the influences of the exogenous forces of a cyclical nature which are not accounted for in the K-M regressions. As a truly exogenous variable, it is assumed to be uncorrelated with the residuals of any of the true reduced-form equations.

We first will demonstrate the source of bias in K-M's results. In our view, (9.1) is the wrong equation to estimate; in principle we should estimate (9.3), even though in practice, lacking a time series for R_t, we may not be able to do this. When K-M estimate (9.1) instead of (9.3), however, they introduce a serious bias into their results. We can represent this bias algebraically by taking moments of equation (9.1) with L_t:

(9.4) $$M_{YL} = a_1 M_{LL} + M_{UL}.$$

Krzyzaniak and Musgrave recognize that an estimate derived from (9.4) will contain a bias because a rise in U_t will cause profits to be higher and therefore raise L_t, the tax yield divided by the capital stock. They therefore adopt the procedure of using Z_t^*, the effective tax rate, as an instrumental variable for L_t in the estimation process. This leads to the following equation:

(9.5) $$M_{YZ^*} = a_1 M_{LZ^*} + M_{UZ^*},$$

where the estimate is based on the assumption that M_{UZ^*} is zero.

But if (9.3) is the true reduced-form equation for Y_{gt}, then the U of equation (9.1) is equal to $b_2 R_t + \omega_t$, and $M_{UZ^*} = b_2 M_{RZ^*}$, which cannot be presumed to be zero, given the high correlation of Z_t^* with cyclically sensitive variables. The expected bias in K-M's estimate a_1 of the true reduced-form coefficient of L_t, assuming $M_{Z^*\omega} = M_{R\omega} = 0$, is equal to

(9.6) $$(a_1 - b_1) = \frac{M_{YZ^*}}{M_{LZ^*}} - b_1 = \frac{b_2 M_{RZ^*}}{M_{LZ^*}}.$$

This bias is positive and likely to be significant in magnitude, since the true influence of R_t on profit rates is surely strong and since Z_t^* is so highly positively correlated with cyclical variables in the period of their sample.

We now proceed to explore, in an analogous fashion, the biases involved in the use of (9.2) as an equation for estimating b_1. To do this we must postulate a true reduced-form equation for E_t, which we have recognized to be an endogenous variable of the system. Let this equation be:[2]

$$(9.7) \qquad E_t = c_0 + c_1 L_t + c_2 R_t + v_t.$$

We solve this equation for the unobservable R_t, expressing it in terms of the observable variables E_t and L_t:

$$(9.8) \qquad R_t = \frac{-c_0}{c_2} - \frac{c_1}{c_2} L_t + \frac{E_t}{c_2} - \frac{v_t}{c_2}.$$

Substituting (9.8) into (9.3) we find

$$(9.9) \qquad Y_{gt} = \left(b_0 - \frac{b_2 c_0}{c_2}\right) + \left(b_1 - \frac{b_2 c_1}{c_2}\right) L_t + \frac{b_2}{c_2} E_t + \left(\omega_t - \frac{b_2}{c_2} v_t\right).$$

This equation is exactly of the form of (9.2), with the cyclical variable E_t as an added explanatory factor serving as a proxy for the unobservable R. Equation (9.2) can be rewritten, keeping ω_t and v_t as distinct components of V_t, as:

$$(9.2') \qquad Y_{gt} = f_0 + f_1 L_t + f_2 E_t + \omega_t - f_2 v_t.$$

Augmented to include the other exogeneous variables used by K-M, plus our additional exogenous variable W_t, this is the regression equation we propose to estimate.

Under the assumptions of this section, the instrumental-variables estimate of f_1 will be a biased estimate of b_1 — the coefficient whose value we really are seeking — for two reasons which correspond precisely to K-M's two objections to Slitor and Goode. In the first place, there is a specification bias, in that f_1 is equal not to b_1 but to $b_1 - (b_2 c_1/c_2)$. The term $-b_2 c_1/c_2$ measures the indirect effect of changes in the tax variable L_t upon Y_{gt}, which is "captured" by E_t when it is introduced, side by side with L_t, as an explanatory variable in the regression. But let us examine the presumptive sign of the adjustment: b_2, measuring the influence of R_t on Y_{gt}, is presumably positive; so also is c_2, measuring the influence of R_t on E_t. But c_1, reflecting the causal impact of L_t on E_t, is surely to be presumed negative. Hence the coefficient for f_1, which

---

[2] If R is a true scalar variable entering both (9.3) and (9.7), (9.7) can be interpreted as the true reduced-form equation for E, and we will so interpret it in the text. If R is considered as reflecting the influences of a series of truly exogenous variables X_i upon Y_{gt}, it will be of the general form $R = \Sigma \beta_i X_i$, where the β_i are weights reflecting the relative influence of the individual X_i upon Y_{gt}. The true reduced-form equation for E_t would presumably give different weights to the individual X_i, which might be summarized in a scalar variable Q $(= \Sigma \gamma_i X_i)$. Equation (9.7) in this case is obtained by substituting the regression of Q on R $(Q = g + hR + \varepsilon)$ for Q in the true reduced form for E. As long as the two cyclical variables Q and R are positively correlated $(h > 0)$, as is overwhelmingly likely, all relevant properties of (9.7) remain; the presumed signs of c_1 and c_2 are still negative and positive, respectively, and the correlation between R_t and v_t still has an expected value of zero.

our expression attempts to estimate, is larger in magnitude than b_1, on which our interest centers.

This result can be seen intuitively. If taxes are raised while other exogenous variables, including R, are held constant, Y_{gt} will tend to rise because of the direct effect of taxes on gross rates of return, but will tend to fall because of the dampening effect of higher taxes on total effective demand. The reduced-form coefficient b_1 reflects the net outcome of these two effects. If, on the other hand, we raise taxes while holding employment constant, we must presume that other exogenous forces have operated to compensate the reduction in effective demand which the tax rise would otherwise entail, so f_1 reflects just the first of the two effects contained in b_1.

The second source of error is that the K-M regression techniques applied to (9.2') will produce a biased estimate of f_1. This results from the fact that E_t is, as shown by the reduced-form equation (9.7), a direct function of v_t, hence necessarily positively correlated with it as long as M_{Lv} and M_{Rv} are zero. Since ω_t does not appear in the reduced form for E_t, it will not be correlated with E_t except through such correlation as may exist between ω_t and v_t. We shall assume for the moment that $r_{\omega v}$ is zero. We shall also retain the standard assumption that v_t and ω_t are uncorrelated with the exogenous variables $Z_t{}^*$ and R_t. Employing these assumptions, and taking moments of (9.2') with $Z_t{}^*$ and E_t, we obtain:

$$(9.10) \qquad \begin{aligned} M_{YZ^*} &= f_1 M_{LZ^*} + f_2 M_{EZ^*}; \\ M_{YE} &= f_1 M_{EL} + f_2 M_{EE} - f_2 M_{vE}. \end{aligned}$$

Solution of these equations for f_1 yields:

$$(9.11) \qquad f_1 = \frac{\begin{vmatrix} M_{YZ^*} & M_{EZ^*} \\ M_{YE} & M_{EE} \end{vmatrix}}{\begin{vmatrix} M_{LZ^*} & M_{EZ^*} \\ M_{EL} & M_{EE} \end{vmatrix}} + \frac{\begin{vmatrix} 0 & M_{EZ^*} \\ f_2 M_{vE} & M_{EE} \end{vmatrix}}{\begin{vmatrix} M_{LZ^*} & M_{EZ^*} \\ M_{EL} & M_{EE} \end{vmatrix}},$$

or

$$(9.11') \qquad f_1 = \hat{f}_1 - \frac{f_2 M_{vE} M_{EZ^*}}{M_{LZ^*} M_{EE} - M_{EL} M_{EZ^*}}.$$

Here $\hat{f}_1$ is the standard instrumental-variables estimate of f_1; its expected value exceeds the true value of f_1 by $f_2 M_{vE} M_{EZ^*}/(M_{LZ^*} M_{EE} - M_{EL} M_{EZ^*})$.

The presumed sign of this bias is positive, f_2 and M_{vE} having presumptively positive signs, and M_{EZ^*} and the denominator having positive signs for the sample data.

Thus we have shown that both of the biases referred to by K-M in their reply to Slitor and Goode are likely to be positive, an instrumental-variables estimate of f_1 tending to overestimate its true value, and f_1 itself exceeding b_1 because of the specification error involved in using E_t as a proxy for R_t. We therefore proceed to estimate equations similar to those estimated by K-M, but including E_t as a proxy for exogenous cyclical forces, confident that the expected biases in the coefficient of L_t are both positive and hence that the amount of shifting of the corporation income tax is likely to be overstated. Needless to say, the whole analysis of this section applies equally well to K-M's Model B, where Z_t or Z_t^* is the tax variable, as it does to Model A, in which L_t is the tax variable.[3]

In a similar vein, one can easily adjust the analysis of the text to accommodate the presence of additional exogenous variables in the overall model to be estimated. Equation (9.11) states that f_1 is equal to $\hat{f}_1$, the partial regression coefficient of Y on L, given E, plus a bias term which is equal to f_2 times the partial regression of v on L, given E. In both cases, the regressions in question use Z^* as the instrumental variable for L. When the basic equation (9.1) is expanded to include ΔC_{t-1}, V_{t-1}, J_t, and G_t, $\hat{f}_1$ in (9.1) should be interpreted as the partial regression coefficient of Y on L, given E_t, ΔC_{t-1}, V_{t-1}, J_t, and G_t, and the bias term becomes f_2 times the partial regression coefficient of v on L, given these same variables. This partial regression is, of course, more likely to have the presumptive sign than the one treated in the text because it measures the relationships between $f_2 v$ and L, holding other potentially relevant exogenous variables constant.

IV

Krzyzaniak and Musgrave present the following estimates (1963, Table 6–1, regression 2) for the regression of Y_{gt} on the set of independent variables listed above, using Z_t^* as an instrumental variable.

$$(9.12.1) \qquad Y_{gt} = .2577 + .3013 \Delta C_{t-1} - .4228 V_{t-1} - .7721 J_t$$
$$- .1083 G_t + 1.5110 L_t \quad (r^2 = .96).$$

Following their procedures and using their data but adding E_t and W_t as

---

[3] If we relax the assumption of zero correlation between ω and v, (9.11[1]) would read:

$$f_1 = f_1 + M_{EZ^*}[(M_{\omega v} - f_2 M_{vE})/(M_{LZ^*} \cdot M_{EE} - M_{EL} M_{EZ^*})].$$

The sign of the bias in f_1 will be positive in all cases where $M_{\omega v}$ is negative, and as long as $f_2 M_{vE} > M_{\omega v}$ when the latter is positive. This last condition can be written $f_2 s_v s_E r_{vE} > s_\omega s_v r_{v\omega}$, and this can in turn be transformed into a form easier to interpret:

$$\frac{\bar{E} f_2}{\bar{Y}} \frac{s_E}{\bar{E}} r_{vE} > \frac{s_\omega}{\bar{Y}} r_{v\omega}.$$

$\bar{E} f_2 / \bar{Y}$ is the elasticity of the profit rate with respect to the employment rate, $s_E / \bar{E}$ is the coefficient of variation of the employment rate, and $s_\omega / \bar{Y}$ is the standard error of the residual of the reduced form explaining variations in Y, expressed as a percentage of $\bar{Y}$. There is a strong presumption that this condition will be met. The elasticity of profits with respect to employment is well over unity; $s_E / \bar{E}$ is the coefficient of variation of the employment rate itself, while $s_\omega / \bar{Y}$ is the coefficient of variation of Y after movements explained by L and R have been removed; and r_{Ev} is likely to be larger than $r_{v\omega}$, since the relation between v and E is a directly functional one, while we have no reason to presume even the sign of the correlation between v and ω, and certainly none to suppose its magnitude to be large. For all these reasons, we expect $\hat{f}_1 > f_1$ even when $M_{v\omega}$ is positive. And even under the remote possibility that $\hat{f}_1 < f_1$, it is extremely unlikely that this would outweigh the specification bias that makes $\hat{f}_1 > b_1$. We thus can remain virtually certain that the expected value of f_1 exceeds b_1, even when positive correlation between ω and v is allowed for.

independent variables, we obtain:

(9.12.2)
$$Y_{gt} = -.3097 + .0774\Delta C_{t-1} + .1938V_{t-1} - 1.2038J_t$$
$$(.1517) \quad (.1269) \qquad (.1828) \qquad (.1848)$$
$$- .2102G_t + 1.024L_t + .6178E_t \quad (r^2 = .99);$$
$$(.0691) \qquad (.1895) \qquad (.1669)$$

(9.12.3)
$$Y_{gt} = -.4198 + .2631\Delta C_{t-1} + .1301V_{t-1} - 1.2814J_t$$
$$(.2545) \quad (.2330) \qquad (.2398) \qquad (.2753)$$
$$- .1019G_t + .6002L_t + .7693E_t + .0258W_t \quad (r^2 = .98).$$
$$(.1524) \qquad (.6410) \qquad (.3064) \qquad (.0245)$$

The coefficient of L_t falls progressively as we add E_t and W_t to the list of explanatory variables, becoming statistically insignificantly different from zero when both E_t and W_t are present. (The number in parentheses below each coefficient gives its standard error of estimate.) This is precisely what one would expect to happen if L_t in (9.12.1) were acting as a proxy for the forces represented by E_t and W_t. That its coefficient should decline when the additional variables are added, if it were originally acting as a proxy for them, is obvious. That the standard error of the coefficient of L_t should rise is also probable, once it is recognized that if E_t and W_t are indeed capturing some of the same forces that were imbedded in L_t, they will be to that extent collinear with L_t, a situation likely to raise the standard error of the coefficient of L_t as compared with the case in which E_t and W_t are not present in the regression.

Comparable results emerge when we apply similar adjustments to the K-M procedure for Model B. Equation (9.13.1) is a regression of the K-M type, using $Z_t{}^*$ as the tax variable. Equations (9.13.2) and (9.13.3) show how the coefficients are altered by the addition of E_t and W_t as explanatory variables.

(9.13.1)
$$Y_{gt} = .386 + .291\Delta C_{t-1} - .494V_{t-1} - 1.971J_t - .220G_t$$
$$(.098) \quad (.347) \qquad (.386) \qquad (.400) \quad (.212)$$
$$+ .481Z_t{}^* \quad (r^2 = .87);$$
$$(.104)$$

(9.13.2)
$$Y_{gt} = -.498 + .015\Delta C_{t-1} + .350V_{t-1} - 2.128J_t$$
$$(.304) \quad (.291) \qquad (.416) \qquad (.322)$$
$$- .259G_t + .273Z_t{}^* + .908E_t \quad (r^2 = .92);$$
$$(.170) \qquad (.108) \qquad (.302)$$

(9.13.3)
$$Y_{gt} = -.537 + .358\Delta C_{t-1} + .134V_{t-1} - 1.577J_t$$
$$(.246) \quad (.265) \qquad (.345) \qquad (.326)$$
$$- .050G_t + .073Z_t{}^* + .934E_t + .041W_t \quad (r^2 = .95).$$
$$(.156) \qquad (.113) \qquad (.244) \qquad (.015)$$

Here the reduction in the coefficient of $Z_t{}^*$ is even more dramatic, as one moves from (9.13.1) to (9.13.2) and (9.13.3), than was the case with that of L_t in equations (9.12.1)–(9.12.3).

We have performed numerous experiments similar to those presented above, using alternative forms of the basic equations and alternative definitions of some of the variables. The results uniformly confirm the conclusions derived above, that the tax rate has not had a significant influence on before-tax rates of profit. This is perhaps most dramatically illustrated by regression (9.14), in which only E_t, W_t, and $Z_t{}^*$ appear as explanatory variables.

$$(9.14) \quad Y_{gt} = -.584 + .819E_t + .073W_t - .101Z_t{}^* \quad (r^2 = .84).$$
$$\phantom{(9.14) \quad Y_{gt} = } (.195) \quad (.255) \quad (.017) \quad (.114)$$

Not only is the tax rate statistically insignificant in explaining variations in gross-of-tax profit rates, once E_t and W_t are introduced, but the sign of its (insignificant) effect is negative!

It should be noted, moreover, as the analysis of part III shows, that our estimates of the coefficients of L_t and $Z_t{}^*$ are, for two distinct reasons, likely to be biased in a positive direction.

We turn now to the interpretation of the coefficients of L_t and $Z_t{}^*$ in regressions of the types presented above. We believe that the forces working toward equilibrium in the capital market will tend to produce responses in the rate of return to capital in noncorporate forms which are similar to those of the rate of return to corporate capital. Hence if, as a consequence of a change ΔZ in the corporation tax rate, the gross-of-tax yield Y_{gt} on corporate capital remains unchanged, the net-of-tax yield will fall by $Y_{gt} \Delta Z$. Although initially there may be no effect on the yields of noncorporate investments, there will now be a tendency for investors to prefer these alternative forms of capital assets. Once sufficient time has elapsed to permit equilibrium in the capital market to be restored, it is to be presumed that the net rate of return will have experienced similar changes in all uses of capital. If, then, we interpret the coefficients of regressions (9.12.3), (9.13.3), and (9.14) to reflect comparisons in which the capital market has approached equilibrium, we must consider what they mean in terms of the incidence of the corporation tax.

Obviously, if the net yield of capital falls by $Y_{gt} \Delta Z$, in both corporate and noncorporate uses, as a consequence of the tax change ΔZ, capital will have borne more than the full burden of the tax change. Capital in both corporate and noncorporate uses will have lost the percentage ΔZ of its initial income, while the government will have gained only ΔZ times the amount of income accruing to corporate capital. Since in the United States approximately half of the total income from capital is generated outside the corporate sector (principally in farming and residential housing), a coefficient of zero for either L_t or $Z_t{}^*$ would imply, under the assumption of capital market equilibrium, that capital was bearing approximately twice the burden of the tax change. A coefficient of unity for L_t, on the other hand, would imply that the net-of-tax return on capital was unchanged, the tax presumably being reflected in a rise in the prices of the products of the corporate sector. This situation can be interpreted as a case of consumers bearing the burden of the tax or, what amounts to the same thing, as a case in which labor and capital bear the tax in proportion to their contributions to the national income. The case of capital just bearing the full burden of the tax occurs when the net-of-tax rate of return falls by approximately $.5 \Delta L$ with a reduction of this amount in the rate of return to all capital (corporate plus noncorporate) adding up to the total burden of the tax as long as the total net income from capital is twice the amount of such income generated in the corporate sector. In order for this result to occur, the gross-of-tax rate of return to corporate capital must rise by .5 ΔL; hence a coefficient of .5 for L_t implies that capital bears approximately the full burden of the tax. This is almost precisely the figure emerging from our regression (9.12.3).

To interpret the coefficient of Z_t^* in equation (9.13.3) above, let us first note that this coefficient implies that an increase of 10 percentage points in the rate of tax will lead to an increase of .0073 in Y_{gt}. If Y_{gt} were initially 15 percent (approximately the average figure for the K-M sample), it would rise to 15.73 percent, and the net rate of return would fall by .84 percentage points, reflecting the rise of 0.73 percentage points in Y_{gt} minus the extra tax collection of 1.573 percentage points. This fall in the net rate of return is larger than the rise in the gross rate of return, reflecting that capital in this case is apparently bearing somewhat more than the full burden of the tax. The full burden, as indicated above, would tend to be borne by capital if the fall in the net rate of return to capital were about equal to the rise in the gross rate of return to corporate capital.

We cannot be certain that the assumption of a well-functioning capital market is the appropriate one for interpreting our results. However, it is important to point out that a regression analysis of this type in effect compares the *levels* of the variables at each observation with those at every other observation in the sample; it does not compare year-to-year changes. Add to this the fact that the tax rate has moved generally upward through the period rather than, for example, oscillating around a flat trend line. We feel reasonably confident that by the 1950s the economy had adjusted to the fact of high corporation tax rates and that in the 1930s it had pretty well adjusted to the relatively lower rates then prevailing. If this is the case, the bulk of the variance being explained in our regressions was between positions reasonably close to long-run equilibrium, and the assumption that the capital market did function to reflect in the noncorporate rate of return the influence of tax changes is closer to being correct than the alternative assumption of no linkage between changes in the corporation tax rate and the rate of return on capital outside the corporate sector. We therefore would draw the conclusion from regressions (9.12.3) and (9.13.3) that capital probably bears close to the full burden of the corporation income tax, and possibly somewhat more than the full burden.

V

To summarize, we have shown that the K-M estimates of the effect of changes in the corporation income tax rate upon the gross rate of return to capital in the corporate sector are subject to a strong positive bias. The gross rate of return has been high, during the period they examine, in times of prosperity and of mobilization or war; it has been low in times of depression or recession. Coincidentally the corporation tax rate was at its lowest levels during the depression years, reached its peaks during World War II and the Korean war, and remained at relatively high levels during the prosperous years of the late fifties. By failing to introduce variables which adequately capture the influence of cyclical and wartime phenomena, K-M have produced estimates in which a good part of the effects of these phenomena upon profit rates is attributed to changes in the corporation income tax rate.

When we introduce a cyclical variable — the employment rate — and a wartime dummy variable as added explanatory variables in the K-M regressions, the estimated effect of changes in the tax rate upon the profit rate falls dramatically. Instead of implying the more than 100 percent shifting of the corporation tax which K-M found, our estimates imply that capital bears approximately 100 percent of the burden of the tax.

In part III we examine in detail K-M's objections to the use of the employment rate (which we recognize to be an endogenous variable of a broader system) as a proxy for the exogenous forces producing cyclical movements. We show there that our estimates are subject to two types of bias, both of which lead to an overstatement of the effect of tax rate changes on the gross profit rate. The fact that these biases are positive only strengthens our argument that the K-M estimates grossly overstate the true effects of tax changes on profits; and if the biases in our estimates are important in magnitude, it suggests that capital may indeed be bearing more than the full burden of the corporation income tax.

We remain impressed by the difficulties, brought out in the introduction to this essay, of making inferences concerning tax incidence from time-series data. In particular, we note that we have not undertaken the task of exploring alternative formal models which could conceivably improve upon the basic K-M framework. We have instead operated within that framework, modifying it only to the extent of incorporating the cyclical and wartime variables. Within this focus, we feel that we have shown unequivocally that the K-M procedure, corrected so as to reduce the bias stemming from the proxy role of their tax variables, does not lead to their conclusion of more than 100 percent shifting of the corporation income tax but, rather, to the conclusion that capital bears approximately the full burden of that tax.

It is noteworthy, however, that our results suggest that the incidence of the corporation income tax lies within the range obtained by Harberger [1962], using an entirely different approach. He developed a general equilibrium model of two sectors (corporate and noncorporate), in which the corporation income tax was viewed as a tax on the use of capital in the corporate sector. In that model, the incidence of the tax was shown to depend critically on three key parameters: the elasticities of substitution (a) between the products of the two sectors, (b) between labor and capital in the production of the corporate sector's product, and (c) between these same two factors in the production of the noncorporate sector's product. Then, applying a range of plausible values for these three elasticities, Harberger estimated that the plausible range for capital's share of the total burden of the corporation income tax lies between 90 and 120 percent.

Thus, to the extent that one is willing to accept the general framework set out by K-M and to run the risks of time-series analyses, one might construe the present paper as providing an independent confirmation of Harberger's earlier results. We are too skeptical to make such a claim, however, and rest our case with the assertion that K-M's conclusions are not valid.

REFERENCES

Goode, Richard. "Rates of Return, Income Shares, and Corporate Tax Incidence," in M. Krzyzaniak (ed.), *Effects of Corporation Income Tax*. Detroit: Wayne State Univ. Press, 1966.

Harberger, Arnold C. "The Incidence of the Corporation Income Tax," *J.P.E.*, Vol. LXX (June 1962). [This volume, Chapter 7.]

Krzyzaniak, Marian (ed.). *Effects of Corporation Income Tax*. Detroit: Wayne State Univ. Press, 1966.

Krzyzaniak, Marian, and Richard A. Musgrave. *The Shifting of the Corporation Income Tax*. Baltimore: Johns Hopkins Press, 1963.

——. "Discussion," in M. Krzyzaniak (ed.), *Effects of Corporation Income Tax*. Detroit: Wayne State Univ. Press, 1966.

Slitor, Richard. "Corporate Tax Incidence: Economic Adjustments to Differentials under a Two-Tier Tax Structure," in M. Krzyzaniak (ed.), *Effects of Corporation Income Tax*. Detroit: Wayne State Univ. Press, 1966.

Appendix I   Corporation Tax Shifting: A Response

Marian Krzyzaniak and Richard A. Musgrave

We welcome the growing interest in empirical approaches to corporation tax incidence, of which the recent paper by Cragg, Harberger, and Mieszkowski ([1967]; referred to below as C-H-M) is the latest evidence. In evaluating our earlier results (Krzyzaniak and Musgrave [1963]), the authors claim to have shown "unequivocally that the Krzyzaniak-Musgrave procedure, corrected so as to reduce the bias stemming from the proxy role of their tax variables, does not lead to their conclusion of more than 100 percent shifting of the corporation income tax, but rather to the conclusion [previously arrived at by Harberger] that capital bears approximately the full burden of the tax" (see Cragg, Harberger, and Mieszkowski [1967], p. 821). We do not think that their case sustains this claim.

INTRODUCTION OF EMPLOYMENT VARIABLE

C-H-M hold that our lagged nontax variables do not sufficiently reflect the current state of economic pressure, and that our current tax-rate variable acts as a proxy for such pressure. The degree of shifting is thus believed to be overstated, and to remedy this, C-H-M introduce a current-pressure variable, defined as the employment rate E_t. Following previous comments by Goode [1966] and Slitor [1966], introduction of such a variable reduces the shifting coefficient for our L_t formulation, but (see C-H-M, equation [9.12.2]) the coefficient remains significant and still sustains the hypothesis of full shifting.

However, C-H-M hold that this result still leaves a significant upward bias, and offer a proof for this. We do not find their proof of upward bias conclusive,[1]

---

[1] The first step in C-H-M's argument is to show that a_1 in their equation (9.1) is biased upward. According to their equation (9.6), the bias equals $(a_1 - b_1) = b_2 M_{RZ^*}/M_{LZ^*}$. Granting this formulation, we do not follow the conclusion that b_2 must be positive. It would have been helpful to show that b_2 is estimated from

$$b_2 = \frac{M_{LZ^*}M_{YR} - M_{YZ^*}M_{LR}}{M_{LZ^*}M_{RR} - M_{RZ^*}M_{LR}} = \frac{\begin{vmatrix} M_{LZ^*} & M_{LR} \\ M_{YZ^*} & M_{YR} \end{vmatrix}}{\begin{vmatrix} M_{LZ^*} & M_{LR} \\ M_{RZ^*} & M_{RR} \end{vmatrix}}.$$

Granting C-H-M's assumption that all the moments are positive, it does not follow that b_2 must be positive as well. It may be negative, depending on the actual values of the moments. Since

Reprinted with permission from "Corporation Tax Shifting: A Response" by Marian Krzyzaniak and Richard A. Musgrave, and "Corporation Tax Shifting: Rejoinder" by John G. Cragg, Arnold C. Harberger, and Peter Mieszkowski, *Journal of Political Economy*, vol. 78, no. 4 (July/August, 1970), pp. 768–777. Copyright © 1970 by The University of Chicago.

and even if an upward bias existed no evidence is offered that it is of significant magnitude.

Omitting minor points of disagreement,[2] our position on the main issue may be restated briefly. As we suggested earlier, our nontax variables may fail to allow fully for current demand pressure, and the tax-variable coefficient acting as proxy for pressure may have an upward bias.[3] We now add that this bias need not be upward but may be in either direction.[4] But this is only part of the picture. The pressure variable actually introduced by C-H-M is endogenous, so that the resulting estimating equation ceases to be in reduced form. Since the current-pressure variable may be affected by the very tax changes whose effect is to be measured, the degree of shifting may thus be understated.

C-H-M feel sure that the economy cannot generate a high degree of shifting and that, on balance, their corrections improve the result. We do not share their intuition but consider this the matter under investigation.[5] In time, the issue may be settled by resort to a superior structural system, which leaves no doubt that pressure is accounted for fully through predetermined variables and in which the reduced form is estimated from a fully identified structure. But this C-H-M do not offer. Until such superior model is available, the issue remains open.

INTRODUCTION OF DUMMY VARIABLE

C-H-M believe that during certain war years (1941–1942 and 1950–1952) in particular, high taxes were caused by high profits, and not vice versa. They feel that the combination of war and peace years results in a nonhomogeneous sample, and to deal with this they introduce a dummy variable for the indicated war years. The coefficient of the tax-rate variable is greatly reduced thereby

the R variable is unknown, the values of the moments are also unknown. The possibility of negative bias in a similar situation is illustrated by comparison of equations (2) and (3) in Table 61, p. 44, of our original study, where introduction of the G variable *raises* the L coefficient while giving a *negative* coefficient for G.

The second step in C-H-M's argument is to prove upward bias of f_1 in their equation (9.2). This again involves the claim that b_2 is positive, which we believe to be questionable. Moreover, the second step requires knowledge of the c-coefficients in their equation (9.7) which, being similar to (9.3), raises identification problems for all c.

[2] Several of these points may be noted: (1) The C-H-M choice of the unemployment rate seems inferior to Slitor's use of the GNP gap. (2) It would have been appropriate to use our standard equation (Krzyzaniak and Musgrave [1963], p. 44, equation [3]) rather than that including the G variable, since this is our preferred formulation. (3) If a current-pressure variable is used, use of the lagged variables becomes unnecessary, and they should be dropped. (4) As the C-H-M equation containing E_t is not in reduced form but in structural form, estimation by least squares becomes questionable. (5) It should be added finally, that our interpretation of our earlier finding has been to emphasize not the point estimate of a, say, 1.339 shifting coefficient, but rather the strong support for the hypothesis of high shifting. See Krzyzaniak and Musgrave ([1963], pp. 46–49).

[3] See our response to Goode and Slitor, in Krzyzaniak ([1966], p. 248).

[4] See n. 1.

[5] C-H-M hold that our results, if valid, would call for a complete reformulation of price theory. We think this is an exaggeration. Restrained monopoly pricing, satisficing, sales maximization under profit constraint, signaling among oligopolists, profit-oriented wage bargaining, price umbrellas, all may explain substantial shifting in the context of a more or less traditional price theory (see also Krzyzaniak and Musgrave [1963, chap. 1, and p. 46, n. 4]).

(see C-H-M, equations [9.12.2], [9.12.3]), its standard error is more than tripled, and the t-ratio becomes less than one. While this does not demonstrate zero shifting as C-H-M conclude, it does suggest that the model does not permit us to choose between the hypotheses of zero and full shifting. However, we cannot accept C-H-M's procedure in dealing with the war years.

The C-H-M result is obtained by adding the dummy variable to the prior introduction of the E_t variable. We find that the result differs if the dummy variable is introduced without first adding E_t. This procedure gives a very high and significant shifting coefficient, with an insignificant coefficient for the dummy variable.[6] C-H-M's results thus hinge wholly on the compounded effect of introducing both the E_t and dummy variables. As these variables are highly collinear with the other variables in the system,[7] it is not surprising that the value of the coefficients should change sharply and become insignificant.

While we do not know whether or how the shifting process differed between war and peace years, we are prepared to test this possibility.[8] To us, a more constructive approach is to omit the war years and to re-estimate our earlier equation for the nonwar years only. We find that the shifting coefficient remains high and significant and does not differ greatly from that for the total period.[9] If the E_t variable is added, the shifting coefficient remains above one, but its significance is reduced.[10] However, the loss of significance is not nearly so great as results in the C-H-M formulation (equation [9.12.3]).

A further and better way of testing C-H-M's hypothesis of nonhomogeneity is to retain all years in the equation but to estimate separate shifting coefficients

[6] The resulting equation is

$$Y_t = .2028 + .0158\Delta C_{t-1} - .0553 V_{t-1} - .6837 J_t - .3001 G_t - .014 W_t$$
$$[.0638] \quad [-.1995] \quad [-4.550] \; [-2.1171] \; [-.8517]$$
$$+ 1.8619 L_t, \quad R_a = .984.$$
$$[5.4430]$$

The t-scores are reduced and overshifting becomes very high, reflecting collinearity of W_t with other variables in the equation.

[7] See Farrar and Glauber [1967], who show that dummies turn collinear with other variables already at low correlation levels.

[8] C-H-M at one point suggest that during the war period the correlation may have run from high profits to high tax rates rather than vice-versa. This is indeed a nightmarish possibility for anyone concerned with incidence analysis. If tax rates are endogenous, the incidence concept dissolves. In this case, nothing is gained by introducing W. The only way out is to omit the period. If C-H-M do not claim reversal of causation but only a change in the nature of the reaction to taxes, there are several ways to account for this, among which introduction of W seems to us the weakest.

[9] Using the peace years only, we obtain

$$Y_t = .3315 + .6523\Delta C_{t-1} - .6101 V_{t-1} - 1.0199 J_t + 1.2853 L_t, \quad R_a = .957,$$
$$[2.1145] \quad [-2.0796] \quad [-3.0642] \; [3.0772]$$

for our preferred equation, and

$$Y_t = .2615 + .2754\Delta C_{t-1} - .1478 V_{t-1} - .7358 J_t - .5125 G_t + 1.9838 L_t,$$
$$[1.4682] \quad [-.8720] \quad [-3.0778] \; [-3.4863] \quad [3.9061]$$
$$R_a = .985,$$

if G is included.

[10] Adding E, this becomes

$$Y_t = -.1802 + .2245\Delta C_{t-1} + .0590 V_{t-1} - .8755 J_t - .4086 G_t + .4897 E_t$$
$$[1.2000] \quad [.2863] \; [-3.4829] \; [-2.5280] \quad [1.5661]$$
$$+ 1.1524 L_t, \quad R_a = .975.$$
$$[1.9432]$$

for the two sets of years. The results show that the shifting coefficients do not differ greatly between the two periods, and remain significant.[11] All this renders one skeptical about whether the presumed nonhomogeneity indeed exists. Application of Chow's test supports this skepticism and shows that the years in our sample are fairly homogeneous.[12] In all, these results suggest that inclusion of the war years in the total sample is justified and that introduction of a dummy variable is not called for.

RELATION TO HARBERGER MODEL

C-H-M then proceed to use their tax coefficient of about .5 to verify Harberger's [1962] earlier model. This is not the place to consider the realism of that model, nor do we want to query why C-H-M bother to verify it with a coefficient which they show to be totally insignificant. Our concern is only with whether this conclusion (assuming their coefficient of .5 to be significant) is in fact relevant to Harberger's earlier reasoning.

The essence of the earlier Harberger model is that introduction of the corporation tax (or of a rate increase) leads to capital flow from the corporate to the unincorporated sector, thereby raising corporate rates of return before tax in order to equate net rates of return in both sectors. This means that the adjustment is made over a period sufficiently long to permit the required capital flow. Our model, and with it the C-H-M estimate, derive the tax-rate coefficient from a system in which the tax rate is unlagged. While use of an unlagged tax variable does not mean that the entire effect must occur in the same year (see Krzyzaniak and Musgrave [1963], p. 64), it does suggest a process which is quite speedy and which hardly permits occurrence of the capital flow needed to implement Harberger's adjustment mechanism. Yet, the C-H-M reasoning implies that the adjustment was of this sort.

C-H-M do not raise this point explicitly, but the issue seems to be touched on in a brief passage, where it is argued "that a regression analysis of this type in effect compares the *levels* of the variables at each observation with those at every other observation in the sample; it does not compare year to year changes" (Cragg, Harberger, and Mieszkowski [1967], p. 820). We are unable to follow the reasoning involved in this statement, or to discover the statistical theory on which it is based. If the time-series regression yields significant coefficients for an unlagged variable, while experiments with lagged variables fail to do so, one is justified in concluding that the effects come about in a

---

[11] The resulting estimate for our preferred form is

$$Y_t = .2856 + .4940\Delta C_{t-1} - .5557V_{t-1} - .7531J_t + 1.1951L_t^{(1)} + 1.3416L]_t^{(2)},$$
$$[2.7576] \quad [-2.7772] \quad [-3.6060] \quad [5.250] \quad [11.0145]$$
$$R_a = .973,$$

where $L_t^{(1)}$ applies for peace years, being set equal to zero in war years (1941, 1942, 1950, 1951, 1952), and vice versa for $L_t^{(2)}$.

[12] Estimating Chow's equality-of-coefficients test for equation line 4, table 6-1, p. 44, in Krzyzaniak and Musgrave [1963], we obtain $F_o = 1.135$, while the critical value at 95 percent (with 5 and 15 degrees of freedom) is 2.9 (see Johnston [1963], p. 138).

relatively short period. It is highly unlikely, therefore, that Harberger's capital-flow process is involved.

REFERENCES

Cragg, John G., Arnold C. Harberger, and Peter Mieszkowski. "Empirical Evidence on the Incidence of the Corporation Income Tax," *J.P.E.* 75 (December 1967): 811–821. [This volume, Chapter 9.]

Farrar, Donald E., and Robert R. Glauber. "Multicollinearity in Regression Analysis: The Problem Revisited," *Rev. Econ. and Statis.*, vol. 49, no. 1 (February 1967).

Goode, Richard. "Rates of Return, Income Shares and Corporate Tax Incidence," in *Effects of Corporation Income Tax*, edited by Marian Krzyzaniak. Detroit: Wayne State Univ. Press, 1966.

Harberger, Arnold C. "The Incidence of the Corporation Income Tax," *J.P.E.*, vol. 70 (June 1962). [This volume, Chapter 7.]

Johnston, J. *Econometric Methods.* New York: McGraw-Hill, 1963.

Krzyzaniak, Marian, ed. *Effects of Corporation Income Tax.* Detroit: Wayne State Univ. Press, 1966.

Krzyzaniak, Marian, and Richard A. Musgrave. *The Shifting of the Corporation Income Tax.* Baltimore: Johns Hopkins Press, 1963.

Slitor, Richard E. "Corporate Tax Incidence: Economic Adjustments to Differentials under a Two-Tier Tax Structure," in *Effects of Corporation Income Tax*, edited by Marian Krzyzaniak. Detroit: Wayne State Univ. Press, 1966.

Appendix II   Corporation Tax Shifting: Rejoinder

John G. Cragg, Arnold C. Harberger, and Peter Mieszkowski

If there is anything in our paper which the response of Krzyzaniak and Musgrave (hereafter referred to as K-M) has caused us to regret, it is the sentence from which they quote in their initial paragraph. It is, and has from the beginning been, our judgment that the pitfalls associated with estimating corporation-tax incidence from time-series data, in K-M fashion, are too numerous and serious for the results to be trustworthy. Section I of our paper concludes: "we do not in any way contend that our modifications of the K-M procedures and experiments adequately cope with the difficulties listed above. Our purpose, in fact, is the much more modest one of showing that making highly plausible and theoretically justified modifications in experiments of the K-M type leads to a reversal of the main conclusions and that, therefore, at the very least, serious doubt is cast on the validity of K-M's conclusions." And our concluding paragraph reads: "Thus, to the extent that one is willing to accept the general framework set out by K-M and to run the risks of time-series analyses, one might construe the present paper as providing an independent confirmation of Harberger's earlier results. We are too skeptical to make such a claim, however, and rest our case with the assertion that K-M's conclusions are not valid." Even the paragraph containing the offending phrase begins: "We remain impressed by the difficulties, brought out in the introduction to this essay, of making inferences concerning the incidence from time-series data." Yet the phrase is there, its spirit is out of tune with our basic position, and we (particularly the middle author, whose temptation is probably most responsible for this lapse) are sorry. Our purpose was to demonstrate, without accepting K-M's framework, how sensitive were their results to plausible and indicated changes. Given our skepticism about the framework itself, it was inappropriate for us even to hint that our experiment might conceivably be taken to confirm Harberger's earlier results.

With the above expiation, we are in a better position to confront K-M's result that an alternative method of dealing with the years of war and mobilization (1941–1942, 1950–1952) — simply leaving them out — produces a shifting coefficient substantially higher than that obtained by us. This simply confirms what we were trying to say in our paper. Making modest and apparently quite plausible changes in specification, grossly different results are obtained. This suggests, as we claim, that one should be skeptical and cautious about the framework generating such fragile and volatile outcomes.

While we find that when K-M eliminate the observations for 1941–1942 and 1950–1952, their results simply underline one of our main points, the same can not be said for their calculation of separate coefficients for $L_t^{(1)}$ and $L_t^{(2)}$

in their equation (5), footnote 11. Here we must demur outright. Our contention is that the years in question exhibited (for reasons extraneous to corporation taxes themselves) high profits and high taxes as compared with normal years. Our argument thus refers to the *intercept* of the profit function; we do not say anything about whether, within this small subset of years, the profit-tax function had a significantly different *slope* from that of other years. We are therefore both unperturbed and unconvinced by the K-M finding that the coefficients of $L_t^{(1)}$ (for the peace years) and $L_t^{(2)}$ (for 1941–1942, 1950–1952) are not significantly different from each other. We find it more appropriate to use a single tax variable L_t, and either to introduce a dummy variable for the years in question (as we do) or to throw out these observations entirely (as K-M do in their equation [2]).

Our final point relates to the fact that there is an upward bias in estimates of the tax-shifting coefficient derived from equations of the K-M type, even when they are "corrected," as we suggest, to include a variable reflecting the degree of employment (or some other indicator of the cyclical stage of the economy). K-M fault us for running regressions in which the employment variable (endogenous to the system) appears on the right-hand side. But in point of fact all of section III of our paper is devoted to a demonstration that, precisely for this case, upward biases of two types exist.

The first type is a specification bias. To demonstrate that it exists, we postulate a true (but possibly unobserved) exogenous cyclical variable, R, which appears along with the tax rate (and possibly other exogenous variables) in the reduced-form equation (9.7) determining the employment rate, E:

$$(9.7) \qquad E_t = c_0 + c_1 L_t + c_2 R_t + v_t.$$

This equation is solved for R_t, and the result is substituted into the true reduced-form equation (9.3) determining Y_{gt}, the gross-of-tax rate of return in capital:

$$(9.3) \qquad Y_{gt} = b_0 + b_1 L_t + b_2 R_t + \omega_t.$$

The resulting equation is:

$$(9.9) \qquad Y_{gt} = \left(b_0 - \frac{b_2 c_0}{c_2}\right) + \left(b_1 - \frac{b_2 c_1}{c_2}\right) L_t + \frac{b_2}{c_2} E_t + \left(\omega_t - \frac{b_2}{c_2} v_t\right).$$

We are interested in the coefficient of L_t. The true causal influence of L_t on Y_{gt} is measured by b_1 in the true reduced-form equation. The coefficient of Y_t estimated from (9.9) will be subject to a specification bias of $-b_2 c_1 / c_2$. Since c_2 and b_2 (measuring the impact of our cyclical variable on employment and profit rates, respectively) are positive, and since c_1 (measuring the true impact of increased tax rates on employment) is presumably negative, the net effect is for the ill-specified coefficient of L_t in equation (9.9) to be greater than the correctly specified coefficient of L_t in equation (9.3). On this point it appears that K-M did not understand fully what we were doing. In our discussion it is clear that the coefficients of equations (9.3) and (9.7) are the true (not estimated) reduced-form coefficients; yet, when K-M argue that the sign of the bias might be negative as well as positive (their n. 1), they act as if b_2 referred to an estimated coefficient. To this we can only respond that it is not the case. K-M may conceivably (though we doubt it) be willing to assert that the *true* impact of an exogenous increase in the cyclical variable upon gross-of-tax profits can plausibly be negative, but we must insist that what they say in footnote 1 about the corresponding estimated impact simply is not relevant to our argument.

The second type of bias is estimation bias, stemming from the fact that the employment variable E_t is endogenous. In our equation (9.11′) we derive an expression for this estimation bias:

$$(9.11')\qquad \hat{f}_1 - f_1 = \frac{f_2 M_{vE} M_{EZ^*}}{M_{LZ^*} M_{EE} - M_{EL} M_{EZ^*}}.$$

Here f_1 is the true coefficient of L_t, equal to $(b_1 - b_2 c_1/c_2)$ in equation (9.9). It is already upward biased due to specification error. The quantity $\hat{f}_1$ is the instrumental-variables estimate of f, when Z_t^* is used as the instrument for L_t. K-M assert (p. 769) that "the pressure variable actually introduced by C-H-M is endogenous, so that the resulting estimating equation ceases to be in reduced form. Since the current-pressure variable may be affected by the very tax changes whose effect is to be measured, the degree of shifting may thus be understated." The expression for bias in equation (9.11′) contains one "true" coefficient (f_2, measuring b_2/c_2 in [9.9′] and presumed to be positive), one unobservable sample moment M_{vE} (measuring the presumably positive relation between disturbances in equation [9.3] and the level of employment), and four observable sample moments (M_{EZ^*}, M_{LZ^*}, M_{EE}, and M_{EL}). K-M's comment, cited above, appears to conjecture that a rise in the tax rate would reduce profits not only directly but also indirectly, through dampening economic activity. The true total effect, they seem to say, would be greater than the direct effect as measured by f_1. There can be no doubt that the causal chain postulated by them is plausible; however, it must be recognized that it is a statement about M_{EZ^*} in equation (9.11′). And M_{EZ^*} is an observable sample moment, which happens to have a positive sign, rather than the negative one that their hypothetical causal chain postulates. We will not deny that in some conceivable future samples of U.S. data, M_{EZ^*} will turn out to be negative, leading to a negative rather than positive estimation bias in the tax-shifting coefficient. But in their own sample M_{EZ^*} is positive — in our view because of the fortuitous historical accident that corporation income tax rates were low in the 1930s (when there was substantial slack in the economy) and high in the late 1940s and 1950s (when full employment prevailed save for relatively mild recessions). This is both the reason why we feel that a cyclical or, as K-M put it, a "pressure" variable must be included *and* the reason why, when it is included, the tax-shifting coefficient is subject to an upward estimation bias.

REFERENCE

Krzyzaniak, M., and R. A. Musgrave. "Corporation Tax Shifting: A Response," *J.P.E.* 78 (pt. 1, July/August 1970): 768–773. [This volume, Chapter 9, Appendix I.]

VIII

The next article was prepared as a comment on four different studies attempting to estimate the results of the tax stimuli (more liberal depreciation allowances and the investment tax credit) that were introduced by the Kennedy administration in the early 1960s. These four studies — by Robert E. Hall and Dale W. Jorgenson, Charles W. Bischoff, Robert M. Coen, and Lawrence R. Klein and Paul Taubman — and my comment are all published in *Tax Incentives and Capital Spending*, edited by Gary Fromm (Washington, D.C.: The Brookings Institution, 1971).

In contrast to Chapter 9, which concentrates on the specific study under review, Chapter 10 contemplates some fundamental issues in the theoretical and empirical analysis of changes in institutional arrangements (in this case new tax provisions) that are suggested by the papers being discussed. The key issue concerns the assumptions that one can make concerning the principles guiding day-to-day economic policy — in this particular case monetary policy. The analysis is carried out under three alternative assumptions regarding monetary policy: (i) that the monetary authorities operated in such a way as to generate a time path of income that would be the same as it would have been in the absence of the tax incentives; (ii) that they behaved so as to make the time path of the money supply the same in the presence of the incentives as it would have been in their absence; and (iii) that the target variable of the monetary authorities was neither income nor the money supply but rather the level of interest rates, and that this latter variable would have followed the same track in the presence of the special incentives as in their absence.

The effects of the tax incentives on important economic variables will differ substantially, depending on which of these hypothetical rules is followed by the monetary authorities. If the income time path is held the same, the effect of the incentives is to raise interest rates and to improve the balance of payments. If, on the other hand, interest rates are constrained to follow a given track, the incentives lead to an increase in real income and a deterioration of the balance of payments. Finally, when the money supply is the variable whose time path is held constant, the results are an increase in income, and a rise in interest rates, with an uncertain net effect on the balance of payments.

Of course, one may be quite certain that actual Federal Reserve policy in the post–tax-incentive period did not follow any simple rule like (i), (ii), or (iii), but was much more complicated. An accurate delineation of the effects of the tax changes is therefore practically impossible in the absence of a detailed knowledge of the twists and turns of monetary policy. Despite the complexity of the problem, however, I believe that the crude evidence is sufficiently strong to support the conclusion that at least one principal effect of the tax incentives was to alter the composition of investment — drawing a significant amount of investible funds out of residential construction and into those uses (business plant and equipment) covered by the incentive provisions.

Chapter 10

Tax Stimuli

and Investment Behavior

I cannot conceive that, even as little as five years ago, a book of this type would have come anywhere near this one [*Tax Incentives and Capital Spending*] in linking the discussion of concrete policy issues to the subtleties of modern economic theory, to the nuances of interpreting particular data series, and to the details of advanced econometric method. Economics is becoming more and more a science, and economists are more and more professional in its practice. These authors are among the leaders in this exceedingly healthy development.

Having said that, I cannot help reflecting on the disparity of the results emerging from the four treatments of the relation of tax incentives to investment behavior. It is naïve to expect there to be only one way in which economic science can be brought intelligently to bear upon a given set of data to answer a given question. Several models, each soundly based, may still have differing implications, because theory has yet to achieve — if, indeed, it ever will — a unique set of propositions on which all professional economists agree. And where divergent theories are tested on a given body of data, the data might not be sufficiently extensive or robust to show that one approach is superior to another. Alternative basic series may likewise exist, each with its own defects; economists may choose differently among them, and may elect alternative ways of adjusting and using the series to correct for the error components they conceive to be most important. Finally, the matter is still further complicated when distributed lags enter the postulated relationships in a significant way; here the choice of the precise type of lag distribution to be imposed can itself have strong bearing on the results.

The basic trouble is that, in much of their work, economists are destined to deal with a limited body of data. In statistical terms, they have limited degrees of freedom. For the data to tell them anything, they must make arbitrary judgments about specification of the model itself, forms of functional relationships, nature of lag distributions, and the like. Once the investigator makes these judgments, he is in a sense their prisoner; they become the "maintained hypotheses" under which his econometric exercises are carried out. Working within such a framework, the economist can find the results that yield him the best fit for a particular body of data; they may have high levels of significance

Reprinted with permission from Arnold C. Harberger, "Discussion," in *Tax Incentives and Capital Spending*, edited by Gary Fromm. © 1971 The Brookings Institution, Washington, D.C.

and good explanatory power, and in this sense be better than any alternative results that can be drawn from the same data within the same framework. But they may, unfortunately, be closely tied up with the framework of maintained hypotheses, in the sense that a modest change in the latter may produce a quite different set of best results.

A long-standing commonplace of scientific method holds that there are in principle an infinite number of hypotheses capable of explaining a given finite body of data. Two points determine a straight line, but an infinite number of parabolas, circles, ellipses, and hyperbolas will also fit those points. In econometric work, complicated functional forms have traditionally been ruled out on essentially a priori grounds, but even so the specification of functions — their form, the determination of which explanatory variables will be introduced in them, and so forth — has been an extremely important issue. As analysts have moved forward to incorporate lag structures in their work, the number of possible hypotheses that might be entertained to explain a given body of data has multiplied as well, thus raising the probability that two — or even four or six — authors, approaching the same question with somewhat different basic models, will each come up with results indicating that his approach is consistent with the data.

COMPARISON OF APPROACHES

These remarks are relevant to comparing the work under discussion. Of the four, the Klein and Taubman paper has the least restrictive investment function, in the sense that fewer restrictions derived from economic theory are imposed in the derivation of that function. Where distributed lags are used by Klein and Taubman, they are in the main arbitrarily drawn from Shirley Almon's study,[1] and applied to three distinct classes of industries (manufacturing, regulated, and other). But a few unexplained variations occur in the treatment of different sectors. For manufacturing, an Almon-lagged capital stock variable is used, along with others, to explain investment; for the regulated industries an unweighted two-quarter moving average of lagged capital stock is used; for the remaining sector, the variable is simply last quarter's capital stock. A lagged capital utilization variable appears in the equation explaining manufacturing investment, but not in those for the other two sectors. A cash flow variable likewise appears in the manufacturing equation but not in the others. While these discrepancies of approach may have sound justifications, the failure of the authors to make them explicit leaves the reader wondering to what degree the equations presented were the result of an extensive process of experimentation, within a rather loose theoretical framework, in search of the best fit.

On the other hand, Klein and Taubman appear to have taken greater pains to justify the particular data series they have used, and to accommodate their analysis to the nuances of the investment-stimulating legislation, than have the other authors.

By way of contrast, the paper by Hall and Jorgenson adopts the explicit

---

[1] Shirley Almon, "The Distributed Lag between Capital Appropriations and Expenditures," *Econometrica*, Vol. 33 (January 1965), pp. 178–96.

framework of neoclassical capital theory, and imposes on the model derived from that framework the restrictive assumptions of (1) competition, (2) Cobb-Douglas production functions, (3) exponential depreciation of capital goods, and (4) a constant before-tax discount rate. The solid theoretical foundation for Hall and Jorgenson's work strikes me as a distinct advantage. Except for the assumption of a constant before-tax discount rate, the other restrictions appear also to have some independent justification. The assumption of competition is clearly violated in the real world, but the results would be much the same if it were replaced by an assumed constant degree of monopoly; only if the degree of monopoly were itself a function of the tax changes would a serious problem be involved here. The Cobb-Douglas production functions are defended on the ground that a significant body of empirical evidence appears to be consistent with the Cobb-Douglas hypothesis, although the authors recognize that some studies suggest an elasticity of substitution between capital and labor of less than one. The assumption of the exponential depreciation of capital goods has great advantages of mathematical convenience in a model of the type Hall and Jorgenson employ, and appears, like the assumption of Cobb-Douglas production functions, at least not to have been controverted by the weight of existing evidence.

A constant before-tax discount rate is, however, another matter. In accepting it, Hall and Jorgenson implicitly make an extreme and implausible assumption about the shifting of the corporation tax, namely, that with the imposition of an increase in the tax, the after-tax rate of return will fall by the full amount of such increase, and will rise by the full amount with a decrease in the tax rate. This result would be plausible if the corporation income tax struck all income from capital equally, but it is not plausible for the U.S. case, in which the corporation income tax applies to the income from only about half the capital in the economy. All income from capital in unincorporated enterprise (predominantly housing and agricultural capital) is exempt from the corporation income tax, and that part of corporate capital that is financed by debt also is exempt. As a consequence, so long as equilibrium prevails in the capital market before and after a change in the corporation income tax, one would expect an increase in the corporation tax rates to depress the after-tax rate of return on all capital, and a decrease in the tax rate to enhance it. But it is indeed extreme to assume that the after-tax rate of return to corporate equity capital falls by the full amount of the tax, for then equilibrium in the capital market would require a corresponding fall in the rate of interest on debt capital and in the rate of return obtained in the noncorporate sector. Capital as a factor of production would under these circumstances bear substantially more than the full burden of the tax.[2] It is far more plausible to assume that capital bears approximately the full burden of the corporation income tax, which

---

[2] In the United States, the capital impact would be approximately twice the full tax burden. For an elaboration of this point see Arnold C. Harberger, "The Corporation Income Taxes," in *International Encyclopedia of the Social Sciences*, Vol. 15 (Macmillan, 1968); Arnold C. Harberger, "The Incidence of the Corporation Income Tax," *Journal of Political Economy*, Vol. 70 (June 1962), pp. 215–240; and John G. Cragg, Arnold C. Harberger, and Peter Mieszkowski, "Empirical Evidence on the Incidence of the Corporation Income Tax," *Journal of Political Economy*, Vol. 75 (December 1967), pp. 811–821. [This volume, Chapters 6, 7, and 9.]

means that the after-tax rate of return to corporate equity capital would rise by approximately half of any decrease in the tax rate, or fall by approximately half of any increase in that rate, with the rates of return to noncorporate and corporate nonequity capital falling or rising equally with the after-tax yield on corporate capital in the case, respectively, of a rate increase or a rate decrease.

The effect of assuming a constant before-tax discount rate is therefore to exaggerate considerably the effect of tax stimuli upon investment, because it ignores their indirect influence on investment through rises in the rate of interest. I shall return to this issue.

Bischoff's paper is in much the same spirit as Hall and Jorgenson's, although somewhat less restrictive in its assumptions. The basic differences are that (1) Bischoff does not impose a Cobb-Douglas production function but instead fits the more flexible constant-elasticity-of-substitution function; (2) Bischoff permits the lag pattern of investment response to changes in relative prices to be different from the lag pattern of response to output changes, whereas the Hall and Jorgenson procedure effectively imposes the same lag pattern in the two cases; and (3) Bischoff permits the discount rate governing investment decisions to respond to changes in market interest rates, whereas Hall and Jorgenson do not. Bischoff's estimates of the elasticity of substitution that yield the best fits are sufficiently close to unity that one cannot attribute significant differences between his results and those of Hall and Jorgenson to his relaxation of the Cobb-Douglas assumption.

Far more important is Bischoff's allowance for different lag patterns of response to changes in relative prices and in output. Bischoff's Table 3.11 reveals a rapid response of investment to output changes, initially more than double the steady-state response and remaining greater than the steady-state response for eleven quarters. On the other hand, Table 3.11 also indicates that the response of investment to price changes (which include changes in equipment cost, interest rate, and taxes) is slow, starting with a small negative effect relative to the steady-state response and taking nine quarters to build up to 90 percent and eleven quarters to reach 100 percent. These results suggest that Hall and Jorgenson have probably overestimated the effectiveness of the tax incentives in stimulating investment; their common pattern of lagged response of investment to changes in price and output probably approximates a weighted average of Bischoff's slow response to price changes and his rapid response to output changes, and hence overstates the speed of reaction to price changes and understates that to output movements.

Bischoff's approach also has an advantage over Hall and Jorgenson's in that it permits the cost-of-capital variable to be influenced by movements in the market interest rate and in the dividend yield on stocks, as well as by tax changes. It is quite clear that the estimates in both papers of investment responsiveness are dominated by output changes, Bischoff's probably substantially less so than Hall and Jorgenson's, as his price variable captures additional (and thoroughly valid) sources of movement in the cost of capital.

But let it be noted that, like Hall and Jorgenson's, Bischoff's estimates of the actual effect of tax concessions on investment fail to allow for the effects of the concessions on interest rates. Whereas Hall and Jorgenson assume the before-tax rate of return in corporate capital to be constant, and measure the influence of tax incentives on this basis, Bischoff assumes in effect that in the absence of tax concessions the interest rate and dividend yield would have followed the same time path as they actually did in the presence of the concessions. Bischoff's treatment of interest rates and stock yields as exogenous is thus subject to the same criticism as Hall and Jorgenson's treatment of the before-tax rate of return as given.

Coen's approach is more general than both Bischoff's and Hall and Jorgenson's in that (1) Coen does not postulate an explicit form for the production function; (2) Coen directly estimates separate coefficients for his new orders (corresponding to output) and price variables, whereas the user cost (price) variable and the output variable enter Bischoff's and Hall and Jorgenson's estimated equations multiplicatively, so that their separate influences are either equal (Hall and Jorgenson) or constrained by a single estimated coefficient (Bischoff); and (3) Coen introduces cash flow as a determinant of investment, while Bischoff and Hall and Jorgenson do not. Coen's model is less general than Bischoff's in that Coen imposes a single exponential lag structure according to which investment responds to price and output stimuli.

Unlike Klein and Taubman and like Hall and Jorgenson and Bischoff, Coen derives his estimated equation directly from a theoretical framework that incorporates profit maximization. He handles the cash flow variable (which is indeed difficult to incorporate in a maximizing model) most ingeniously, by postulating that variations in cash flow do not influence the target capital stock determined by price and output, but rather affect the speed with which that target level is approached. He differs from Bischoff and Hall and Jorgenson in imposing an exponential adjustment lag, whereas they obtain their lag structure from the data; but he adds some flexibility by incorporating a fitted expectations lag (the same for the price and new orders variables). I doubt, however, that these differences are of great importance in accounting for the differences in results.

I suspect that the important difference between Coen's approach on the one hand and Bischoff's and Hall and Jorgenson's on the other is the manner in which the user cost and output variables enter the equation; and it is difficult to say in this case that one approach is clearly better than the other. If the data were perfect, I think there would be little doubt that Coen's formulation would be preferable. For both Hall and Jorgenson and Bischoff, the lag-adjusted price and output series enter multiplicatively in the equation explaining investment; a single coefficient applies to their product. While admittedly something is lost in linearizing a product like, say, $(p/c)_t Q_t$ into $(\overline{p/c}) Q_t + (p/c)_t \bar{Q}$, I do not feel that the loss is likely to be great. And if it is not great, performing the linearization and introducing $(p/c)_t$ and Q_t separately can be regarded as a test of the validity of the fundamental assumption that $(\overline{p/c}) Q_t$ and $(p/c)_t \bar{Q}$ have the same coefficient. A formulation similar to Coen's can in this sense be regarded as providing a test of one of the basic assumptions of both Bischoff and Hall and Jorgenson, so long as the data are strong enough for this task.

Unfortunately, that is unlikely to be the case. Zvi Griliches, who first called this point to my attention, has expressed the judgment that the average measurement error in the user cost variables employed by these authors can easily be as high as 20 to 25 percent of the mean of such variables. In common, I believe, with most other observers, I share his qualms. If he is correct, when output and user cost are introduced as separate variables in a regression, the coefficient of user cost will be biased strongly toward zero because of its high error component. Coen's results, which indicate a much smaller effect of the tax stimuli than Bischoff's or Hall and Jorgenson's, can be explained in this way, provided one is willing to postulate a sufficiently high error component in his user cost variable.

The Hall and Jorgenson and Bischoff results are less influenced by this error, because by hypothesis they get information on the coefficient of user cost from variations in output as well as in user cost (price). Error variability is a significantly smaller fraction of the total variability of $(p/c)_t Q_t$ than it is of the total variability of $(p/c)_t$ alone; hence the coefficient of the $(p/c)_t Q_t$ variable is less biased than that of $(p/c)_t$. Similarly, one can say that the substantial variations in output that took place over the estimating period bring a lot more information to bear on the estimate of the user cost coefficient than Coen's approach will allow. Thus if one is willing to accept the theoretical framework of Bischoff or Hall and Jorgenson, with its implication that the output and price variables *should* be joined together, one can easily be led by econometric considerations to prefer their results to Coen's. But if one rejects the framework implying that $(p/c)_t Q_t$ is the right variable, or accepts that framework tentatively but judges the issue of measurement error to be of minor importance, then one would be inclined to regard Coen's results as superior.

My final point in connection with Coen's work is that he, like Hall and Jorgenson and Bischoff, measures partial rather than total effects of the tax incentives, in the sense that he does not allow for the effects of these incentives themselves on interest rates.

CONSEQUENCES OF THE TAX MEASURES

This section explores the likely macroeconomic consequences of the series of tax measures under consideration, and inquires what the four papers have to say about them. It is not unfair to characterize most proponents of the legislation at the time of enactment as thinking that the measures would increase investment in the U.S. economy in relation to some measure of its overall scale, such as gross national product (GNP). The facts, however, quite clearly belie this key expectation. Whereas in the years 1955 through 1961, gross private domestic investment bore an average relationship to GNP of 15.3 percent, the corresponding average from 1962 onward (including the first half of 1967) is 15.0 percent.

How can this apparent failure of the tax stimuli actually to stimulate be explained? The answer lies largely in the truism that investment must equal savings for the economy as a whole. This means, in national accounting terms, that gross private domestic investment plus net foreign investment must equal gross private savings plus the government surplus. The tax measures under consideration, including the general tax reduction of 1964, produced no clear incentive to savings. Each entailed a reduction in the revenues the government might expect from a given level of GNP, and each entailed a corresponding rise in private disposable income out of a given GNP. But since increments to disposable income are not all saved, the net effect of the tax stimuli has very likely been a reduction in total saving (private plus government) as a fraction of GNP. This, indeed, is what the crude data show, with national saving averaging 16.0 percent of GNP in the 1955–1961 period and 15.9 percent in the 1962–1967 period. (The difference between national saving and gross private domestic investment is net foreign investment, which increased from an average 0.7 percent of GNP in 1955–1961 to an average .9 percent in 1962–1967.)

Once the issue of the savings rate is brought into the picture, it becomes quite obvious that those who expected the tax stimuli substantially to increase overall investment (and saving) in relation to GNP were doomed from the beginning to disappointment. This does not mean, however, that the measures must be written off as failures. Once the overall savings constraint is accepted, it is clear that the probable effect of the tax stimuli was a shift in the composition of total investment rather than a significant change in its relation to GNP. Such a compositional shift did in fact occur. From an average of 4.8 percent of GNP in the 1955–1961 period, residential construction fell to an average 3.9 percent in the 1962–1967 period. Counterbalancing this, other private domestic nonresidential investment (principally plant and equipment spending) rose from 9.8 percent of GNP in the earlier period to 10.2 percent in the later period, and was the principal beneficiary of all of the tax measures under consideration.

To the extent that the observed compositional shift of investment was the consequence of the tax stimuli, they should be given good marks, for it is obvious that the marginal productivity of capital in the nonresidential sector of the economy is substantially higher than it is in the housing sector. Tax provisions alone guarantee this; the relevant marginal productivity in the corporate sector is gross of corporate taxes, property taxes, and personal taxes, while in the bulk of the housing sector it does not even include personal taxes. To put it another way, the yield to an individual of a corporate investment is the marginal productivity of that investment less all the taxes that have to be paid out of that marginal product. In owner-occupied housing, the relevant yield is something like the mortgage rate, say 6 percent, reduced by the individual's marginal tax rate. Thus one can applaud the effects of the tax incentives to investment while recognizing that they may not have accomplished the global objective many believe they were intended to produce.[3]

[3] One should not make the mistake here of assuming that a stimulus to residential investment helps the poor at the expense of the rich. The available evidence on housing demand indicates an income elasticity in excess of unity. See Margaret G. Reid, *Housing and Income* (University of Chicago Press, 1962), and David Laidler, "Income Tax Incentives for Owner-Occupied Housing," in Arnold C. Harberger and Martin J. Bailey (eds.), *The Taxation of Income from Capital* (Brookings Institution, 1969).

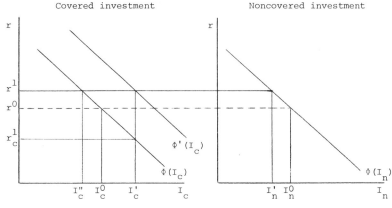

FIGURE 10.1

*Effects of Tax Incentives on Covered and Noncovered Investment,
Assuming Actual Time Path of Income.*

What follows is an attempt, with the aid of some simple models, to isolate the effects of the tax stimuli on what may be called "covered investment," that is, those items of investment that benefited directly from the measures under consideration. In the first example, it is assumed that, in the absence of the tax stimuli, the monetary authorities would have been able to manage their policies so as to achieve the same level of income in each year as that actually attained. There is in this case no "income effect" of the tax measures, only a redistribution of investment from the noncovered to the covered category.

Figure 10.1 depicts investment I as a function of the interest rate r for both the covered c and noncovered n categories. It is assumed that, in the absence of the tax stimuli, the interest rate required to achieve the actual level of income would have been r^0. In the presence of the tax measures, the interest rate required to produce this same level of income is r^1. As a consequence of the tax measures, therefore, noncovered investment falls from I_n^0 to I_n'. Covered investment, however, is subject to two influences. As a consequence of the rise in the interest rate, it would normally tend to fall from I_c^0 to I_c'', but the tax measures shift the investment demand curve to the right, causing a net increase from I_c^0 to I_c'. Another way of interpreting the adjustment is to conceive of the tax stimuli as giving an implicit subsidy to covered investment. This subsidy can be converted into an equivalent reduction in the interest rate, equal to $(r^1 - r_c^1)$. Under this interpretation the effect of the rise in the interest rate itself would again be to reduce covered investment to I_c'', and the partial or direct effect of the tax stimuli would have been movement along $\Phi(I_c)$ increasing investment from I_c'' to I_c'.

All four analyses follow this second interpretation, in that they convert the tax measures into equivalent reductions in the interest rate or — what amounts to much the same thing — the user cost of capital. But three of the four take as the effect of the tax stimuli what I have called the partial or direct effect, and make no allowance for the rise in interest rates caused by these same tax measures. Thus, the Hall and Jorgenson, Bischoff, and Coen measures of the increase in investment caused by the stimuli correspond to $I_c' - I_c''$ in Figure 10.1, not to $I_c' - I_c^0$, which represents the total effect. Klein and Taubman, on the other hand, indicate that their results stem from inserting the tax stimulus $(r^1 - r_c^1)$ into the Wharton Econometric Forecasting Unit model, and solving for the resulting increase in gross fiscal nonresidential investment. Their answer thus corresponds, in a sense, to the general equilibrium answer of $I_c' - I_c^0$, but their underlying model was different from the one discussed here, as they obtain different time paths of GNP with and without the tax stimuli, while this model assumes the course of GNP to be unaffected by them.

In a second simple model, in which the tax measures can have an effect upon GNP, it is assumed that the time path of the quantity of money would have been the same in the presence or absence of the tax measures. This is analogous to saying that the *LM* curve of the traditional Keynesian or neo-Keynesian analysis would be unaffected by the policies in question. Here the tax stimuli result in a rightward shift of the *IS* curve, causing both income and the interest rate to rise. The effect on covered investment is depicted in Figure 10.2. The indirect effect of the measures through the induced change in the interest rate is given by a movement along $\Phi(I_c)$ from A to B; the indirect effect through the induced change in income is given by a shift of the investment demand curve from $\phi(I_c)$ to $\phi'(I_c)$ and is reflected in a movement from B to C; and the direct price effect, which Hall and Jorgenson, Bischoff, and Coen attempt to measure, is given by a movement along $\phi'(I_c)$ from C to E. (This last step can equivalently be considered a shift of the investment demand from C to F.) The total effect of the tax stimuli on covered investment is thus given by $I_c' - I_c^0$. The effect on noncovered investment is indeterminate, consisting of a reduction caused by the rise in the interest rate and an increase caused by the rise in GNP.

A third possible policy alternative is that in the absence of the tax measures the time path of interest rates would have been the same as that which actually developed, a not implausible assumption in the light of the key role of the

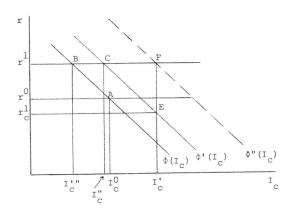

FIGURE 10.2

Effects of Tax Incentives on Covered Investment, Assuming Actual Time Path of Money Supply.

interest rate in the defense of the U.S. balance of payments. Under this alternative, no part of the upward drift of interest rates that has taken place since 1962 is attributed to the tax measures since, by assumption, it would have happened even in their absence. The role of the tax measures is then to prevent this tightening of credit markets from having the negative effect on economic activity that it would normally entail. Analytically, in this case, starting from the position (probably of less than full employment) that the economy would have reached with the same interest rate but in the absence of the tax measures, the effect of the measures is to produce a rightward shift of the *IS* curve, and a concomitant rightward shift of the *LM* curve, so as to permit equilibrium at a higher level of income with the same interest rate. The effect on covered investment is shown in Figure 10.3. Here the change in this category of investment occasioned by the tax stimuli consists of two steps: a move from *A* to *B* occasioned by the induced increase in income, and a move from *B* to *C* representing the direct price effect of the tax incentives.

This discussion serves only to open up a series of issues that lamentably were not treated by any of the authors. Hall and Jorgenson, Bischoff, and Coen simply bypass all general equilibrium considerations and concentrate on attempting to measure the direct price effect of the incentives. They therefore cannot purport to say anything about the total effect. The total effect must be less than the direct effect where alternative monetary policy would have kept the time path of income the same; it must be greater than the direct effect where alternative monetary policy would have kept the time path of interest rates the same; and it can be either greater or less than the direct effect in the case where the alternative policy would have maintained the same time path of the money supply — all this in the context of the simple models outlined above, and referring only to covered investment.

Klein and Taubman, on the other hand, though unique in working within a general equilibrium framework, fail to spell out the key assumptions about policy and behavior underlying their solution, and do nothing at all to explore the implications of the tax incentives under different assumptions about

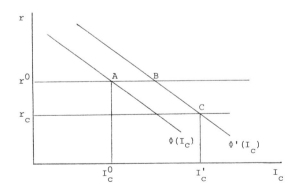

FIGURE 10.3
*Effects of Tax Incentives on Covered Investment, Assuming Actual
Time Path of Interest Rates.*

monetary policy. On the first point, they are clearly in a better position than any reader to distinguish the key behavioral and policy forces that, in the Wharton model, contribute important elements to their solution. Had they done this, they could have given at least a rough idea of the nature, in their model, of the principal indirect effects of the tax stimuli on both covered and noncovered investment. They could also, of course, have stated explicitly the main policy assumptions on which their solution is based, so that readers could readily judge their plausibility.

On the second point, I would like to have seen alternative solutions based on different policy assumptions, analogous but not necessarily equivalent to the three cases discussed above. I have no doubt that with a sufficiently easy monetary policy the actual time path of GNP could have been approximately replicated even in the absence of the tax incentives. It is therefore of some interest to explore this case. On the other hand, the preoccupation of the monetary authorities with the balance of payments makes it unlikely that they would have pursued such a policy; on this ground the equal-interest-rate case is worth exploring. Even more interesting would be a model in which the actual time path of the balance of payments was replicated, and its consequences for GNP, interest rates, and covered and noncovered investment derived, on the assumption the tax incentives did not exist. But this is probably asking too much, as I know of no way reliably to capture, in an econometric equation, the volatile function explaining the capital account of the balance of payments. All the difficulties encountered in explaining private domestic investment — and many more — are present when the capital account is the dependent variable.

In sum, therefore, the quality of the work presented here is very high, but the analyses leave unfinished and unclear the picture of the quantitative effects of the tax incentives that have been examined. I remain prone to the same rough judgment about these incentives that I have held for several years: that they played an important role in permitting us to come reasonably close to full employment in the presence of a strong balance-of-payments constraint; that they accomplished this by creating a situation in which the interest rate level consistent with full employment was significantly higher than it otherwise would be; that, viewed against alternative ways of achieving full employment, these tax stimuli produced a massive shift of investment from the noncovered sector (principally residential housing) to the covered sector, without much change in total investment; and that, viewed against the alternative of maintaining the same interest-rate or balance-of-payments posture that obtained, the incentives probably accounted for a significant increase in total investment and in income.

IX

The next two chapters concern the special tax treatment of mineral industries and represent my contribution to the debate surrounding such treatment. Probably the main thrust of this contribution is to call attention to the influence of special tax provisions on the amount of resources allocated to the affected activities and to the losses in economic efficiency which this entails. My focus in both articles represented a departure from the standard critique of percentage depletion and related preferential provisions affecting minerals. This critique can be summarized as follows: the big mineral enterprises and particularly the big oil companies get rich at the expense of the U.S. Treasury (or of taxpayers in general). In response to such attacks, the companies in question have regularly cited data comparing their rates of return on invested capital with those prevailing in other industries to show that their rates of yield did not differ much from the average. This rebuttal served at least to blunt the force of the standard critique and to generate legislative changes which, far from narrowing the scope and the force of special tax provisions, tended over time to extend these privileges to an ever-wider set of minerals. Starting from percentage depletion for oil and gas in 1926, coal, metals, and sulphur were added in 1932; fluorspar, rock asphalt, and ball and sagger clay came into the list in 1942; other additions were made in 1944, 1947, and 1951 (when even sand, gravel, slate, and stone came to be included); and finally, in 1954, percentage depletion treatment was extended to "all other minerals," with some stated exceptions.

The position that I have taken is to accept more or less at face value the industry's contention that their rates of return on capital are not out of line. Under these circumstances the effects of the incentives do not work themselves out in excessive profits, but rather in excessive amounts of resources being dedicated to the affected activities. My purpose, then, is to measure the degree of implied subsidy that the special tax provisions provide. My first effort at this (Chapter 11, which appeared in a Congressional tax compendium titled *Federal Tax Policy for Economic Growth and Stability* (Washington, D.C.: Joint Committee on the Economic Report, 1955), was based on relatively crude data, and its estimates, at least for oil and gas, are superseded by those of Chapter 12, which was published in the *Proceedings of the Second Energy Institute* (Washington, D.C.: The American University, 1961). I have for this reason omitted the mathematical appendix to Chapter 11, material which is reworked and improved upon in Chapter 12. The text of Chapter 11 was left unaltered, however, as it brings out the historical and institutional background of the controversy, whereas Chapter 12 does not, and also enters more directly into certain aspects of the debate (e.g., those referring to risks and to national defense considerations) that are not treated in Chapter 12.

Chapter 11

The Taxation
of Mineral Industries

In this paper I propose to outline the incentives given by our tax laws to mineral industries. It will be shown that these incentives lead to a situation in which it takes $2 million of capital invested in mineral exploration to produce as much product as $1 million of capital invested in other industries. Our tax laws also foster the uneconomic expansion of mineral production and give mineral holdings artificially high values.

These effects can be avoided through the gradual elimination of percentage-depletion provisions in favor of cost depletion and through the gradual merging of the rate of tax on capital gains with that on ordinary incomes. In the concluding sections of the paper, arguments for special treatment of mineral industries on grounds of their special riskiness and on grounds of their special contribution to our defense potential are examined.

NEUTRAL TAX TREATMENT

The corporation income tax operates chiefly as a tax on the return to invested capital. Such a tax would clearly not be neutral if the return to capital in some uses were free of tax. For example, if the tax rate were 50 percent, and if investment in the untaxed industries were carried to a point where the return was, say, 10 percent, then in the taxed industries investment would be carried only to a point where the return before tax was 20 percent. Investors would in each case be getting a 10-percent return after tax, but the economy as a whole would suffer as a result of the differential treatment of different uses. Projects yielding only 10 percent would be willingly undertaken in the untaxed industries, while projects yielding 19, 18, and 17 percent would be rejected as potential investments in the taxed industries. A lower tax rate, striking all industries equally, would yield the same amount of revenue, yet would not lead to a situation in which high-return uses of capital were foregone and low-return uses undertaken as a result of the tax laws. So long as we intend to retain the corporation income tax as a part of our fiscal structure, we should therefore

Reprinted from Arnold C. Harberger, "The Taxation of Mineral Industries," *Federal Tax Policy for Economic Growth and Stability* (Washington, D.C.: Joint Committee on the Economic Report, 1955), pp. 439–449.

strive to design its provisions in such a way that the return to capital is taxed equally in all uses and industries.

NONNEUTRAL TREATMENT OF CAPITAL GAINS

Practically everybody is familiar with the effects of the special provisions for capital-gains taxation, because they are present, also, in the individual income tax. The purchase of growth stocks increasing in value at 6 percent per year is preferable to the purchase of stocks paying dividends at 6 percent per year but which do not increase in value. Particularly for taxpayers in the higher brackets, it is worth while to incur substantial costs in order to find ways of transmuting income into capital gains. Actually, only the most arbitrary distinctions can be made between income and capital gains. If at the beginning of a year two taxpayers have $20,000 of net assets, and at the end of the year they both have $23,000 of net assets, and if during the year they both spend $7000 for consumption, by what rationale can we justify separate tax treatment of the two, even though one might have had $10,000 in "income," and the other an accrual of $10,000 in capital gains? In this context it is sometimes argued that capital gains do not come in a steady flow, but for many taxpayers neither does income flow in steadily. Such arguments really favor the extension of the provisions in our tax laws that permit taxpayers to average their incomes over time, not the special treatment of capital gains.

For many industries the possibilities of treating the returns to their capital as capital gains are inconsequential, but for some industries, including mineral exploration, they are extremely important. Successful oil wells and other mineral finds can be sold, and the difference between their sale price and their cost treated as a capital gain. If this procedure were followed in the mineral exploring industry, and if all costs were considered in computing the capital gain, the return to capital in mineral exploration would be taxed at only 25 percent as compared with the 52-percent tax applying to ordinary corporate income. This would give a substantial incentive to mineral exploration. If in the economy as a whole the return to capital after tax were 10 percent, investment in mineral exploration (taxed at 25 percent) would be carried to the point where it yielded around 13 1/3 percent before tax, while in industries unable to take advantage of the special rate on capital gains, investment would be carried only to the point where it yielded around 20 percent before tax. Projects yielding 19, 18, 17 percent would be foregone in most industries, while activities yielding only 13 1/3 percent would be willingly undertaken by mineral explorers.

CAPITAL GAINS AND THE EXPENSING OF COSTS

The above example far understates the incentive which our tax laws offer to mineral explorers who sell their finds as capital gains. It assumes that the capital-gains tax of 25 percent applies to the difference between the value of successful finds and all the costs incurred. That is, it assumes that the government takes 25 percent of the gross return to the explorer, and shares in his costs to the tune of 25 percent. Actually our present laws provide for the government's sharing to the tune of 52 percent in most of the costs of mineral exploration, because most exploration costs are deductible from ordinary income in the computation of income subject to tax.

Consider first the costs of unsuccessful explorations. From the standpoint of economy as a whole, the costs of unsuccessful searches are part of the cost of finding new deposits, but individual searches are treated separately for tax purposes. Hence the costs of unsuccessful searches become losses, to be written off against ordinary income before computing taxes. The riskier is the type of exploration in question, the larger will be the fraction of the total costs of unsuccessful exploration which finds a 52-percent tax offset in this way.

Some of the costs of successful explorations can also be written off as expenses against ordinary income. These writeoff possibilities are the result of special provisions of the tax laws. In the case of petroleum, a substantial fraction of the costs of successful wells are written off as expenses under the heading "Intangible Development Costs." In the case of mineral deposits, all development expenses after the existence of commercial ore is established are deductible. Such expenses do not, however, include the costs of plant and equipment.

The unequal tax treatment of revenues and expenses leads to the paradox that companies can make a substantial amount of money on exploration even if their revenues from exploration (before taxes) are just barely equal to their costs of exploration (before tax offsets). If $1 million in exploration expenditures carries with it $500,000 of tax offsets, and leads to finds worth $1 million in the marketplace, with corresponding capital gains taxes of $250,000, what would be a marginal investment under neutral tax treatment becomes an extremely profitable one.

Such extremely profitable outlets for capital will not last for long in a free market economy. Capital will flow into profitable uses until their rate of return after taxes is brought into accord with the rate of return to investors of capital in the economy generally.

If the rate of return on capital in the economy is 10 percent, investments will tend to be made in any line of activity up to the point where the returns from those investments after taxes, discounted at 10 percent, are equal to their costs after tax offsets.

Let us now compare two possible ways of producing capital assets worth $1 million: one by means of mineral exploration and the other by producing machines. Machine producers will be willing to spend up to $1 million to make machines whose discounted value is $1 million. But mineral explorers will be willing to spend, on the average, up to $1.5 million in order to provide discovered reserves worth $1 million. The explorers would obtain a tax offset of about $.75 million on their costs, leaving costs net of taxes at $.75 million. On their revenues, the explorers would pay $.25 million in capital gains taxes, leaving revenues net of taxes also at $.75 million.

Thus capital-gains treatment plus the expensing of exploration costs would lead to a situation in which $1.5 million worth of capital would be willingly spent in order to find $1 million worth of reserves. Alternatively put, if $1 million of capital were transferred out of mineral exploration into other uses, such as manufacturing, the economy would give up $.67 million of reserves and gain in its place $1 million worth of manufactured goods, both evaluated at the normal rate of return. Looked at either way, the combination of capital-gains treatment and expensing of exploration costs leads to a shocking waste of the nation's capital resources.

DISCOVERY DEPLETION

Although, as we have seen, the available option of capital gains treatment for mineral discoveries gives extremely strong incentives to exploration, we do not in fact observe frequent sales of mineral discoveries as capital gains. The reason for this is that still stronger incentives to exploration are available under the label of "percentage depletion," and when percentage depletion is used the discoverers have a strong incentive to retain and operate their properties.

It is convenient to begin the discussion of percentage depletion with an analysis of its historical forbear, known as discovery depletion. The earliest provisions for the depletion of mineral properties provided for a deduction from income for tax purposes, analogous to depreciation, of a certain fraction of the cost of the property in question. Where the property was in existence in 1913, provision was made (in the 1916 act) for the use of the market value of the property in 1913 in lieu of cost as the basis for depletion allowances. Since, because of the riskiness of mineral exploration, the value of successful finds usually greatly exceeds the costs of the successful finds alone, this provision was welcomed by the owners of properties which had been discovered before 1913.

Properties discovered after 1913 were not treated in this way; their depletion allowances had to be based upon cost. The apparent disparity of treatment of properties discovered before and after 1913 led to the adoption in 1918 of a provision allowing depletion based on the fair market value of the property at the date of discovery or within 30 days thereafter, in lieu of depletion based on cost. This was called discovery depletion.

Discovery depletion can best be viewed as a means of avoiding the capital-gains tax altogether. If the 1918 provisions applied today, and a discoverer spent $1 million on exploration in order to find deposits worth $1 million in the market, he would obtain tax offsets of about $500,000 on his costs, but would have to pay no tax at all on the value of his discoveries, so long as he retained and operated them himself.

If we compare discovery depletion with capital-gains treatment and with neutral tax treatment for the case where $1 million is spent to find $1 million in reserves, we find that in all three cases tax offsets of some $500,000 are obtained on the basis of the costs incurred. But while gross revenues would in effect be taxed at $500,000 under neutral tax treatment, they would be taxed at $250,000 under capital-gains treatment, and they would not be taxed at all under discovery depletion.

With discovery depletion, as with any other provisions, investment in exploration would tend to be pressed to the point where the discounted value of discoveries, net of tax, equaled the cost of discoveries, net of tax offsets. $1 million of capital investment would represent only about $500,000 of costs after tax offsets, and investment in mineral exploration would accordingly be pressed to the point where $1 million of investment resulted in the discovery of only $500,000 worth of reserves. Yet the investors would be making the ordinary rate of return on their capital, and would have no cause to regret this outcome.

PERCENTAGE DEPLETION

Percentage depletion grew out of discovery depletion when it was found difficult to obtain good estimates of the market values of all discovered properties as of the date of discovery. To overcome the administrative burden of estimating the value of each individual property, provision was made for allowing as depletion a certain percentage of the gross value of the output of the property, value being taken at the mine or wellhead. The percentage was different for different minerals, and was chosen so as to accord roughly with the actual experience under discovery depletion. Thus the percentage depletion provisions of the 1926 and 1932 acts attempted to allow roughly the same amounts of depletion as would have been allowed under the earlier discovery of depletion provisions; the main purpose of the acts was to make the computation of depletion easier and less subject to controversy. The percentage of gross income allowed in the case of oil was 27 1/2; in sulfur, 23; in metals, 15; and in coal, 5. Provision was also made that the amount of depletion should in no case exceed 50 percent of the net income from the property.

Since percentage depletion was the direct outgrowth of discovery depletion, and attempted to approximate its effects, it should be no surprise that an analysis of percentage depletion yields much the same results as the above analysis of discovery depletion. Because the computations are rather complicated, I have placed them in an appendix,* but the results for typical minerals are summarized here:

Whereas under discovery depletion it would be worthwhile for an explorer to spend $2 million to find $1 million worth of reserves, under percentage depletion it appears that to find $1 million worth of reserves an explorer would be willing to spend $1.95 million for oil, $2.11 million for sulfur, $2.13 million for iron, $1.96 million for copper, $2.27 million for lead and zinc, $2.30 million for coal. Estimates are based on data provided by the Treasury for 1946 and 1947, and on approximations of the average length of life of wells and mines in the various minerals. They are accordingly not precise, but can be taken to confirm the conclusion that the effects of percentage depletion on exploration are not substantially different from those of discovery depletion.

EFFECT OF OUR TAX INCENTIVES

There can be no doubt that our present tax laws give strong incentives to mineral exploration, but this does not mean that we have a great deal more exploring activity than would take place under neutral tax treatment. In the case of some minerals, such as petroleum, the annual volume of exploring activity is great, and here there is good reason to suppose that our tax incentives have rather substantially affected the amount of exploration. With other

* [A later article which supplants the original appendix appears as the next chapter in this volume.]

minerals, such as coal, reserves already known are ample to fill the needs of our economy for hundreds of years, and accordingly there is very little exploration for new deposits. Obviously the tax incentives under discussion here cannot have had a very substantial effect on the amount of exploration for coal. What is true of coal is probably equally true of sand and gravel and a number of the minor minerals that have recently (1951) been granted percentage depletion. Minerals like copper, lead, and zinc probably occupy an intermediate position, exploration for them having responded less than in the case of petroleum but more than in the case of coal as a result of our tax incentives.

Our analysis has indicated that to the extent that exploration is increased in response to current tax provisions, it involves a very substantial waste of resources, with capital devoted to exploration producing only about one-half as much value of product as the same capital would if devoted to ordinary industrial investment. But what happens if little or no additional exploration takes place in response to the special tax provisions? Here the predominant effect is either to increase the value of mineral holdings or to increase the rate of extraction. To the extent that the value of mineral holdings is increased, their owners have received, as a result of the special tax provisions, a "gift" from the Treasury. To the extent that the rate of extraction is increased beyond the point which would be dictated by neutral tax treatment, a waste of resources is involved which is closely analogous to that discussed above in the case of exploration.

These two effects are alternatives. If on the one hand, as may be true in the case of coal, our national output can be greatly expanded without any increase in unit costs, then tax concessions like percentage depletion operate to increase production and drive down prices. Mine owners end up with little more profit than they had before, and consumers get coal more cheaply, say for $9 per ton instead of $10. What looks here like a benefit to consumers really is not, however, for the economy is paying, in terms of the resources used to extract the coal, $10 per ton while consumers use coal to the point where it is only worth $9 a ton to them. But consumers in their role as taxpayers will be paying extra taxes to cover the concession of $1 per ton.

If on the other hand national output cannot readily be expanded, as may be the case with lead, prices will not fall significantly as a result of the tax concession, and the concession will accordingly lead to increased profits and hence to increases in the value of mineral holdings.

Thus if the waste of resources involved in increasing production beyond the level it would attain under neutral taxation is great, then the "gift" to mine owners in the form of enhanced capital values will be small. But if the increase of production beyond its level under neutral taxation is small, the "gift" to mine owners will be large, and indeed will be the predominant result of the tax concession.

POLICY RECOMMENDATIONS

Our present tax laws thus have three possible effects on the minerals industries: To increase the profits and capital values of the owners of mineral deposits; to increase the production of minerals to a point where, but for tax concessions, cost would exceed the value produced; and to increase exploration for minerals to the point where, but for tax concessions, the value of discoveries would be only about half the cost of exploration. The relative importance of these three effects varies from mineral to mineral, but regardless of which effect is dominant, our present policy is unwise. It cannot have been the intent of Congress to make owners of mineral deposits richer at the expense of the rest of the community, and it is clearly unwise to foster the use of resources in either mineral production or mineral exploration when those resources would be much more productive elsewhere in our economy.

I accordingly strongly recommend and urge that every effort be made to place the tax treatment of mineral industries on a par with that of other industries. This should be accomplished:

1. By the gradual reduction and eventual elimination of percentage depletion provisions, leaving strict cost depletion as the sole basis for recovery of capital values in mineral extraction.
2. By the gradual reduction and eventual elimination of the differences that now exist between the tax treatment accorded to capital gains and that given to ordinary income. I envisage here the gradual raising of the maximum rate of tax on capital gains from its present level of 25 percent to the rate applying to ordinary corporate income.

Although a considerable improvement over our present position could be made simply by eliminating the percentage depletion options which are now available, there would still remain the strong incentives to mineral exploration that stem from the special treatment of capital gains, and which were outlined in the early sections of this paper. Thus a rather significant overhaul of our tax structure is necessary before the taxation of mineral industries can be thoroughly rationalized.

RISK AND SMALL ENTERPRISE

It will be recalled that most of the incentive to mineral exploration outlined above came from the fact that the costs of exploration were deductible against ordinary income, while the fruits of exploration received tax treatment which was more favorable than that accorded to ordinary income. A small firm with little or no income against which to offset its exploration costs is thus placed at a severe disadvantage as compared with a large firm having substantial income, either from mineral extraction or from some other source. This disadvantage would still remain if the policy recommendations outlined above were put into effect. However, it could be substantially mitigated by allowing firms to carry forward the losses made on unsuccessful explorations against the income to be obtained from future successes. Then small firms would be at a disadvantage only if their explorations over a long period of time did not yield discoveries equal in value to the costs incurred. A certain share of the costs of such firms would be without tax offsets, while all the costs of the corresponding large firms would be offset against income subject to tax.

It is sometimes argued that our present tax provisions for mineral industries are desirable because of the special risks that such industries are alleged to face. Especially risky enterprises, like specially risky securities, are said to require a rate of return somewhat higher than that prevailing on investments of moderate risk. If the required rate of return were 15 percent after taxes in petroleum exploration, but only 10 percent after taxes in most other industries, then the search for oil would stop at a point where the capital invested yielded 15 percent. By transferring capital from other uses, where it was earning 10 percent, to oil exploration, the economy would gain until the point was reached where capital yielded only 10 percent in the oil business.

The difficulty here is that a yield of 10 percent after taxes in the oil industry cannot be achieved if the required rate of return is 15 percent. More oil can indeed be obtained by tax concessions, which operate as a gift from the rest of the economy to the oil explorers of, say, 5 percent per annum on the capital invested in oil exploration. But such a gift is merely a hidden price paid for the extra oil. If the rest of the economy wants more oil, it should be willing to pay for it by way of a higher market price.

In our present world, in which most minerals are available in the world market, it would indeed be unnecessary for extra oil to be obtained through the payment of price premia to domestic explorers as incentives to risk taking. It would be much cheaper for the rest of the economy simply to buy whatever extra oil it desired in the world market. If in the process market prices would be bid up, more domestic oil would also be forthcoming, but oil users would have the knowledge that they were paying no greater price than was necessary to provide them with the amount of oil they wanted. Hence there is no justification for the use of tax concessions as a device for overcoming the reluctance of domestic mineral enterprises to incur risk, at least not in a peacetime economy.

In point of fact, there are good reasons to believe that the riskiness of mineral exploration has been exaggerated. In petroleum, which is often cited as an extremely risky industry for exploration, there have developed a wide range of contractual devices by which the risks of exploration can be shared. Exploring companies can sell off 90 percent or more of the interest in the wells which they themselves drill, and with the proceeds buy fractional interests in wells drilled by others. In the light of these possibilities, the fact that nine out of ten exploratory wells are dry seems less of a deterrent to exploration than it might at first glance appear. Additional evidence is provided by the fact that bankruptcies are not widespread among even moderate-sized petroleum companies. And the rate of return on capital, for the petroleum industry as a whole, appears to accord closely with that applying in other segments of the American economy. So even if the risks are substantial, it appears that investors demand no special premium of significant size for taking "long shot" rather than "sure shot" gambles. And in a way it would be surprising if they did require a special premium, for worldwide experience with gambling and lotteries suggests that many people are willing to risk their capital at long odds even when the aggregate winnings fall far short of the aggregate of wagers.

Thus even if mineral exploration is especially risky, in the sense that the risks cannot be pooled to leave the individual investor in a position of only moderate risk, and even if investors demand special premia for special risks, there is no justification for special tax concessions to mineral enterprises on this account. But our scattered evidence suggests that even if individual explorations are risky there is no reason to presume on that account that special risk premia are required; indeed it suggests that the possibilities of risk pooling are sufficiently great to cast doubt on the assumption that exploration need be especially risky to the investor or investing company.

SPECIAL INCENTIVES FOR NATIONAL DEFENSE

Our national defense is such a primary objective that citizens are willing to incur great costs on its account. But especially with a defense budget as large as ours is today, we should be strongly interested in seeing to it that we are getting the maximum amount of defense potential for our money, or to put it another way, that we are not paying more than is necessary for the amount of defense potential that we are getting. True economy, in this area as in others, requires scrutinizing each individual action to make sure that we are getting the most for our money.

It is my conviction that our present tax treatment of mineral industries has no justification in a peacetime economy. Hence it can be justified, if at all, only in terms of its contribution to national defense. But it would indeed be surprising if percentage depletion were the best way to provide for our defense needs of coal and sand and gravel as well as oil and copper and lead. Some minerals are domestically available in great abundance and can be extracted easily. These should need no special treatment on defense grounds. Other minerals are abundantly available, but their rate of extraction can be expanded only slowly. Here the maintenance of stockpiles or of standby capacity might be warranted. Still other minerals are increasingly hard to find in the United States, and we are relying increasingly on foreign sources of supply for them. These minerals, of which petroleum, copper, lead, and zinc are examples, pose the hardest problems for national defense. Should we create incentives to extract our waning supplies more rapidly, so as to have a high output available for an immediate emergency, but at the risk of failing supplies for a more distant conflict? Should we restrict current production and maintain stockpiles of known reserves in the ground, and incur the costs of recruiting and training a labor force to mine them in the event an emergency should strike? Should we rely exclusively on stockpiles above ground, incurring what in some cases might be substantial storage costs? Or should we attempt, in our defense preparations, to assure the comparatively safe transportation of the minerals from nearby foreign sources, such as Canada, Mexico, and Venezuela?

It is not within my competence to answer the above questions. They are questions of great importance to our nation, yet they have not been given adequate study. Such study is necessary before the best minerals policy for national defense will be found. One may reasonably wonder, however, whether a tax policy such as we have at present would have a place in any rational scheme of providing for our defense needs. Certainly it is not in our defense interests to enhance the capital values of those who happen to own mineral deposits. It is dubious at best whether we should provide incentives to increase the production and use of our waning supplies of scarce minerals. And it is almost certainly wrong for us to foster the use of $200 worth of our resources to find $100 worth of mineral deposits, which then will more than likely be extracted and consumed before a national emergency strikes. Yet these are the effects of our present tax laws. I accordingly do not believe that the present provisions can be supported even on national-defense grounds.

Chapter 12

The Tax Treatment
of Oil Exploration

I

Some years ago I presented an analysis of the problem of percentage depletion, in which I developed what I believe to be the theoretical structure which is relevant for this problem, at least in those cases where the role of exploration is of primary importance.[1] I do not plan to recapitulate here the overall lines of argument presented in my earlier paper. I do, however, plan to present once again the approach outlined in the mathematical appendix of the earlier paper, for several typographical errors in the published version of that appendix have created unnecessary difficulties for many readers. More important, the numerical examples given in my earlier paper were based on fairly rigid assumptions, some of which have been challenged by other writers.[2] In this paper I take a much more cautious approach, and rather than attempting precise numerical estimates for the key factors involved, I allow for rather broad ranges. These ranges are wide enough to include, I believe, all plausible possibilities. Individual cases which might fall outside these ranges would be so rare as to be truly exceptional, and not representative of the typical pattern of effects.

In order to avoid the complexities entailed in trying, within a single theoretical model, to deal with all the widely different types of activity now covered by

[1] See Arnold C. Harberger, "The Taxation of Mineral Industries," in U.S. Congress, Joint Economic Committee, *Federal Tax Policy for Economic Growth and Stability* (Washington, D.C.: Government Printing Office, November 1955), pp. 439–449. [This volume, Chapter 11.]

[2] See especially Peter O. Steiner, "Percentage Depletion and Resource Allocation," U.S. House of Representatives, Committee on Ways and Means, *Tax Revision Compendium* (Washington, D.C.: Government Printing Office, December 1959), Vol. II, pp. 949–966. Steiner objected to the assumptions which I made about the fraction of exploration costs which were expensed, and about the ratio which depletion allowances typically bore to net income from producing wells. There are a few points in Steiner's treatment which I believe are open to discussion, but the issues are so minor that their introduction here would tend to obscure the main points which this paper attempts to make. The ranges which are given in the present paper for the ratios in question are sufficiently wide that they easily include those used by Steiner.

Reprinted with permission from Arnold C. Harberger, "The Tax Treatment of Oil Exploration," *Proceedings of the Second Energy Institute* (Washington, D.C.: The American University, 1961), pp. 256–269.

percentage depletion provisions, I shall limit the scope of this paper to the case of petroleum. Most of the analysis does have broader applicability, but each separate activity has certain peculiar characteristics of its own which would require at least a special discussion of how the model should be interpreted, if not an alteration of the basic model itself. By focusing on the case of oil, I shall be able to bring explicitly into the treatment certain key features of that particular industry.

One key feature of this industry is the highly competitive nature of exploration for oil. Large numbers of firms, of all different sizes, are engaged in this activity. Given the competitiveness of oil exploration, it has always been a puzzle to me how so many writers, in treating percentage depletion, have assumed that the depletion provisions lead to the firms in the industry making exorbitantly high profits. My contention is that competition in oil exploration is sufficient to keep the rate of return on investment in that activity broadly in line with the rate of return on investment in other sectors of the economy. The rate of return to which I refer is of course net of taxes and tax offsets.

The riskiness of oil exploration does of course lead to wide differences in the experience of individual enterprises. But it cannot be denied that if capital in oil exploration yielded, on the average, 20 percent net of taxes, while in most other activities it yielded only 10 percent, there would be a great rush of capital into oil exploration. This would tend to drive down the rate of return toward 10 percent. Perhaps in the end there would remain some differential (reflecting a risk premium), but the available evidence does not suggest that this premium, if it exists at all, is of substantial magnitude. The rate of return, net of taxes, on capital invested in oil exploration corporations, is not substantially greater than the rate of return on investment in other corporations.

The equalization of the after-tax rate of return between oil exploration and other activities probably applies at the corporate level. There are a great many corporations engaged in oil exploration, and they are all, broadly speaking, subject to the same marginal tax rate. They constitute a sufficiently large mass of capital to be able to bring the rate of return on oil exploration to the point where "corporate" capital would be neither especially advantaged nor especially disadvantaged by either shifting into or out of the oil exploration activity. But if this is the case for corporations (with a 52 percent marginal tax rate), it is likely to be true that individuals in the 70 or 80 or 90 percent tax bracket will find that they really can get a higher after tax rate of return by investing in oil exploration than by investing in other directions. The limits to the amount that they invest in oil exploration will be dictated by considerations of portfolio balance and of risk rather than by purely rate-of-return considerations.

II

In this section and the next I present the mathematical demonstration of the proposition that investment in oil exploration is probably pushed substantially beyond the margin which can be considered as "economic" for the society as a whole.

Consider two capital assets, one a machine and the other an oil well. Let them be equivalent in the sense that the streams of income expected to stem from them, net of other costs but before taxation, are identical. These streams, under competitive conditions, measure the value of the services of these assets to the final users of their products, and hence to the economy. Let the present value of each of these income streams be Y, using as the rate of discount that rate which reflects the typical net-of-tax yield on capital in the economy.

Generally speaking, one would expect that potential purchasers of these two assets would be willing to pay the same price for either of them. However, tax considerations do enter the picture. The machine must be depreciated for tax purposes according to normal procedures, while in the case of the oil well, the special provisions for percentage depletion may be involved. In either case, however, the price which a firm would be willing to pay for an asset should equal the discounted value of the *net* income stream expected to flow from that asset. This consists of the discounted value (Y) of the before-tax income stream, less the discounted value (W) of the tax payments associated with this asset.

In the case of normal depreciation we have

$$W_1 = t(Y - dR_1).$$

Here t is the rate of corporation income tax which is applicable, d is a discount factor, and R_1 is the (as yet unknown) price paid for the asset. The discount factor, d, simply takes account of the fact that the present value of \$1,000 spread out over a period of time in the future is less than \$1,000. The price paid for the asset is the dollar total which can be written off as depreciation over the life of the asset. But the present value of these writeoffs is only a fraction (d) of the initial price. This fraction will be smaller, the higher is the rate of discount and the longer is the life of the asset.

In the case of percentage depletion, we have

$$W_2 = t(Y - pY) = tY(1 - p).$$

Here p is the fraction which depletion allowances bear to net income before depletion. One should bear clearly in mind that p is *not* the statutory 27 1/2 percent, which applies not to net income before depletion but to the gross value of the output of the asset (the well) at its site. Our statutes do provide that the allowance for percentage depletion may never exceed 50 percent of the net income from the asset at its site; hence p, in the case of oil, must lie somewhere above 27 1/2 percent but may in no case exceed 50 percent.

It is instructive to inquire whether, for the purchaser of an existing producing well, it would normally be preferable to use the option of percentage depletion. I assume here that the prospective flow of output from the well is correctly estimated at the time of its purchase. If cost depletion is to be used, the present value of the after-tax income stream, and hence the price which buyers would be willing to pay for the well, will be

$$R_1 = Y - W_1 = Y - t(Y - dR_1).$$

Solving this, we find:

$$R_1 = \frac{Y(1 - t)}{1 - td}.$$

If percentage depletion is to be used, the price buyers would be willing to pay for the well is

$$R_2 = Y - W_2 = Y - t(Y - pY) = Y(1 - t + tp).$$

Since p must lie between 27 1/2 and 50 percent, it can be seen that R_2, with a 52 percent tax rate, must lie between $.623Y$ and $.74Y$.

R_1, on the other hand, will be $.48Y/(1 - .52d)$ with a 52 percent tax rate. Plausible assumptions about discount rates, useful life of wells, and patterns of depreciation lead to values of d well within the range of .5 to .75.[3] And this range for d in turn implies a range for R_1 of from $.649Y$ to $.787Y$.

The overlap between the ranges for R_1 and for R_2 signifies that it is not at all surprising that when producing wells are purchased the buying companies very often opt for cost depletion. In fact the ranges indicated suggest that cost depletion may be slightly preferable to percentage depletion when a well is operated by a company which purchased rather than discovered it. The approach presented here is therefore certainly not at variance in this respect with assertions made by industry experts that cost depletion is used in perhaps the majority of cases of wells purchased by operating companies.

Actually, the differences between percentage depletion and cost depletion are probably not great in cases *of purchased wells*. The difference becomes important in those cases where the discoverers of wells retain them in their possession for operation. In the remaining cases, where the discovering company sells the successful wells to producing companies, it is the capital gains provisions of our tax laws rather than the percentage depletion provisions which create artificial incentives for oil exploration.

III

In the cases of both capital gains treatment and percentage depletion treatment of the fruits of exploration, the cost side of the picture is of great importance. In the case of most business assets, their cost of acquisition is clearly and easily defined. In the case of producing oil wells, especially the successful exploratory wells, the cost is not so readily obtained. In an economic sense, the cost of finding successful wells includes the costs of all the unsuccessful searches as well. Yet this is not easily allocable among the successful wells, certainly not for purposes of tax accounting.

Our tax laws take the view that the costs of a successful exploratory well are simply those costs directly incurred in finding it — and in fact the bulk of these costs are allowed to be expensed immediately rather than being capitalized and entering into the "basis" on which a possible capital gain might be computed upon the sale of the well.

[3] The range allowed for d is really very substantial. If we assume a 10-year life and straight-line depreciation, any rate of discount between about 5.5 percent and 15.5 percent would yield a d within the range given. Looking at it another way, if we assume a discount rate of 8 percent and straight-line depreciation over the life of the asset, any asset life between 7 years and 18 years will yield a d within the given range. Taking a 10 percent rate allows us to have any asset life between 5 and 15 years and still remain within the given range. The formula for d is $d = [1 - (1 + i)^{-n}]/ni$, where n is the effective life of the asset and i is the rate of discount.

Ordinarily, the capital gain on an asset sold by a business firm is computed by deducting from the sale price of the asset its actual original cost less depreciation to the date of sale. On the difference a special tax rate of 25 percent applies. In the case of a successful oil well a very different situation emerges. All the costs associated with the dry holes drilled in the course of the search may be written off against ordinary income, as may most of the costs of the successful find. The result is that even when the value of the find is substantially less than the total costs incurred, the company may make a handsome profit.

Suppose that costs are $1,200,000, of which $1,000,000 are allowable as expense. This $1,000,000 of expense carries with it a tax offset of $520,000 for any company with significant net income from other operations. Suppose that the remaining $200,000 are costs associated with the successful well, which are not allowed as expense and which therefore become the "cost basis" of the successful well for the purpose of computing capital gains. Let the successful well be sold for $1,000,000. A capital gains tax of $200,000 (25 percent of $800,000) must be paid upon the sale of the well. From the standpoint of the economy as a whole $1,200,000 worth of resources have been used to find a property worth $1,000,000 — clearly a losing operation. But from the standpoint of the company as a private venture — and because of our tax laws — there is a gain of $120,000 ($1,000,000 receipt from sale plus $520,000 of tax offsets less $1,200,000 costs less $200,000 capital gains tax).

The case is even worse when syndicates of individuals in high income tax brackets do the exploring. Assuming the same cost situation, and individuals in, say, the 80 percent income tax bracket or above, the tax offset would be over $800,000. The individuals could gain even if the successful well sold for as little as $600,000. Their profit would be at least $100,000 ($600,000 receipt from sale plus at least $800,000 in tax offsets less $1,200,000 costs less $100,000 capital gains tax). What for the economy is a disastrous waste of resources (spending ·$1,200,000 to find something worth only $600,000) is for these individuals a quite acceptable investment. The simple way to avoid this inducement to economic waste is to recognize the special provisions made for expensing on the cost side of the exploration picture, and in the light of these special provisions to disallow capital gains treatment on any sale of oil property.

Most exploration is not done for the purpose of subsequent sale and capital gain, however. It is done rather by producing companies which then operate the successful wells they find, almost invariably under the percentage depletion provisions of the tax law. Cost considerations are important here, too, since once again the costs of dry holes plus a large part of the costs of successful wells can be expensed against ordinary income, and thus obtain tax offsets in addition to whatever offsets accrue through percentage depletion.

Ordinary business investment will tend, in any line of activity, to be pushed to the point where the present value of the net-of-tax stream of income expected to accrue from an asset (R_1) is equal to the cost of the asset (C_1). Hence we have, for an ordinary business investment yielding an income stream whose present value is Y:

$$C_1 = \frac{Y(1-t)}{(1-td)}.$$

In the case of oil exploration by producing companies, we have the same tendency. Exploration will tend to be carried to the point where the present value of net-of-tax receipts is equal to the present value of costs, net-of-tax offsets. The present value of the net-of-tax receipts is given by $R_2 = Y(1 - t + tp)$. This expression incorporates the tax offset involved in percentage depletion itself, but not that involved in the expensing of the bulk of exploration costs. We shall allow for this on the cost side, assuming that these tax offsets apply to some 80 percent of costs. Thus, if actual costs are C_2, costs net of these tax offsets are $C_2(1 - .8t)$. Competitive forces will thus press toward an equilibrium in which

$$C_2(1 - .8t) = Y(1 - t + tp), \quad \text{or in which}$$

$$C_2 = \frac{Y(1 - t + tp)}{(1 - .8t)}.$$

We can now ask the question, how different is the amount of resources which will normally be used to obtain a given income stream in oil exploration from the amount of resources which will typically produce the same income stream via ordinary business investment? To answer this question, we assume Y (the present value of the income stream) to be the same in both cases, and simply take the ratio of C_2 to C_1.

This yields

$$\frac{C_2}{C_1} = \frac{(1 - t + tp)(1 - td)}{(1 - .8t)(1 - t)}.$$

With a 52 percent tax rate, and various values for p and d, this ratio behaves

TABLE 12.I

Values of C_2/C_1 under Alternative Assumptions

p	.275	.35	.5
d			
.5	1.64	1.75	1.95
.65	1.47	1.57	1.75
.75	1.36	1.44	1.61

as shown in Table 12.1. The range of these estimates indicates that in order to obtain an equivalent income stream, between 1.36 and 1.95 times as many resources will typically be used in oil exploration by producing companies as in ordinary business investment.[4]

IV

I cannot believe that it was the intention of our lawmakers to create such strong artificial incentives to oil exploration as appear through percentage depletion and/or the procedure of selling successful wells for capital gains. On the one hand, it is hard to see how this could have been their intention when, at least in the published economic literature, the magnitude of these incentives has not been estimated until recently. On the other hand, even if recently developed analyses had been available to the lawmakers at the time when percentage depletion allowances were first enacted, their choice in adopting percentage depletion would not mean their endorsement of incentives of the present scale. For income tax rates were then much lower than they are today, and the magnitude of the special incentives entailed in percentage depletion depends strongly on the applicable rate of income tax.

The following table reveals this dependency very clearly. In it, values of C_2/C_1 are calculated for different tax rates, assuming $d = .65$ and $p = .35$ (as in the central cell of Table 12.1).

TABLE 12.2

Values of C_2/C_1 under Alternative Tax Rates
(percentage depletion, assuming $d = .65$, $p = .35$)

Tax rate	C_2/C_1
.1	1.056
.2	1.126
.3	1.218
.4	1.342
.5	1.519
.6	1.789
.7	2.250
.8	3.200

Whereas with a 50 percent tax rate, percentage depletion gives incentives to use roughly 1 1/2 times as many resources as need be used in other investments to obtain the same income stream, the figure is only 1.056 times when the tax

---

[4] Altering the assumption that 80 percent of the total costs of exploration obtain tax offsets independently of percentage depletion does not change the general conclusions derived from Table 12.1. Changing this percentage to 90 would alter the ratios in Table 12.1 upward by about 10 percent; changing the percentage to 70 would alter them downward by about 8 percent. Steiner's data (*op. cit.*, p. 960, Table 3, especially rows a_1 and a_2) suggest that any alteration should probably be upward toward 90 percent rather than downward toward 70 percent.

rate is 10 percent and 1.126 times when the tax rate is 20 percent. Thus, until the middle 1930s (when corporation taxes began to approach their current levels), the special incentives stemming from percentage depletion were of a comparatively small magnitude. With the subsequent successive increases in the corporation tax rate, petroleum exploration has been automatically placed in a much more favored position relative to other kinds of investment activity. I would contend strongly that it was not the design of our legislators to bring about this increasing favoritism toward petroleum exploration. Tax rates were raised because of pressing needs for additional revenue, and the basic structure of provisions for depletion was simply left untouched as rates were altered. But this had the effect of greatly enhancing the relative advantage enjoyed by petroleum exploration as an outlet for investment.

Exactly the same sort of dependency of the relative advantage for petroleum exploration on the level of tax rates appears when the effects of capital gains taxation are analyzed. Assume that buyers of already discovered wells uniformly choose to use cost depletion rather than percentage depletion, and as a consequence are willing to pay the same price for a well producing a given income stream as purchasers would pay for other kinds of capital equipment yielding the same income stream. Differences in the amounts of resources used to produce the income streams thus emerge only on the cost side. In the case of ordinary capital equipment the costs (C_1) incurred to produce a stream whose present value is R_1 will tend to be equal to R_1. When petroleum exploration is undertaken for purposes of capital gain it is the present value of costs net of taxes and tax offsets which will tend to be equal to R_1. If costs in this case are equal to C_3, and 80 percent of these costs can be written off against ordinary income, while the remaining 20 percent provide the "cost basis" for computation of capital gain, we have, in equilibrium:

$$C_3 - t(.8C_3) + t'(R_1 - .2C_3) = R_1,$$

where t is the tax rate on ordinary income and t' is the special tax rate applying to capital gains.

TABLE 12.3

Values of C_3/C_1 under Alternative Tax Rates
(capital gains, assuming $t' = 1/2t$, or $t' = .25$, whichever is less)

Income tax rate (t)	C_3/C_1
.1	1.044
.2	1.097
.3	1.164
.4	1.250
.5	1.364
.6	1.596
.7	1.923
.8	2.419

Using the fact that for ordinary investments yielding income streams of present value R_1, C_1 tends to be equal to R_1, we may write:

$$C_3(1 - .8t - .2t') = C_1(1 - t'),$$

or

$$\frac{C_3}{C_1} = \frac{(1 - t')}{(1 - .8t - .2t')}.$$

It can be seen from a comparison of Table 12.3 with Table 12.2 that the incentive given to petroleum exploration by the capital gains provisions of our tax laws is almost as great, for any given tax rate, as that given by the percentage depletion provisions. Moreover, the differential incentive given by the capital gains provisions is like that given by percentage depletion in that it increases with the tax rate, from small values when the tax rate is in the neighborhood of 10 or 20 percent to high values when it is 50 percent and more. The conclusion appears inescapable that strong incentives for excessive investment in petroleum exploration really came into being in the last few decades, as income tax rates were raised toward their present high levels. To bring the relative incentives for petroleum exploration back to the level at which they were when percentage depletion was first enacted would entail, at present corporation tax rates, a very substantial reduction in the current 27 1/2 percent depletion rate, and a very substantial increase in the tax rate applicable to capital gains on oil properties.

X

Chapter 13, which appeared in *The Taxpayer's Stake in Tax Reform* published in 1968 by the Chamber of Commerce of the United States is essentially a straightforward exposition of the principles underlying the taxation of value added, together with a modest plea for its consideration as a permanent component of the United States tax system. This is a *modest* plea because the arguments for a value-added tax are much stronger when it is viewed (as was the case in the European countries, which have by now largely shifted to the value-added tax) as a substitute for a preexisting turnover tax than when it is viewed as a wholly new component of the system.

As Chapter 15 indicates, I place only small weight on the possible beneficial effect of a value-added tax on the balance-of-payments position of the United States. Its principal benefit, I believe, would be as a potential source of increases in revenues when these are needed in a hurry (as was the case, for example, in the Korean War) and as a highly responsive instrument of flexible fiscal policy in the short run.

I have encountered no arguments against the value-added tax in the above terms. Rather, its opponents seem to have concentrated their fire on the likely regressive incidence of the tax. On this matter no issues of economic analysis are involved, but only questions of values on the one hand and political judgment on the other. On the value side, I share with opponents of the value-added tax the belief that the tax system should be progressive. But I would argue that judgments concerning progressivity are more relevant when applied to the whole tax system (or even better, to the whole tax-expenditure system) than when applied to each component separately. A tax system can have some substantial regressive components, and still be quite, or even very, progressive overall. This does not argue in any sense that there should be regressive components in a tax system, but only that where a particular tax (like the value-added tax) has very substantial advantages of its own (neutrality with respect to resource allocation, ease of administration, flexibility with respect to changing revenue needs), the fact that taken alone it is somewhat regressive in its incidence should not be taken as a decisive argument against it.

Here is where the issue of political judgment enters. If one views the ultimate incidence of the tax system as the product of a series of historical accidents — first one tax is imposed, then another, then a rate structure is changed, etc. — the addition of one new regressive component (in this case the value-added tax) will automatically make the system as a whole more regressive. This is the position taken by a number of opponents of the value-added tax.

On the other hand, it is possible to take the view that the political and social climate prevailing in any given period largely determines the degree of progressivity of the tax and expenditure systems, more or less independently of the particular components making up, say, the tax system. Thus the imposition of value-added tax could be accompanied, or reasonably shortly followed, by either an increase of the exemption level on the personal income tax, or by a closing of some tax loopholes that benefit mainly the higher brackets, or by a variety of other devices which would tend to preserve the progressivity of the overall structure, or to make it reflect changing political pressures and forces much as it would have done anyway, even in the absence of a value-added tax.

I do not have very firm feelings about which of these alternative sets of political judgments is more nearly correct or relevant, but my leaning is toward the view that the overall degree of progression is determined in a fashion that is largely independent of the presence or absence of any particular tax. Certainly I can say that it is when I more or less explicitly or consciously accept the approximate validity of this view of the political process that I feel most easy and comfortable in advocating a value-added tax for the United States.

Chapter 13

A Federal Tax on Value Added

The idea of a value-added tax is still strange to most Americans, and it is only natural that this should lead to its being greeted with trepidation and suspicion. Our first task, therefore, is to set out the basic concept of the value-added tax, and to relate it to more familiar types of taxation. Then, as the second step in our analysis, we shall outline the principal arguments for and against the value-added tax, and attempt to assess their overall merits and weaknesses as well as any particular advantages or disadvantages that such a tax might have for the United States. Finally, we shall turn to issues related to the design and adminis-tration of a value-added tax.

THE NATURE OF VALUE-ADDED TAXATION

In its National Policy Statement, *A Better Balance in Federal Taxes on Business* (April, 1966), the Committee for Economic Development stated (p. 20):

> We urge that serious consideration be given to the introduction of a flat rate tax on all the value added in business activity in the United States. To assure that the tax rate can be set at a low enough rate to minimize distortions, this tax should be as broadly based as is administratively feasible. By a tax on value added we mean an unduplicated tax on the increase in the value of products as they pass through successive firms in the production and distribution process.

The key element of value-added taxation is clearly stated by the CED: The base of such a tax is the *increase in value* of products as they pass through successive stages in the production and distribution process. The farmer pays tax on the difference between the value of the wheat he produces and the cost of the seeds, fertilizers, etc. used in producing the wheat. The miller pays tax on the difference between the value of the flour he produces and the cost of the wheat and other material inputs that went into its production. The baker pays tax on the dif-ference between the value of the bread he produces and the cost of the flour and other materials consumed in making it. Finally, the retailer pays tax on the difference between the retail value of bread he sells and the cost to him (at wholesale) of acquiring the bread. Thus if the tax were levied at the rate of

From *The Taxpayer's Stake in Tax Reform*, copyright 1968, Chamber of Commerce of the United States. Reproduced by permission.

229

5 percent of value added at each stage of the process, it would end up having collected, in separate stages, 5 percent of the retail value of bread. It is an *unduplicated* tax in the sense that once tax has been paid on a "part" of the economic activities involved in producing bread, that "part" is never taxed again in subsequent stages of production.

The principles reflected in the above example of bread apply equally well to other products. Of the final tax of 5 percent of the value of an automobile, a part would have been paid by coal mining companies, other parts by steel firms, by tire makers, by glass makers, by copper companies, etc., and finally the parts corresponding to them would be paid by the auto manufacturer and the dealer. Of the final tax of 5 percent on meat, a part would have been paid by the rancher, a part by the cattle-fattener, a part by the meat packer, a part by the wholesaler, and a part by the retailer. If the tax were fully general, and struck all productive activities in the economy, it would end up having taxed away 5 percent of value of the final goods and services produced by the private sector of the economy; in other words, it would have taken 5 percent of the private sector's contribution to the Gross National Product.[1] Each business firm would have paid tax on its contribution to the GNP, which is simply the difference in value between its output and the costs of those materials and intermediate products which were purchased from other firms for use in making that output.

Now let us examine the relationship between value-added taxes and other, more familiar taxes. The value-added tax just described, which is called the product type, is most closely related to a retail sales tax of a very general kind — so general as to cover all goods and services acquired by consumers, plus all acquisitions of investment assets by business firms. The value-added tax strikes all final goods and services produced by the private sector of the economy, while the fully general retail sales tax strikes all final goods and services acquired by the private sector. The differences between the production and the acquisitions of the private sector are of two types: (a) sales to the public sector, and (b) transactions with foreign countries.

With respect to (a), these sales would be taxed under the value-added tax and presumably exempt under the sales tax. The difference, however, is of little practical moment. If the public sector were to pay tax under the sales tax alternative, it would also receive the revenues in question; there is thus no basic difference between the situation in which the public sector pays and receives a 5 percent tax on the final goods and services it acquires, and that in which it pays and receives no tax on these acquisitions. The only point at which the difference has relevance concerns the different levels of government. Under a federal value-added tax, state and local governments would in effect pay tax to the federal government on their purchases; under a federal final sales tax, these purchases would presumably (though not necessarily) be exempt. Thus, while the situation of the public sector as a whole is the same under final sales and

---

[1] The above statement is precisely true only for the so-called product type of value-added tax, but the general principle that a fully general value-added tax is equivalent to a tax on some corresponding macroeconomic total applies also to value-added taxes of the income and consumption types. These are discussed in detail below.

value-added taxation, the distribution of fiscal burdens and revenues within it may be somewhat different.

With respect to (b), under a general final sales tax, export sales would presumably be exempt, while under a value-added tax striking all production done within the country, tax would automatically have been paid on the great bulk of the value of exports long before the items in question reached the export stage or were even known to be headed for export. The border-tax adjustments permitted under the General Agreement on Tariffs and Trade are, however, all that is needed to bring about the same end result under either value-added tax or the final sales tax. These adjustments permit the rebating, at the point of export, of any indirect taxes that have been paid in the process of the production of any exported goods or services. They also permit the collection, at the point of import, of a corresponding tax (in our example, 5 percent) on any imported goods and services. In this way a tax which (like the value-added tax) is nominally levied upon production activity can be transformed in effect into a tax on acquisitions of final products by domestic consumers and business firms.

In sum, a general value-added tax of the product type, and incorporating the GATT border-tax adjustments, is for all practical purposes equivalent to a general sales tax on all final goods and services acquired by the private sector.

Up to now we have considered the value-added tax as a levy on the difference between the value of production and the cost of acquiring materials and intermediate products. We can now visualize an income statement for the firm, and ask ourselves of what items does the above difference consist. Basically, this reduces to an issue of deciding what we mean by value of production and what we mean by the costs of acquiring materials and intermediate products. However we decide this issue, we must do so consistently; if an item is counted as part of product when sold to another firm, it must be counted as part of cost when bought from another firm. No serious issues arise here insofar as material goods or direct services (such as legal, accounting, and consulting services) are concerned. If they are bought from an individual or entity not covered by the value-added system, as in the case of the services of a lawyer directly employed by the firm, they are not deductible in the computation of value added.

If they are bought from a firm which is itself covered by the system, they are deductible to the purchasing firm but are treated as part of the value of product of the selling firm. Thus the services of a law firm contracted by a company would be deductible so far as that company was concerned, but the salary paid to the lawyers in question would not be deductible in the law firm's computation of its own tax liability.

A similar issue arises in connection with the treatment of interest payments and rents. In both cases what is involved is the use within a firm of "hired" capital, and the question arises of whether to treat the payments to hired capital similarly to those to hired labor, i.e., to count interest and rent payments as part of value added, or whether to treat them similarly to the purchase and sale of goods and services, thus counting rental and interest income as part of the product of the firm and deducting rental and interest payments to other firms. The second of these approaches is clearly to be preferred, for the fact that the services in question are "hired" is not the relevant distinction. The relevant distinction is whether the payments in question were made to other firms covered by the system or not. If they were, and if the law is appropriately framed, they would already have entered into the calculation of those firms as part of the value of their product, and the other firms would have been liable to tax upon them. The general rule, then, is that all receipts from the provision of goods and services (including interest and rent receipts) are included in the value of production, and all payments to other entities within the value-added system for materials or intermediate goods and services (including interest and rental payments to such entities) are deductible in the calculation of value added.

When a general value-added tax of the product type is imposed, covering the whole (incorporated and unincorporated) business sector of the economy, then, the principal components of the tax base are (a) profits,[2] (b) wage and salary payments,[3] (c) interest and rental payments to individuals, (d) indirect business taxes (other than the value-added tax itself), and (e) depreciation allowances. Together these add up to the Gross National Product generated by the private sector of the economy, so long as the tax is indeed fully general.

When looked at this way, the tax often gives rise to the question of whether it is fair or appropriate to include indirect business taxes and depreciation allowances in the tax base. Without going at this point into the issues involved, let us note that the standard, garden variety type of excise tax in effect is levied on the base of all of the above items plus the costs of materials and intermediate products (including whatever taxes those costs incorporate); hence there are no grounds to justify our being shocked at having depreciation and indirect taxes included in the value-added tax base. Moreover, their inclusion in the base is not a necessary part of value-added taxation, but rather the distinguishing feature of the product type of value-added tax. They can easily be eliminated from the base by allowing firms to deduct them from value added as defined for a product-type tax, before arriving at the base on which their tax will be computed. Doing so, we convert a value-added tax of the product type into one of the income type.

This is perhaps the clearest way to conceive of what is meant by a value-added tax of the income type — as simply a value-added tax of the product type, adjusted so as to make depreciation and indirect business taxes (other than the value-added tax itself) deductible. It is important to note that the income type of value-added tax does not correspond to a tax on business income, but rather to one on all wages and profits in the business sector, plus interest and rents (i.e., the income from capital other than profits) paid by that sector to individuals. These items, for a fully general tax, would add up essentially to the national income generated within the private sector. The tax with which a value-added tax of the income type can most directly be compared is not the corporation profits tax but rather the personal income tax. In effect, the income type value-added tax is simply a proportional income tax on all income generated in the economy, with an exemption for that part generated in the public sector. And since, as indicated before, there is precious little difference between the cases in

---

[2] Sales, and therefore profits, should in principle include goods "sold" by the firm to itself or its owners — e.g., inventory accumulation or withdrawal of part of the firm's product for consumption by owners.

[3] Including payments in kind.

which the government does or does not pay tax to itself, the analogy to a proportional income tax on income generated within the economy is quite close indeed.

The consumption type of value-added tax differs from the income type in that instead of allowing the deduction of depreciation on capital assets it simply permits the cost of such assets to be deducted at the time of purchase. The analogy here is with a proportional tax on consumption, or with a retail sales tax from which investment goods acquired by business firms are exempt. This can be easily seen by proceeding from our earlier analysis of a value-added tax of the product type. We saw there that such a tax (with the GATT border-tax adjustments) was equivalent to a general tax at a flat rate on all final goods and services acquired by the private sector of the economy. If, starting with such a tax, we exempt those goods acquired for investment purposes, we are naturally left with a tax striking only consumption goods.

The concept of a value-added tax, then, though it may be unfamiliar as such to many readers, has close analogies, in its several variants, with (a) a fully general sales tax on final goods and services (product type), (b) a proportional tax on all income generated in the economy (income type), (c) a proportional tax on all consumption goods sold to consumers in the economy (consumption type). The equivalence is so close that it is difficult to conceive of any strong argument for a general value-added tax of one type or another, which is not equally weighty in favor of its non-value-added counterpart. Thus one rarely if ever hears arguments for substituting a value-added tax for an existing sales or income tax; its advocates instead tend to regard it as a substitute for other taxes, against which its superiority stands out more clearly, or as an additional tax in the system.

THE MAJOR ISSUES

The value-added tax clearly has its strongest appeal, and its firmest base of application, in continental Europe, where it has been in effect in France since 1954, is scheduled to be introduced in West Germany this year, and has been recommended for adoption by all Common Market countries. The reason is, I believe, not hard to find, for the continental European countries have traditionally relied heavily on taxes of the turnover type, in contrast to most other advanced economies. The overwhelmingly most important argument favoring the introduction of value-added taxation on the Continent is that the value-added tax is a much more neutral, much more rational substitute for the prevailing (or previously prevailing) turnover tax system.

Under the turnover system, the farmer pays tax on the value of the wheat, the miller pays tax on the value of the flour, and the baker pays tax on the value of the bread. Thus, in effect, the wheat embodied in the bread is taxed three times, the value added in converting wheat into flour is taxed twice, and the value added in making flour into bread is taxed once. All the above assumes, however, that the farmer, the miller, and the baker are three separate business firms. If the miller and the baker merge, the new firm still only pays tax once on the value of the bread; the tax previously paid by the miller on the value of the wheat simply disappears. And if the merged firm were to acquire the farmer's enterprise, his tax too would disappear, leaving only the tax on the bread.

Not only does turnover taxation give obvious incentives to vertical integration, but since not every firm is in a position to become vertically integrated, the system turns out to be one in which the bread produced by ten different bakers will in all likelihood have borne, per dollar of final value, ten different amounts of aggregate turnover tax. To the incentive to integrate vertically we must therefore add the inequity of differential taxation of the same product. Moreover, a bakery which is unintegrated may for want of a better partner integrate with a high-cost mill, paying somewhat more to produce flour in the mill than it could buy the flour for on the open market. This is uneconomic from the point of view of the economy as a whole, but may be a worthwhile move from the bakery's point of view if the extra cost it bears producing its own flour is less that the tax it saves as a consequence of being integrated with the mill. Thus tax-induced inefficiency of production may be added to the charges already levied against the turnover system.

Under the value-added tax, by contrast, it makes no difference what the economic structure of production is; a dollar's worth of bread will in the end pay the same tax. The tax incentive to vertical integration disappears, and with it the inequities for those who cannot merge and the inefficiencies introduced into the operations of some of those who can. Given the fact that turnover taxes in Europe have tended to be quite general in their coverage, making their disadvantages well known and their discriminations widely suffered, it is small wonder that value-added taxation has developed its strongest support and gained its strongest impetus there.

In the United States, Canada, and the United Kingdom, the turnover tax system is and has been essentially nonexistent, and the value-added tax has been viewed either as a substitute for selective excise taxes or as a partial substitute for the corporation income tax. Selective excise taxes on final products, which are the type that have prevailed in these countries, introduce a discrimination at the consumer level against the taxed commodities and in favor of those not subject to excise taxation, and within the group of taxed goods against those subject to the higher rates of tax. Economic inefficiency results, in the sense that a consumer willing to pay $1.20 for an item whose price net of tax would be $1 is denied access to that item if because of the tax its prices is $1.25, even though he pays only $1 for a corresponding untaxed item. The welfare of consumers could be improved by shifting resources out of the no-tax industries and into those subject to selective excises, but the existence of the tax essentially prevents this reallocation of resources from taking place. The way to bring such a reallocation about, at no loss of tax revenue, is to reduce the highest rates of excise tax, introduce low-rate taxes in goods not yet subject to tax, and perhaps raise the low-rate excises as well. In the process of doing this, the economy would be moving toward a general flat-rate tax on all final consumption goods, which as we have seen is equivalent to a general value-added tax of the consumption type. Such a tax is not discriminatory as among the different items consumed. Under a 5 percent tax of this type, all consumer prices contain a tax of precisely 5 percent over cost — regardless of what the consumer buys, he pays $1.05 for each dollar of cost. Once consumers have fully adjusted their consumption to this regime, the efficiency with which they use their income can no longer be improved by commodity-tax adjustments.[4]

Typically, selective excise tax systems do not have nearly the breadth of coverage of the European turnover tax systems, and it is likely that their economic costs are lower as well. On the first ground, self-interested opposition to the taxes is more likely to be confined to a small group of the electorate, and on the second it is harder to arouse strong opposition based simply on concern for public welfare. As a consequence, in spite of there having been considerable academic support and some business support for the substitution of a broad-based, low-rate tax for the selective excises that prevailed in the U.S. for more than a decade, this substitution never took place. When the selective excises were finally nearly eliminated in the tax law of 1964, the move came as part of a package of general tax reductions; no serious consideration was given to their replacement by tax of value-added or similar type.

The strongest organized voice favoring a value-added tax at the present time for the United States is the Committee for Economic Development. Their argument is three-pronged, as indicated in the following quotations:

> The immediate consequences of rising military expenditures in Vietnam require taxes to be raised to prevent inflation. We recommend that a value-added tax on business activity be considered as the measure for raising the necessary revenue. As will become clear, this short-run solution to the immediate revenue requirements is a well-directed first step toward our longer-run plans for the structure of our tax system.

> It is because of its relevance as part of our longer-run tax structure that we have suggested the value-added tax as the tax to meet our immediate revenue needs. . . . We [therefore] recommend that when the international situation makes it possible for federal revenues to be reduced, the value-added tax be kept as a permanent part of our tax structure and that the reduction in revenue should be brought about by corporate income tax reduction.

> The corporate profits tax and the value-added tax also would differ in their effects on the balance of payments. Under present rules of the General Agreement on Tariffs and Trade (GATT), direct taxes such as the corporate income tax may neither be rebated on exports nor added to imports (it being assumed that such taxes are not passed on). Indirect taxes, such as the value-added tax, may be rebated on exports and added to imports (it being assumed that indirect taxes are passed on). A partial shift from the corporate

[4] This assertion must be qualified when distortions other than commodity taxes are present in the system, for then a differential tax or subsidy on specified commodities can work to offset existing distortions. I do not consider this qualification to be of major practical consequence in most cases, but it is conceivable that it might be in some. For further elaboration of this point see Arnold C. Harberger, "Taxation, Resource Allocation, and Welfare" in National Bureau of Economic Research, and The Brookings Institution, *The Role of Direct and Indirect Taxes in the Federal Revenue System* (Princeton: Princeton University Press, 1964), pp. 25–75, and "The Measurement of Waste," *American Economic Review*, May, 1964, pp. 58–76. [This volume, Chapters 2 and 3.]

income tax to a value-added tax offers the potential of stimulating exports and discouraging imports, and thus improving our balance-of-payments position.

Let us consider these arguments in turn. First, as an emergency measure to accommodate an unforeseen increase in government expenditures, the value-added tax has the great advantage of neutrality. The selective excises that were imposed as an emergency measure during the Korean War were highly discriminatory, producing a highly unequal distribution of the extra tax burden they entailed. Moreover, although successive pieces of legislation provided for the automatic expiration of the selective excises, subsequent events led to the continual postponement of their expiration, so that until the ultimate repeal of most of them in 1964, they seemed well on their way to becoming a permanent part of our tax structure. I believe that history demonstrates that there is more than a fair probability of emergency taxes becoming permanent; consequently, the more attention that can be paid to making them worthy elements of the overall structure, the better. The value-added tax wins hands down against the Korean War excises on this criterion.

The disadvantage of the value-added tax as a temporary measure is that it would be an entirely new element in the tax system. The administrative problems of putting it into effect, and of reaching the great numbers of tax-payers that would be involved, seem quite a formidable price to pay if the system is in any case not going to last. As strongly as I advocate the adoption of the value-added system in the United States, I doubt that I could favor its adoption if I knew for *certain* that it would last no more than two or three years. If it had, as I believe it would have, a substantial probability of lasting longer, I would readily argue for its adoption to meet an apparently temporary emergency. But — and this is the most important point — if the tax were once introduced into the permanent structure, it would be a natural vehicle for meeting the revenue requirements of temporary emergencies through changes in rates. In this case the administrative problems of setting the system in motion would be faced only once — thereafter the merits of its neutrality and its broad base (which implies that substantial amounts of additional revenue could be met by small increases in the rate of tax) would dominate.

The second prong in the CED case for a value-added tax is the long-run argument that a substitution of a value-added tax for part of the corporation income tax would enhance the efficiency of the economy. The corporation income tax is an exceedingly discriminatory one: It strikes the income from *equity* capital earned in the *corporate* sector of the economy, and thus discriminates against the corporate sector generally, while giving firms within that sector an incentive to bias their financial structure against equity and in favor of debt, and discriminating against the more venturesome and risk-taking firms because the market provides them only limited access to debt financing. Apart from these discriminations among types of capital, the corporation income tax creates incentives for the corporate sector to use less capital relative to labor than purely economic considerations would dictate. As the CED report states (p. 27) "A value-added tax, on the other hand, would be neutral, as far as any tax can be neutral, among forms and methods of doing business. By taxing the income produced by each of the factors of production alike, it creates no tax-induced incentives to alter production methods.''

There can be doubt that the shift of part of the weight of the corporation income tax to a tax of the value-added type would be conducive to greater economic efficiency, as the CED asserts, and the economist in his role as a national efficiency expert can do nothing but applaud such a move. Yet it is well to point out that a powerful coalition of forces is likely to oppose such a switch. The opponents are fairly obvious — labor, unincorporated businesses, and corporate businesses in which the return to equity capital is a relatively small fraction of value added would take over, directly or indirectly, the burden of which corporations in general were relieved. Among the types of corporations that would oppose the move are those (like public utilities) whose capital structures are heavily weighted toward debt, those (like many apparel firms) that are relatively highly labor intensive, and those (regardless of industry) that are in a relatively precarious financial situation, either sustaining actual losses or making only very low returns on their capital. Indeed, the switch of some part of the corporation income tax to a value-added tax would almost certainly shift some firms from a profit to a loss position, for while it is true that under the corporation income tax firms with losses are not liable for tax, under the value-added tax all firms are assessed a given fraction of their value added, regardless of their profit situation.[5]

As far as labor is concerned, it might at first appear that workers should be neutral as regards whether a given amount of tax is to be raised from businesses by the corporation income tax or by the value-added tax, as "business will pay in any event." But this is obviously short-sighted. Labor should, and labor today surely would, look to the longer-run incidence of the two tax alternatives. With respect to the value-added tax, the long-run incidence of the various types should be clear from the discussion of the previous section. The consumer-type value-added tax will in the long run be borne by consumers; and the income-type tax will be borne proportionately by all factors of production. The product-type tax would tend, paradoxically, to fall more on consumers than the income type, and less on consumers than the consumer type, because in the long run that part of the tax which nominally or initially strikes depreciation will have to be reflected in the prices of products. Labor, then, would be indifferent between value-added and corporation income taxation only if the corporation income tax itself were largely borne by labor, either in its role as a very large part of the consuming public or in its role as a factor of production as such. This is not the place to enter into a detailed analysis of the incidence of the corporation income tax; suffice it to say that both theoretical analysis and empirical evidence strongly suggest that capital bears close to the full burden of the corporation income tax in the United States.[6]

---

[5] In the CED's words "The present method of taxing corporate income tends to shelter the inefficient and tax the efficient" (p. 27). The value-added tax would not entail this discrimination, but this does not mean that inefficient firms will not lobby forcefully against it.

[6] See Arnold C. Harberger, "The Incidence of the Corporation Income Tax," *Journal of Political Economy*, LXX (June, 1962), and John G. Cragg, Arnold C. Harberger, and Peter Mieszkowski, "Empirical Evidence on the Incidence of the Corporation Income Tax," *Journal of Political Economy*, LXXV (December 1967). [This volume, Chapters 7 and 9.]

Thus, though on the grounds of economic efficiency an explicit shift from corporation income to value-added taxation would be highly desirable, such a move is likely to face formidable political opposition.

The third string in the CED's bow was the balance-of-payments argument, which is of even greater current interest today than it was in 1966 when the CED report was written. Indeed, there is a considerable undercurrent of opinion in government and business circles and in the press to the effect that the U.S. is at a competitive disadvantage vis-à-vis Europe because Europe relies more heavily on indirect than on direct taxation as we do, and is therefore able to rebate, under the GATT rules concerning border-tax adjustments, a considerably larger fraction of the internal value of export products. As much of this discussion is in general terms — not explicitly in terms of a tradeoff between a reduction in corporation taxes and the imposition of a value-added tax — I shall first deal with the balance-of-payments implications of the introduction of a new value-added tax, or its substitution for a part of the personal income tax, and then turn to the case of a shift between corporation income and value-added taxation.

The reaction of the balance of payments to the introduction of a new value-added tax depends exclusively on the nature of the overall strategy of monetary policy which is pursued in the wake of the change, and on the economy's reaction to that policy. The ultimate incidence of the tax, as has been indicated, will be broadly proportional across the economy. The question is whether this incidence will be reflected in a structure of costs which is roughly the same as it would be in the absence of the tax, with the tax being reflected in a rise in prices, or at the other extreme whether the structure of prices will be roughly the same as it would have been without the tax, with the tax being reflected in a reduction in the level of costs. In order for the former result to work out, the monetary authorities would have to expand the money supply by more than the normal amount so as to "finance" the consequent rise in prices. If the Federal Reserve were to simply provide for the normal secular expansion of the money supply, this would in the presence of the new tax exert a deflationary pressure on money wages, and other costs. Now it is a well-known fact that the economy does not respond promptly and flexibly to deflationary pressures: instead of prices and costs falling quickly as a consequence of a policy of stringency on the part of the Federal Reserve, the economy tends to slow down, unemployment increases, and real output falls short of its potential. This is precisely what would tend to happen if the Federal Reserve failed to expand in order to "finance" a corresponding price rise following the imposition of a new value-added tax.

I doubt very much that the Federal Reserve authorities would opt for such a course. Maintaining the price level in the face of a 4 percent value-added tax would entail pushing wages and other costs down to a level 4 percent below where they would otherwise be. As far as balance-of-payments effects are concerned, the same result could be achieved by a four percent deflation even without a value-added tax to rebate at the border. Since the Federal Reserve has not taken the deflationary route in the past, we have no ground to predict that it would do so under the circumstances here being considered. Our best prediction is that the Federal Reserve would as much eschew generating internal cost deflation under those circumstances as it has in general in the past. This leads to the conclusion that the likely result of the imposition of a new value-added tax would be that the general price level would rise by the percentage of the tax, but that our export prices would remain essentially constant owing to the rebate of the tax at the border. Likewise, there would be no incentive to shift demand away from domestic goods and toward imports because imports would be subject to a countervailing surcharge of 4 percent at the border, and their prices would rise in step with those of U.S. products in our own national market. If this is the course followed by our monetary authorities, then, the imposition of the new tax is unlikely to have any perceptible effect on our balance of payments.

Where the value-added tax is introduced as a substitute for a part of the personal income tax, more problematical issues arise. In principle, workers should be willing to accept a 4 percent reduction in their money wages (or, what amounts to essentially the same thing, a wage reduction of 1 percent in place of a normal 3 percent increase) in return for a reduction in income taxes of corresponding value to them. If this were the case, domestic prices could remain the same as a consequence of the simultaneous introduction of a value-added tax, and export prices could drop by 4 percent, with a corresponding improvement of our balance-of-payments position. But I doubt that this would happen. In the first place, organized labor is not likely to placidly accept such a tradeoff. Perhaps the wage increases would be less than normal if income taxes were simultaneously reduced, but I find it highly implausible that there would be full reflection of income tax reductions in a reduced wage scale. In the second place, a fairly large segment of the labor force pays little or no income taxes. A policy of general wage reductions to reflect the reduction in income tax collections would leave this group clearly worse off, and give rise to a strong center of political opposition to the tax substitution scheme. I conclude, then, that the value-added versus personal income tax substitution might lead to some improvement in our balance-of-payments position, but that our exports are likely to have a significantly smaller price advantage than the percentage rate of the value-added tax.

Finally, I come to the balance-of-payments effects of a shift to the value-added tax at the expense of a part of the corporation income tax. This tax switch would favor the corporate sector vis-à-vis the noncorporate sector. Noncorporate sector products would tend to rise in price, reflecting the newly-imposed value-added tax, while corporate sector products would tend to fall, because that sector would gain corporate tax relief equal to the full yield of the value-added tax, while it would be called upon to pay only its share of that yield under the value-added tax as such. It is not clear that corporate-sector prices would fall immediately, but the greater profits generated by the tax switch would give an incentive for corporations to expand output, and as output in fact expanded, the price fall would come about.

The substitution of the value-added tax for a part of the corporation income tax accordingly has favorable balance-of-payments consequences, if monetary policy is assumed to be unaffected. As import prices would rise by the full percentage of the value-added tax, consumers would shift some of their demand from imported goods to substitute commodities produced by the corporate sector. On the export side, the prices of corporate-sector products — even including the value-added tax — would tend to be lower than before, and the rebating of the value-added tax upon exportation would either make their foreign prices fall still more or else give companies a strong profit incentive to expand the quantity exported at the same price through sales promotion efforts in foreign markets.

It is clear, therefore, that of the three alternatives we have explored which do not entail reductions of wages and other costs, the present one is likely to have the most favorable balance-of-payments consequences. But one must be careful not to exaggerate these effects: even in this most favorable set of circumstances, the balance-of-payments benefits to the United States would be significantly smaller than those of a devaluation of the same percentage as the value-added tax. That is to say, a value-added tax of 4 percent cannot yield as great balance-of-payments effects as a 4 percent devaluation. I am afraid that many of the proponents of a shift toward indirect taxation as a measure to improve our balance of payments have greatly exaggerated the likely benefits that would ensue. It is quite possible, as was indicated earlier, that internal prices would rise to reflect a new value-added tax; in this case there would be no perceptible balance-of-payments effects at all. And even in the favorable case just examined the effects would be small unless the value-added tax carried a rate significantly higher than 3 or 4 percent. It should also be noted that the higher the rate of value-added tax, the stronger would be the political opposition, mentioned earlier, to having its revenue consequences offset by a reduction in the corporation income tax rate.

I come now to what I believe is the most important advantage of a value-added tax: its potential as an instrument of flexible fiscal policy. Economists have long been aware of the power of fiscal policy as a means of influencing the general level of activity in the economy and of averting untoward movements in the price level. Volumes have been written, and an untold number of speeches made on this subject, yet precious little has been done. The source of the difficulty is, I believe, plainly and painfully evident. It is now nearly a year since the President called for a tax surcharge, and in spite of the pleadings of Administration officials, the bulk of the economics profession, many enlightened businessmen, and the Federal Reserve itself, nothing has been done. The last great fiscal policy move made by the United States — the tax revision of 1964 — came at the end of nearly two years of Congressional discussion and debate. With this kind of Congressional delay, even the idea of a flexible fiscal policy seems utopian.

Obviously, there are many reasons why Congress has been reluctant to accede rapidly to Presidential requests in the fiscal field. The Constitution places fiscal powers in Congress's hands, and our legislators have jealously guarded them. The assessments of Congressmen and Senators of the need for tax changes may differ within each body, giving rise to extended debate, and the majority view of Congress may differ from that of the Administration, as may be the case at the present time. These problems are obviously not going to be resolved by a new tax gimmick, and it would be foolhardy to claim so. But I believe that having a value-added tax in the system would greatly facilitate the flexible use of fiscal policy, for two reasons.

In the first place, there are many ways of changing the income tax law; thus, when a proposal is made for a specific set of changes, there usually emerge, in Congress, groups that feel that a change ought to be made, but of a different type — changing exemption levels rather than rates, making the changes more progressive or less progressive, etc. Moreover, when an adjustment of the personal income tax is contemplated, political considerations usually dictate that a change in the corporation tax rate also be made, giving rise to debate as to how the benefits of the tax cut should be distributed between corporations and individuals. Small wonder, then, that when it examines possible income tax changes, Congress takes a lot of time! In contrast to this situation, a change in the value-added tax would in principle only entail varying the rate of tax. The Pandora's box of alternative possibilities that emerges when the income tax is at issue is totally avoided, and it is only reasonable to suppose that Congress would be able to act with much greater dispatch. As a general tax at a low rate, shared broadly by the whole community, the value-added tax is therefore a prime candidate as the preferred fiscal instrument for countercyclical manipulation. Moreover, the insulation from politics provided by its generality and neutrality makes it again the obvious vehicle for Congress' granting to the President limited discretionary power to change the rate of tax for countercyclical purposes.

The second ground for preferring the value-added tax as an instrument of flexible fiscal policy is the administrative simplicity with which its rate could be changed. Taxpayers could simply be instructed to change the rate of tax which they applied to the value added calculated on their tax returns. Especially if the tax were of the consumption type, thus requiring no depreciation accounting, it would not be a serious burden on businesses to file, say, quarterly tax returns, and in this event a decision made within any quarter to change the rate of tax could already have its effect by the end of that quarter.

From this analysis of the issues involved in a federal tax on value added, I find no reason to modify the conclusions I drew in an earlier paper on the subject:

> In sum, the value-added tax has considerable merit as a revenue-raising device. It is admirably suited as an instrument for achieving emergency increases in tax revenue, and it is also an excellent tool in framing a flexible and countercyclical fiscal policy. A low-rate tax on value added, preferably of the consumption type, could therefore be an important addition to our federal tax system. (*Challenge*, Nov./Dec., 1966, p. 46)

THE DESIGN AND ADMINISTRATION OF A VALUE-ADDED TAX

The first major issue concerning design and administration is whether a value-added tax should be of the product, income, or consumption type. I feel that the overwhelming weight of the arguments on this issue favor the consumption type of tax. Under a product type of tax, purchases of materials and intermediate products are deductible, but investment goods acquisitions are not. Therefore, a distinction must be made between investment goods and other inputs; such a distinction is necessarily arbitrary, and can give rise to litigation and other enforcement difficulties. Also, the "natural" treatment of inventories under a product-type tax is to consider as inputs those materials actually used up in the production process during the tax period, and to treat increments to inventory as investments by the firm. This embroils the tax authority in all of the knotty problems of inventory accounting, and places corresponding burdens on the companies in connection with the preparation of their tax declarations.

The income-type tax is even worse. Not only does it require the distinction to be drawn between investment goods and other inputs, but it also requires the depreciation of past investments. The tax authority here becomes involved with all the issues with respect to admissible depreciation rates and patterns that we have become familiar with in connection with the income tax. And as with the product-type tax, the natural treatment of inventories would require inventory accounting to support a firm's tax declarations.

By way of contrast, the consumption-type tax is the model of administrative simplicity. All purchases by a firm from other firms covered by the value-added system are deductible at the time of acquisition, regardless of whether they are investment goods or direct inputs into production. Since both investment goods and other inputs are deductible, there is no need to distinguish the part of the purchases made during a period that went to increase inventories from the part that fed the production line; hence no inventory accounting is necessary as an underpinning to the tax calculation. Strict cash accounting of all purchases from other firms is all that is necessary. It is this simplicity which makes it reasonable to think of quarterly collections under a consumption type of value-added tax; thus enhancing its usefulness as a countercyclical weapon.

The second issue of design and administration is that of coverage. While a fully general tax has great theoretical appeal, the burdens of administration and compliance can be substantially reduced, with only a minor sacrifice of yield, by exempting farmers and retailers. The exemption of farmers would not reduce the yield, because since farmers would not be in the system, purchases by food processors and other firms from farmers would not need to be treated as allowable deductions by those firms in calculating their own tax liability. In effect, the food processors and other firms buying from farmers would get their farm products more cheaply, but then would be required to pay the tax not only on their own value added but on that of the farmer.[7]

A definite loss in revenue would, on the other hand, be involved in the exemption of retailers, but it might be deemed worthwhile in the light of the substantial savings of administrative effort that would be involved. Clearly, if

[7] Actually, under this system, revenues would be somewhat greater than under a fully general tax, because the food processors, paying tax "for" the farmers, would not be able to deduct the value of farmers' purchases from other firms. In practice, a rule-of-thumb deduction for such purchases might be allowed, however. This could be accomplished, under, say, a 4 percent value added, by allowing the food processors to apply a 3 percent rate to their purchases from farmers as against a 4 percent rate on their value added. Exempting farmers would also entail a slight loss of revenue, offsetting part of the gain referred to above, stemming from direct sales from farmers to consumers (or to retailers in the case where the latter group is also exempt).

retailers were to be exempt, a firm line would have to be drawn between activities qualifying as retailing and those reflecting earlier stages of the production and distribution process.

My own view is that if the value-added tax were of the consumption type, its administration would be sufficiently easy that it would be worthwhile to keep both farmers and retailers within the value-added system. Only for a product- or income-type tax would I recommend the exemption of these two groups.

My final point in connection with administration concerns the reinforcement which the value-added tax gives to the administration of the personal and corporate income taxes. Each firm making its declaration of value-added tax would have to list its purchases from other firms. If these firms were identified by code numbers, it would be a relatively simple matter, using modern computer technology, to obtain an independent assessment of a firm's sales to other businesses from the declarations of its customers. Enforcement is not, to my knowledge, a serious problem where large corporations are concerned, but small, closely held corporations and unincorporated enterprises generally are believed to practice a significant amount of tax evasion. Thus, not only is the value-added tax meritorious in its own right, but it also would contribute to the effectiveness of the administration of the two most important existing sources of federal revenue.

SELECTED BIBLIOGRAPHY

Bronfenbrenner, M. "The Japanese Value-Added Sales Tax." *National Tax Journal*, III (December 1950).

Bronfenbrenner, M., and K. Kogiku. "The Aftermath of the Shoup Tax Reform, Parts I and II." *National Tax Journal*, X (September and December 1957).

Brown, H. G. "The Incidence of a General Output or a General Sales Tax." *Journal of Political Economy*, XLVII (April 1939).

Due, John. "The Value-Added Tax." *Western Economic Journal*, Vol. III, No. 2 (1965).

Harberger, A. C. "Let's Try a Value-Added Tax." *Challenge*, XV (November/December 1966).

Papke, James A. "Michigan's Value-Added Tax after Seven Years." *National Tax Journal*, XIII (December 1960).

Shoup, Carl. *Second Report on Japanese Taxation*. Japan Tax Association, 1950.

———. "Theory and Background of the Value-Added Tax." In *Proceedings of the Forty-Eighth Annual Conference on Taxation* (National Tax Association, 1955).

Sullivan, Clara K. *The Tax on Value-Added* (1965).

XI

Chapters 14 and 15 were prepared as reports for the Department of Commerce in 1965. Though they were rather widely circulated, both in and out of government circles, they have never before been published. Both chapters deal with the issue of GATT-type border-tax adjustments, the first one in the context of a "classical" model characterized by full employment and a fully operative international adjustment mechanism, and the second one in the context of a Keynesian model with fixed wages and exchange rates and with no automatic tendency for balance-of-payments adjustment. Given the nature of the two types of models, it seems appropriate to identify that of Chapter 14 with long-run equilibrium and that of Chapter 15 with relatively shorter-term variations under a fixed exchange-rate system.

In each case, specific mathematical models are developed which are then applied both to analyze indirect taxes of a fully general type and to treat the more likely case in which such taxes have only partial coverage. The implications of the possible substitution of indirect taxation (on which border-tax adjustments are allowable under the GATT rules) for corporation income taxation (against which GATT rules do not permit border-tax adjustments) are also explored in both cases.

Chapter 14

The Trade Effects

of Alternative Tax Systems

The purpose of this chapter is to provide a theoretical framework for the analysis of the effects of different tax systems on the pattern of international trade. It is particularly concerned with the trade effects of a shift of (some of) the weight of taxation from direct, personal income taxes to indirect taxes, where the indirect taxes in question are subject to the GATT rule which permits "equalizing" import tariffs to be levied on imports of items which are struck by indirect taxes and which allows for the rebating of indirect taxes on items that are exported. Some attention will also be paid to the trade effects of a shift from direct, personal taxes to corporation income taxes to see what similarities exist between these effects and those stemming from a shift from personal taxes to indirect taxes.

THE ROLE OF ABSOLUTE PRICE-LEVEL MOVEMENTS

Much discussion on the subject is clouded by an issue that has little or nothing to do with the effects of taxation as such — namely, the behavior of the absolute price level and the rate of exchange. Suppose, for example, that a general value-added tax of 20 percent is imposed on all goods and services produced in an economy, replacing a general income tax of 20 percent. Furthermore, suppose that in the course of the economy's adjusting to this change, the general price level of goods produced in the economy is allowed to rise by 25 percent. Obviously, if the exchange rate is not permitted to change, the country will tend to import more and export less. But if the exchange rate (the price of foreign currency) is also allowed to rise by 25 percent, there will be no incentive to increase imports or reduce exports. Given a monetary policy that allows prices to rise by 25 percent, we have trade effects favorable to imports and unfavorable to exports so long as the exchange rate is held constant, and we have no trade effects so long as the exchange rate is permitted to rise to correspond to the rise of internal prices.

Analogously, we can assume that when the shift is made from a direct tax of 20 percent to an indirect, general value-added tax of 20 percent, the monetary policy pursued is such that internal prices (gross-of-tax) are not permitted to rise. Now we have no trade effects if the exchange rate is held constant. But now nominal income accruing to factors of production has fallen from 100 to 80. If the exchange rate were to be allowed to fall in this case by 20 percent, reflecting the fall in unit factor costs of domestically produced goods, incentives favoring imports and discriminating against exports would again be produced. And, of course, if the exchange rate were to be raised, the incentives would work in the opposite direction.

It appears that almost anything can happen, depending on the monetary and exchange-rate policies pursued. But — and this is the first important point I want to make — we get the *same* effects from given policies even if we not change the tax system at all — i.e., if we stick with a straight, 20 percent personal income tax. Here, if the internal price level is allowed by monetary policy to rise from 100 to 125, there will emerge incentives against exports and in favor of imports unless the exchange rate is also raised by 25 percent. If the price level and the exchange rate are kept stable at 100 there are no trade effects, and if the price level is kept stable while the exchange rate is allowed to fall to 80 there are again the same trade effects as would emerge with a price level of 125 and an exchange rate of 100. Given the fact that we get the same trade effects from given combinations of monetary and exchange-rate policy, regardless of whether we make the shift from direct to indirect taxes or not, it seems to me to be completely misleading to attempt to attribute such effects to the tax change itself; they reflect the monetary and exchange-rate policy of the country rather than its tax policy.

The situation is essentially similar when a general indirect tax is imposed on domestic buyers of final products rather than the domestic producers. Here, however, exchange adjustments create trade effects when the price level is allowed to rise to reflect the indirect tax, while downward exchange-rate adjustments are necessary to prevent trade effects if monetary policy holds the price level constant. If prices paid by domestic buyers rise from 100 to 125, prices paid for the country's exports by foreigners (which do not include the tax), stay put at 100. Likewise, if prices paid by domestic buyers for imports rise from 100 to 125, prices received by foreign suppliers also stay put at 100. Thus only if the exchange rate is kept at its prior level will there be no incentives to change the levels of imports or exports. On the other hand, if a monetary policy is followed which maintains the (gross-of-tax) price level at 100, prices received by domestic producers will have to fall to 80, and there will be incentives for export expansion. Likewise, prices of imports will tend to rise (gross-of-tax), and import quantities to fall. These trade effects can be avoided (still assuming a monetary policy which maintains the price level at 100), by an appreciation of the country's currency (i.e., a fall in the exchange rate to 80). When the exchange rate is at 80 per unit of foreign currency, the net-of-tax prices of both imports and exports can fall to 80 in domestic currency, while their foreign currency prices stay constant. This point is clearly seen by Musgrave and Richman in their paper "Allocation Aspects: Domestic and International."[1] They implicitly assume the exchange rate is kept constant, and state that a general indirect tax imposed

---

[1] National Bureau of Economic Research and The Brookings Institution, *The Role of Direct and Indirect Taxes in the Federal Revenue System* (Washington, D.C.: The Brookings Institution, 1964), p. 104.

on domestic buyers of all final products (which is equivalent to a value-added tax with GATT-rule treatment) will have no trade effects if the general price level is allowed by monetary policy to rise to reflect the tax, but will have trade effects if monetary policy does not allow this price-level adjustment. I would add only that regardless of what happens to the price level, an exchange-rate adjustment can be found that will render nil the trade effects of a shift from direct to general indirect taxation of final products at the domestic buyer level.

A BASIC ASSUMPTION:
BALANCE-OF-PAYMENTS ADJUSTMENT

The key question to be faced here is how to isolate the effects of a change in the tax system upon the pattern of trade, when the pattern of trade is so heavily influenced by both monetary and exchange-rate policies. The answer I propose is a simple one, and, I believe, the only one that can plausibly be defended: we must assume that monetary and exchange-rate policies are such as to bring about equilibrium in the balance of payments. This has been the assumption made in the international trade literature on the pure theory of tariffs and trade restrictions, and it was also adopted in an insightful paper, recently produced by the Office of Tax Analysis of the U.S. Treasury,[2] which deals with problems similar to those treated here.

One question which arises in connection with the assumption of balance-of-payments equilibrium is that it appears at first sight to assume trade effects away. Nothing could be further from the truth. A tariff policy which greatly restricts imports will by itself produce balance-of-payments equilibrium at a very low level of trade; a policy which heavily subsidizes exports will produce equilibrium at a much higher level of trade than a "neutral" tax policy, etc. Other tax policies can (and in general will) affect the "equilibrium" level of trade through their various influences upon the demand for and the supply of importable goods and exportable goods. Within these categories, the tax system can differentially affect different commodities, curtailing, for example, the level of trade in some importables and exportables, while expanding the volume of trade in other items in these same broad groups. To interpret these trade effects upon the rest of the world, we can reasonably assume that if exports by country A of a particular commodity are increased as a consequence of country A's tax policy, the effect will be to curtail to some extent the production of and trade in competing commodities by other countries, and conversely. Similarly, if tax policy leads to a reduction of imports of a good by country A, other countries' exports of that good will tend to be curtailed. Thus if we can estimate the pattern of effects of country A's tax system on its imports and exports, we can also indicate which exports of which other countries are likely to have been hurt or helped by that tax system.

A second question that also arises in connection with the assumption of balance-of-payments equilibrium concerns its realism. Can we realistically assume that an adjustment mechanism is at work which actually brings about

[2] U.S. Treasury, Office of Tax Analysis, "The Foreign Trade Effects of Changes in Domestic Tax Systems" (mimeo., March 5, 1964).

continued equilibrium in a country's balance of payments? Obviously not. But on the other hand, can we realistically assume that an adjustment mechanism is absent? I would say even more obviously not. The world economy has probably doubled in "size" during the postwar period; vast changes have taken place in the technologies and the structures of production of the different national economies; internal price levels and wage levels have exhibited vastly different movements in different countries; the composition of trade itself has changed very significantly in a number of countries. If the basic changes that produced these and other effects had somehow worked themselves out *without* there existing any tendency for balances of payments to be brought somewhere "near" equilibrium, I think there can be no doubt at all but what gold movements and international liquidity crises would have emerged that would utterly dwarf those that in fact have occurred. Something has obviously been helping to keep balances of payments under some sort of control. We have had currency depreciations and currency appreciations; we have had differential price-level movements; interest rate policies have been manipulated so as to affect the movement of capital and thus at least assuage existing pressures on particular countries' balances of payments. These forces have maintained, I believe, a reasonable degree of order in the world payments picture in spite of disturbances that in and of themselves would be very disruptive of that order. I cannot see how one can say that the world payments system has somehow been able to adjust to such powerful changes as the emergence of Italy and Japan as major exporters of new products, as the differential inflations that have occurred in the various major trading countries, while it has not tended to adjust to the comparatively minor impact on trade of having one type of tax system rather than another in one or more countries. Imperfect though the adjustment mechanism is, it is surely working. And it is doing a reasonable job of accommodating disturbing forces that are far greater than the kinds of tax changes we are analyzing here. Hence as we proceed to analyze the effects of alternative tax systems, we are on much safer ground assuming balance-of-payments adjustment than we would be if we attempted somehow to rule adjustment mechanisms out of the picture.

THE RELATION OF TAX INCIDENCE
TO THE QUESTION AT HAND

Having already shown that it is unwarranted to attribute absolute price-level differences to the presence or absence of a particular type of taxation, we can now rather easily dispose of another issue that has weighted down much previous work on the subject of this chapter. As part of the erroneous concentration on absolute price-level effects, the point of view is often expressed that if a tax is shifted forward it tends to hamper trade, while if it is shifted backward it does not. The March 5, 1964, Treasury paper effectively disposes of this view, but its presentation is, in my view, somewhat marred by the association of shifting with absolute price-level movements. The shifting and incidence of taxation is a question which can and should be explored in the framework of relative rather than absolute prices. A perfectly general value-added tax, for example,

248

has the same ultimate incidence regardless of whether the price level is permitted to rise to 125, keeping factor incomes constant at 100, or if the price level is kept constant at 100, allowing factor incomes to fall to 80, provided that the exchange rate is appropriately adjusted in the second case. The Treasury study comes to the correct conclusion that the price-level response does not matter, but in doing so it calls the case of a rising price level a case of forward shifting, and the case of a falling price level one of backward shifting. The study makes no fundamental mistake, only, perhaps, an inelegant use of terms, yet in doing this it tends to perpetuate the association of the shifting/incidence question with absolute price-level effects.

The Musgrave-Richman paper, on the other hand, clearly sees that monetary policy is the key element in governing price-level movements when it treats the value-added tax (p. 104). On this subject, the paper's flaw is that it does not allow for any adjustment mechanism; hence it arrives at different answers depending on the monetary policy followed. (When exchange rate adjustments are later briefly mentioned (p. 110), the possibility of their "neutralizing" a value-added tax is noted, but even here the connection between the nature of monetary policy on the one hand and the necessity or nonnecessity of devaluation on the other, is not brought out.)

The Musgrave-Richman paper takes a different tack, however, when it analyzes the effects of corporation income taxes (pp. 112–113). Here, when the corporation income tax is assumed to be shifted, this is taken to imply that the absolute price level rises to reflect the tax; when the corporation income tax is assumed not to be shifted, the absolute price level is taken to remain constant. When the authors compare corporation tax treatment with a value-added tax alternative, they make alternate assumptions concerning whether the value-added tax also is (or is not) reflected in the absolute price level. We have been told earlier that these consequences of value-added taxation depended on monetary policy (i.e., not on incidence), yet when the corporation tax is discussed it appears to be incidence rather than monetary policy that is bringing about the absolute price-level effects.

Let me here assert flatly that there is no direct association between the incidence of the corporation income tax and the level of the general price level in the economy. The corporation income tax can be entirely shifted, and the price level can go up or down; it can be entirely borne or more than completely borne by capital, and the price level can go up or down. The shifting question concerns the percentage shares of capital and labor in the national income, while the price-level question concerns the nominal size of the pie which is being divided. The price level can go up, and capital can obtain either a smaller, the same, or a bigger net-of-tax share of the pie, and likewise if the price level goes down. Moreover, *regardless of its incidence*, the corporation income tax is guaranteed by accounting procedures to be "part" of the price of the products of corporate enterprise. But this does not mean that if the tax were taken off, the price level would decline by the proportion that corporate tax receipts bear to national income. We simply must maintain the clear independence of questions of shifting and incidence from questions of general price-level determination, and I believe we are well advised to take the further step adopted here of assuming an international adjustment mechanism to be at work. This last assumption automatically makes the level of a country's general price level irrelevant to the effects of particular types of taxation in that country.

INDIRECT TAXES DO HAVE TRADE EFFECTS

In general, one can expect that a set of indirect taxes will have trade effects. If the indirect taxes are placed on the production of the affected commodities, and so long as the indirect taxes are not completely general, the normal effect will be to restrict the production of the taxed commodities, to expand imports of competing goods, and to contract exports of the taxed commodities. If, on the other hand, the indirect taxes are placed on the consumption of the affected commodities, and again so long as the indirect taxes are not completely general, the normal effect will be to restrict the consumption of the taxed commodities, to reduce imports of competing goods, and to expand exports of the taxed goods. Taxes on consumption (or, what is the same thing, taxes on production with GATT-rule border-tax adjustments) thus produce incentives in the direction of expanding exports and contracting imports of the taxed goods, while taxes on production without border-tax adjustments generate incentives for the expansion of imports and the contraction of exports of the affected commodities.

The balance-of-payments adjustments induced by these types of taxes will be the reverse of the direct effects. For consumption taxes, balance-of-payments adjustment will require contraction of other exports and expansion of other imports — effects which can be brought about by internal inflation and/or by currency appreciation. For production taxes, balance-of-payments adjustment will require expansion of other exports and contraction of other imports — which can be brought about by internal deflation and/or currency depreciation. One cannot say, a priori, whether the total ultimate effect of either kind of tax upon trade will be positive or negative, but one can outline the key forces that are involved.

If consumption taxes fall exclusively on importables, the normal effect will be to decrease trade; if they fall exclusively on exportables, the normal effect will be to increase trade. If production taxes (without border-tax adjustments) fall exclusively on importables the normal effect will be to increase trade, and if they fall exclusively on exportables, the normal effect will be to decrease trade. Beyond this no simple generalizations can be made.

The procedure for finding the general solution in any specific case is, however, clear. Let commodities 1 to k be exportables, commodities k to n be importables, and commodities n to q be purely domestic goods. Measure the commodities in units of foreign currency (on the assumption that their foreign currency price is beyond the control of the country in question). Let H_{ij} be $\partial X_i / \partial t_j$, measuring the effect of a change in the tax rate on commodity j upon the production of commodity i. Likewise, let G_{ij} be $\partial C_i / \partial t_j$, measuring the effect of a change in the tax rate on j upon the consumption of commodity i. Let $E_i (= X_i - C_i)$ be exports (imports if negative) of commodity i, and let D_i represent $\partial X_i / \partial r$ — measuring the effect of a change in the exchange rate upon production of i; and let B_i represent $\partial C_i / \partial r$ — measuring the effect of a change in the exchange rate upon the consumption of i. The effect of a given pattern of taxes upon exports of i will be $\sum_j (H_{ij} - G_{ij})t_j + (D_i - B_i)\,\Delta r$, and the effects upon total exports will be

$$\sum_{i=1}^{k} \sum_{j=1}^{q} (H_{ij} - G_{ij})t_j + \sum_{i=1}^{k} (D_i - B_i)\,\Delta r.$$

The relevant expression for Δr is obtained by the requirement of equilibrium in the balance of trade, i.e.

$$\sum_{i=1}^{n} \sum_{j=1}^{q} (H_{ij} - G_{ij})t_j + \sum_{i=1}^{n} (D_i - B_i)\,\Delta r = 0.$$

To see how this general analysis applies in a simple case, assume that a consumption tax is imposed on only one export good, j. This will produce a negative effect on consumption of that good ($G_{jj} < 0$), and will in and of itself have no effect on the production of that good ($H_{jj} = 0$), because the price facing producers is simply the world price translated at the prevailing exchange rate. Thus the "impact effect" of the tax will be to expand exports of good j, producing on that account a favorable tendency in the balance of trade. The restoration of equilibrium in the balance of trade requires an appreciation of the currency which will produce effects restricting exports and expanding imports, operating generally over all commodities. These induced effects upon exports will in part offset the expansion in exports of good j, but not fully, because the induced effects upon imports will do some of the offsetting. The net effect is therefore an expansion in exports of good j, a contraction of other exports, and an expansion of imports of all kinds. (Even this simple case could be complicated by the cross-effects of the tax on good j upon the production and consumption of other commodities. If these cross-effects are significant upon other traded items, the tax on j could conceivably result in a net contraction of trade. I plan to investigate this possibility further.)

COMPARISON OF THE TRADE EFFECTS OF INDIRECT TAXES AND OF TARIFFS

Whatever may be the effects of a set of indirect taxes upon trade, they are likely to be substantially less than the effects of taxes at the same rates falling on trade alone — i.e., production or consumption taxes will have less effect upon trade than tariffs. To establish this proposition we need only note that the effects of a tariff can be duplicated by a similar tax on the consumption of the tariffed commodity (whether imported or domestically produced), and a simultaneous subsidy to the domestic production of the tariffed good. The trade effects of a tariff are therefore composed of two parts: a disincentive to consumption which could be reproduced by a consumption tax; and an incentive to domestic production which could be reproduced by a production subsidy. An indirect tax on consumption will give us the first of these effects, while an indirect tax on production will cause changes in trade similar in magnitude (though opposite in sign) to the second of these effects.

It is likely that in most cases the production effects of tariffs are greater than the consumption effects; therefore, as a guide to our judgment, we may assume that a set of consumption taxes on importables would have somewhat less than half of the effect upon trade that would ensue from a set of tariffs on the same commodities at similar rates to the consumption taxes. However, the effects on trade of existing consumption-type indirect tax systems are likely to be still smaller than this, for these tax systems also strike exportables, and in this area they operate to increase trade. Therefore, unless an indirect tax system is heavily concentrated on either importables or exportables, its trade effects are likely to be only a small fraction of the trade effects of tariffs at similar rates.

TRADE EFFECTS OF CORPORATION INCOME TAXES

Corporation income taxes can be viewed as partial value-added taxes — striking only that part of value added which is represented by the income from corporate equity capital. They operate to reduce production in the corporate sector, as against what it would otherwise be, to stimulate production in the noncorporate sector, and to alter factor intensities in favor of labor in the corporate sector and in favor of capital in the noncorporate sector. It is highly unlikely that the last-mentioned effect of corporation taxes on relative factor intensities has any significant bearing on the trade effects of these taxes. The principal trade effects will stem mainly from the production incentives created by the tax, and will be similar to the trade effects of production-type value-added taxes. To the extent that the corporate sector is concentrated mainly in the production of exportables, the effect of corporation income taxation will likely be to decrease trade; to the extent that the corporate sector is concentrated mainly in the production of importables, it is likely that corporation income taxation will increase the volume of trade. The effects upon trade of the corporation income tax are likely to be very similar to those of an alternative set of indirect taxes on value added, where the tax on value added in any activity would equal the fraction which corporate tax payments now bear to value added in that activity.

This similarity of the trade effects of the corporation tax and of a corresponding set of value-added taxes suggests that border-tax adjustments are just as justifiable for the corporation tax as for value-added taxes. Before exploring this idea, let me state briefly the "justification" for border-tax adjustments. It is *not* that these adjustments render indirect taxes neutral with respect to trade, but rather it is that the trade effects of indirect taxes striking the consumption of goods of a given type (regardless of their place of origin) are likely to be smaller than the trade effects of taxes of similar size striking the production of those same goods within the country imposing the tax. Border-tax adjustments simply perform the function of transmuting taxes levied nominally upon production into taxes which are in effect taxes on consumption of the affected commodities.

If we have a tax on value added in a given set of industries, we can view that tax as striking the returns to all factors of production occupied in those

252

industries, and we can view the border-tax adjustments as placing a counter-vailing tax on competitive imports and as rebating the taxes on returns to factors of production for those goods that are reported. The same procedure can be applied when the tax does not strike the returns to all factors of production but only, say, the returns to corporate equity capital.

The objections to the making of border-tax adjustments for corporation income-tax payments appear to be mainly practical rather than theoretical ones. Although, in general, corporation taxes are levied as a flat percentage of profits, the ratio which they bear to the price of the product varies with relative factor intensities, with the capital structure of the companies concerned, and with the rate of return to equity capital. Thus, a 50 percent tax on the return to equity capital might represent 10 percent of the price of some cotton textiles, and 20 or 30 percent of the price of other cotton textiles. What rate would be appropriate as the countervailing duty on imports of textiles? There is no obvious answer to this question, but it presages some of the difficulties that would accompany any attempt to make border-tax adjustments for the corporation income tax. Other difficulties emerge in connection with the rebating of the tax for export purposes, as it is not known how much corporation tax has been paid at each of the various stages through which a product has passed before finally being exported.

A final point in this connection is that the corporation income tax is not likely to be concentrated heavily in either the exportables or the importables industries. Since its effect in the case of exportables is trade-contracting, and in the case of importables is trade-expanding, the presence of these offsetting forces upon trade may well produce a rather small net effect.

SOME INDICATIONS AS TO THE SIZE OF TRADE EFFECTS OF INDIRECT TAXES

A fully general indirect tax striking all production in the economy at a single rate would presumably have no effects on trade, on production or on consumption (recall that we are comparing this indirect tax with an alternative way, e.g., an income tax, of raising the same revenues). The same statement can be made for a fully general indirect tax striking all purchases of final goods and services. Thus as far as fully general taxes are concerned, one need not worry about trade effects, regardless of the "type" of tax. By the same token, for fully general taxes there can be no serious defense for border-tax adjustments — they convert production taxes into consumption taxes, but so long as one is speaking of fully general taxes there will be no trade effects from either set; the border-tax adjustments would appear in this case to be superfluous and therefore unnecessary.

When one gets down to indirect taxes that are not fully general, however, trade effects may occur, and border-tax adjustments may affect their magnitude. The following analysis sketches the principal effects for a relatively simple case.

Suppose, initially, that indirect taxes are levied only on products which happen to be either exportables or importables. Assume, furthermore, that the country in question cannot affect the world prices of either of these classes of goods. This assumption enables us to juxtapose the demand function for imports and the supply function for exports, by measuring the quantities of both imports and exports in terms of their foreign-currency values. The level of trade will be determined by the intersection of these two functions, as in Figure 14.1. Altering the tax system will, presumably, shift these functions and thus alter the equilibrium level of trade. We must thus inquire into how various methods of taxation will affect the location of the functions in question.

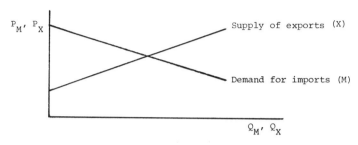

FIGURE 14.1

Consider first the demand for imports. This function will be the difference between the demand function for importables (I) and the supply function for these goods. Taking the price of home goods (neither exportable nor importable) as the numeraire, we write the demand function for importables as

(14.1) $$I^d = a_0 + a_1(P_I + T_I) + a_2(P_E + T_E),$$

where T_I and T_E are the unit taxes on the consumption of importables and of exportables, respectively, and P_I and P_E are their net-of-tax prices, which must be equal to each other because of the choice of units in which exportables and importables are measured. Assume also that, given the price of home goods, the locally produced supply of importables is a function solely of the price received by producers. Thus

(14.2) $$I^s = b_0 + b_1 P_I.$$

The demand function for imports can therefore be written as

(14.3) $$M^d = I^d - I^s = (a_0 - b_0) + (a_1 + a_2 - b_1)P_I + a_1 T_I + a_2 T_E.$$

In like manner, we write the demand function for exportables:

(14.4) $$E^d = c_0 + c_1(P_E + T_E) + c_2(P_I + T_I).$$

The supply function for exportables is

(14.5) $$E^s = e_0 + e_1 P_E,$$

254

and the supply function for exports:

(14.6) $X^s = E^s - E^d = (e_0 - c_0) + (e_1 - c_1 - c_2)P_I - c_1 T_E - c_2 T_I,$

recalling at this last step that $P_E = P_I$.

Denoting, for simplicity, $(a_0 - b_0)$ by f_0, $(a_1 + a_2 - b_1)$ by f_1, $(e_0 - c_0)$ by g_0, and $(e_1 - c_1 - c_2)$ by g_1, we can equate M^d and X^s to obtain

(14.7) $f_0 + f_1 P_I + a_1 T_I + a_2 T_E = g_0 + g_1 P_I - c_1 T_E - c_2 T_I.$

This yields

(14.8) $$P_I = \frac{(f_0 - g_0) + (a_1 + c_2)T_I + (a_2 + c_1)T_E}{g_1 - f_1}$$

and

(14.9)

$$M = f_0 + \frac{f_1(f_0 - g_0) + f_1(a_1 + c_2)T_I + f_1(a_2 + c_1)T_E}{(g_1 - f_1)} + a_1 T_I + a_2 T_E,$$

where $M (= X)$ now represents the equilibrium volume of trade. Thus, as compared with a situation in which no indirect taxes are levied, the change in the level of trade resulting from having taxes of T_I and T_E per unit on the consumption of importables and exportables, respectively, will be

$$\Delta M = \frac{f_1(a_1 + c_2)T_I + f_1(a_2 + c_1)T_E + (g_1 - f_1)a_1 T_I + (g_1 - f_1)a_2 T_E}{(g_1 - f_1)}$$

(14.10)

$$\Delta M = \frac{(f_1 c_2 + g_1 a_1)T_I + (f_1 c_1 + g_1 a_2)T_E}{(g_1 - f_1)}$$

To analyze this expression, we must determine the presumptive signs of the relevant parameters

$f_1 =$ price slope of import demand function — negative

$g_1 =$ price slope of export supply function — positive

$a_1, c_1 =$ own-price slopes of demand functions for importables and exportables — negative

$a_2, c_2 =$ cross-price slope of demand functions for importables and exportables — positive

$\dfrac{f_1 c_2 + g_1 a_1}{g_1 - f_1} =$ partial effect of T_I upon trade — negative

$\dfrac{f_1 c_1 + g_1 a_2}{g_1 - f_1} =$ partial effect of T_E upon trade — positive.

The partial effects of T_I and T_E upon trade are seen each to be a weighted average of an own-price demand effect and a cross-price demand effect. If we set $[-f_1/(g_1 - f_1)] = w_1$, and $[g_1/(g_1 - f_1)] = w_2$, we can express the partial

255

effect of T_I upon trade as $w_1(-c_2) + w_2a_1$, and the partial effect of T_E upon trade as $w_1(-c_1) + w_2a_2$.

These two effects are likely to be quite similar in magnitude, though opposite in sign. Our problem, with the assumptions that have been made including a fully employed economy, precludes the existence of first-order income effects. The price-slopes a_1, a_2, c_1 and c_2 therefore represent substitution effects, and we can write $a_1 + a_2 + a_3 = 0$; $c_1 + c_2 + c_3 = 0$, defining a_3 as $\partial I^d/\partial P_3$, and c_3 as $\partial E^d/\partial P_3$, with P_3 representing the price of home goods. Thus we have

$$\text{Partial effect of } T_I \text{ upon trade} = w_1c_1 + w_2a_1 + w_1c_3,$$
$$\text{Partial effect of } T_E \text{ upon trade} = w_1(-c_1) + w_2(-a_1) + w_2(-a_3).$$

These expressions differ only in respect of their third terms. The partial effect of T_E upon trade will tend to be greater than that of T_I if first $a_3 > c_3$, i.e., exportables are better substitutes for home goods than importables, and second $w_2 > w_1$, i.e., the elasticity of supply of exports is greater than the elasticity of demand for imports, and conversely.

We now turn to the analysis of the trade effects of indirect taxes that are levied on the production rather than the consumption of the affected commodities. Taking R_I and R_E as the unit taxes on importables and exportables, respectively, we have, recalling that $P_I = P_E$,

(14.1') $\qquad I^d = a_0 + (a_1 + a_2)P_I$

(14.2') $\qquad I^s = b_0 + b_1(P_I - R_I)$

(14.3') $\qquad M^d = I^d - I^s = (a_0 - b_0) + (a_1 + a_2 - b_1)P_I + b_1R_I$

(14.4') $\qquad E^d = c_0 + (c_1 + c_2)P_I$

(14.5') $\qquad E^s = e_0 + e_1(P_I - R_E)$

(14.6') $\qquad X^s = E^s - E^d = (e_0 - c_0) + (e_1 - c_1 - c_2)P_I - e_1R_E.$

Equating X^s and M^d, and defining f_0, f_1, g_0, g_1 as before, we have

(14.7') $\qquad\qquad f_0 + f_1P_I + b_1R_I = g_0 + g_1P_I - e_1R_E.$

This yields

(14.8') $\qquad P_I = \dfrac{(f_0 - g_0) + e_1R_E + b_1R_I}{(g_1 - f_1)},$

and

(14.9') $\qquad M = f_0 + \dfrac{f_1(f_0 - g_0) + f_1c_1R_E + f_1b_1R_I}{(g_1 - f_1)} + b_1R_I.$

Thus, as compared with a situation with no indirect taxes, the change in the level of trade stemming from the taxes R_I and R_E on the production of importables respectively, will be

$$\Delta M = \dfrac{f_1e_1R_E + f_1b_1R_I + (g_1 - f_1)b_1R_I}{(g_1 - f_1)}$$

(14.10') $\qquad \Delta M = \dfrac{f_1e_1R_E + g_1b_1R_I}{g_1 - f_1}$

$$\Delta M = w_1(-e_1)R_E + w_2b_1R_I.$$

256

Our results, as expected, show that the effect upon trade of a production tax on exportables will be negative, and that of a production tax on importables positive.

We are now in a position to compare the relative magnitudes of the effects of taxes striking production. This comparison is relevant because the effect of border-tax adjustments is to convert a production-based tax into a consumption-based tax. Taking exportables first, we can see that a consumption-based tax will increase trade by $[w_1(-c_1) + w_2 a_2] T_E$, while a production-based tax will decrease trade by $w_1 e_1 R_E$. Thus if the responsiveness of production of exportables to price changes is sufficiently greater than the responsiveness of their consumption, i.e., if $w_1 e_1 - w_1(-c_1) > w_2 a_2$, the production-based tax will have a greater effect upon trade than the consumption-based tax. Now taking importables, we find that a consumption-based tax will decrease trade by $[w_2(-a_1) + w_1 c_2] T_I$, while a production-based tax will increase trade by $w_2 b_1 R_I$. Thus if the responsiveness of production of importables to price changes is sufficiently greater than the responsiveness of their consumption, i.e., if $w_2 b_1 - w_2(-a_1) > w_1 c_2$, a production-based tax of given magnitude will have a greater effect upon trade than a consumption-based tax of similar magnitude. The same conclusion holds in both instances. I believe it is highly likely that production of both exportables and importables is substantially more sensitive to price changes than their consumption. If this judgment is correct, the conclusion to be derived is that border-tax adjustments in and of themselves tend to reduce the magnitude of the trade effects stemming from indirect taxes.

Chapter 15

Short-Run Effects

of Border-Tax Adjustments

I. INTRODUCTION AND SUMMARY

Largely because of the balance-of-payments difficulties that the United States has been facing in recent years, there has been increasing interest in the workings of border-tax adjustments. According to existing GATT rules, a country can rebate, on exportation of a commodity, the indirect taxes that have been paid in the course of the production of that commodity. Likewise, countervailing import surcharges can be levied on imports of types similar to domestically produced goods in the course of whose production indirect taxes are levied. These countervailing surcharges represent, in principle, the equivalent of the indirect taxes paid by the corresponding internally produced commodities.

Though the United States applies border-tax adjustments on those goods on which it levies indirect taxes, the fact remains that the weight of such adjustments is considerably less here than in most European countries because the latter rely more heavily on indirect taxation than the United States does. This fact gives rise to queries whether the United States could not improve its balance of payments by shifting some of the weight of its taxation from direct taxes (on which GATT rules do not permit border-tax adjustments) to indirect taxes (on which such adjustments are allowed). The discussion in this regard generally focuses on the substitution of a broad-based indirect tax (such as a value-added tax or manufacturers' excise tax) for some part of the personal income tax or of the corporation income tax. Also of current interest are the possible balance-of-payments effects of tax changes that are being contemplated in other countries.

These issues provide the motivation for this discussion, and consequently its focus is on the balance-of-payments effects of border-tax adjustments under various conditions. The qualification, "short-run" appearing in the title is intended mainly to call attention to the fact that no automatic adjustment mechanism (such as flexible exchange rates or differential price-level changes among countries) is assumed to be at work keeping in balance the international payments and receipts of the country in question. When such an automatic adjustment mechanism is at work, and working well, there is no longer any point in analyzing the effects of such measures as border-tax adjustments on the balance of payments. The relevant issues turn on other variables such as the total volume of trade.[1] However, under the present conditions of the world economy, we obviously face an adjustment mechanism which is at best sluggish and imperfect. Under these conditions, as we well know, serious balance-of-payments problems can emerge, and it becomes a matter of interest to inquire into the balance-of-payments effects of alternative policy measures.

The assumed absence of an automatic adjustment mechanism obviously places the analysis in a world where neither flexible exchange rates nor the relative wage and price movements incorporated in traditional gold-standard analysis operate to produce balance-of-payments equilibrium. We build these characteristics into the analysis which follows by assuming that exchange rates remain fixed and that the level of wage rates in the country in question is independent of the policy changes that are treated.

On the basis of the assumptions of constant exchange rates and given wage rates, we build a macroeconomic model to determine the effects of various tax changes on the balance of payments. Although this model is simple, it incorporates all the key forces relevant to our problem. As is characteristic of mathematical models, it enables us to be certain that our conclusions follow logically from our assumptions, and that our argument does not entail internal contradictions.

The model presented takes two forms, one designed for an economy operating at less-than-full employment and the other designed for an economy in which full employment is maintained. Underlying the less-than-full employment model, a monetary policy is assumed which supplies to the economy the amount of money required for accommodating the levels of output and demand that result from the maintenance of the given wage rate and of a constant interest rate. In this model, therefore, monetary policy can be considered as passive — introducing neither inflationary nor deflationary forces into the economy, but permitting other forces, such as border-tax adjustments, to exert their own stimulating or depressing effects without attempting to offset them. Likewise, in the less-than-full employment model, fiscal policy as such plays a passive role. For example, when an increase in indirect taxes is assumed to take place in the model, direct taxes are assumed to decrease so as to keep total government revenue constant. Increases or reductions in budget surpluses or deficits being thus ruled out, the only changes in income that stem from fiscal actions occur because of changes in the *form* of taxation, not as a result of changes in its total amount.

Lying behind the full-employment variant of the model, on the other hand, are active monetary and/or fiscal policies. Here, if an assumed tax change — such as the introduction of border-tax adjustments — would create an increase in the total demand for the products of the economy, monetary and fiscal policy actions are assumed which offset this effect so as to leave the total demand for the country's output equal to its full-employment supply. The composition of

---

[1] In Chapter 14, I have analyzed the effects of border-tax adjustments under conditions in which balance in international payments prevails both before and after the changes being considered.

output among different classes of goods can change in this model, but the aggregate output of the economy cannot.

Given the fact that the two variants of the model entail quite different assumptions about monetary and fiscal policies, it is noteworthy that the principal conclusions stemming from the two variants are identical with regard to the direction of the balance-of-payments effects of the various policies analyzed here. This stability of our conclusions in the face of varying assumptions about monetary and fiscal policies makes them considerably more useful and forceful than they otherwise might be. A brief review of these conclusions follows.

In section II the case of a truly general value-added tax is analyzed. It is shown there that the imposition of such a tax, counterbalanced by a corresponding reduction in direct taxes, would leave the balance of trade unchanged. Prices of final products would rise by the full amount of the tax, but purchasers of such products would have the requisite purchasing power because of the concomitant reduction in income taxes. If, on the other hand, the same tax substitution were made without border-tax adjustments, a deterioration of the balance of trade would result. Similarly, if border-tax adjustments were removed, after having been in effect for a general value-added tax, the balance of trade would worsen. But if new border-tax adjustments were applied to a general value-added tax that had previously been in effect without them, the balance of trade would improve. The most important conclusion of section II is that stated first — put simply, no balance-of-payments effect is to be expected from the introduction of a new and fully general value-added tax with border-tax adjustments.

In section III the analysis is complicated to take account of different effective rates of indirect tax on goods which are internationally traded and on those which are not. Here it is shown that the balance-of-trade effects of imposing new indirect taxes on the two classes of goods depends on which class is taxed at the higher effective rate. If, as is overwhelmingly likely to be the case, international goods carry a higher effective rate of tax than nontraded goods, then some improvement in the balance of trade will result, so long as border-tax adjustments are made. If border-tax adjustments are not made, however, the imposition of a new indirect tax on either of the two classes of goods will result in a deterioration of the trade balance. As before, the introduction of border-tax adjustments on an already existing tax system, where the adjustments were not previously applied, must lead to an improvement in the balance of trade.

The above conclusions of section III are derived from an analysis of the less-than-full employment variant of the basic model. In section IV the analysis is extended to the full-employment case, and it is shown that the conclusions summarized above apply without modification.

Whereas in the earlier analysis no distinction was made between a situation in which a new indirect tax is offset by a reduction in personal taxes and a case in which it is offset by a reduction in corporate taxes, section V extends the analysis to cover this specific issue. It is shown there that while the immediate balance-of-trade effects are likely to be the same regardless of whether personal or corporate taxes are reduced, the reduction of corporate taxes is likely to produce effects on capital flows and, in the longer run, secondary effects on the trade balance, both of which operate to improve the balance of payments. Thus, so far as balance-of-payments effects are concerned, corporate tax reduction is preferable to personal tax reduction.

II. THE CASE OF A GENERAL VALUE-ADDED TAX

The assumption of constant wages, together with the traditional assumption that wages represent overwhelmingly the most important variable cost of production in the short run, enables us to express the quantity supplied of any category of goods as a function of its price alone. As we are focusing on the balance-of-trade consequences of tax measures, it is convenient to group commodities in two broad categories — international goods and domestic goods. International goods consist of both importables and exportables, and it will be assumed that the country in question has no significant influence on the world price of these goods. With this assumption, the unit of each international good can be chosen as that amount which sells for, say, one dollar in world markets (the dollar here representing foreign currency), and the balance of trade of the country in question can accordingly be expressed as the difference between its quantities supplied and demanded of international goods.

As a general value-added tax will fall with equal weight on all components of cost, its impact on the cost curve of any sector will be to raise it by the percentage rate of tax. By itself this would lead to a reduction in output everywhere in the economy, and would thus generate unemployment and downward pressures on wages. But if the value-added tax were imposed as a replacement for a part of an already existing income tax, these results would be obviated. Suppose that the total demand for goods before the tax change were $100 million, that at the same time a value-added tax of 10 percent was introduced, and that income-tax rates were so adjusted as to reduce income-tax yields by $10 million. Under these circumstances, with border-tax adjustments, the equilibrium of the economy would end up exactly the same, in real terms, as it was before. All prices would rise by 10 percent, relative prices would remain unchanged, earned incomes would remain unchanged but disposable incomes would rise by an amount sufficient to "finance" the same real purchases as were made previously. If border-tax adjustments were not made, relative prices would change, with international goods becoming relatively cheaper than domestic goods, inducing an increase in demand for and a reduction in supply of international goods and a corresponding deterioration in the balance of trade. In this case, then, border-tax adjustments are necessary in order to prevent a deterioration of the balance of trade, and do not confer on the country in question any net balance-of-payments advantage.

The result is quite different when one considers the case of a value-added tax which is already in existence, and to which the economy has already fully adjusted. Here the truth seems to be that "whatever is, is right," so far as balance-of-payments effects are concerned. If the existing value-added tax does not entail border-tax adjustments, and the economy has already fully accommodated itself to this setup, then the arbitrary introduction of border-tax adjustments will result in the expansion of exports and the contraction of imports and will thus improve the balance-of-payments position of the country in question. If, on the other hand, the existing value-added tax were one incorporating border-tax adjustments, the elimination of these adjustments would cause a balance-of-payments deficit, while their maintenance would be required to preserve the status quo in the balance of payments.

Let me attempt to summarize by citing three rather stylized examples — the United States, Germany, and France. If the United States were to impose a value-added tax while simultaneously reducing income taxes and holding wages to their normal course, the result would be a deterioration in the United States balance of payments unless the value-added tax were accompanied by border-tax adjustments, in which case the potential detrimental effect of the value-added tax on the balance of payments would be neutralized. Here border-tax adjustments appear to be "good" in the sense that their introduction imposes no burden either on the balance of payments of the United States or on that of the rest of the world.

Now consider the case of Germany. Germany has a rather highly developed system of indirect taxes, based on the turnover or "cascade" system. Border-tax adjustments are made in Germany, but it is generally agreed that these adjustments are only partial. Because indirect taxes are paid in various stages of the productive process, it is necessary to estimate the amount of such taxes that are "incorporated" in a given type of good being exported. The Germans use rough rules-of-thumb in this estimation, and these rules-of-thumb are conservative in the sense that they on the average underestimate the total amount of tax that has been paid on account of an export good as it passed through its various stages of elaboration. Germany is now contemplating a shift to the French system of value-added taxation. Assuming the new value-added tax to be a general one at a flat rate, there will be no need for rules-of-thumb to guess at the amount of indirect tax that has been paid on account of an export good, for it can then be presumed that, say, 10 percent of its market value has in fact been paid at one or another stage in the elaboration process. Thus a 10 percent rebate upon exportation will be called for. This rebate will be greater than the rebates being paid under the current rule-of-thumb system and will accordingly confer balance-of-payments advantages upon Germany, so long as wages are held to their "normal" course. It is as if Germany had had, up to now, a value-added tax without full rebates, had adapted her economy to this setup, and now introduces increased rebates on exports. Here the increased rebates do confer a net balance-of-payments advantage to Germany and a corresponding disadvantage to the rest of the world.

The French case is one in which the value-added tax has been a part of the tax system for some time, with full border-tax adjustments being made. If now the French were to abolish the border-tax adjustments while maintaining the value-added tax as it is, they would thereby induce a substantial deterioration of their balance of payments, and a corresponding improvement in that of the rest of the world. Thus, border-tax adjustments appear to be "neutral" (a) when new indirect taxes are being introduced (the United States example), or (b) when old indirect taxes already involve border-tax adjustments (the French example). Border-tax adjustments appear to be nonneutral when they are newly applied on indirect taxes to which the economy has already accommodated itself in the absence of border-tax adjustments (the German example).

III. TAXES WITH UNEQUAL IMPACT ON INTER-NATIONAL AND DOMESTIC GOODS: CONSTANT WAGE RATES AND LESS-THAN-FULL EMPLOYMENT

Although it is typically the purpose of value-added taxation to apply indirect taxes in a nondiscriminatory fashion to as wide a spectrum of goods as possible, no actual tax system has achieved the goal of striking *all* the value produced in an economy. Service activities, in particular, tend to be exempted from indirect taxation, even in very broad-based tax systems, and often agricultural production is also exempt. Moreover, many countries discriminate among activities according to the "luxury" or "necessity" character of their principal products. The net result of the failure to tax all activities, and of differential taxation of some, is that international goods and domestic goods are normally not taxed equally. Because of the great importance of the services as a component of domestic goods, the presumption is that domestic goods are typically taxed at lower *average* rates than international goods. In this section we therefore inquire into the short-run balance-of-payments effects of various tax policies, operating on the assumption that the effective rate of indirect taxation upon domestic goods will be no greater than that on international goods. For this analysis, we take the effective tax on a final product to be the sum total of indirect taxes paid in the process of producing it; thus, the taxes allocated to automobiles include those paid on the steel, rubber, copper, glass, etc., that are used to make the automobiles. This assumes implicitly that materials and intermediate goods enter into the production of products at higher stages in fixed proportions, certainly a highly plausible approximation.

Apart from materials, labor is taken to be the only factor of production that is significantly variable in the short run. This is a standard assumption for short-run analysis of this type, which stems from the fact that capital equipment cannot typically be transferred from one industry to another — as labor can — in a short period of time, and that the augmentation of the capital stock of an industry through investment typically is a time-consuming process. These assumptions permit us to describe the supply of any final good as a function of its net-of-tax price and of the wage rate paid to labor. Since we have adopted the convention of investigating the reactions of the economy to tax changes under conditions in which the course of wages is independent of such tax changes, we can treat the quantities supplied as functions of the net-of-tax price alone.

Thus we have

(15.1) $$dI^s = e_1\, dp_1 \quad (e_1 > 0)$$

(15.2) $$dH^s = e_2\, dp_2 \quad (e_2 > 0)$$

where I^s refers to the supply of international goods, and p_1 to their net-of-tax price, and H^s refers to the supply of domestic goods and p_2 to their net-of-tax price.

On the demand side, let us first proceed on the assumption of a less-than-full-employment situation with constant interest rates. Demand for each good will then depend upon its relative price and the level of real income (y). We take the initial level of prices as being unity; this is simply a matter of choosing the units in which we measure the goods, and places no constraint upon the results.

We therefore have

(15.3) $dI^d = b_1(dp_1 + t_1 - dp_2 - t_2) + c_1\,dy \quad (b_1 < 0; c_1 > 0)$

(15.4) $dH^d = b_2(dp_2 + t_2 - dp_1 - t_1) + c_2\,dy \quad (b_2 < 0; c_2 > 0).$

Here $(dp_1 + t_1 - dp_2 - t_2)$ represents the change in the price of international goods relative to domestic goods, where t_1 is the effective rate of tax on international goods and t_2 the effective rate of tax on domestic goods. Similarly, $(dp_2 + t_2 - dp_1 - t_1)$ represents the change in the relative price of domestic goods stemming from the imposition of taxes at the rate t_1 on international goods and at the rate t_2 on domestic goods.

The responses of demand for the two goods to changes in relative price are measured by b_1 and b_2, respectively. The interpretation of these coefficients depends upon one's assumptions about how the tax system accommodates the changes in indirect taxes implied by the imposition of t_1 and t_2. The most convenient — and, I believe, the most relevant — assumption in this regard is that direct taxes are reduced, as indirect taxes are imposed, so as to keep the total tax receipts of the government unchanged. Under these circumstances, b_1 and b_2 must be interpreted as reflecting the substitution effect only, and they must be equal in magnitude (see appendix for the proof of this statement), and, of course, negative in sign.

The change in real income, dy, is measured by the sum of the changes in the real output of the economy, measured at initial prices, which it will be recalled are set equal to unity. Thus we have

(15.5) $$dy = dI^s + dH^s.$$

Also, while there is no requirement in this model for trade to be balanced — indeed, we are seeking to measure the effects of tax changes on the trade balance — we do require the equilibration of supply and demand for domestic goods. Thus

(15.6) $$dH^d = dH^s.$$

This completes the model for the case of less-than-full employment, and we can now proceed to analyze the consequences of different tax changes.

A. *The Introduction of New Indirect Taxes Levied on the Purchaser.* When indirect taxes are levied on the purchaser, the price paid by domestic buyers for international goods rises by the amount of the tax, while the price received by local producers of international goods remains unchanged. This is the consequence of the fact that the foreign price of international goods is taken as given, and of our assumption of a fixed exchange rate. We therefore have, in this case, that the price received by producers of international goods (net-of-tax) remains unchanged, or $dp_1 = 0$. The system reduces to

(15.1') $$dI^s = 0$$

(15.2') $$dH^s = e_2\, dp_2 = dy$$

(15.3') $$dI^d = b_1(t_1 - dp_2 - t_2) + c_1\, dy$$

(15.4') $$dH^d = b_2(dp_2 + t_2 - t_1) + c_2\, dy = dH^s$$

Solving for dp_2, we find that

(15.7)
$$e_2\, dp_2 = b_2\, dp_2 + b_2 t_2 - b_2 t_1 + c_2 e_2\, dp_2, \quad \text{or}$$
$$dp_2 = \frac{b_2(t_2 - t_1)}{e_2(1 - c_2) - b_2}.$$

Substituting into (15.3'), we have

$$dI^d = b_1(t_1 - t_2) - \frac{b_1 b_2(t_2 - t_1)}{e_2(1 - c_2) - b_2} + \frac{c_1 e_2 b_2(t_2 - t_1)}{e_2(1 - c_2) - b_2}$$

$$dI^d = \frac{e_2(1 - c_2)b_1(t_1 - t_2) + c_1 e_2 b_2(t_2 - t_1)}{e_2(1 - c_2) - b_2}.$$

Recalling that $b_2 = b_1$, this can be expressed as

(15.8)
$$dI^d = \frac{e_2(1 - c_2 - c_1)b_1(t_1 - t_2)}{e_2(1 - c_2) - b_1},$$

and the change in the balance of trade can be written

(15.9) $$dI^s - dI^d = \frac{-e_2(1 - c_2 - c_1)b_1(t_1 - t_2)}{e_2(1 - c_2) - b_1} \qquad [(1 - c_2 - c_1) > 0].$$

The relevance of (15.9) to our discussion stems from the fact that to levy indirect taxes upon the purchaser of a product is equivalent to levying the same taxes on the producer of the product and simultaneously introducing border-tax adjustments. Consider a good selling in the world market for $1. If a tax of 10 cents a unit is levied on domestic producers of that good, they will receive a net-of-tax price of 90 cents. But if border-tax adjustments are made on exportation of the product, they will receive $1 per unit, as before, on the exported portion of their production. But this in turn means that any part of their product that they sell domestically will also sell for $1, net of tax, since two different prices cannot apply to the same good in the same market. (I pass over here the possibilities of monopoly pricing, and particularly of discriminating monopoly as between the foreign and domestic markets.) Thus the burden of a tax levied on the producers of exportable goods is in effect borne by the domestic purchasers of them, when border-tax adjustments are made, just as would be the case if the tax were directly levied on domestic purchasers. Similarly, if a tax is levied on producers of an importable good selling for $1 in world markets and if border-tax adjustments are made, the countervailing duty paid on imports of that good will cause its internal price to rise by the amount of the tax, and producers will receive the world price as their net-of-tax receipt per unit sold. This, too, is just what would happen if the tax had been levied directly on domestic purchasers of the commodity. Finally, so far as purely domestic goods are concerned, it is a matter of indifference whether an indirect tax is levied nominally on the producer or nominally on the purchaser; the change in the "label" of the tax should have no economic effects.

Thus, the problem that has been analyzed, whose results are given in equation (15.9), is really the problem of the balance-of-trade effects of the introduction of new indirect taxes accompanied by border-tax adjustments. The principal results are as follows:

1. If a truly general value-added tax were introduced, so that $t_1 = t_2$, there would be no effect on the balance of trade so long as border-tax adjustments were made. This confirms the assertion made to this effect in the preceding section.
2. If new indirect taxes are imposed (together with border-tax adjustments) in the "typical" pattern, with the taxes falling more heavily on international goods than on domestic goods (i.e., $t_1 > t_2$), the balance of trade of the country in question will necessarily be improved, the extent of the improvement being proportional to the excess of t_1 over t_2.

B. *The Introduction of New Indirect Taxes Levied on the Producer, Without Border-Tax Adjustments.* If indirect taxes are introduced without border-tax adjustments, the price received (net-of-tax) by local producers of international goods will fall by the amount of the tax. Thus, in our model, $dp_1 = -t_1$. Introducing this into the general model yields

$$(15.1'') \qquad dI^s = -e_1 t_1$$

$$(15.2'') \qquad dH^s = e_2 \, dp_2$$

$$(15.3'') \qquad dI^d = b_1(-dp_2 - t_2) + c_1 \, dy$$

$$(15.4'') \qquad dH^d = b_2(dp_2 + t_2) + c_2 \, dy = dH^s$$

$$(15.5'') \qquad dy = -e_1 t_1 + e_2 \, dp_2.$$

Equating dH^s and dH^d, we obtain

$$e_2 \, dp_2 = b_2 \, dp_2 + b_2 t_2 + c_2 e_2 \, dp_2 - c_2 e_1 t_1,$$

or

$$dp_2 = \frac{b_2 t_2 - c_2 e_1 t_1}{e_2(1 - c_2) - b_2}.$$

Substituting into (15.5'') and (15.3''), we get

$$dI^d = (-b_1 + c_1 e_2) \left(\frac{b_2 t_2 - c_2 e_1 t_1}{e_2(1 - c_2) - b_2} \right) - b_1 t_2 - c_1 e_1 t_1,$$

266

and

$$dI^s - dI^d = -e_1(1 - c_1)t_1 + b_1 t_2 - \frac{(c_1 e_2 - b_1)(b_2 t_2 - c_2 e_1 t_1)}{e_2(1 - c_2) - b_2}$$

(15.10)
$$= \left[-e_1(1 - c_1) + \frac{(c_1 e_2 - b_1)c_2 e_1}{e_2(1 - c_2) - b_2} \right] t_1$$

$$+ \left[b_1 - \frac{(c_1 e_2 - b_1)b_2}{e_2(1 - c_2) - b_2} \right] t_2.$$

Using the fact that $b_1 = b_2$, and defining $s = (1 - c_1 - c_2)$, (15.10) can be simplified to

(15.11)
$$dI^s - dI^d = \frac{e_1 s(b_1 - e_2)t_1 + e_2 s b_1 t_2}{e_2(1 - c_2) - b_1}.$$

Since b_1 is negative, and all the rest of the parameters positive, it is clear that the balance of trade must deteriorate as a consequence of a tax on producers, regardless of whether the tax is levied on producers of international goods or on producers of domestic goods or both. The conclusion of this part of the analysis is strong:

3. If new indirect taxes are levied, falling nominally upon producers, and without being accompanied by border-tax adjustments, they will necessarily lead to a deterioration of the trade balance of the levying country.

C. *The Introduction of Border-Tax Adjustments in Connection with Already Existing Taxes.* The introduction of border-tax adjustments amounts, as has been indicated before, to the conversion of a tax levied upon producers into a tax levied on purchasers. The balance-of-trade effects of such a change can therefore be ascertained by subtracting the balance-of-trade effects of a tax on producers from the balance-of-trade effects of a tax on purchasers. We therefore subtract equation (15.11) from equation (15.9). Recalling that $(1 - c_1 - c_2) = s$, we obtain

(15.12)
$$dI^s - dI^d = \frac{-e_2 s b_1 t_1 - e_1 s(b_1 - e_2)t_1}{e_2(1 - c_2) - b_1} = \frac{(e_1 e_2 - b_1(e_1 + e_2)]s t_1}{e_2(1 - c_2) - b_1}.$$

This expression is necessarily positive. It is independent of t_2, as should be the case, for it is impossible to make border-tax adjustments for purely domestic goods. Thus we conclude:

4. The introduction of border-tax adjustments on an already existing tax system must have favorable effects on the balance of trade.

IV. TAXES WITH UNEQUAL IMPACT ON INTERNATIONAL AND DOMESTIC GOODS: CONSTANT WAGE RATES AND FULL EMPLOYMENT

We can now proceed to check on whether the four principal conclusions arrived at in the preceding section are valid when the model is altered so as to permit the continuous maintenance of full employment. If full employment is to be maintained, the production of home goods must go up whenever the production of international goods declines, and vice versa. This requires, to a close approximation, that $dI^s = -dH^s$, or $dy = 0$.

Thus, if a tax is imposed which causes a reduction in the production of international goods, something must happen to create a corresponding increase in the demand for home goods. This "something" will not, in general, happen automatically; policies must be followed that will produce this result. Obviously, there is some choice among alternative policies that will achieve this end — both monetary and fiscal policies are in principle suited to the purpose, and they can be used singly or in combination. But we need not here inquire as to the precise nature of the policy mix that will be used to generate and maintain full employment. The only restriction that we will place on that mix is that it operates in such a way that when it is expansionary, both the demand for home goods and the demand for international goods will increase, and vice versa when the policy is restrictive. We will call dE the change in expenditures (measured at initial prices) brought about by such policies and will assume it to be divided in the fractions g_1 and g_2 between international and domestic goods. The "full-employment" system of equations thus reads:

$$(15.1) \qquad dI^s = e_1 \, dp_1$$

$$(15.2) \qquad dH^s = e_2 \, dp_2$$

$$(15.3^*) \qquad dI^d = b_1(dp_1 + t_1 - dp_2 - t_2) + g_1 \, dE$$

$$(15.4^*) \qquad dH^d = b_2(dp_2 + t_2 - dp_1 - t_1) + g_2 \, dE$$

$$(15.5^*) \qquad dI^s = -dH^s$$

$$(15.6^*) \qquad dH^s = dH^d$$

For a tax on the home good (t_2), with no taxes on the international good, we have $t_1 = 0$, $dp_1 = 0$, $dI^s = 0$, $dH^s = 0$ [from (15.5^*)], and therefore $dH^d = 0$, and $dp_2 = 0$. We obtain dE from (15.4^*):

$$0 = b_2 t_2 + g_2 \, dE; \qquad dE = \frac{-b_2 t_2}{g_2}.$$

Substituting into (15.3^*), we obtain

$$dI^d = -b_1 t_2 - \frac{g_1 b_2 t_2}{g_2}.$$

Therefore

$$dI^s - dI^d = \frac{(g_2 b_1 + g_1 b_2)}{g_2} t_2,$$

and since $b_1 = b_2$, and $(g_1 + g_2) = 1$, we have

$$(15.13) \qquad dI^s - dI^d = \frac{b_1 t_2}{g_2}.$$

268

For a tax on purchases of international goods we have $t_2 = 0$ and $dp_1 = 0$, $dI^s = 0$, $dH^s = 0$, and therefore $dH^d = 0$ and $dp_2 = 0$. Again obtaining dE from (15.4*), we get

$$0 = -b_2 t_1 + g_2 \, dE; \qquad dE = \frac{b_2 t_1}{g_2}.$$

Substituting into (15.3*), we obtain

(15.14)
$$dI^d = b_1 t_1 + \frac{g_1 b_2 t_1}{g_2}, \quad \text{and}$$

$$dI^s - dI^d = -b_1 t_1 - \frac{g_1 b_2 t_1}{g_2} = \frac{-b_1 t_1}{g_2}.$$

Amalgamating (15.13) and (15.14) for the case of taxes on both purchases of home goods and purchases of international goods, we have

(15.15)
$$dI^s - dI^d = \frac{-b_1(t_1 - t_2)}{g_2}.$$

This expression is zero when $t_1 = t_2$, and positive when $t_1 > t_2$. Therefore conclusions (1) and (2) from page 266 above apply to the full-employment case just as well as to the less-than-full-employment case.

For a tax on production of the international good, we have $dp_1 = -t_1$. Since dH^s must equal $-dI^s$, we obtain $dp_2 = e_1 t_1 / e_2$. Equating dH^d with dH^s, we get

$$e_2 \, dp_2 = b_2 \, dp_2 + g_2 \, dE,$$

so

$$dE = \frac{(e_2 - b_2)}{g_2} \, dp_2 = \frac{(e_2 - b_2) e_1 t_1}{e_2 g_2}.$$

We now substitute into (15.3*) to obtain

$$dI^d = \frac{-b_1 e_1 t_1}{e_2} + \frac{g_1(e_2 - b_2) e_1 t_1}{e_2 g_2}$$

and

(15.16)
$$dI^s - dI^d = -e_1 t_1 + \frac{b_1 e_1 t_1}{e_2} - \frac{g_1(e_2 - b_2) e_1 t_1}{e_2 g_2}.$$

This result is unambiguously negative, as was the result in equation (15.13), for a tax on home goods. (There is no difference in effect between a tax levied nominally on producers of home goods and the same tax levied nominally on purchasers of home goods.) Thus the third conclusion reached above, that a tax levied on producers always leads to a deterioration of the trade balance, remains valid for the full-employment case.

Finally, to check on the validity of the fourth conclusion we simply subtract expression (15.16) from expression (15.14). This tells us what would happen if a tax on producers of international goods were converted into what is in effect a tax on consumers of such goods via border-tax adjustments. Since (15.16) is unambiguously negative, and (15.14) unambiguously positive, the net result of such a shift must be an improvement in the trade balance. Thus all four of the conclusions reached in section III for the less-than-full-employment case apply without modification to the full-employment case as well.

V. AN EXTENSION OF THE ABOVE ANALYSIS: VALUE-ADDED TAX VS. CORPORATION INCOME TAX

As the United States seeks ways of improving its balance-of-payments position, it is frequently suggested that some of the weight of the tax system be shifted from direct to indirect taxes. It is asserted or implied, when this suggestion is made, that the possibility of introducing border-tax adjustments concomitantly with new or increased indirect taxes will result in a significant improvement of the balance of trade. As we have seen, this conclusion is probably unwarranted when indirect taxes are substituted for personal income taxes. On the one hand, if the indirect tax were a truly general value-added tax, or if it, without being general, struck domestic and international goods at roughly the same effective rate, the presumption is that there would be no balance-of-trade effects. On the other hand, if the tax were nongeneral, and at the same time struck international goods at higher effective rates than domestic goods, there would be a favorable effect on the balance of trade, but it would be related not to the level of the effective rate of new taxation on international goods but to the excess of that rate over the effective rate of new taxation on domestic goods. Thus, for example, suppose that a 10 percent tax were placed on value added over a broad sector of the economy, but with some exemptions. Let us assume, that, say, 20 percent of all value added in the production of international goods, and 50 percent of all value added in the production of domestic goods turned out to be exempt from the tax. Then one would have an effective rate of tax of 8 percent on international goods and of 5 percent on domestic goods. The consequent "leverage" for improving the balance of trade would be the 3 percent differential between these two rates rather than the 10 percent tax that was actually being rebated upon exportation and charged as a countervailing duty on importation. The balance-of-trade effects would accordingly be only some 30 percent of those that would be calculated on the basis of a presumably full stimulus from the 10 percent border-tax adjustment. There would be favorable effects, to be sure, but they would not be nearly so substantial as a naive approach to the problem would lead one to expect.

What differences are introduced into this set of conclusions when we assume that new indirect taxes are counterbalanced by a reduction in the corporate rather than the personal income tax? This question asks, in effect, whether the reduction of corporate taxes will result in a lower internal price level of international goods than would a reduction of equal magnitude in personal income taxes. I see no reason to presume that this would be the case in the short run. The prevailing prices for goods represent the equilibrium of supply and demand in their respective markets. Only if a reduction in the corporation tax (as against the personal income tax) would cause the supply function for international goods to shift to the right, could such a presumption be sustained. But in the short run, corporate profits are not reflected as a cost underlying the supply function, but rather as the residual share which emerges after all other costs are met. Since corporate profits are not a component of short-run marginal costs, an alteration in the tax rate on them will not influence short-run marginal costs, hence will not affect the short-run supply functions of the affected industries.

I would thus maintain that for a strictly short-run analysis of the balance of trade the presumption is that the results obtained in the preceding sections hold regardless of whether the new indirect taxes are counterbalanced by a corporate or a personal tax reduction. However, the medium- and longer-run effects of corporate tax reduction do appear to be more favorable to the balance of trade than those of personal tax reduction, and there might be significant short-run effects on the balance of payments as distinct from the balance of trade. Both of these results stem from the fact that a reduction in corporate taxes makes investment in the corporate sector more profitable than it otherwise would be. The greater profitability of the corporate sector will stimulate investment there, and will presumably draw some funds into such investment which otherwise would have been placed abroad by financial institutions, etc. This effect will lead to an improvement in the balance of payments on capital account, which could take place quite rapidly. It should be pointed out here, however, that this effect would not apply to direct investment abroad, since the reduction in corporate taxes would presumably enhance the profitability of such investment as well as the profitability of purely local investment. Nonetheless, I would anticipate that, in the net, an improvement in the balance of payments would result. If full-employment policies are pursued, it is almost certain that the equilibrium rate of interest will rise as a consequence of the reduction in corporate tax rates, and this in turn should have a favorable effect on the balance of payments, causing a net diversion of some funds from the foreign to the internal market.

As investments in the corporate sector reach the productive stage, there will be an increase in the supply of corporate products and a reduction in their price, as an equilibrium is gradually brought about between profit rates in the corporate sector (which were specially favored by the corporate tax reduction) and other rates of return to capital in the economy. Broadly speaking, this price readjustment would entail a lowering of the prices of the products of the corporate sector and a raising of the prices of the products of the noncorporate sector. Since corporate sector products are much more predominantly international goods, in the terminology of this paper, than noncorporate products, the net result of this relative price shift would be an improvement in the balance of trade.

This last assertion can be demonstrated rigorously within the framework of the model developed in this paper. Since we are here concerned with working out the longer-run adjustment to a change in the tax system, we are dealing with a set of reactions that occur after the new tax setup is in existence; thus we need not introduce tax changes explicitly into this part of the analysis.

Instead we shall assume that, as a consequence of the incentives to invest in corporate sector, we observe over time a rightward shift of k_1 in the supply function of international goods, and a leftward shift of k_2 in the supply function for domestic goods. The model then becomes, for the full-employment case:

(15.1**) $$dI^s = e_1\, dp_1 + k_1$$

(15.2**) $$dH^s = e_2\, dp_2 - k_2$$

(15.3**) $$dI^d = b_1(dp_1 - dp_2) + g_1\, dE$$

(15.4**) $$dH^d = b_2(dp_2 - dp_1) + g_2\, dE$$

(15.5**) $$dI^s = -dH^s$$

(15.6**) $$dH^d = dH^s.$$

Since the world price of international goods is given, $dp_1 = 0$. From (15.1**), (15.2**) and (15.6**), we obtain $dp_2 = (k_2 - k_1)/e_2$. From (15.1**), (15.5**) and (15.6**), we get $dH^d = -k_1$. Substituting this and the expression for dp_2 into (15.4**), we obtain

$$-k_2 = \frac{b_2(k_2 - k_1)}{e_2} + g_2\, dE, \quad \text{or}$$

$$dE = \frac{-e_2 k_1 - b_2(k_2 - k_1)}{e_2 g_2}.$$

Substituting for dp_2 and dE in (15.3**), we have

$$dI^d = \frac{-g_2 b_1(k_2 - k_1) - g_1 e_2 k_1 - g_1 b_2(k_2 - k_1)}{e_2 g_2},$$

which, using the fact that $(g_1 + g_2) = 1$ and $b_1 = b_2$ can be simplified to

$$dI^d = \frac{-b_1(k_2 - k_1) - g_1 e_2 k_1}{e_2 g_2}.$$

The expression for the change in the trade balance then becomes

(15.17) $$dI^s - dI^d = \frac{e_2 g_2 k_1 + b_1(k_2 - k_1) + g_1 e_2 k_1}{e_2 g_2} = \frac{e_2 k_1 + b_1(k_2 - k_1)}{e_2 g_2}.$$

This expression is unambiguously positive so long as $k_1 > k_2$. This last condition means that the rightward shift in the supply curve of international goods set in motion by the reduction in corporate taxes cannot be more than outweighed by the leftward shift in the supply curve of domestic goods stemming from the same cause. This is certainly not a very stringent condition, and even if it were not met, this would only mean that one of the two terms in (15.17) would be negative, not that the change in the trade balance would necessarily itself be negative.

For the case of less-than-full employment the model corresponding to an upward shift of k_1 in the supply function for international goods and a downward shift of k_2 in the supply function for domestic goods consists of equations

(15.1**), (15.2**), (15.6**), plus

(15.3***) $$dI^d = b_1(dp_1 - dp_2) + c_1\, dy$$

(15.4***) $$dH^d = b_2(dp_2 - dp_1) + c_2\, dy$$

(15.5***) $$dy = dI^s + dH^s.$$

Here again, the assumption of constant exchange rates requires that $dp_1 = 0$. From (15.1**), (15.2**), and (15.5***) we obtain

$$dy = (k_1 - k_2) + e_2\, dp_2.$$

From this, plus (15.2**) and (15.4***), we have

$$dp_2 = \frac{k_2 + c_2(k_1 - k_2)}{e_2(1 - c_2) - b_2}.$$

Substituting into the expression for dy, we have

$$dy = (k_1 - k_2) + \frac{e_2 k_2 + e_2 c_2(k_1 - k_2)}{e_2(1 - c_2) - b_2}$$

$$dy = \frac{e_2 k_1 - b_2(k_1 - k_2)}{e_2(1 - c_2) - b_2}.$$

Now substituting into (15.3***), we obtain

$$dI^d = \frac{-b_1 k_2 - b_1 c_2(k_1 - k_2) + c_1 e_2 k_1 - c_1 b_2(k_1 - k_2)}{e_2(1 - c_2) - b_2}.$$

Now using $dI^s = k_1$, we have for the change in the balance of trade

$$dI^s - dI^d = \frac{k_1 e_2(1 - c_2) - k_1 b_2 + b_1 k_2 + b_1 c_2(k_1 - k_2) - c_1 e_2 k_1 + c_1 b_2(k_1 - k_2)}{e_2(1 - c_2) - b_2}$$

which, using the fact that $b_1 = b_2$, can be reduced to

(15.18) $$dI^s - dI^d = \frac{(1 - c_1 - c_2)[k_1 e_2 - b_1(k_1 - k_2)]}{e_2(1 - c_2) - b_2}.$$

This expression, like (15.17) is necessarily positive so long as $k_1 > k_2$. We can accordingly conclude that the secondary stimulus to the balance of trade, stemming from the increases in corporate sector output induced by a reduction in the corporation income tax will clearly be positive, except in the most unlikely event that the downward shift in supply of noncorporate goods and services greatly outweighs the upward shift in supply of corporate products. This is true both for the case of a less-than-full-employment economy and for an economy in which a full-employment policy is continuously pursued, subject always to the course through time of wage rates being unaffected by the policy measures here analyzed.[2]

[2] As I have reflected further upon the model presented in section V, I have been troubled by one aspect of it. When $k_2 \neq k_1$, the full-employment output of the economy should grow, and we should allow for an income effect on demand for both home goods and international goods. I have subsequently worked out this case, and find that when this effect is allowed for, an unambiguous improvement in the trade balance results from the investment incentives associated with a corporate tax reduction in the full-employment case. The model as presented need not be modified if k_2 is assumed equal to k_1.

Appendix A Note on Substitution Terms

Let us express the demand for home goods as a function of absolute prices and of disposable income, Y, in money terms:

$$(15.A1) \qquad dH^d = b_{22}(dp_2 + t_2) + b_{21}(dp_1 + t_1) + c_2\, dY.$$

Here b_{22} measures the responsiveness of home-goods demand to a change in the price of such goods, with other prices and disposable income held constant. Likewise, b_{21} measures the responsiveness of home-goods demand to changes in international goods prices, with other prices and disposable income held constant. These coefficients are related in the following way to the corresponding coefficients (denoted by primes) measuring the responsiveness of demand to relative price changes holding real income constant:

$$b_{22} = b_{22}' - c_2 H^d$$
$$b_{21} = b_{21}' - c_2 I^d.$$

This stems from the fact that a rise of Δp_2 in the price paid by purchasers of home goods lowers real income by $H^d\, \Delta p_2$, and a rise of Δp_1 in the price paid by buyers of international goods lowers real income by $I^d\, \Delta p_1$, in each case assuming that other prices and money income are held constant. The income effect of a change in price on the demand for home goods is simply c_2 times the change in income thus measured, and the substitution effect is the remaining part of the total effect. Similarly, in the demand function for international goods, expressed in absolute price and money-income terms,

$$(15.A2) \qquad dI^d = b_{11}(dp_1 + t_1) + b_{12}(dp_2 + t_2) + c_1\, dY,$$

we have

$$b_{11} = b_{11}' - c_1 I^d, \quad \text{and} \quad b_{12} = b_{12}' - c_1 H^d.$$

Turning now to the change in disposable income, we have, assuming initial equilibrium in the market for home goods ($H^d = H^s$) and the balance of trade ($I^d = I^s$), $dY = dy + I^d(dp_1 + t_1) + H^d(dp_2 + t_2)$.

The change in disposable income thus breaks down into a part due to the change in real output (dy); a part due to the reduction of direct taxes, $I^d t_1 + H^d t_2$, to counterbalance the increase in yield of indirect taxes ($I^d t_1 + H^d t_2$), and a part due to changes in prices received by producers ($I^s\, dp_1 + H^s\, dp_2$), which, under our assumption of initial equilibrium, is equal to ($I^d\, dp_1 + H^d\, dp_2$).

Inserting the expressions for b_{22}, b_{21}, and dY in (15.A1),

$$(15.A3) \qquad dH^d = (b_{22}' - c_2 H^d)(dp_2 + t_2) + (b_{21}' - c_2 I^d)(dp_1 + t_1)$$
$$+ c_2\, dy + c_2 I^d(dp_1 + t_1) + c_2 H^d(dp_2 + t_2).$$

Since the terms in I^d and H^d cancel, (15.A3) can be reduced to

$$(15.A4) \qquad dH^d = b_{22}'(dp_2 + t_2) + b_{21}'(dp_1 + t_1) + c_2\, dy.$$

Similarly, we can substitute for b_{11}, b_{12}, and dY in (15.A2) to obtain

$$(15.\text{A}5) \qquad dI^d = (b_{11}' - c_1 I^d)(dp_1 + t_1) + (b_{12}' - c_1 H^d)(dp_2 + t_2)$$
$$+ c_1\, dy + c_1 I^d(dp_1 + t_1) + c_1 H^d(dp_2 + t_2).$$

Again, the terms in I^d and H^d cancel, yielding

$$(15.\text{A}6) \qquad dI^d = b_{11}'(dp_1 + t_1) + b_{12}'(dp_2 + t_2) + c_2\, dy.$$

Now, it is a well-known property of substitution effects that the response of a commodity to a 1 percent rise in its own price is the negative of the sum of the responses of that commodity to a 1 percent rise in all the other prices in the system. Thus, recalling that units are so chosen as to set initial prices equal to unity, we have $b_{11}' = -b_{12}'$, and $b_{22}' = -b_{21}'$. Likewise we have the property of substitution terms that the partial derivative of one good with respect to the price of another must equal the partial derivative of the second with respect to the price of the first.[1] Hence we have $b_{12}' = b_{21}'$. Using these properties we can see that (15.A4) can be rewritten

$$(15.\text{A}7) \qquad dH^d = b_{22}'(dp_2 + t_2 - dp_1 - t_1) + c_2\, dy,$$

and (15.A6) can be rewritten

$$(15.\text{A}8) \qquad dI^d = b_{11}'(dp_1 + t_1 - dp_2 - t_2) + c_1\, dy.$$

(15.A7) and (15.A8) correspond exactly to equations (15.4) and (15.3) in the text, with b_{22}' being there relabeled b_2 and b_{11}' relabeled b_1. Moreover, from the facts that $b_{22}' = -b_{21}'$, $b_{11}' = -b_{12}'$, and $b_{12}' = b_{21}'$, it is easily seen that $b_{11}' = b_{22}'$, or, in the notation of the text, $b_1 = b_2$. Q.E.D.

When trade is not initially balanced, equation (15.3) of the text becomes

$$dI^d = b_1(dp_1 + t_1 - dp_2 - t_2) + c_1\, dy + c_1 B\, dp_1,$$

and equation (15.4) of the text becomes

$$dH^d = b_2(dp_2 + t_2 - dp_1 - t_1) + c_2\, dy + c_2 B\, dp_2,$$

where B equals the initial balance of trade (positive for a surplus and negative for a deficit). The analysis of section III.A of the text remains completely unmodified, for in this part $dp_1 = 0$, and the above equations are reduced back to (15.3) and (15.4). The analysis of sections III.B and III.C becomes more complicated in the case of initial imbalance but conclusions (3) and (4), reached in these sections, remain unchanged for the case of an initial deficit. Sections IV and V remain completely unchanged when initial imbalance in trade is introduced, section IV because the demand functions (15.3*) and (15.4*) are not affected by initial imbalance, and section V because, for the effects analyzed there, $dp_1 = 0$.

---

[1] For a derivation of the properties of substitution terms used here, see J. R. Hicks, *Value and Capital*, 2d ed. (Oxford: Clarendon Press, 1946), pp. 309–311.

XII

The following chapter was prepared for and presented at a Conference on Fiscal Policy for Economic Growth in Latin America, which was held in Santiago, Chile in December, 1962, under the auspices of the Joint Tax Program of the Organization of American States, the Inter-American Development Bank, and the United Nations Economic Commission for Latin America. The conference was concerned with measures of tax reform that might be feasible for meeting the revenue needs of the Latin American countries in the decade of the 1960s, and the paper accordingly focused on this issue. In this context, it should not be surprising that this chapter reveals more than most of the others in this volume about my value orientation with regard to tax policy and is correspondingly less involved in theoretical details.

The general line of argument runs as follows. We take as given the fact that the personal income tax is subject to substantial and widespread evasion, the degree of evasion varying significantly among different groups of taxpayers. It would therefore be inequitable to look to this tax alone as a source of overall progressivity in the tax system. Accordingly, it is proposed that a system of excise taxes be instituted that is itself progressive, to help ensure that even those categories of higher-income taxpayers who are able to shirk on their income-tax payments will still not elude the tax net entirely.

In a similar spirit is the notion that the income from capital should, at least in the Latin American context, be taxed more heavily than the income from labor. What is proposed here is that the effort be made to tax the income from capital equally in all its uses. This avoids discrimination among uses involved in the corporation income tax as such by imposing supplementary taxes at approximately equal rates on the income from capital that is in forms other than corporate equity.

The taxation of residential and agricultural properties takes on special importance. Here, in what has been the most widely discussed aspect of the paper, I propose (though not for the first time) the economist's solution to the problem of property valuation — namely, market-enforced self-assessment. This is a scheme whereby property owners declare the taxable value of their properties, subject to the sole constraint that their declaration implies an offer of sale to any buyer who is willing, bona fide, to pay X percent more than the owner's self-declared valuation for the property. Although this proposal has given rise to some heated debates, my own reaction has been one of pleasure and, to an extent, surprise at its ability to survive these controversies. If nothing else, the self-assessment proposal dramatically calls attention to the inequities usually involved when assessment is done arbitrarily and without a direct and automatic relationship to the true market value of the property.

Chapter 16

Issues of Tax Reform
for Latin America

INTRODUCTION

I should like to begin this paper with a statement of its scope and objectives. The topic assigned to me is a general one which could easily be interpreted to cover a hodgepodge of separate, essentially unrelated issues. I do not want this paper to be such a potpourri; yet at the same time I do want to meet the requirements of the title by covering more than one or two limited issues of tax reform. In drawing the line between very narrow focus, on the one hand, and "complete coverage," on the other, I shall deal briefly with two matters connected with the general philosophy with which tax problems are approached and shall then concentrate on two substantive areas which appear to me as likely candidates for tax reform in Latin America. The two matters of general philosophy are (a) the problems and goals of tax planning in Latin America and (b) alternative views of the role which elimination or reduction of tax evasion can play in meeting the future tax needs of Latin American countries. The two substantive areas for tax reform that I shall consider explicitly are (c) possibilities for the development or expansion of progressive excise tax structures and (d) possibilities for improving and rationalizing the taxation of income from capital.

I should like also to point out in this introduction that it is virtually impossible to discuss issues of tax reform without at the same time making a series of value judgments, either explicitly or by implication. I have tried to base the discussion which follows on value premises which are widely held: that a tax system should be progressive, that it should not interfere significantly with the achievement of an efficient allocation of resources, that it should not artificially direct investment into low-productivity uses, that it should provide adequate revenue to meet expected levels of government expenditure without chronic resort to inflationary financing, and that it should, on equity grounds, tax income from capital somewhat more heavily than income from labor. I have also argued that a tax system

Reprinted with permission from Arnold C. Harberger, "Issues of Tax Reform for Latin America," in *Joint Tax Program, OAS/IBD/ECLA* (Baltimore: The Johns Hopkins Press, 1965), pp. 110–121.

should be so designed as to minimize the injustices resulting from the differential capacities of different groups to evade particular taxes. Those readers who object to some or all of these premises are likely, on this account, to disagree with some of the conclusions drawn from the analysis which follows. I can only at this point express my hope that most readers will find the premises sufficiently congenial to provide a reasonable basis for a discussion of issues of tax reform.

SOME ISSUES OF GENERAL PHILOSOPHY

Given that the demands of economic development and social improvement will almost certainly require that an increasing fraction of the national income be channeled through the public sector, the tax authorities should develop a planning mechanism by which they attempt to foresee and provide for the necessary increases in revenue. It seems obvious that adequate tax planning should be part of any overall, coordinated development policy; indeed, tax planning would probably be one of the most rudimentary and least difficult parts of such a policy. Yet many Latin American countries have conspicuously failed in the past to levy taxes sufficient to cover their existing levels of government expenditure. Adequate public sector support for future growth will require substantially increased expenditure even in such traditional areas of public sector activity as education, road building, and public utilities. Increases in health and welfare expenditures are also likely in the future as governments take increasing interest in the welfare of the poorer classes. If these added tasks of the public sector are to be accomplished without disrupting the economies of the countries concerned, there must occur a drastic improvement in the capacities of many governments to raise revenue. What I have here called tax planning — the sorting out of alternative ways of achieving needed revenue increases and the decision in advance as to which ways appear most acceptable — is simply the first step toward obtaining such a drastic improvement.

Given that unforeseen contingencies are likely to arise, requiring on occasion rapid increases in tax receipts, the tax-planning authorities should maintain a series of specific plans as to how they would suggest raising given amounts of extraordinary revenue within given periods of time. In addition to the budget instability which might come from natural disasters, etc., many Latin American countries face potential instability due, on the one hand, to the variability of the international prices of their principal exports and, on the other hand, to the tendency for public sector wage levels to move in brusque and discontinuous jumps and in response to circumstances and pressures that cannot always be foreseen. If periodic budgetary crises are to be surmounted, the tax authorities must have available to them, in moments of crisis, acceptable ways of capturing such short-run increases in revenue as the situation appears to require. This can be done only on the basis of a reasonable amount of advance planning.

Up to a certain point, evasion must be accepted as a continuing phenomenon. Some taxes are more susceptible to evasion than others, and some groups can more easily evade any given tax than others. The maintenance of adequate tax equity is accordingly more likely if each individual's or group's tax burden is distributed among a number of taxes with distinct tax bases rather than concentrated heavily on particular taxes which some groups may have an extraordinary capacity to evade. This classical principle of taxation is well observed in the regressive components of most existing tax structures but inadequately observed in their proportional and progressive components.

This should not be taken to condone laxity in tax administration or to suggest that much existing evasion cannot be eliminated. It should be taken instead to suggest that 100 percent compliance is an absurd goal for tax planning and that the design of a tax system, even with the best administration, should recognize that the capacity for evasion will differ significantly among groups.

It should also be recognized that such gains in yields as can be achieved by improved administration are likely to accrue only slowly through time. The idea that improved administration will provide funds to meet an immediate crisis or contingency is surely erroneous; yet this is, in fact, the ground on which the opposition to many proposed increases in taxation in Latin America rests its case. To consider the reduction of evasion as a means for providing short-run increases in revenue is itself a gross evasion of responsibility. It is probably also true that the demands for increased revenue which will arise in the next decade or so in Latin America will substantially exceed the additional revenue that can be obtained through improved administration within this longer period.

THE CASE FOR A PROGRESSIVE EXCISE TAX STRUCTURE

A progressive structure of excise taxes has much to recommend it as a way of meeting part of the foreseeable increase in revenue needs while at the same time reducing the relative importance of inequities due to evasion. Increasing the rates of personal income taxation would yield added revenue, but attempting to meet the entire burden of increased taxation in this way would augment the inequity between those who are able and willing to evade this tax and those who comply with their full obligations. Increasing the regressive component of the tax structure would, on the other hand, result in an unjust division of the burden of added taxation among income groups.

A progressive structure of excise taxes is also an almost ideal basis for meeting unexpected contingencies. The rates of these taxes may be raised or lowered on short notice, and the administration of these changes is comparatively simple. Moreover, if the excise tax structure is reasonably progressive, a just sharing of the burden of meeting contingencies can be reasonably assured by an across-the-board percentage adjustment of rates in the excise tax structure as a whole. Up to now, in Latin America, contingencies have typically been met by increases in the regressive components of the tax structure (cigarettes, sales tax, etc.) or by inflationary finance.

The case for progressive excise taxation is a good one, but the well-known arguments favoring nondiscriminatory (e.g., income) as against discriminatory (e.g., excise) taxes remain valid. The benefits of progressive excise taxation in terms of equity, administrative feasibility, and aptness for meeting contingencies are bought at a cost in terms of the distortion of individual choices among commodities. This cost increases with the rate of tax and with the substitutability of products which are taxed (or taxed at high rates) for products which are not taxed (or taxed at low rates). In the design of a progressive excise tax structure, care should accordingly be taken to avoid excessively high rates of tax and the effort should be made to tax products which are close substitutes for each other at similar rates. As a rough approximation, it may be stated that tax rates higher than the 30 to 40 percent range should be subject to careful scrutiny, as there is a presumption that beyond this range indirect taxes can impose substantial costs by artificially distorting the choices confronting individual consumers.

It is recognized that the Latin American countries have for a long time had progressive import duties. These were levied not for the purpose of protecting domestic industries but for the dual purpose of restraining the use of foreign exchange for luxury consumption and of obtaining a just distribution of the total tax burden. The second of these objectives corresponds well with the arguments made above; indeed the correspondence is complete in the case where imports are the only source of supply of the goods included in the progressive tariff structure. However, when domestic production of goods suitable for luxury taxation exists, a progressive import-tariff structure on these same goods yields less revenue (due to the substitution of domestic for imported goods) and serves less well than before the purpose of achieving progressiveness and equity in the tax structure. Latin American countries have been slow to place excise taxes on locally produced luxury consumption goods. This may not have been an important step to take in a period when there was little or no local production of these goods, but today, with luxury consumer goods production growing in virtually every Latin American country, and large in magnitude in several, it merits the most serious consideration.

Special attention should be given to the taxation of automobiles. It is implicit in what has already been said that in those countries where there is local production of automobiles, this production should be subject to excise taxation, though not, of course, necessarily at the same rates as the tariffs applying to imported cars. But a tax on locally produced cars, together with an import duty on cars imported through commercial channels, leaves out a source of supply which has been quite important in many Latin American countries: namely, those cars which are imported duty-free by foreign diplomats or other functionaries or by returning nationals fulfilling certain requirements. These privileged groups receive, in effect — as personal capital gains — large sums that might otherwise have accrued as tax revenues to the government. There are a number of ways of coping with this unfortunate state of affairs. One which I find particularly appealing, and which fits well in an overall scheme of progressive excise taxation, is a system of progressive license or use taxes on automobiles. To illustrate, the annual license tax for a new Cadillac might be $1,000; for a 10-year-old Cadillac it might be $200; that for a new Jeep might be $200; and that for a 10-year-old Jeep might be $20. Such a system could be made much more neatly progressive than any prevailing system of import duties on automobiles, and it would at the same time greatly limit the extent of capital gains which the privileged groups mentioned above would be able to extract from the Latin American countries.[1]

THE SPECIAL TAXATION OF INCOME
FROM CAPITAL

I entitle this section "The Special Taxation of Income from Capital" because I mean to isolate for consideration those taxes or tax provisions whose tax base is either the amount of capital, the income from capital, or parts thereof, in particular sectors or activities, or generally. A tax striking all value added in the economy at an equal rate hits both the income from labor and the income from capital; it is therefore not a special tax on income from capital in the sense in which I am using the term. Likewise, a progressive personal income tax which takes the same amount from all individuals of given income, regardless of whether that income came from capital or from labor, is not a special tax on income from capital. On the other hand, a tax on corporation income, in cases where income received as interest, dividends, and possibly as capital gains is additionally taxable as the personal income of the recipient, is clearly a special tax on the income from capital. So also is a property tax, in cases where the income of the property owner is additionally taxable under the personal income tax law. I shall also consider in this section special treatments, whether favorable (exemptions) or unfavorable (surtaxes or special additional taxes), falling on property or on the income from property in specific sectors or industries. This set of distinctions is simple to make for countries with a unified personal income tax structure, but some adjustments of the basic data are required before it can be applied to countries where "category taxes" are in force. For example, in a country where the category rate for wages and salaries is 10 percent and the category rate for corporate profits is 50 percent, the analysis of this section would treat the system as consisting of a basic tax rate of 10 percent plus a special tax of 40 percent on corporate profits. A more complex system with a category rate of 10 percent for wages and salaries received by persons, of 20 percent for dividend income of persons, and a 50 percent rate for corporation income would be treated in this analysis as consisting of a basic tax rate of 10 percent and a special tax rate for corporation income of between 40 and 50 percent (the precise rate depending on the fraction of profits paid out in dividends). Actual systems are still more complex than this, and the required adjustments would necessarily vary from case to case, but the basic principle for adjustment is simple: one only has to find the total tax paid out of income from capital in each line of activity (and perhaps by type of capital), estimate the amount by which total tax receipts would fall if the recipients of income from capital had received the same sums as additional labor income, and express

[1] This proposal does not preclude a simultaneous direct attack upon the problem of capital gains by the privileged groups, such as requiring that cars imported duty-free either be re-exported or, at the option of the owner, be sold to the government of the host country at their original purchase price or at their original purchase price minus a reasonable charge for depreciation.

this difference as a percentage of the income from capital in the activity (or of the type) involved. The result is the rate of special taxation of income from capital in that line of activity or of that type.

The principal argument for the special taxation of income from capital runs in terms of equity. A man receiving a given income as the fruit of his own labor "deserves" it more than a man receiving the same income as the return to his capital. This argument is particularly strong where inheritance and/or gift taxes are low or ill enforced, for then the income received from capital will in large measure be income coming from assets which were built up by people other than the income recipient himself and which were transferred to him without the prepayment of a tax reflecting the recipient's less meritorious claim to income from them.

The argument above could be used to justify special taxes on income from capital at rates which were progressive according to the amount of income from capital received by an individual or according to the amount of property owned by an individual. The equity argument does not, however, easily justify rates of taxation of income from capital according to the sector or activity in which the income is generated or according to the type of claim (stocks, bonds, etc.) which the ultimate income receivers may own. Given that, in practice, most "special" taxes on the income from capital take a certain percentage of the affected income or (what amounts to much the same thing) a certain percentage of the value of the affected capital, we may conclude that equity considerations would be well met if tax rates were designed so as to take roughly the same fraction of income from capital of all types and in all activities or alternatively to take each year roughly the same fraction of the value of capital of each type and in each activity.

Considerations of resource allocation argue even more forcefully than considerations of equity for the application of equal rates of special taxation to the income from capital in all sectors. Even in poorly organized capital markets, there exists a strong tendency toward the equalization of the net (after tax) rates of return on capital of different types and in different activities. For a variety of reasons (risk differentials, inadequate information, indivisibilities, legally protected monopoly positions, dynamic change in the conditions of technology and of demand), actual equalization of net rates of return is never achieved in the real world. But it remains true that investment decision makers prefer a 20 percent net rate of return to one of 10 percent and that unless they are unaware of the differential or are otherwise prohibited from exercising their preference, they will tend to concentrate new allocations of funds and resources in the high-return sector, driving down the rate of return there and simultaneously tending to raise the rate of return in the low-yielding sector. Where the rate of tax on income from capital is the same in all sectors, this tendency is an exceedingly healthy one from the standpoint of economic efficiency and the promotion of economic growth. The contribution of a unit of capital to the national income can (with some qualifications) be measured by its gross-of-tax rate of return. If, in the above example, the tax rate applying to income from capital were 33 1/3 percent, the contribution of additional capital to the annual national income would be roughly 30 percent of the value of the capital in the high-return sector and roughly 15 percent of the value of the capital in the low-return sector. Concentration of new allocations of capital in the high-return sector would accordingly tend to enhance the rate of economic growth. And such concentration is the natural consequence of the preference of investment decision makers for high rates of return.

Suppose, however, that in the sector with a 30 percent gross-of-tax rate of return a tax amounting to half the income from capital is levied and that in the sector with a 15 percent rate of return no tax at all is applied. Then the net rate of return will be 15 percent in both sectors, and there will be no tendency to concentrate new investment in the high-return sector. The presence of differential rates of taxation (here 50 percent and zero percent, respectively) produces and tends to maintain an inefficient pattern of resource use and reduces the contribution of capital investment to economic growth. There is a strong presumption that virtually any pattern of taxation which strikes the income from capital at different rates in different sectors or activities will have similar effects. Desirable results in terms of economic efficiency and economic growth are produced when there is a tendency to equalize gross-of-tax rates of return, while the natural operation of market forces tends to equalize net-of-tax rates of return. When the rates of tax applying in all activities are the same, the market forces are harnessed to promote the objectives of efficiency and growth. When different rates of tax apply in different sectors or activities, the natural operation of market forces tends to frustrate the achievement of maximal efficiency and growth.

I appreciate that the discussion above may sound a bit too idealized for direct application to the situations of many Latin American countries. Market imperfections there may be too big to warrant great reliance on the effectiveness of the tendency for equalization of net rates of return. Accordingly, in this paragraph, I discuss the policies which would be desirable for the achievement of the objectives of efficiency and growth in the presence of substantial capital market imperfections. These objectives clearly demand the concentration of new investment in areas with a high (gross-of-tax) rate of return. If capital does not flow naturally into such areas, it is a reasonable objective of tax policy to attempt to induce such a flow. This could be achieved by taxing the income from capital more heavily in sectors and areas with low rates of return and less heavily in sectors and areas with high rates of return. But this is precisely the opposite pattern of discrimination from that which prevails in most Latin American countries. The sectors in which capital is taxed at low effective rates (e.g., real estate and agriculture) are precisely the sectors in which capital has relatively low marginal productivity, while the sectors in which capital is taxed at high effective rates (e.g., industry) are precisely the sectors of relatively high marginal productivity. Thus, the prevailing tax systems discriminate in the opposite way from that which would presumably be required to correct for capital market imperfections.

Imperfections in the labor market appear to work in the same direction as imperfections in the capital market. The use of the gross-of-tax rate of return to capital as a measure of the social marginal productivity of capital in a sector is correct when the wages paid by the sector reflect the alternative productivity of the labor it employs. If a sector pays wages which are higher than the alternative productivity of its labor, the social rate of return on the capital employed in that sector will exceed the gross-of-tax rate of return perceived by the enterprises in that sector; and if a sector pays wages which are lower than the alternative productivity of its labor, its social rate of return on capital will be less than the gross-of-tax rate of return which it perceives. I believe I am correct in stating that in every Latin American country the agricultural, service, and construction sectors have relatively low wage scales, whereas the industrial and mining sectors have relatively high wage scales. I believe, moreover, that these differentials persist even after differences in capacities and skills are taken into account. That is, agriculture, the service industries, and construction pay less for *equivalent* labor than do manufacturing and mining. I conclude, therefore, that the social rate of return on capital is likely to be lower than (or at most equal to) the perceived gross-of-tax rate of return to capital in agriculture, services, and construction, whereas the social rate of return almost certainly exceeds the perceived gross-of-tax rate of return in industry and mining. The pattern of taxes on income from capital which would tend to correct for these labor market imperfections would entail rates of tax on the income from capital in agriculture and real estate which were higher than the rates applying to income from capital in manufacturing and mining. Once again, the prevailing tax structures create incentives in precisely the opposite direction from what would be required to correct for existing market imperfections.

Granted (a) that the estimation of the degree (as distinct from the direction) of market imperfections and the design of a tax structure to offset them would be exceedingly difficult tasks; (b) that the move to a system of equal taxation of income from capital in all sectors would itself entail a major and fundamental reform of existing tax structures; and (c) that the gradual elimination of imperfections in the labor and capital markets, itself a desirable goal of economic policy, would render a pattern of equal, nondiscriminatory taxation preferable to a discriminatory system — I propose as a proximate *and* long-term goal of tax reform in Latin America the special taxation, at roughly equal rates, of all income from capital, regardless of type or source. By "special" taxation I mean, to reiterate, that after the payment of special taxes, all net income from capital accruing to individuals would be fully taxable as personal income to them. In still other words, the policy I propose is a policy of conscious but nondiscriminatory double taxation of all income from capital.

Before turning to problems connected with the implementation of this proposal, let me suggest the possible orders of magnitude of its yield. It is conservative to estimate that in most Latin American countries somewhere between 30 and 40 percent of the national income accrues to capital. It is unlikely that in any Latin American country capital earns (before taxes) less than 30 percent of the national income; on the other hand, it is highly likely that in at least a few Latin American countries capital's return (before taxes) amounts to more than 40 percent of the national income. The potential yield of a tax which took 20 percent of all income from capital would (conservatively) lie between 6 and 8 percent of the national income; and the potential yield of a tax which took 30 percent of all income from capital would likely be between 9 and 12 percent of the national income. Thus, without resort to "exorbitant" rates of tax, this proposed reform could by itself overcome the chronic fiscal disequilibrium of many Latin American countries and at the same time provide the fiscal base for an expanding contribution of the public sector to economic and social development.

In dealing with problems of implementation, I shall discuss (a) the taxation of income from owners' equity in the corporate sector, (b) the taxation of income from owners' equity in the noncorporate sector, (c) the treatment of interest payments, (d) possible special provisions relating to income from agriculture, (e) possible special provisions relating to income from real estate, and (f) problems connected with valuation of capital. In order to give some flavor of realism to the discussion, and because at certain points the relative magnitudes of different tax rates become a matter of some importance, I shall assume that the goal of policy is to take, by means of special taxes, something like 30 percent of all income from capital. Needless to say, the order in which the various provisions are discussed below does not reflect their order of priority or importance.

The special taxation of income from corporate equity capital is already an established part of virtually all national tax systems. The vehicle by which this is accomplished is the corporation income tax. To achieve this part of the overall objective would require nothing more than the imposition of a 30 percent rate of tax on all corporate income. The most important way in which current practice in Latin America fails to meet this goal lies in the frequent exemption of income in particular lines of activity from the corporation income tax. Such exemptions are often claimed to promote economic development because they help corporations in new lines of activity over their difficult early years. There is a grain of truth in this assertion, but it should be noted (a) that the most difficult early years are those in which the corporations in question sustain losses — years in which they would have no taxable income in any case; and (b) that with a moderate (e.g., 30 percent) rate of tax even a new corporation is not grossly penalized when its investments begin to bear fruit and produce net income. Against the dubious claims made in favor of exemptions, we must weigh the following facts: (a) although exemptions are easy to grant, they appear to be considerably more difficult to remove; (b) in the short run, at least, exemptions tend to create within the corporate sector certain islands of privilege, wherein abnormally high private returns to capital can be earned even though the social returns to capital are not abnormally high and may be abnormally low; (c) in the long run, at least, exemptions tend to attract excessive amounts of capital to the affected industries, thus promoting an inefficient allocation of the economy's scarce capital resources. I conclude that the nondiscriminatory treatment of income from corporate equity capital is an important part of a program aimed at achieving the nondiscriminatory taxation of all income from capital.

Countries with a category tax system are in a good position to adopt the measures required to capture the desired fraction of the return to capital in unincorporated enterprises, for in these countries some special tax on the income of unincorporated enterprises typically already exists. Countries without a category tax system would do well, in this respect at least, to adopt similar measures. If we take for granted that a tax on the income of unincorporated enterprises does exist or will be imposed, we may confront the real difficulty facing the taxation of income from capital in this area: namely, the difficulty of apportioning the income of an unincorporated enterprise between "return to proprietors' labor" and "return to capital." It is fruitless, I believe, to hope for a precise method of apportionment, given the number and the variety of types of unincorporated enterprises in any country and given the difficulties of administrative control over their record keeping. I would therefore propose, as a second-best solution, the introduction of a progressive special tax on the income of this broad class of enterprises. It is to be presumed that the contribution of proprietors' labor to the total income of the enterprise will tend to be larger in those enterprises with small total incomes and smaller in those with large total incomes. One might think of a minimum rate of special taxation of 10 percent (applying to enterprises with low total incomes and presuming, implicitly, that some two-thirds of the total income of these enterprises is due to proprietors' labor) and of a maximum rate of around 25 percent (applying to enterprises with high total incomes and presuming, implicitly, that only one-sixth of the total income of these enterprises is due to proprietors' labor), with appropriate gradations in between. The rate of special tax applied to the total income of unincorporated enterprises should in no case exceed the rate applied to corporate income, because the income of unincorporated enterprises invariably includes some return to the labor of proprietors. If the proposed progressive tax were to be adopted, it would be necessary to take some measures to prevent tax avoidance by the artificial splitting up of enterprises. One step in this direction might be a requirement that all unincorporated enterprises owned by a single tax-paying unit (person or family) be treated for tax purposes as a single enterprise.

The interest paid by an enterprise on bank loans, other loans, or bonds is just as much a part of the income from capital generated by that enterprise as the profits accruing in it. One simple way of assuring that interest payments would be subject to the special tax on income from capital would be to disallow their deduction as a cost in computing the income (corporate or noncorporate) subject to special taxation. This simple device has much to recommend it. My only reason for considering alternative measures stems from my confidence that some of the main recipients of interest payments (banks and other financial intermediaries) are more reliable taxpayers (in the sense of being less prone or able to evade or avoid their tax liabilities) than some of the entities that pay interest to them. In short, it may be administratively simpler for the government to capture the tax "due" to it on the interest paid by enterprises by taxing that interest when it is received by banks and other financial intermediaries than by taxing it at the source of payment. Likewise, in a country in which interest payments on industrial bonds are significant and in which bond issues must be publicly registered, the tax on bond interest might be made payable to the fiscal authorities at the time of each periodic interest payment.[2]

---

[2] If interest paid to financial intermediaries and interest paid on bonds were to be taxed separately, as suggested here, an issue arises as to whether the tax should be paid by the borrowing

If in line with this proposal, interest paid to banks and financial intermediaries and possibly interest paid on bonds are subject to distinct tax treatment, there are two alternatives for the treatment of other interest payments. The first is to allow the deduction, for purposes of computing income subject to the taxes on corporate and unincorporated enterprises, only of such interest costs as were paid to banks and financial intermediaries or on bonds. Other interest payments would not be deductible and hence would automatically be taxable at ordinary income tax rates. Alternatively, other interest payments could be made deductible, but a special tax could be levied on such interest payments (other than those on bank loans, bonds, etc.) for which deduction was claimed. The rate of tax applicable to these other interest deductions could in no case be greater than the rate of tax applicable to corporate or noncorporate income (else no enterprise would claim deductions, and the system would reduce to that discussed under the first alternative).

Under any system of taxing interest payments, it would be necessary to accord special treatment to financial intermediaries. If the interest paid by enterprises to banks is subject to a special tax, the interest paid by banks to their depositors should not also be subject to a special tax.

There is no strong argument for treating the return to capital in agriculture differently from the return to capital in other activities. Corporations operating within agriculture could easily be subjected to the same tax treatment as other corporations, and ordinary (unincorporated) farms could be treated in the same way as other unincorporated enterprises. The difficulties of assessing farm income are great, however, and they have led some countries to impute farm income on the basis of the value of the property. This same procedure can be used for approximating farm income within a system, such as that proposed in this paper, designed to strike all income from capital with special taxes at roughly equivalent rates. If, for example, the annual income from agricultural property was imputed to be 7 percent of the value of the property, the special tax on the annual return to capital in agriculture could be set at, say, 2 percent of the value of the property. It is important to realize here that the value of the property assessed should include not only the value of the land but also the value of all improvements, equipment, and inventories. For example, the value of irrigation canals, barns, machinery, orchards, vineyards, and livestock should be included in the capital sum on the basis of which income from property is imputed. And unless an additional special tax is levied on the imputed income from residential housing in rural areas, the value of residences should also be included in the total from which income is imputed. It is also

---

enterprise, in addition to the contractual interest, or whether the tax should fall on the recipient. This issue is not a serious one as far as the long-run results of the tax are concerned, for the long-run results depend only on the existence of the tax and not on which group is nominally liable for its payment. In the short run, however, there are real differences in incidence, depending on which group is nominally liable. The appropriate policy on this issue would depend on whether it was deemed important that the special tax on interest payments have its full impact in the short run and whether one group or the other seemed a more likely subject for bearing the short-run impact of the tax, from the standpoint of the general policy of the country concerned. The long-term effect could be achieved without having any special short-term impact on either group, simply by making the tax on bank (bond) interest payments payable only on the interest on loans made (or bonds issued) after the law became effective.

important to realize that the special tax we are discussing here is not a substitute for the personal income tax. If income subject to personal tax is also imputed, then, using the same figures as in the above example, 5 percent of the value of the property (7 percent imputed yield less 2 percent paid in special tax) would be the annual imputed income from property on the basis of which personal income tax would be levied.

In the case of residential housing, the income obtained from rented properties could be treated in just the same way as other return to capital and taxed at the rates of special taxation applicable to the (corporate or unincorporated) enterprises concerned. The income from owner-occupied houses would, however, have to be imputed; or, what amounts to essentially the same thing, the special tax, at least on owner-occupied residences, would have to be expressed as a percentage of the value of the property. Administrative considerations might dictate giving the same treatment to all residences, whether or not they are owner-occupied. In this latter case, an annual tax of, say, 2 percent of the value of the property might be levied on all residences. If this were done, however, it would not be correct to subject interest payments on mortgages to an additional tax.[3]

As in the case of other forms of income from capital, the income (actual or imputed) from residential property should be subject to personal income taxation in addition to the special taxation just considered. Rental income is everywhere subject to personal income taxation, so we need not discuss it further here. The imputed income from owner-occupied residences, however, is not subject to personal income taxation in many countries; the purpose of this paragraph is to emphasize that it should be. The failure to tax imputed income on owner-occupied residences introduces an extraordinarily regressive component into a country's tax system. The poor owner-occupier, whose marginal personal income tax rate is zero, receives no benefit from the exemption of imputed income. The middle-class owner-occupier, whose marginal personal tax rate is, say, 20 percent, receives a benefit equal to 20 percent of the rental value of his dwelling as a result of the exemption of imputed income. The wealthy owner-occupier, whose marginal personal tax rate is, say, 50 percent, receives a benefit equal to half the rental value of his dwelling. Not only is the exemption of imputed rental income inequitable; it also creates artificial incentives for investment in luxury housing, an area where (precisely because of the exemption) the marginal productivity of capital is likely to be low and also where investment is unlikely to carry with it the beneficial external effects (associated with improved techniques and possibly with transfers of labor from sectors of low to sectors of high marginal productivity) that might be expected normally, for example, from investment in industrial capital equipment.

[3] This same proviso holds in the case (discussed in the paragraph above) in which the special tax on income from property in agriculture is based on the value of the property rather than on the actual income received. Where the tax is on actual income and interest payments are deductible in the computation of income subject to tax, there *should* be — according to the principle of roughly equal special taxation of all income from capital — a special tax on interest payments. Where interest payments are not deductible in computing the income subject to special taxation, or where that income is imputed on the basis of the value of the property, there *should not* be a special tax on interest payments.

If taxes are to be levied, or income imputed, on the basis of the value of agricultural and/or residential properties, it is important that assessment procedures be adopted which estimate the true economic value of property with reasonable accuracy. Assessment procedures have been notably weak in most Latin American countries and are badly in need of reform. The economist's answer to the assessment problem is simple and essentially foolproof: allow each property owner to declare the value of his own property, make these declared values a matter of public record, and require that an owner sell his property to any bidder who is willing to pay, say, 20 percent more than the declared value. This simple scheme is self-enforcing, allows no scope for corruption, has negligible costs of administration, and creates incentives, in addition to those already present in the market, for each property to be put to that use in which it has the highest economic productivity. The beauty of this scheme, so evident to economists, is not, however, appreciated by lawyers, who object strongly to the idea of requiring the sale of properties, possibly against the will of their owners. The economist can retort here that if owners value their property at the price at which they would be willing to sell, they should not be unwilling to sell at a price 20 percent higher. But there are also other ways of accommodating the objections of the lawyers. Perhaps the simplest way is to create, within the office in charge of property assessments, strong incentives against underassessment — penalizing assessment officers whenever properties assessed by them sell for prices substantially above the assessed value and rewarding assessment officers with "good" records (i.e., whose assessed values turn out to be reasonably close to the actual sales prices of those properties which are sold). Within a framework which stimulates high assessed values, the interests of the property owner can be protected by permitting him to make a bona fide offer of sale and to use as the assessed value in this case a figure 20 percent below his offer price. Under this procedure, a property owner is never required to be in the position of being *forced* to sell, although he may *voluntarily* place himself in that position if he considers the value put on his property by the assessing officers to be too high. Regardless of which of the two assessment schemes outlined above is adopted, it would be important for assessed values and/or the offer prices placed on their properties by owners to be linked to a price index, so as to avoid the possibility of owners' being required to sell their properties simply because inflation had rendered unrepresentative prices which, when they were initially set, reflected fairly accurately the true market values of the properties in question.

CONCLUSION

I believe that the proposals outlined in this paper would provide the basis for tax systems sufficiently robust to meet the demands of the next decade in most Latin American countries. Where more than 30 percent of the national income accrues to capital, it should not be excessively difficult to capture 6 percent of the national income through the special taxation of income from capital. If a serious effort is made to develop a system of progressive excise taxation, it should be possible to capture an additional 6 percent of the national income as revenue from this source (this could be accomplished, for example, by taxing one group of commodities accounting for 10 percent of the national income at a rate of 30 percent, by taxing another group of commodities accounting for 10 percent of the national income at a rate of 20 percent, and by taxing a third group of commodities accounting for 10 percent of the national income at a rate of 10 percent). In addition to these taxes, it should not be difficult to obtain a yield equal to a further 6 percent of the national income from the personal income tax. With 6 percent of the national income being taken in special taxes on the return to capital, and allowing something like 4 percent of the national income for corporate saving and the return to capital owned by government, we can estimate that some 90 percent of the national income would accrue as income of persons after the special taxation of return to capital. Two-thirds of this amount could be exempted entirely and the remainder taxed at progressive rates averaging out to 20 percent, and the yield would still be 6 percent of the national income. Thus, without resort to excessively high rates of taxation, it should be possible to garner something like 18 percent of the national income out of the two sets of taxes treated in this paper, plus the personal income tax. Moreover, these components of the tax structure would definitely be progressive. Additional revenue would still be obtainable from import duties, from taxes (as in Chile) or exchange profits (as in Brazil) on certain export commodities, and from social security taxes. And side by side with a genuinely progressive set of taxes such as those discussed above, some resort to broad-based taxes on sales or value added could be had without introducing serious injustices into the total tax structure. In short, the reforms suggested in this paper can contribute substantially to improve the equity of tax structures, to provide for required secular increases in revenue, and to create the possibility for a rapid and equitable response of the tax system to unforeseen contingencies.

XIII

The Royal Commission on Taxation, generally known (after its chairman) as the Carter Commission, produced for Canada in 1966 one of the most profound and comprehensive proposals for general tax reform that has ever been issued. It is rare that a public document should itself stand as a landmark in the intellectual development of a subject, but this one surely does. This final chapter gives my overall appraisal of the report and then engages in a rough, empirical exercise which attempts to estimate the potential capital-market effects of the Carter Commission proposals.

Chapter 17

A Landmark in the Annals
of Taxation

The Report of the Royal Commission on Taxation is without doubt a landmark among public documents — of any nation — setting forth policy prescriptions in the tax field. No such document, to my knowledge, has ever equalled its combination of positive attributes — scope, comprehensiveness, consistency, depth of theoretical and empirical analysis, and respect for the basic economic criteria of efficiency and equity. The Commission and its staff deserve our greatest respect and admiration for a monumental achievement. If their Report leads, as it should, to the kind of basic reform of the Canadian tax system which it recommends, they will have performed a tremendous service for the Canadian economy and society. Moreover, I am confident that adoption of their proposals will make the Canadian tax system one that will be emulated by other countries all over the world. Movements for tax reform are powerful in many areas — especially in the Latin American countries which I know at first hand. The economics profession is gaining strength and influence in these countries, and their political climate is increasingly favorable to changes aimed at strengthening and revitalizing their economies. I am sure that, seeing the proposed Canadian system in operation, more than one or two of these countries will find in it the type of reform — even-handed in its equity and conducive to economic efficiency and growth — that they are seeking. And I myself would hope that the new Canadian system would also stimulate my own country to surmount the many political obstacles that stand in the way of fundamental tax changes, and introduce reforms moving our tax system in the direction so clearly and cogently signalled by the Royal Commission's Report.

I. A GENERAL OVERVIEW

It is not easy briefly to characterize a report of such scope, but I would venture to say that its keystones are the recommended integration of the corporation and personal income taxes on the one hand and the recommended adoption of

Reprinted with permission from Arnold C. Harberger, "A Landmark in the Annals of Taxation," *The Canadian Journal of Economics* (February, 1968, Supplement), pp. 183–194.

the comprehensive income tax base on the other. The first of these key recommendations entails, for all practical purposes, the abolition of the corporation income tax, and it is to this aspect that I will turn first. It has always been a source of puzzlement to me how the income from equity capital invested in corporations ever came to be chosen as the relevant base for any tax at all, let alone a tax with rates of the order of magnitude of 50 percent. One might argue on grounds of equity that wealth as well as income is relevant as a measure of ability to pay, and thus justify a special tax, in addition to the ordinary income tax, falling on wealth. In the same vein one might justify a special tax striking the income from wealth rather than wealth itself. But this latter system would be a far cry from the corporation income tax, which isolates just one component of the income from wealth — corporate net earnings — and levies on it a discriminatory tax at a high rate.

Sometimes one hears the argument that the corporation income tax is justified as a payment to the government for the privilege of incorporation. The only sense that can be made of this argument — if it is regarded as justifying the tax from a social welfare point of view — is that corporations engender external diseconomies in amounts which are proportional to their profits — clearly an absurd contention! Indeed, it is highly likely that the use of capital in the corporate sector, far from producing external diseconomies, generates external benefits on a scale far surpassing that of other uses of capital. The corporate form enables large sums of capital to be assembled, permits the exploitation of economies of scale which would otherwise remain unexploited, fosters the development of a capital market in equities which otherwise would not exist, and prevents the type of monopoly power that extremely wealthy families would have in its absence. Moreover, the corporate sector has clearly been one of the principal generators of technical advance, which in turn has been one of the major forces of economic progress in all modern economies, and has been responsible for a considerable share of the rise in living standards of consumers. In so far as consumers have obtained very substantial benefits from technical progress, it is clear that the economic agents responsible for generating such progress have not enjoyed the full fruits of their efforts; an externality of major proportions is present here.

For the reasons just stated, it is clear that the integration of the corporate and personal tax system would be a major achievement which would promote a more rational allocation of resources within Canada and provide a climate more conducive to economic growth.

The Report's recommendation of a comprehensive personal income tax base is equally deserving of our applause. Economists have long recognized that the most consistent and relevant definition of income is the amount which the unit in question could consume while conserving the value of its capital assets. This obviously includes income in kind, accruing capital gains, and gifts and inheritances received. The Report attempts to incorporate all of these items in the income tax base, permitting an ample resort to averaging in order to avoid discrimination against households with volatile income streams. The only serious compromise reflected in the Report's recommendations in this regard is its opting for the taxing of capital gains on realization rather than on accrual.

The reasons for the Report's position on this matter are administrative convenience and political acceptability. It is indeed difficult for the tax authorities to verify whether reported accruals for tax purposes were approximately equal to movements of market values of assets, except for such assets as corporate securities with regularly quoted market prices. Moreover, the prospective burden on taxpayers of estimating for tax purposes the changes in their asset values each year would surely detract some political support from the proposal as a whole. And, indeed, the best approach to accrual taxation of capital gains — self-assessment by the taxpayer with a commitment to sell to anyone who bids a certain percentage over the taxpayer's declared value — would probably raise serious legal problems as well as alienate many potential supporters of the program.

One should also note that the Report does go part of the way toward accrual taxation, for corporate savings are indeed to be included in the personal tax base, and reflected in a corresponding change of the taxpayers' "cost basis" for the purpose of computing subsequent capital gains or losses. Thus a stockholder whose shares had gained in value an amount reflecting the cumulated retained earnings per share over the period he had held the stock would have, on the sale of the stock, neither a capital gain or loss for tax purposes. He would, in effect, have paid tax on his capital gains, roughly as they accrued.

Compromise is evident, too, in a few other areas. Though the Report recommends tightening the taxation of mineral industries, the proposed treatment for these industries is still significantly more favorable than that accorded to others. Likewise, the recommended tightening of the limits of bank reserves for bad debts, while a step in the right direction, still permits deduction for tax purposes of up to three times the amounts that would reflect the actual loss experience of the banks for certain classes of loans. In a similar vein, we have the recommended exemption from tax of capital gains on the sale of houses, up to a lifetime limit of $25,000, and the recommended annual ($100 for children and $250 for adults) and lifetime ($5,000 per individual) exemptions of gifts from outside the family unit. Strict economic considerations could never justify these decisions, particularly when it is recognized that the value of the exemptions to the taxpayer is proportional to his marginal tax rate.

Compromise of a sort is also involved in the Commission's recommendations of five-year block averaging and of the institution of non-interest-bearing income adjustment accounts. Cumulative lifetime averaging is evidently fairer than the proposed system and is no more difficult to administer. And it has the great advantage of eliminating the necessity for the taxpayer with windfall gains to opt for an averaging strategy — a strategy which entails, among other things, predictions as to what will be the future course of the taxpayer's income and which therefore can prove to be against the taxpayer's best interest if his expectations are not in fact fulfilled. The compromise in this case stems from the fact that Canada already has block averaging for fishermen and farmers; the public is therefore likely to be less distrustful of a system whose workability has been proved than of a better system which is completely new.

In using the word compromise in connection with the above imperfections of the proposed system, I do not mean to criticize the Commission for having opted as it did. Compromise is often essential for reaching political decisions, and the imperfections referred to are certainly of minor importance compared with the vast superiority of the proposed system, taken as a whole, over the present one. I mean instead to indicate that from a purely technical point of view the Commission's Report, in the minor ways in which it can be faulted, must be faulted for not going quite far enough rather than for going too far.

II. A KEY MACROECONOMIC ISSUE

In this part, rather than investigate details of the proposed reform, I would like to turn attention to one key macroeconomic issue which is critical to foreseeing the ultimate consequences of adopting the Commission's proposals. This issue is, in brief, what will happen to interest rates and stock prices in Canada? In section A I explore the probable consequences of a situation in which interest rates are unaffected by the tax change; in section B I pursue the implications of stock prices being unaffected by the change; and in section C I attempt a judgment as to the likely course of interest rates and stock prices if the Report's recommendations are adopted.

A. *Assuming Interest Rates Unaffected.* At the present time, I believe that something close to equilibrium prevails in the securities markets of Canada and the United States, in the sense that the relationship between earnings yields on stocks and interest rates on bonds in each of the countries appears to have reached something close to its long-run equilibrium. Both types of yield are modestly higher in Canada than in the U.S., the premium perhaps reflecting the price that must be paid by Canada to attract American capital. The available evidence indicates that the net flow of capital to Canada is highly responsive to small changes in the premium.

In this section we make the extreme assumption that the supply of debt capital to Canada, at the prevailing premium of interest rates, is essentially infinitely elastic. We assume, both here and in subsequent sections, that the over-all equilibrium of the capital market requires that the after-tax earnings yield on stocks be closely related to (though not identical with) the after-tax yield on bonds for the typical shareholder. It follows from these assumptions that there would be a clear tendency for the prices of Canadian equities to rise, as a result of the proposed effective abolition of the corporation income tax as far as Canadian shareholders are concerned.

This rise in equity prices would take place in advance of the actual entry into force of the new tax laws. It would begin as soon as a significant group of owners of capital was ready to bet on the possibility of adoption of the Report's proposals, and it would surely be virtually complete by the time most people were convinced that the proposals would be adopted. During the interval, anyone who believed that the Report's recommendations would be implemented would have an incentive to speculate on the expected rise of Canadian share prices. Canadian bondholders would tend to switch to stocks; Canadians with investments abroad would tend to repatriate capital for investment in the stock market; and foreigners willing to speculate on the anticipated rise of the Canadian market would bring in new funds for that purpose.

If the inflows from abroad were considerable, there would be a correspondingly great readjustment in the composition of Canada's balance of payments, the equity inflows being counterbalanced by reductions in Canada's foreign indebtedness (under the assumption of an infinitely elastic supply of debt capital to Canada).

Once the rise in share prices had taken place, foreigners would tend to sell their holdings of Canadian equities. Under the proposed tax set-up, these shareholders would face a tax regime essentially the same as the one prevailing today. The rise in share prices would present them with a capital gain, and in this sense they have no grounds to argue that they would be treated unfairly under the new system. But their earnings per share (unlike those of Canadian stockholders) would be no different under the new system than under the old. The possibility of selling Canadian shares with earnings/price ratios of, say, 4 percent, and of buying, say, shares in United States companies with earnings/price ratios of 6 percent, would surely be attractive to these foreign shareholders. Thus, the benefit of the new system to them consists only of the prospective rise of Canadian share prices. Once this had taken place, it would be to their advantage to sell to Canadians.

A similar change would take place in the incentives for Canadian capital to be held abroad, once the rise in share prices had taken place. The Report proposes that portfolio investors in foreign securities be given the option of claiming a 30 percent arbitrary gross-up and tax credit. "Because United States and United Kingdom corporations would ordinarily be deemed to have paid foreign taxes at least to the extent of 30 percent, Canadians holding portfolio investment in (such) corporations . . . could in general obtain 30 percent credit. . . . The dividend return from these shares would become more attractive than it is now, and this would mitigate the effect of full taxation of share gains."[1] Thus a Canadian shareholder of an American company with earnings (after United States corporation tax) of $10 per share, would have to pay Canadian tax on the basis of earnings of $13 per share, with a tax credit of $3. A Canadian holder of a Canadian share with earnings of $10 would simply pay income tax on that amount (owing to full integration). Thus if earnings after United States corporation tax are capitalized into share prices at the same rate as Canadian earnings before the Canadian corporation tax (which, after all, is no tax at all to Canadian shareholders but simply a withholding device), there would be no incentive for Canadians to repatriate their foreign investments and there might indeed be an incentive for Canadian capital to move abroad.

Turning now to foreign direct investments in Canada, two cases should be distinguished: (a) those foreign companies which, because of the scale of their operations, their "know-how," or the degree of differentiation of their products, possess enough monopoly power to preclude any reasonable possibility of serious competition by Canadian companies, and (b) those which are vulnerable to Canadian competition. The former group, if they maintain existing earnings

---

[1] IV, 535–536.

rates on invested capital, will be able to function much as they do under the present system. The latter group will, over time, be under pressure from Canadian competition to "go Canadian." This pressure will arise because Canadian companies will have access to a market for cheap equity capital. Earnings on Canadian equities, not being subject to corporation income tax, will reach an equilibrium level too low to attract foreign capital into competitive ventures in which its earnings would continue to be subjected to double taxation. By "going Canadian" the foreign companies could take advantage of the Canadian equity market, and restore their competitive position vis-à-vis local firms. As compared with the alternative of their drawing their new equity capital from abroad, this would of course entail a falling off in the rate of foreign direct investment, and indeed quite probably a significant shift of existing foreign companies to Canadian ownership. The reduction of inflow of direct investment is likely to be abrupt for the "competitive" companies, as they will be faced with prospects of declining net earnings over time. The tendency to liquidate foreign direct investments and to shift the operations to Canadian ownership is likely to be more gradual, as existing earnings rates are reduced through time in the face of expanded Canadian competition.

One can anticipate, therefore, rather volatile balance-of-payments movements at the outset, first a speculative inflow of equity capital as stock prices are bid up, and then an outflow as foreign portfolio investments in stocks are liquidated and as direct investment in "competitive" foreign companies falls sharply. The flow of direct investment over the longer term will probably remain substantially below current levels, in part because of a tendency to shift existing foreign companies more and more into Canadian hands. In this longer-term situation, the incentives affecting the choices of Canadian investors abroad are not likely to produce a reduction in outflow nearly sufficient to offset the other items mentioned. On the assumption of an elastic supply of foreign debt capital, of course, the flows of equity capital described above would be offset by opposite flows on debt capital account.

The major distributive consequences of implementing the Carter Commission's recommendations are to be found in (a) the capital gains and losses that will be generated by the shift, and (b) the reduction in the rate structure of the personal income tax. If, as we assume in this section, the interest rate remains unchanged, recipients of interest income will be benefited by having to pay lower rates of personal tax on that income. Thus the after-tax interest rate, which is the rate at which after-tax income is capitalized into bond prices, will rise, and the capitalization rates relevant for setting the prices of other capital assessts such as stocks and real estate will increase correspondingly.

If the prices of all capital assets were to be unaffected by the tax change, the effects of the change on Canadian owners of capital would be limited to those stemming from the reduced rate structure. But asset prices will surely change under the assumption of constant interest rates. On the one hand, real estate prices are likely to fall, owing to the fact that capital gains on real estate, previously untaxed, would be treated as income under the proposed system. On the other hand, as has been indicated earlier, stock prices are likely to rise as a result of the net effect of (a) elimination of the corporation income tax as far as Canadian shareholders are concerned, and (b) the taxation as income of capital gains on shares. In so far as capital gains on equities are a reflection of retained earnings, the net effect of (a) and (b) must be positive, for under this assumption retained earnings under the present system are taxed at the corporate tax rate of 50 percent, while under the proposed system they would be taxed at the shareholder's personal marginal rate, which would be less than or equal to the maximum proposed personal rate of 50 percent.

B. *Assuming Stock Prices Unaffected.* In making the assumption that stock prices are unaffected, I mean it to apply to the broad average of such prices, not to those of individual classes of equities. This clarification is necessary, for it is clear that the proposed changes will tend to have a greater positive effect on the prices of shares which up to now have had high dividends relative to earnings and consequently small expectations of capital gains than on the prices of shares with low pay-out ratios and high capital gains prospects. We assume, then, that the price of the "representative" share will not be influenced by the change, and that the representative share equally well reflects the portfolios of foreign and domestic shareholders.

Once it is assumed that stock prices are unaffected, we must abandon the assumption of section A regarding interest rates, for it was shown there that if interest rates remained constant, the prices of equities would tend to rise. In order for equity prices to be unaffected, Canadian interest rates must therefore rise relative to those in the United States. Such a rise is, of course, fully consistent with a high (though not infinite) elasticity of supply of foreign debt capital to Canada.

Under these circumstances, the process of adjustment to the tax change is quite different from that outlined in section A. Foreign portfolio investors now have no special incentive to invest in Canadian shares in anticipation of a capital gain, and since there is no change in share prices relative to the yields that foreign shareholders receive, there is no direct pressure for them to divest themselves of their Canadian equity holdings once the process of capitalizing expected changes in net-of-tax earnings into stock prices is complete.

Canadians, however, will have an incentive to shift from bonds to stocks, and foreigners to divest themselves of their existing holdings of Canadian bonds, in anticipation of the fall in the prices of these bonds which is implied by the expected rise of Canadian interest rates. Once the capitalization process is complete, the relative attractiveness of bonds and stocks for Canadians will be the same as before, but for foreigners Canadian bonds (which have risen in yield) will be relatively more attractive than Canadian stocks. Perhaps on this score there will be some reduction in foreign holdings of Canadian equities to counterbalance their increased holdings of Canadian bonds. There should also be some repatriation of Canadian capital held abroad as a consequence of the higher yields available in Canada.

The pressures on foreign companies competitive with Canadian ones to "go Canadian," which were potentially powerful under the assumptions of section A, are here non-existent; indeed, the competitive position of these foreign companies may be enhanced. If for given gross-of-tax earnings Canadian share prices do not rise, the cost of equity capital to Canadian companies will remain as before; since foreign companies will under the proposed system be subject to essentially the same tax treatment as now exists, their cost of equity capital will also be unaffected. On the debt capital side, however, Canadian companies will face higher interest rates, while foreign companies, to the extent that they can raise debt capital for their Canadian operations in foreign markets, may be able to avoid some or all of this increase in the cost of such capital. Foreign direct investments are therefore in a distinctly superior position under the assumptions of this section than under those of section A.

Movements in the capital account of the balance of payments are likely to be significantly less if equity prices remain constant than if they rise significantly. To verify this, assume that as expectations of the tax shift develop, investors anticipate a rise in the prices of stocks which is significantly smaller than that implied in section A by the assumption of constant interest rates. There would now be an initial speculative inflow of capital from abroad, but of smaller magnitude than that anticipated in section A. The balance-of-payments pressures at this point would lead to a reduction of the Canadian short-term interest rate so as to induce a compensating movement in the foreign debt capital account. Once equity prices had risen, there would be an outflow of foreign equity capital similar to, but smaller in magnitude than, that envisaged in section A. This would be counterbalanced by a rise in the inflow of foreign debt capital, the attraction of which would require a rise in Canadian interest rates, granted that we are now supposing that the supply of debt capital to Canada is not infinitely elastic. The case covered explicitly in this section can be viewed as the limiting case of the present example, in which the rise in stock prices is negligible in magnitude.

The distributive consequences of the assumptions of this section are more adverse to capital in the short run, and more favorable in the long run than would be the case if interest rates were unaffected. Real property values will fall more sharply, and bond prices will now fall rather than remaining stable. In the long run, of course, the higher yield on savings will benefit capitalists on whatever new savings they place in the market and on the reinvestment of the proceeds of maturing bonds.

C. *Prospects for Interest Rates and Share Prices.* We take as the cornerstone of our assessment of the prospects for the future the strong link between the bond markets of New York and Toronto. At the time of writing (Spring 1967) the yields of long-term Canadian obligations average about 6 percent, with government obligations yielding about 5 1/2 and private bonds about 6 1/2 percent. These yields exceed those on comparable U.S. securities by something less than 1 percent, a relationship that has characterized the two markets for some time. The premium of Canadian rates over American rates is, of course, not constant, variations in this premium being the principal instrument by which the Bank of Canada controls the country's balance of payments.

It is clear from the preceding two sections that the likely direction of movement of interest rates will be upward. Section B's assumptions directly implied a higher rate, and section A's implied a substantial increase in the flow of debt capital to the U.S. assuming an infinite elasticity of supply of such capital. Since we know that the relevant elasticity is not infinite, it is clear that the actual production of an increased flow of funds would require an increase in the premium of Canadian over American rates.

We now introduce the judgment that the increase in the premium could not plausibly be more than one full percentage point. In the context of today's bond market, this would mean an average long-term bond rate in Canada of some 7 percent, compared to a U.S. average rate of a little over 5 percent. This is clearly an extremely large (and to my knowledge unprecedented) value of the differential.

Finally, we make two alternative assumptions about the relationship between net-of-tax bond yields and net-of-tax stock yields for the typical stockholder. These are (a) that net stock yields are some multiple, m, of net bond yields, and (b) that net stock yields are equal to net bond yields plus an additive risk premium, a. Under the first assumption, the current relationship between gross-of-tax bond yields, r_B, and gross-of-tax earnings-price ratios on equities, r_E, will be

$$(17.1) \qquad mr_B(1 - t) = .5r_E[\delta(1.2 - t) + (1 - \delta)] + \gamma$$
$$= .5r_E[1 + \delta(.2 - t)] + \gamma.$$

The .5 factor preceding r_E reduces the earnings rate before corporation income tax to an earnings rate after corporation taxes. The dividend payout ratio, δ, is augmented by 20 percent to reflect the existing 20 percent tax credit accorded to dividends, and the marginal personal tax rate, t, is then applied to dividends. Retained earnings [equal to $.5r_E(1 - \delta)$ per dollar of stock held] are assumed to generate normal capital gains of like amount. Capital gains over and above the amounts generated by retained earnings (what the Report calls "goodwill gains") are reflected in the additive term γ, which is the percentage per year by which stock prices are expected to rise due to causes other than retained earnings.

Similarly, the prospective relationship between bond yields and earnings-price ratios (designated by primes) under the proposed system will be, on assumption (a):

$$(17.2) \qquad mr_B'(1 - t') = r_E'(1 - t') + \gamma(1 - \lambda t').$$

Here t' is the marginal tax rate of the typical shareholder under the proposed system; equation (17.2) reflects the fact that this rate applies equally to interest received from bonds and to corporate earnings on equities owned by the taxpayer. Goodwill gains would also be subject to tax under the proposed system, but only upon realization; hence a discount factor λ is applied to reflect the fact that the present value of the taxes to be paid on capital gains accruing today is less than the undiscounted value of such taxes.[2]

---

[2] If a stock is gaining in value at 2 percent per year, the stockholder can actually consume this amount by selling 2 percent of his holdings each year. If he does this each year, even though he in effect consumes the entire amount of accruing capital gain, he only pays tax on 2 percent of his as-yet-unrealized gains.

If corporate earnings before taxes, accruing on the basis of shares currently outstanding, are (as is to be expected) unaffected by the tax change, we can substitute E/P for r_E in (17.1) and E/P' for r_E' in (17.2), thus deriving expressions relating stock prices (P and P') to their relevant determinants:

(17.3)
$$P = \frac{.5E[1 + \delta(.2 - t)]}{mr_B(1 - t) - \gamma}$$

(17.4)
$$P' = \frac{E}{mr_B' - [\gamma(1 - \lambda t')/(1 - t')]}.$$

We assume that the typical shareholder[3] now has a marginal tax rate of 50 percent, and that the typical company pays out 40 percent of its after-tax earnings in dividends. We take .06 as an approximation of the current level of r_B, and .125 as our estimate of the current ratio of before-tax corporate earnings to share prices for the typical corporation. It is difficult to estimate γ — the goodwill-gains term. In principle this should reflect expected rises in the value of real property held by the corporation, plus expected gains due to future inflation, plus gains stemming from investments with greater-than-normal real yield. The rise of stock prices in the last two decades should probably not be taken as a guide for estimating γ, as that rise mainly reflects a reduction in the risk premium on shares and hence a reduction in m. I shall tentatively assume that γ for the typical company is .005, but shall later make additional calculations for atypical companies for which γ can be greater.

We now insert the above values of the various parameters into (17.1) to obtain

$$m(.06)(.5) = .5(.125)[1 + .4(.2 - .5)] + .005$$

or $.03m = .06$. The implied value of m is therefore 2.

---

[3] The term "typical shareholder" is a shorthand notation for a rather elusive concept. It refers to that class of shareholders which is at the margin determining the relative prices of securities. An example is the relationship between interest rates on tax-exempt bonds and those on taxable bonds in the U.S. If taxable bonds yield 6 percent and tax-free bonds yield 4 percent, the typical investor would have a marginal tax rate of 33 1/3 percent. The comparison between bonds and shares is somewhat more complicated because of the existence of a risk premium. We show in the text that with a ratio of 1:16 of after-corporation-tax earnings to share prices, a bond rate of 6 percent, and a dividend payout rate of 40 percent, a marginal tax rate of 50 percent implies indifference between stocks and bonds at the margin if the multiplicative risk premium is 2. Similarly, a marginal tax rate of 70 percent yields indifference at the margin when $m = 3.05$, and a marginal tax rate of 30 percent implies indifference when $m = 1.5$. In an oversimplified world in which all investors had the same m, equilibrium in the capital market would determine a marginal tax rate, t^*; all investors with marginal tax rates above t^* would invest in shares; all with marginal tax rates below t^* would invest in bonds. The real world is more complicated, in that investors diversify their portfolios rather than concentrate them as they would if they operated on a strict criterion of expected net-of-tax yield. None the less, the basic idea of "typical" investors as comprising that group whose behavior determines the setting of security prices is a very useful concept for analysing security markets. The "typical" investor is not the average investor, and his tax rate is not the weighted average of the marginal tax rates of all investors. He is instead a member of that income group which is "at the margin" in determining security prices. It is to be presumed that this group will be somewhere near the middle of the population of shareholders, weighted by the number of shares they own; our assumed values of t and t' reflect this presumption.

Under the proposed tax regime, we assume that the marginal tax rate of the typical shareholder would be .4, and that λ, the discount factor applying to taxes paid on goodwill gains, would be .5. Terms E, m, and γ are assumed to be the same as under the present system. Substituting the relevant values into (17.3) and (17.4), we find that P'/P is equal to 1.10. The rise in stock prices, which appeared on casual analysis in section A to be potentially very great in magnitude, turns out to be almost negligible, even if interest rates remain constant. And if r_B' rises to 7 percent (our upper limit), P'/P will be .935, and stock prices will actually fall.

For stocks with higher rates of expected goodwill gains, the prospects are even dimmer, for under the present system these gains are entirely exempt from tax, while under the proposed system they would be subject to tax. For the same values of the other parameters as were assumed above, a value of γ of .0175 will produce $P' = P$ in the case where r_B' remains at .06. Any higher value for γ will produce $P' < P$ even if interest rates remain constant. And if r_B' rises to .07, $P' < P$ for all positive values of γ.

Turning now to the model with an additive risk premium, we have the following basic equations:

$$(17.5) \qquad r_B(1 - t) + a = .5r_E[1 + \delta(.2 - t)] + \gamma$$

$$(17.6) \qquad r_B'(1 - t') + a = r_E'(1 - t') + \gamma(1 - \lambda t').$$

Substituting $r_B = .06$, $t = .5$, $r_E = .125$, $\delta = .4$, and $\gamma = .005$ into (17.5) we obtain our estimate of $a = .03$.

Transforming (17.5) and (17.6) into a form similar to (17.3) and (17.4), we find

$$(17.7) \qquad P = \frac{.5E[1 + \delta(.2 - t)]}{r_B(1 - t) + a - \gamma}$$

$$(17.8) \qquad P' = \frac{E(1 - t')}{r_B'(1 - t') + a - \gamma(1 - \lambda t')}.$$

From these equations and the assumed parameter values, we estimate P'/P to be 1.21 on the assumption that $r_B = r_B' = .06$, and to be 1.10 under the assumption of $r_B = .06$, $r_B' = .07$.

As we vary γ, holding the other parameters constant, we find that P'/P falls as γ rises, reaching unity when $\gamma = .028$ under the assumption that $r_B = r_B' = .06$, and when $\gamma = .017$ under the assumptions that $r_B = .06$, $r_B' = .07$.

The picture that emerges from this analysis is indeed reassuring. In a general way, one cannot rule out that tax changes as far-reaching and revolutionary as those proposed in the Report could drastically upset price relationships in the capital market and at the same time engender massive movements in the capital account of the balance of payments which would be difficult indeed to cope with. We find, however, that the particular pattern of tax changes proposed will, under plausible assumptions about the capital market mechanisms of Canada and the United States, have only a minor impact on stock prices in general.[4] The prices of particular securities will certainly move more than our estimates of the general average, those with currently high pay-out ratios rising more than the average, and those with currently very low pay-out ratios perhaps even falling. But the movement in the general level of the stock market promises to be no greater than 20 percent, and probably less than that, as a consequence of the tax shift. Movements of this kind have taken place in periods of less than a year many times in the past, creating no obvious trouble for the Canadian economy. There are no grounds to presume, therefore, that the capital market movements associated with the tax shift, or their balance-of-payments implications, ought to be matters of serious concern. It is a tribute to the perspicacity of the framers of the Report that the implementation of their recommendations promises to be so smooth.

III. CONCLUSION

I must repeat at this point my profound regard for the monumental task that has been completed by the Commission and its staff. Implementation of the recommendations of their Report would make the Canadian tax system a model for the world, and would provide a framework for economic progress that is both equitable and conducive to the efficient functioning of the economy. Transitions from one tax system to another are bound to entail some problems of adjustment, and this case is no exception. But the problems in this case appear to be minor indeed, and the rewards to the economy from taking the steps recommended by the Commission are great — great enough to justify by far Canada's accepting the limited problems that the transition may entail.

[4] A question may arise in the minds of some readers as to whether pension funds (which would be tax exempt under the Royal Commission proposals) will not so dominate the securities market that they determine share prices. I doubt that this would be the case for two reasons: (a) pension funds do not typically concentrate their holdings in equities; hence the total volume of equity investment accounted for by the funds will be only a fraction of their total holdings, and (b) in order for pension funds to determine equity prices, if their risk premiums are comparable to those of private citizens, they would have to effectively drive private shareholders out of the market and essentially monopolize the holding of Canadian equities.

If the pension funds demand for holding equities risk premia that are substantially higher than those required by private investors, the two groups may simultaneously be "at the margin" between stocks and bonds, but in this case the calculations based on private investor equalization of net-of-tax yields will remain valid predictors of market behavior.